For information about permission to reproduce selections from this book, write to Permissions, W. W. Norton & Company, Inc., 500 Fifth Avenue, New York, NY 10110.

**Desktop composition by Justine Burkat Trubey
Manufacturing by the Courier Companies, Inc.**

Library of Congress Cataloging-in-Publication Data

Lown, Patricia Twohill.
    All New York : the source guide / by Patricia Twohill Lown
and David Amory Lown ; illustrations by Françoise McAree.
        p.   cm.
    Includes index.
    ISBN 0-393-04541-2
    1. Decorative arts—New York (State)—New York—Directo-
ries.   2. Artisans—New York (State)—New York—Directories.
3. Interior decoration—New York (State)—New York—Directories., Travel—New York I. Lown, David. II. Title.
NK838.N37L68 1997
745'.025'7471—dc21   97-10631
                                                          CIP

W. W. Norton & Company, Inc., 500 Fifth Avenue, New York, NY
10110
http://www.wwnorton.com

W. W. Norton & Company Ltd., 10 Coptic Street, London CW1A 1PU

1 2 3 4 5 6 7 8 9 0

INTRODUCTION

New York is the most marvellous and the most overwhelming city in the world. It is, at one and the same time, the most culturally sophisticated and the most innocent. The streets are awash with people all day and all night, some on voyages of discovery and acquisition and others simply drifting. Visitors who keep their eyes and ears open and are not afraid to become part of the teeming masses soon discover the true essence of the city. Its museums, theatres, concert halls and opera houses are the best the world has to offer.

For those who use this book and are searching for "things" of beauty or comfort, there are breathtaking choices. Antiques, art and collectibles have come here from all parts of the world. And, most important, four centuries of immigrants have brought with them, not only the treasures and traditions of their homelands, but the skills and crafts handed down over several thousand years.

Every culture and every different language enriches every other, but, finally, New York City has become the world's center of dynamic creativity.

Gathering the information for this book has been a daunting task. The authors have followed the format and structure of their previous work, *Tout Paris*, as closely as possible. Selections were measured by several criteria: quality, courtesy, accessibility, authenticity and reliability. If, by some oversight, a favorite supplier or artisan has been left out, please feel free to write to the publisher.

A very special thanks to our Research Assistant, Joan Mullen, for her enormous contribution and her irrepressible good nature.

Finally, the authors want to thank the people of New York City. Communicating with the artists, the artisans, the dealers and merchants who are involved every day with creating, restoring and selling things of beauty and value has been one of life's great pleasures.

CATEGORY INDEX

ANTIQUE DEALERS

Shopping for antiques can be a lot of fun. Browsing through the antique shops, the flea markets, the street fairs, the Armory and Chelsea Pier shows and, finally, the auction houses provides some of life's greatest pleasures.

But, fun aside: where the "real antique" is concerned, there's usually a considerable investment involved. When a valuable antique or collectible has a doubtful pedigree, there can be a lot of unhappiness. Most dealers are reliable, but skilled artisans are so good these days that a piece of furniture can be created that looks as authentic as a 300-year-old original.

The very best dealers belong to associations which publish rules of honest dealing for members. They will, without question, provide certificates of authenticity or provenance. With this in hand, the buyer has a measure of protection, but he should always remember that authentication is an inexact science and even the best of experts can be taken in.

The best advice we can give is never buy in haste. Look at something, fall in love with it, walk away, think about it for a day or two, then repeat the process. If you decide you can't live without it, then go back again and negotiate, negotiate, negotiate.

——————— **THE UPPER EAST SIDE OF MANHATTAN** ———————

⚏ A LA VIEILLE RUSSIE, INC.

781 Fifth Avenue, New York, NY 10022 • Tel: (212) 752-1727 • Mon-Fri 10:00-5:00, Sat 10:30-4:00 • Paul Schaffer, Peter L. Schaffer, Mark A. Schaffer • French, Russian and German spoken • Prices high to very high

A superb collection of Russian Imperial treasures. 18th-century Russian and French furniture, antique jewels, snuff boxes, Faberge, Russian icons and art objects. Silver, enamels, porcelains, paintings.

⚘ DIDIER AARON, INC.

32 East 67th Street, New York, NY 10021 • Tel: (212) 988-5248 • Fax: (212) 737-3513 • Mon-Fri 9:30-6:00 • Herve Aaron, President • French and Spanish spoken • Prices very high

Rated as one of the "best of the best" in Paris. 18th- and 19th-century European furniture and works of art. Old Masters and 19th-century paintings, drawings and decorations.

ACANTHUS

22 East 80th Street, New York, NY 10021 • Tel: (212) 570-6670 • Fax: (212) 570-5173 • By appointment • Brian T. Aitken • French and Italian spoken • Prices high

Greek and Roman art.

ROBERT ALTMAN

1148 Second Avenue, New York, NY 10021 • Tel: (212) 832-3490 • Fax: (212) 832-4679 • Mon-Fri 11:00-5:00 • Robert Altman and Kim Walter • Some French spoken • Prices high • Trade only

18th- to 20th-century decorative Continental and American antiques. Their own exclusive line of floor lamps.

⚘ L'ANTIQUAIRE & THE CONNOISSEUR INC.

36 East 73rd Street, New York, NY 10021 • Tel: (212) 517-9176 • Fax: (212) 988-5674 • Mon-Fri 9:00-5:30 • Helen Fioratti • Italian, French, German and Spanish spoken • Prices high • 20% professional discount

Continental European 15th- through 18th-century furniture, fine and decorative art: Byzantine mosaics, medieval sculpture, antique textiles. French and Italian ceramics. Mrs. Fioratti is a true connoiseur and her book on French furniture proves it.

ANTIQUARIUM FINE ANCIENT ARTS GALLERY, LTD.

948 Madison Avenue, New York, NY 10021 • Tel: (212) 734-9776 • Fax: (212) 879-9362 • Tue-Fri 10:00-5:30, Sat 10:00-5:00 • Robin F. Beninson, Director • French spoken • Prices medium to very high • Professional discount • Major credit cards

Museum quality classical Egyptian and Near Eastern antiquities, ancient jewelry and ancient glass.

ARIADNE GALLERIES

970 Madison Avenue, New York, NY 10021 • Tel: (212) 772-3388 • Fax: (212) 517-7562 • Mon-Fri 10:00-6:00 • Prices high

Superb antiquities, Greek, Roman and Byzantine art, objets d'art and jewelry.

CHRYSTIAN AUBUSSON INC.

315 East 62nd Street, 3rd floor, New York, NY 10021 • Tel: (212) 755-2432 • Mon-Fri 9:30-5:00 • French and German spoken • Prices high • 25% trade discount

18th- and 19th-century French furniture, mirrors and decorative accessories.

BETTY JANE BART ANTIQUES

1225 Madison Avenue, New York, NY 10128 • Tel: (212) 410-2702 • Mon-Sat 11:00-5:30 • French spoken • Prices medium • 20% professionl discount

17th- and 18th-century French, Italian and Spanish furniture, mirrors, screens, chandeliers and painted furniture.

ELLEN BERENSON ANTIQUES AND FINE ARTS, INC.

988 Lexington Avenue, New York, NY 10021 • Telfax: (212) 288-5302 • Mon-Fri 10:30-6:00, Sat 11:00-5:30 • Ellen Berenson • French spoken • Prices medium to high • 10-20% professional discount • Major credit cards

Antique European, American and Oriental furniture and painted furniture. European and Oriental porcelain; antique lighting; paintings. Oriental rugs.

◪ BLUMKA GALLERY

101 East 81st Street, New York, NY 10028 • Tel: (212) 734-3222 • Fax: (212) 249-1087 • By appointment • Anthony Blumka • Prices high

Medieval and Renaissance works of art, furniture and art objects.

R. LOUIS BOFFERDING

Upper East Side • Tel: (212) 744-6725 • By appointment • Some French spoken • Prices high • Professional discounts

18th century European furniture, art and decorative objects. French furniture and objects from the 1930s and 40s. Furniture designed by 20th-century interior designers such as Elsie de Wolfe, Syrie Maugham, Jean Michel Frank.

BRAHMS NETSKI ANTIQUE PASSAGE LTD.

234 East 60th Street, New York, NY 10022 • Tel: (212) 755-8307 • Fax: (212) 755-8305 • Mon-Fri 10:00-6:00 • Michael Netski, Ronnie Brahms • French spoken • Prices medium to high • 20% professional discount

Antique to 20th-century furniture and accessories.

A.R. BROOMER, LTD.

1050 Second Avenue, #81, New York, NY 10022 • Tel: (212) 421-9530 • Fax: (212) 758-3840 • Mon-Sat 10:30-6:00 • Prices medium • Amex, Visa and MC

16th- to 19th-century European works of art. 17th- and 18th-century Chinese blue-and-white porcelain.

MERCIA BROSS—CAROL LYNFORD ANTIQUES LTD.

160 East 56th Street, New York, NY 10022 • Tel: (212) 355-4422 • Mon-Sat 11:00-6:00 • Some French spoken • Prices medium • 15% professional discount

English and Continental antiques, objets d'art and ceramics.

NANCY BROUS ASSOCIATES, LTD.

1008 Lexington Avenue, New York, NY 10021 • Tel: (212) 772-7515 • Fax: (212) 753-9587 • Mon-Fri 10:00-6:00, Sat 11:00-5:30 • Prices medium • Major credit cards

Antique English furniture, especially Victorian: sconces, bell jars. Specialist in antique bamboo furniture.

BURGIO ANTIQUES

509 Madison Avenue, 2nd floor, New York, NY 10022 • Tel: (212) 906-9179 • Fax: (212) 906-9180 • By appointment

Superb collection of European antiques.

BURKE'S ANTIQUES INC.

1030 Lexington Avenue, New York, NY 10021 • Tel: (212) 570-2964 • Fax: (212) 396-1001 • Mon-Fri 10:00-5:30, Sat 11:00-4:00 • Diane Calamari • Prices high • 20% professional discount • Major credit cards

Specialist in Victorian and Edwardian small items of unusual decorative furniture and accessories, porcelain, glass and brass.

LE CADET DE GASCOGNE

1015 Lexington Avenue, New York, NY 10021 • Telfax: (212) 744 5925 • Mon-Fri 10:00-6:00 • Gilbert Gestas, President • Prices medium to high.

18th- to 19th-century French antiques and paintings.

LEE CALICCHIO LTD.

134 East 70th Street, New York, NY 10021 • Tel: (212) 717-4417 • Fax: (212) 717-5755 • Mon-Fri 11:00-5:00 • And by appointment

Neoclassical antiques and art objects from the late 18th and 19th centuries.

CARNEGIE HILL ANTIQUES

1309 Madison Avenue, 2nd floor, New York, NY 10128 • Tel: (212) 987-6819 • Mon-Sat 11:00-6:00 (Closed Wed and Sun) • Erzsebet H. Black • Hungarian spoken • Prices medium • 15% professional discount

18th- and 19th-century Continental and English furniture, art and accessories.

RALPH M. CHAIT GALLERIES, INC.

12 East 56th Street, New York, NY 10022 • Tel: (212) 758-0937 • Fax: (212) 319-0471 • Mon-Sat 10:00-5:30 • Allan S. Chait, President; Steven J. Chait, Director; Mrs. Marion C. Howe, Manager • Prices high • Major credit cards

Fine Chinese works of art; Neolithic to 1800 A.D.

THE CHINESE PORCELAIN COMPANY

475 Park Avenue, New York, NY 10022 • Tel: (212) 838-7744 • Fax: (212) 838-4922 • Mon-Fri 10:00-6:00, Sat 11:00-5:00 • Khalil Rizk, Conor Mahony, Margaret Kaelin, Laurie Augenti

Asian ceramics, works of art and sculpture, European furniture and decorations.

COLLECTANIA

1194 Lexington Avenue, New York, NY 10028 • Tel: (212) 327-2176 • Fax: (212) 727-9160 • Sharon Rossano • French spoken • Prices medium • 10% professional discount • Amex and MC

Charming collection of antiques and decorative objects, pillows, trimmings.

COTSWOLD ANTIQUES, LTD.

1187 Lexington Avenue, New York, NY 10028 • Tel: (212) 472-0701 • Mon-Fri 10:00-5:00, Sat-Sun by appointment • Wally Gibbs • Spanish spoken • Prices medium • Professional discount • Major credit cards

19th-century English and Continental furniture, chandeliers and lamps. They specialize in custom made Pole Lamps.

D & B ANTIQUES, INC.

Upper East Side Warehouse • Tel: (212) 249-1543 • Fax: (212) 717-6309 • By appointment only • Deborah Whitenack • Prices medium to high

English and Continental 18th- and 19th-century furnishings. Upholstered furniture a specialty.

♔ DALVA BROTHERS, INC.

44 East 57th Street, New York, NY 10022 • Tel: (212) 758-2297 • Fax: (212) 758-2607 • Mon-Sat 9:30-5:30 • David L. Dalva II, President; Leon J. Dalva, President; Jean A. Dalva; David L. Dalva III • Prices high to very high

Superb collection of 18th-century French and Italian furniture, porcelain, sculpture, clocks and works of art.

DEVENISH & COMPANY, INC.

929 Madison Avenue, New York, NY 10021 • Tel: (212) 535-2888 • Fax: (212) 535-2889 • Mon-Sat 9:30-5:30 • Prices high to very high

Very high quality English and French 18th-century furniture, paintings and objets d'art.

DIMSON HOMMA

20 East 67th Street, New York, NY 10021 • Tel: (212) 439-7950 • Fax: (212) 439-7960 • Mon-Sat 11:00-6:00 and by appointment • Rise Dimson and Robert Homma • French spoken • Prices high • Trade discount • Major credit cards

Eclectic mix of museum quality antiques, art objects from Ming Dynasty; porcelain, African ceremonial pieces, sports memorabilia and mouth-blown tumblers. First-edition books.

DAVID DUNCAN ANTIQUES

227 East 60th Street, New York, NY 10022 • Tel: (212) 688-0666 • Fax: (212) 644-8134 • Mon-Fri 10:00-6:30, Sat-Sun 2:00-6:00 • Prices high

18th- and 19th-century French furniture and decorative objects. Some English.

EAGLES ANTIQUES

1097 Madison Avenue, New York, NY 10028 • Tel: (212) 772-3266 • Mon-Fri 9:30-5:30, Sat 10:00-5:30 • Mrs. Carol Feinberg, Owner; Christopher Dziadosz, Manager • Prices medium to high • 20% professional discount

18th-century Georgian formal furniture, Regency formal furniture, decorative objects. Chinese porcelain. Excellent selection of antique pillows. Restoration of antique furniture and pillows. Will travel to country houses.

ECLECTIC COLLECTOR

1201 Lexington Avenue, New York, NY 10028 • Tel: (212) 249-4277 • Fax: (212) 249-4326 • Mon-Sat 11:00-6:00 • Alfred Van Lelyveld • French, Dutch, Chinese and Japanese spoken • Prices medium • 20% professional discount • All major credit cards

18th-, 19th- and 20th-century furniture and decorative arts mainly from Europe but with a mingling of Asian and African.

ELLIOTT GALLERIES

155 East 79th Street, New York, NY 10021 • Tel: (212) 861-2222 • Mon-Fri 10:00-5:30 • Allan Bloom • Prices medium to high • Trade discounts

18th century through the Ashcan School of the 1930s. Furniture and decorative objects.

EVERGREEN ANTIQUES

1249 Third Avenue, New York, NY 10021 • Tel: (212) 744-5664 • Fax: (212) 744-5666 • Mon-Sat 11:00-7:00 • Italian, Spanish and German spoken • Prices high • Major credit cards

An extensive collection of 19th-century Continental and Scandinavian furniture and accessories, including Biedermeier and Provincial furniture.

HUBERT DES FORGES, INC.

1193 Lexington Avenue, New York, NY 10021 • Tel: (212) 744-1817 • Mon-Fri 10:00-6:00 • French spoken • Prices medium

19th- and 20th-century lamps and sconces; Majolica and objets d'art. 1920s and 1930s Italian gilded metal tasselled furniture.

FRENCH & CO.

17 East 65th Street, New York, NY 10021 • Tel: (212) 535-3330 • Fax: (212) 772-1756 • Mon-Fri 9:00-5:00 • Martin Zimet • French and Italian spoken • Prices medium to high

18th-century English and French furniture. Old Master to 19th-century European paintings.

BARRY FRIEDMAN, LTD.

32 East 67th Street, New York, NY 10021 • Tel: (212) 794-8950 • Fax: (212) 794-8889 • Tue-Sat 10:00-6:00, Mon by appointment • Scott Cook, Director • French, German, Italian and Spanish spoken • Prices high

European decorative arts from the Bauhaus, De Stijl, Art Nouveau, Art Deco and leading Modernist movements.

GARDNER & BARR, INC.

213 East 60th Street, New York, NY 10022 • Tel: (212) 752-0555 • Fax: (212) 355-6031 • Mon-Sat 11:00-6:00 • Mark Scott • French spoken • Prices medium • Major credit cards

Large and beautiful selection of vintage Venetian glass.

DAVID GEORGE ANTIQUES

165 East 87th Street, New York, NY 10128 • Tel (212) 860-3034 • Fax: (212) 941-1009 • Mon-Thu, Sat 10:30-5:30 • Prices medium • Major credit cards

Continental and English furniture; Chinese and Japanese antiques, smalls.

GILBERT GESTAS

1015 Lexington Avenue, New York, NY 10021 • Tel: (212) 744-5925 • Mon-Fri 10:00-6:00 • Spanish spoken • Prices high • Professional discount

Early 19th-century furniture and objects. Bronze, gilt clocks, animal sculpture, bronze and marble busts.

₩ CORA GINSBERG

19 East 74th Street, New York, NY 10021 • Tel: (212) 744-1352 • Fax: (212) 879-1601 • By appointment

Extraordinary collection of antique textiles, needlework, costumes and decoration.

PRICE GLOVER, INC.

59 East 79th Street, New York, NY 10022 • Tel: (212) 772-1740 • Fax: (212) 772-1962 • Mon-Fri 10:00-5:00 • Price Glover, President; Isobel Glover, Vice President • Prices high • 20% professional discount

18th- and 19th-century English lighting and decorative arts.

F. GOREVIC & SON, INC.

635 Madison Avenue, New York, NY 10022 • Tel: (212) 832-9000 • Fax: (212) 832-1509 • Mon-Sat 10:00-5:30 • Charles Gorevic, President; Roger Gorevic • Prices medium to high

Antique English and Continental silver, old Sheffield plate, antique jewelry and works of art.

JAMES GRAFSTEIN LTD.

236 East 60th Street, New York, NY 10022 • Tel: (212) 754-1290 • Fax: (212) 838-0525 • Mon-Fri 11:00-5:00 • James Grafstein • French spoken • Prices medium • Trade only • 20% discount

French and Continental furniture and decorations of the 18th and 19th centuries.

GUILD ANTIQUES

1089 & 1095 Madison Avenue, New York, NY 10028 • Telfax: (212) 472-0830 • Mon-Sat 10:00-5:00 • Prices medium • Visa and MC

18th- and 19th-century English furniture; 18th-century Chinese export porcelain; 18th- and 19th-century English and European mirrors, English porcelain and paintings and decorative accessories.

HARVEY & CO. ANTIQUES

250 East 60th Street, New York, NY 10022 • Tel: (212) 888-7952 • Fax: (212) 753-3919 • Mon-Fri 10:00-5:00, Sat 12:00-4:00 • Michael F. Patrick • Prices medium • 25% trade discounts • All credit cards

19th-century opulent furniture, lighting, accessories and silver.

JAMES HEPNER ANTIQUES

130 East 82nd Street, New York, NY 10028 • Tel: (212) 737-4470 • Fax: (212) 737-4782 • Mon-Fri 11:00-5:30, and by appointment • French spoken • Prices high • 25% professional discount

Sculpture, furniture and paintings from the Roman period to Art Moderne with a concentration on the 17th, 18th and 19th centuries.

LINDA HORN

1015 Madison Avenue, New York, NY 10021 • Tel: (212) 772-1122 • Fax: (212) 288-0449 • Mon-Sat 10:00-6:00 • Prices high • Professional discount • Amex, Visa and MC

19th-century antiques from England, France, Belgium, including furniture, armoires, tables, gilt mirrors, small silver items, tea caddies, unusual brass objects. Chandeliers and decorative accessories. Extraordinary window displays.

CLINTON HOWELL ANTIQUES

19 East 74th Street, New York, NY 10021 • Tel: (212) 517-5879 • Fax: (212) 517-4826 • Mon-Fri 10:00-5:00 • Clinton Howell • French spoken • Prices very high • 20% professional discount

Especially fine 18th-century English furniture and works of art.

JAMES II GALLERIES

11 East 57th Street, 4th floor, New York, NY 10022 • Tel: (212) 355-7040 • Fax: (212) 593-0341 • Mon-Fri 10:00-5:30, Sat 10:30-5:00 • Barbara Munves • Prices very high • Major credit cards

19th-century English decorative arts: china, glassware, silver, collectibles, silver-mounted perfume bottles, sterling silver frames.

⚏ LEO KAPLAN, LTD.

967 Madison Avenue, New York, NY 10021 • Tel: (212) 249 6766 • Fax: (212) 861 2674 • Mon-Sat 10:00-5:30 • Leo Kaplan, President; Ruth Kaplan, Alan Kaplan, Susan Kaplan • French spoken • Prices low to high • Professional discounts • Major credit cards

English, French and Russian antiques and works of art. 18th-century pottery, porcelain, paperweights, enamels and cameo glass.

LANGHAM LEFF GALLERY

19 East 71st Street, New York, NY 10021 • Tel: (212) 288-4030 • Fax: (212) 288-4342 • Mon-Sat 11:00-5:00 • Tracy Lake • French spoken • Prices high • Trade discount • Major credit cards

Furniture and decorative objects from the 16th to the early 20th centuries; 17th- to early 20th-century fine art.

BERNARD & S. DEAN LEVY, INC.

24 East 84th Street, New York, NY 10028 • Tel: (212) 628-7088 • Fax: (212) 628-7489 • Tue-Sat 10:00-5:30 • Amy Roth

Fine American 17th-, 18th- and early 19th-century antiques, American silver, needleworks, folk art and paintings.

H. M. LUTHER, INC. ANTIQUES

35 East 76th Street, New York, NY 10021 • Tel: (212) 439-7917 • Fax: (212) 505-0401 • Mon-Sat 10:00-5:00 • Prices high

18th- and 19th-century English and Continental furniture. 19th-century Japanese bronzes, ormolu.

MALMAISON ANTIQUES

253 East 74th Street, New York, NY 10021 • Tel: (212) 288-7569 • Fax: (212) 517-7652 • Mon-Fri 9:00-5:00 • Roger Prigent, Owner • French spoken • Prices medium • 20% trade discount

Early 19th-century French, American and Russian Empire furniture, paintings, sculpture and accessories. Art Deco of the 30s and 40s.

MANHATTAN ART & ANTIQUES CENTER

1050 Second Avenue, New York, NY 10022 • Tel: (212) 355-4400 • Fax: (212) 355-4403 • Mon-Sat 10:30-6:00, Sun 12:00-6:00

Approximately 100 antique shops and art galleries. Open to the public.

THE MERRIN GALLERY

724 Fifth Avenue, New York, NY 10019 • Tel: (212) 757-2884 • Fax: (212) 757-3904 • Tue-Sat 10:00-6:00 • Samuel Merrin, Edward Merrin • Prices high

Egyptian, Greek, Roman, Etruscan and Near Eastern antiquities.

⌘ NESLE, INC.

151 East 57th Street, New York, NY 10022 • Tel: (212) 755-0515 • Fax: (212) 644-2583 • Mon-Fri 9:00-5:00 • Albert R. Nesle, Nancy H. Nesle • Italian, French and German spoken • Prices low to high • Professional discounts

Antique lighting fixtures; 18th- and 19th-century English and French decorative accessories.

⌘ NEWEL ART GALLERIES

425 East 53rd Street, New York, NY 10022 • Tel: (212) 758-1970 • Fax: (212) 371-0166 • Mon-Fri 9:00-5:00 • Spanish spoken • Prices medium to very high

An extra-special and huge collection of French and English antique furniture and decorations; lots of Art Deco.

OBJETS PLUS

315 East 62nd Street, New York, NY 10021 • Telfax: (212) 832-3386 • Mon-Fri 10:00-5:00 • Victor Alonzo and Roger Gross • French, Italian, Portuguese and German spoken • Prices high • Trade only • Trade discounts

18th- and 19th-century French and Continental furniture, mirrors, bronzes, lamps, porcelain and chandeliers.

OBJETS TROUVES ANTIQUES

217 East 60th Street, New York, NY 10022 • Tel: (212) 753-0221 • Fax: (212) 753-0224 • Mon-Sat 10:00-6:00, Sun by appointment • Marianne Johnson-Gill, Owner • French spoken • Prices medium to high • 20% professional discount

18th- and 19th-century French, Continental and English furniture, paintings and decorations. Lower level: French country antiques.

OLD VERSAILLES ANTIQUES

315 East 62nd Street, New York, NY 10021 • Tel: (212) 421-3663 • Mon-Fri 12:00-5:00 • Charles Kriz, President • Prices high • 20% trade discount

18th-century French and Continental furniture, paintings and art objects.

⌘ FLORIAN PAPP

962 Madison Avenue, New York, NY 10021 • Tel: (212) 288-6770 • Fax: (212) 517-6965 • Mon-Fri 9:00-5:30, Sat 10:00-5:00 • Prices high • Professional discount

Superb collection of 18th- and 19th-century European furniture, paintings and decorations.

PARIS ANTIQUES, INC.

315 East 62nd Street, New York, NY 10021 • Telfax: (212) 421-3340 • Fax: (212) 421-3340 • Mon-Fri 11:00-5:00 • Ben Passalacqua • French and Italian spoken • Prices medium • 25% trade discounts

18th- and 19th-century French and Continental furniture and accessories.

PARIS TO PROVINCE

210 East 60th Street, New York, NY 10022 • Telfax: (212) 750-0037 • Mon-Fri 10:00-6:00, Sat 11:00-5:00 • Sally Husk • Prices medium • 20% professional discount

18th- and 19th-century French, English and Continental furniture, paintings and objects of art. Restoration.

AMY PERLIN ANTIQUES

1020 Lexington Avenue, New York, NY 10021 • Tel: (212) 744-4923 • Fax: (212) 717-5326 • Mon-Fri 10:00-5:00 • Amy Perlin • Italian, French and Spanish spoken • Prices medium • Visa and MC

Unusual Continental antiques of the 16th to 19th centuries.

BOB PRYOR ANTIQUES—DECORATIONS

1023 Lexington Avenue, New York, NY 10021 • Tel: (212) 688-1516 • Mon-Sat 10:30-5:30 • Prices medium to high

Specialty: 17th to 19th centuries. Good period brass and scientific instruments, boxes and small collectibles.

GUY REGAL LIMITED

210 East 60th Street, New York, NY 10022 • Tel: (212) 888-2134 • Fax: (212) 888-2136 • Mon-Sat 10:00-6:00 • Elisa B. Losada • French and Spanish spoken • Prices medium to high • Major credit cards

17th- to 19th-century Continental antiques and accessories. 19th-century art.

JAMES ROBINSON, INC.

480 Park Avenue, New York, NY 10022 • Tel: (212) 752-6166 • Fax: (212) 754-0961 • Mon-Fri 10:00-5:00 • Joan Munves Boening, Edward Munves, Jr., Norma C. Munves, M. Kimball Harwood • Prices very high

Remarkable collection of antique silver, porcelain, glass, jewelry and objets de vertu.

ROSENBERG & STIEBEL, INC.

32 East 57th Street, New York, NY 10022 • Tel: (212) 753-4368 • Fax: (212) 935-5736 • Mon-Fri 10:00-5:00 or by appointment • Eric Stiebel, Gerald G. Stiebel, Penelope Hunter-Stiebel • French and German spoken • Prices high

Old Master paintings and drawings, 18th-century porcelain and French furniture. Medieval and Renaissance works of art.

JOHN ROSSELLI INTERNATIONAL

523 East 73rd Street, New York, NY 10021 • Tel: (212) 772-2137 • Fax: (212) 535-2989 • Mon-Fri 9:30-6:00 • Jonathan Gargiulo • Prices medium • 30% trade discount • Trade only

Antique decorative items, one of a kind, American, European 19th-century. Also reproduction furniture custom made.

ROYAL-ATHENA GALLERIES

153 East 57th Street, New York, NY 10022 • Tel: (212) 355-2034 • Fax: (212) 688-0412 • Mon-Sat 10:00-6:00 • Jerome M. Eisenberg, Ph.D., Director • French, Spanish and Rumanian spoken • Prices high • All major credit cards

Greek, Etruscan, Roman, Egyptian, Near Eastern antiquities. European sculpture through 1800, Old Master drawings, Islamic, Southeast Asian and Oriental works of art, Pre-Columbian and tribal art. Greek, Roman and Byzantine coins.

ISRAEL SACK

730 Fifth Avenue, New York, NY 10019 • Tel: (212) 399-6562 • Fax: (212) 399-9552 • Mon-Fri 9:30-5:00 • Polish spoken • Prices high • Professional discount

17th- and 18th-century American furniture and decoration. Excellent quality.

N. SAKIEL & SON

Gallery 88, 1050 Second Avenue, New York, NY 10022 • Tel: (212) 832-8576 • Mon-Sat 10:30-6:00, Sun 12:00-6:00 • Larry Sakiel

Antique Continental furniture, decorative accessories, bronzes, porcelain and antique silver.

SCHLESCH GARZA ANTIQUES

158 East 64th Street, New York, NY 10021 • Tel: (212) 838-3923 • Fax: (212) 838-9329 • Mon-Fri 10:00-4:00 • Portuguese, Danish, Swedish, Spanish, some German and French • Trade discounts

Rare and fine 18th-century Baltic furniture: Danish, German, Swedish, Norwegian, Russian. Chinese export furniture of the 18th century. Chandeliers and mirrors of the 18th century.

SENTIMENTO, INC.

306 East 61st Street, 3rd floor, New York, NY 10021 • Tel: (212) 750-3111 • Fax: (212) 750-3839 • Mon-Fri 10:00-6:00 • Toby Landey • Prices medium • 20% trade discount

French, English and Continental furniture and decorative accessories, mainly 18th and 19th centuries; original drawings.

S.J. SHRUBSOLE

104 East 57th Street, New York, NY 10022 • Tel: (212) 753- 8920 • Fax: (212) 754-5192 • Mon-Fri 9:30-5:30, Sat 10:00-5:00 • E.N. Shrubsole, President; B.H. Langstaff, Senior Vice President; J.M. McConnaughy, Vice President; Timothy Martin, Antique Jewelry Specialist • Prices high to very high • Major credit cards

A very special source for extremely high quality antique English silver, early American silver, old Sheffield plate, antique jewelry, gold boxes and glass.

SLATKIN & CO.

131 East 71st Street, New York, NY 10021 • Tel: (212) 794-1661 • Fax: (212) 794-4249 • Mon-Sat 10:00-6:00 • Mark Flesher • French spoken • Prices high • Amex, Visa and MC • They also have a boutique at Bergdorf Goodman

A selection of 19th-century French antique furniture, 18th- and 19th-century reproduction furniture, desk and boudoir accessories.

A. SMITH ANTIQUES, LTD.

235 East 60th Street, New York, NY 10022 • Tel: (212) 888-6337 • Fax: (212) 754-5674 • Mon-Fri 10:00-5:00 • Brian A. Gurney • Prices high • 20% professional discount

18th- and 19th-century English and Continental furniture, art and accessories.

SOLEIMANI ANTIQUE GALLERY

58 East 79th Street, New York, NY 10021 • Tel: (212) 717-6500 • Fax: (212) 717-1486 • Mon-Sat 10:00-6:00 • Benjamin Soleimani • French, Italian and Spanish spoken • Prices medium • All major credit cards

18th- and 19th-century French and Continental furniture. Some paintings, prints and posters.

STAIR & COMPANY

942 Madison Avenue, New York, NY 10021 • Tel (212) 517-4400 • Fax: (212) 737-4751 • Mon-Fri 9:30-5:00, Sat 11:00-4:00 • Prices very high • 20% professional discount

Very, very high quality English furniture and works of art from the 18th and early 19th centuries. Chinese export porcelain.

WILLIAM STRAUS

1435 Lexington Avenue, New York, NY 10128 • Tel: (212) 410-5682 • By appointment

15th- to 20th-century furniture and works of art.

TOUT LE MONDE

1178 Lexington Avenue, New York, NY 10028 • Tel: (212) 439-8487 • Fax: (212) 439-8490 • Mon-Sat 10:00-6:00 • Howard Crash, Patricia Reger • Prices medium to high • 20% professional discount • Major credit cards

Antique furniture, decorations, mirrors, paintings, decorative objects, manuscripts. Large collection of silver.

TURNER ANTIQUES

Gallery 2, 160 East 56th Street, New York, NY 10022 • (212) 935-1099 • Mon-Sat 10:00-6:00 • William Turner • Prices medium to high • 20% professional discount

Late 19th-century English and American furniture, decorative arts: Aesthetic, Neo-Gothic, Anglo-Japanese.

EARLE D. VANDEKAR OF KNIGHTSBRIDGE, INC.

305 East 61st Street, New York, NY 10021 • Tel: (212) 308-2022 • Fax: (212) 308-2105 • Mon-Fri 10:00-4:30 by appointment • Paul Vandekar, Elle Shushan • Prices medium • 20% professional discount • Major credit cards

Antique porcelain and pottery, Chinese export, portrait miniatures and lighting.

VICTOR ANTIQUES

223 East 60th Street, New York, NY 10022 • Tel: (212) 752-4100 • Fax: (212) 752-2747 • Mon-Fri 10:00-6:00, Sat 12:00-5:00 • Eliane Lambrechts • Spanish, French, Italian, Portuguese and Arabic spoken • Prices high • 15-30% professional discount

19th-century European antiques and decorative accessories. Upholstery and restoration.

♔ FREDERICK P. VICTORIA & SON, INC.

154 East 55th Street, New York, NY 10022 • Tel: (212) 755-2549 • Fax: (212) 888-7199 • Mon-Fri 9:00-5:00 • Anthony Victoria, President • French and Spanish spoken • Prices high • 20% professional discount

18th-century European furniture and decorative arts. Custom-made reproductions based on originals.

KAREN WARSHAW LTD.

167 East 74th Street, New York, NY 10021 • Tel: (212) 439-7870 • Fax: (212) 439-7871 • Mon-Fri 11:00-5:00 • Prices medium • 30% professional discount • Amex

This is a 19th-century townhouse filled with French and English antique furniture, decorative objects, paintings, accessories, mirrors, lamps, porcelain and sconces. Karen Warshaw also provides an accessory and antique locating service.

CHARLES J. WINSTON & CO, INC.

515 Madison Avenue—41 East 53rd Street, New York, NY 10022 • Tel: (212) 753-3612 • Mon-Fri 9:30-4:30 • John J. Winston • French and Spanish spoken • Prices high • 33 1/3% professional discount. Trade only

French, English and Chinese furniture, chandeliers, sconces, crystal, rock crystal, bronzes.

S. WYLER, INC.

941 Lexington Avenue, New York, NY 10021 • Tel: (212) 879-9848 • Fax: (212) 472-8018 • Mon-Sat 9:30-5:45 • Richard L. Wyler • Prices high • Amex

Superb quality antique silver and English porcelain.

YEW TREE HOUSE ANTIQUES

450 B East 72nd Street, #7F, New York, NY 10021 • Telfax: (212) 249-6612 • Ahna Hogeland and Kevin Kleinbardt • Mon-Fri 11:00-5:30 or by appointment • Prices medium to high • 10-25% professional discount

17th-, 18th- and 19th-century European furniture.

———— THE UPPER WEST SIDE OF MANHATTAN ————

BETTER TIMES ANTIQUES

201 West 84th Street, New York, NY 10024 • Tel: (212) 496-9001 • Thu-Tue 12:00-6:30 • Victor Principe, Pul Oldham • Prices medium to high • Trade discount • MC and Visa

European, English and American furniture from 18th to early 20th centuries. Some reproduction antique furniture.

MORIAH ANTIQUE JUDAICA

16 West 56th Street, New York, NY 10019 • Tel: (212) 245-0101 • Michael P. Ehrenthal, Director

Jewish art and antiques.

JOY SCHONBERG GALLERIES

255 West 88th Street, New York, NY 10024 • Tel: (212) 877-3369 • Joy K. Schonberg

Antique Judaica, archaeology, books, manuscripts and paintings. Silver ceremonial objects.

WELCOME HOME ANTIQUES

556 Columbus Avenue, New York, NY 10019 • Tel: (212) 362-4293 • Mon-Fri 12:00-8:00, Sat-Sun 12:00-6:00 • Robert Levin and Ken Plum • Prices moderate • Professional discounts

American furniture 1830 through 1940. Empire, country, mission, primitive.

ABE'S ANTIQUES

815 Broadway, New York, NY 10003 • Tel: (212) 260-6424 • Mon-Fri 9:30-5:30 • Prices medium to high • Trade only • 20% professional discount • Major credit cards

19th-century French furniture, chandeliers, mirrors, clocks, fireplaces, andirons and screens.

♔ AGOSTINO ANTIQUES, LTD.

808 Broadway, New York, NY 10003 • Tel: (212) 533-3355 • Fax: (212) 477-4128 • Mon-Fri 9:00-5:00 • Salvatore Trupiano, Richard Keller • Italian spoken • Prices medium to high • 20% professional discount

Fine 18th- and 19th-century English and French furniture and decorative accessories. Also an exclusive line of antique furniture reproductions.

CASITA

48 East 12th Street, New York, NY 10003 • Tel: (212) 253-1925 • Mon-Fri 10:00-6:00, Sat 12:00-5:00 • Jack Emanuelson • Some French and Spanish spoken • Trade discount

French furniture: Louis XV, Louis XVI and Directoire period and style and decorative objects. A good choice of antique fabrics, especially Toiles de Jouy.

♔ PHILIP COLLECK LTD.

830 Broadway, New York, NY 10003 • Tel: (212) 505-2500 • Fax: (212) 529-1836 • Mon-Fri 10:00-5:30 and by appointment • Diana O. Jacoby, Mark Jacoby • Prices medium to very high

18th-century English furniture and decorative arts, English lacquer, Chinese export furniture and mirrors.

L'EPOQUE

30 East 10th Street, New York, NY 10003 • Tel: (212) 353-0972 • Fax: (212) 353-0957 • Mon-Fri 10:00-5:00 • Peter Balint • French and Hungarian spoken • Prices high • Professional discount

17th- to 19th-century French furniture.

GEORGE N. ANTIQUES

67 East 11th Street, New York, NY 10003 • Tel: (212) 505-5599 • Fax: (212) 353-3051 • Mon-Fri 10:30-5:30 • George N. Brody • Spanish spoken • Prices medium • 1/3 discounts to the trade • Major credit cards

18th-century American, English and Continental furniture and decorations.

BERND GOECKLER ANTIQUES, INC.

30 East 10th Street, New York, NY 10003 • Tel: (212) 777-8209 • Fax: (212) 777-8302 • Mon-Sat 9:00-6:00 • Bernd Goeckler speaks French, German and Swiss-German • Prices medium • 20% trade discount

18th- and 19th-century furniture, lighting and accessories.

HYDE PARK ANTIQUES

836 Broadway, New York, NY 10003 • Tel (212) 477-0033 • Fax: (212) 477-1781 • Mon-Fri 9:00-5:30, Sat 10:00-2:30 • Bernard Karr • Some Spanish, German, French and Portuguese spoken • Prices high • Professional discount

English furniture, mirrors, porcelain, paintings and decorative accessories from the 18th to early 19th centuries.

HOWARD KAPLAN ANTIQUES

827-831 Broadway, New York, NY 10003 • Tel: (212) 674-1000 • Fax: (212) 228-7204 • Mon-Fri 9:00-5:00 • Richard Larson • Prices very high • Professional discount • MC and Visa

Several floors of antiques and other objects. French, English, Italian, 18th- and mostly 19th-century furniture. Large tables and overscale buffets. Leather upholstery. Bedroom and bistro shop. Custom lamp shades. Custom tables from 200-year-old wood. On-site upholsterer trained by Jansen in Paris. French room installations. Finally a stock of old woods.

KARL KEMP & ASSOC., LTD.

29 East 10th Street, New York, NY 10003 • Tel: (212) 254-1877 • Fax: (212) 228-1236 • Mon-Fri 10:00-5:30, Sat 12:00-5:00 • French, German and Spanish spoken • Prices medium to high • 20% professional discount

Neoclassical antiques, specializing in Empire, Biedermeier, French Art Deco furniture. Consulting services for collectors.

KENSINGTON PLACE ANTIQUES

80 East 11th Street, New York, NY 10003 • Tel: (212) 533-7652 • Tel: (212) 533-6378 • Mon-Fri 9:30-5:00 • Robert Holme • French and Spanish spoken • Prices medium to high • Professional discount

18th- and 19th-century English, French and Italian furniture.

KENTSHIRE GALLERIES, LTD.

37 East 12th Street, New York, NY 10003 • Tel: (212) 673-6644 • Fax: (212) 979-0923 • Mon-Fri 9:00-5:30, Sat 10:30-3:00 • Robert Israel, Fred Imberman • Spanish spoken • Prices high • 25% professional discount • They also have an Antique shop in Bergdorf Goodman • Major credit cards

Huge gallery with 18th- and early 19th-century English furniture, furnishings, paintings, porcelains, and decorative objects. Antique and period jewelry.

THE LITTLE ANTIQUE SHOP

44 East 11th Street, New York, NY 10003 • Tel: (212) 673-5173 • Mon-Fri 10:00-5:00, Sat 11:00-4:00 • Luigi Boscain • Prices medium • Professional discount

Nice collection of interesting screens, lots of Art Deco, good quality boxes and art objects, paintings and some very nice marquetry cabinets.

H. M. LUTHER, INC., ANTIQUES

61 East 11th Street, New York, NY 10003 • Tel: (212) 505-1485 • Fax: (212) 505-0401 • Mon-Sat 10:00-5:00 • Prices high • Professional discount

18th- and 19th-century English and Continental furniture. Japanese bronzes of the 19th century, ormolu.

MARTELL ANTIQUES

53 East 10th Street, New York, NY 10003 • Tel: (212) 777-4360 • Mon-Fri 10:00-5:30, Sat 11:00-5:00 • Prices medium

18th- and 19th-century French country furniture. Restoration.

METRO ANTIQUES

80 East 11th Street, New York, NY 10003 • Tel: (212) 673-3510 • Fax: (212) 995-8549 • By appointment • Prices medium to very high

Rare early European antiques and decorative objects.

LAWRENCE MICHAEL ANTIQUES, INC.

832 Broadway, New York, NY 10003 • Tel: (212) 529-8444 • Fax: (212) 505-9931 • Mon-Fri 9:30-5:00 • Dimitri Dedes and Thomas Hutchison • Greek, French and Spanish spoken • Prices medium • 20% professional discount

18th- and 19th-century English, French and Continental furniture and decorations.

ROBIN S. MILLER

Greenwich Village area, 10003 • Telfax: (212) 533-4126 • By appointment only • French and Spanish spoken • Prices medium • 20% professional discount

French furniture, Grand Tour objects, drawings and watercolors of the late 18th and early 19th centuries.

O'SULLIVAN ANTIQUES

51 East 10th Street, New York, NY 10003 • Tel: (212) 260-8985 • Fax: (212) 260-0308 • Mon-Fri 9:30-6:00, Sat 10:00-4:00 • John Clarke • French spoken • Prices high • 15% professional discount

Victorian and Georgian furniture, mainly Irish. Art objects.

PROCTOR GALLERIES, INC.

824 Broadway (at 12th), New York, NY 10003 • Tel: (212) 388-1539 •
Fax: (212) 388-1540 • Mon-Fri 9:30-5:30, Sat 11:00-4:30 • Karin Proctor
• Some French and some Spanish spoken • 25% trade discounts •
Major credit cards

European furniture, European and Oriental art objects, American
and European paintings. Collection begins with Roman sculpture
through 16th to early 19th centuries.

REYMER-JOURDAN ANTIQUES

29 East 10th Street, New York, NY 10003 • Tel: (212) 674-4470 • Fax:
(212) 228-9471 • Mon-Fri 10:00-5:30, Sat 12:00-5:00 • Marie Guerin
• French and Spanish spoken • Prices high • 20% trade discounts

Late 18th- and early 19th-century French and Continental furniture,
objects and lighting. Some furniture and lighting from the 1920s,
1930s and 1940s.

⌗ RITTER-ANTIK, INC.

35 East 10th Street, New York, NY 10003 • Tel: (212) 673-2213 • Fax:
(212) 673-2217 • Mon-Fri 10:00-5:00, Sat 12:00-5:00 • Heinz Leichter,
Dr. D. Gordon • German spoken • Prices high • 20% professional discount

One of the largest and best collections of Biedermeier furniture in
the States. Also selected Neoclassical pieces from the 17th through
the 20th centuries.

ROLAND'S ANTIQUES, INC.

67 East 11th Street, New York, NY 10003 • Tel: (212) 260-2000 • Fax:
(212) 260-2778 • Mon-Fri 9:30-5:00 • Prices medium • Professional
discount

Antiques, architectural items, paintings, monumental sculptures,
stained glass windows, objets d'arts, reproductions.

TURBULENCE

812 Broadway, New York, NY 10003 • Tel: (212) 598-9030 • Mon-Fri
10:00-6:00 • Prices medium to very high

16th- to 19th-century European furniture and decorative arts.

--------- THE LOWER WEST SIDE OF MANHATTAN ---------

ALICE'S ANTIQUES OF SOHO

72 Greene Street, New York, NY 10012 • Tel: (212) 966-6867 • Fax:
(212) 334-3273 • 7 days 11:30-7:30 • Sean Renta • Spanish spoken •
Prices medium to high • Professional discount • Major credit cards

A large selection of antique iron and wood beds from Europe and
America from the 1860s to 1890s. Also antique rugs, furniture and
iron and marble consoles. Full line of custom linen for beds.

ATELIER ANTIQUES

465 Broome Street, New York, NY 10013 • Tel: (212) 925-3820 • Mon-Fri 11:00-7:00, Sat 12:00-6:00 • Jiri Novak • Czech spoken • Prices medium • 20% professional discount • Amex

18th- and 19th-century furniture. Restoration services in their Atelier as well as custom furniture to order.

E. BUK

151 Spring Street, New York, NY 10012 • Tel: (212) 226-6891 • By appointment • Prices medium • 10-25% professional discount

19th- to early 20th-century furniture, lighting and accessories. Prop rentals.

JACQUES CARCANAGUES, INC.

19-21 Greene Street, New York, NY 10013 • Tel: (212) 431-3116 • Fax: (212) 274-8780 • Tue-Sat 10:00-5:30 • Merrin Peress • Spanish, French, Portuguese and Chinese spoken • Prices low to very high • Trade discount • Major credit cards

Extraordinary collection of 18th- to 20th-century antique furniture and home furnishings from Asia. Decorative objects, tribal and ethnic jewelry.

COBWEB

116 West Houston Street, New York, NY 10012 • Tel: (212) 505-1558 • Fax: (212) 505-1730 • Mon-Fri 12:00-7:00, Sat 12:00-5:00 • Jessa Bertsche • Prices medium • Amex, Visa and MC

19th-century furniture and decorative accessories from southern Europe, North Africa, Indonesia and the Philippines.

COCONUT COMPANY

131 Greene Street, New York, NY 10012 • Tel: (212) 539-1940 • Fax: (212) 539-1935 • Mon-Sat 10:30-6:30, Sun 12:00-6:00 • Constantin von Haeften • French, German, Spanish and Japanese spoken • Prices medium to high • 20% professional discount • Major credit cards

19th-century French furniture and accessories. Asian antique and new furniture and artifacts from Thailand, Bali, Burma, including Dutch Colonial furniture. Comfortably proportioned English sofas and an extensive selection of upholstery fabrics.

MICHAEL CONNORS ANTIQUES

39 Great Jones Street, New York, NY 10012 • Tel: (212) 473-0377 • Fax: (212) 477-0096 • Mon-Fri 10:00-6:00 by appointment • Monica P. Gallacher • Spanish spoken • Prices medium to high • Trade only

Colonial West Indian antiques and decorative arts.

ESCABELLE IMPORTS, LTD.

273 Lafayette Street, New York, NY 10012 • Telfax: (212) 941-5925 • Mon-Fri 11:00-7:00, Sat-Sun 12:00-6:00 • Joseph Best and Philippe Sonte, Directors • French spoken • Prices high • 15-20% professional discount • Major credit cards

18th- and 19th-century Neoclassical French furniture and decorative objects with bi-monthly exhibitions of contemporary art.

GREENE STREET ANTIQUES

65 Greene Street, New York, NY 10012 • Tel: (212) 274-1076 • Fax: (212) 941-6081 • Mon-Fri 10:00-6:30, Sat-Sun 12:00-6:30 • Anessa Rahman, Josef Anavian • Prices medium • 15% professional discount • Major credit cards

European 19th-century and Art Deco furniture. Scandinavian Biedermeier. They also restore, refinish and upholster their own furniture.

PENINE HART ANTIQUES & ART

457 Broome Street, New York, NY 10013 • Tel: (212) 226-2761 • Fax: (212) 431-1517 • Tue-Sat 11:00-6:30, Sun 12:00-6:00 • Penine Hart, Manager • French and Korean spoken • Prices medium to high • 10% professional discount • Major credit cards

A broad collection of antiques from the early 1800s through the 1940s, paintings and sculpture by contemporary artists.

HOPE & WILDER

90 Grand Street, New York, NY 10013 • Tel: (212) 966-9010 • Tue-Sat 11:00-7:00, Sun 12:00-7:00 • Elleen Applebaum • Prices medium to high • 10% professional discount • Major credit cards

19th- and early 20th-century American antiques, some English and French: cupboards, dressers, tables, beds, chairs, smalls galore. Upholstered furniture, fabric, slipcovers, custom sewing work.

INTERIEURS

114 Wooster Street, New York, NY 10012 • Tel: (212) 343-0800 • Fax: (212) 343-1229 • Mon 12:00-6:00, Tue-Sat 11:00-7:00, Sun 12:00-3:00 • Laurence Kriegel, Francine Gardner • French spoken • Prices high • Major credit cards

French home furnishings and French antiques. Lighting from France as well as ceramics. Some modern furniture.

EILEEN LANE ANTIQUES, INC.

150 Thompson Street, New York, NY 10012 • Tel: (212) 475-2988 • Fax: (212) 673-8669 • 7 days 11:00-7:00 • Bo Lindstrand • French, German and Swedish spoken • Prices moderate • 10-20% professional discount • Major credit cards

Extraordinary collection of alabaster light fixtures of the 1900s custom wired. Specialists in 1830 to 1930 blonde-wood furniture from Scandinavia and Austria. Custom refinishing and re-upholstery.

LES 2 ILES

104 West 27th Street, New York, NY 10001 • Tel: (212) 604-9743 • Fax: (212) 604-9341 • Mon-Fri 8:00-6:00 and by appointment • Eric Demeret • French, Russian, Spanish and Chinese spoken • Prices low to medium • 20% trade discount

French and Russian antique furniture. High quality restoration and conservation, specializing in veneer marquetry, French polishing and gold leafing. Custom furniture and reproductions.

LYME REGIS, LTD.

68 Thompson Street, New York, NY 10012 • Tel: (212) 334-2110 • Tue-Sat 1:00-7:00, Sun by appointment • Elaine Friedman • Prices medium • 10% professional discount • Major credit cards

18th- and 19th-century small decorative objects, greenware, paintings, pottery and textiles from England and Scotland.

PATERAE, INC.

458 Broome Street, New York, NY 10013 • Tel: (212) 941-0880 • Fax: (212) 941-1009 • Tue-Sat 11:00-7:00, Sun-Mon 12:00-6:00 • Dan Cleary • Mandarin, Cantonese and Spanish spoken • Prices medium • 10% trade discount • Major credit cards

Interesting assortment of furniture and lamps from the 18th century to Art Deco and Moderne.

PETIT MUSEE

276 Fifth Avenue, New York, NY 10001 • Tel: (212) 685-7383 • Fax: (212) 685-0748 • Mon-Sat 9:00-5:30 • David Roy • Spanish and Hebrew spoken • Prices medium • Trade discount • Major credit cards

18th- and 19th-century furniture, tapestries, rugs and paintings.

PIERRE DEUX ANTIQUES

369 Bleeker Street, New York, NY 10014 • Tel: (212) 243-7740 • Fax: (212) 675-8273 • Mon-Sat 10:00-6:00 • John Bermingham • Prices high • 20% professional discount • All major credit cards

18th- and 19th-century French country antiques.

PRIMA SOHO

478 West Broadway, New York, NY 10012 • Tel: (212) 475-4041 • Fax: (212) 475-4177 • Mon-Sun 11:00-7:00 • Lou Carfallo • French and Danish spoken • Prices low to very high • Major credit cards

19th- and early 20th-century furniture, art, accessories, crystal, porcelain, collectibles.

SAN LORENZO FINE ART AND ANTIQUES

123 West Broadway, New York, NY 10013 • Tel: (212) 766-4770 • Fax: (212) 766-4797 • Tue-Sat 11:00-6:00 and by appointment • Catherine Weinstock • Italian, French and German spoken • Prices high • 10-20% professional discount • Visa, MC and Discover

18th- and 19th-century Continental furniture and decoration: textiles; ethnographic objects, contemporary painting.

NIALL SMITH ANTIQUES

96 Grand Street, New York, NY 10013 • Tel: (212) 941-7354 • Mon-Sat 10:00-6:00 • Prices medium to high

19th-century English, Irish and Continental furniture, large scale neo-classic furniture.

TWIN FIRES

110 Greene Street, New York, NY 10012 • Tel: (212) 343-2322 • Fax: (212) 343-0990 • Tue-Sat 11:00-6:00, Sun 12:00-5:00 • Lois Viola • Prices medium to high • Trade discount • Major credit cards

Antique country pine furniture from England and Ireland. Custom reproduction furniture made from old wood and custom woodworking of all kinds.

BRIAN WINDSOR

272 Lafayette Street, New York, NY 10012 • Tel (212) 274-0411 • Mon-Sat 12:00-6:00, Sun 12:00-5:00 • Prices medium • 20% professional discount • All major credit cards

19th- and early 20th-century furniture, decorative objects, garden furnishings.

_____ **OF PARTICULAR INTEREST OUTSIDE** _____
MANHATTAN

THE QUEENS ART AND ANTIQUE CENTER

37-27 32nd Street, Long Island City, NY 11101 • Tel: (718) 784-1959 • Fax: (718) 784-2179 • Tue-Sun 10:00-6:00 • Eva Barta • Hungarian spoken • Prices medium • 10% professional discount • Major credit cards

18th- and early 19th-century furniture, paintings, silver, silver plate and porcelain.

American Antiques and Folk Art

ALEXANDER GALLERY

942 Madison Avenue, New York, NY 10021 • Tel: (212) 472-1636 • Fax: (212) 734-6937 • Tue-Sat 10:00-6:00 • Alexander Acevedo • Spanish spoken • Prices medium to high • Trade discount

18th- and 19th-century American furniture, accessories and paintings. Pre-Columbian and American Indian artifacts.

☘ AMERICA HURRAH ANTIQUES

766 Madison Avenue, New York, NY 10021 • Tel: (212) 535-1930 • Fax: (212) 249-9718 • Tue-Sat 11:00-6:00 • Joel and Kate Kopp, Owners

Antique American folk art. American Indian art, quilts, hooked rugs, weathervanes, painted country furniture.

CARSWELL RUSH BERLIN, INC.

P.O. Box 210, Planetarium Station, New York, NY 10024 • Tel: (212) 721-0330 • Fax: (212) 580-2095 • By appointment only • Carswell Berlin • Spanish spoken • Prices high to very high • 10-15% professional discount

American Classical furniture and accessories 1800-1840. Formal furniture of the period including Sheraton, Empire and Restoration.

GALLERY 532-SOHO ANTIQUES

117 Wooster Street, New York, NY 10012 • Tel: (212) 219-1327 • Fax: (212) 219-1810 • Tue-Sun 12:00-6:30 • Karen Wellkoff • Prices medium • 10% discount • Major credit cards

American arts and crafts, furniture, American lighting, pottery and metalwork.

GIAMPIETRO

50 East 78th Street, #2A, New York, NY 10021 • Tel: (212) 861-8571 • Tue-Sat 11:00-5:30 • Fred and Kathryn Giampietro

Early American antiques, American folk art, painted furniture, art objects and accessories. 20th-century "Outsider" self-taught paintings and sculpture.

SAMUEL HERRUP ANTIQUES

12 East 86th Street, New York, NY 10028 • Tel: (212) 737-9051 • By appointment • Samuel S. Herrup

American antiques and folk art, especially portraits and sculptures, 17th- to 19th-century furniture.

☘ MARGOT JOHNSON, INC.

18 East 68th Street, #1A, New York, NY 10021 • Tel: (212) 794-2225 • By appointment only • Christopher Presser

Museum quality 19th-century American antique furniture and decorations. Specialist in Herter brothers furniture. Porcelain from 1850 to 1900.

☘ LEIGH KENO AMERICAN ANTIQUES

980 Madison Avenue, 2nd floor, New York, NY 10021 • Tel: (212) 734-2381 • Fax: (212) 734-0707 • Mon-Fri 10:00-5:00 • Leigh Keno • Prices very high

Superb 18th-century American furniture and decorative arts.

KENTUCKY

137 Duane Street, New York, NY 10013 • Tel: (212) 349-6577 • By appointment only • Kathy Shorr • Prices low to medium • Major credit cards

KENTUCKY 7

45 East 7th Street, New York, NY 10003 • Tel: (212) 533-0622 • Tue-Sat 12:00-7:00, Sun 2:00-5:00 • Kathy Shorr • Prices low to medium • Trade discount • Visa and MC

Rural American furniture and folk art, prints and paintings from England. Restoration services.

◀ BERNARD & S. DEAN LEVY

24 East 84th Street, New York, NY 10028 • Tel: (212) 628-7088 • Fax: (212) 628-7489 • Tue-Sat 9:30-5:30 • Amy Roth • Prices high

Fine American antiques and art from the 17th-, 18th- and early 19th-century. American silver, needleworks, folk art and paintings.

JUDITH AND JAMES MILNE, INC.

506 East 74th Street, New York, NY 10021 • Tel: (212) 472-0107 • Fax: (212) 472-1481 • Mon-Fri 9:30-5:30 and by appointment • French spoken • Prices medium • Professional discount • Major credit cards

American country antiques, painted furniture, folk art, weather vanes, architecturals, quilts, hooked rugs, garden furniture and decorative accessories.

PANTRY & HEARTH

121 East 35th Street, New York, NY 10016 • Tel: (212) 532-0535 • Fax: (212) 545-0758 • By appointment • Gail Lettick • Prices medium • 10% professional discount

Specialist in American 17th-, 18th- and 19th-century painted and high country furniture, accessories and folk art.

SUSAN PARRISH

390 Bleeker Street, New York, NY 10014 • Telfax: (212) 645-5020 • Tue-Sat 12:00-6:00 or by appointment • Prices medium • 10% trade discount • Major credit cards

Antique Americana specializing in antique quilts, painted 19th-century furniture and folk art.

MARK O. RABUN

115 Crosby Street, New York, NY 10012 • Tel: (212) 226-5053 • Fax: (212) 226-0797 • Mon-Sat 11:00-7:00 • Some French spoken • Prices medium to high • Professional discount

Specialist in the American 19th-century Aesthetic movement, particularly Herter and Godwin. English arts and crafts. Mission oak furniture.

⚕ ISRAEL SACK

730 Fifth Avenue, New York, NY 10019 • Tel: (212) 399-6562 • Fax: (212) 399-9552 • Mon-Fri 9:30-5:00 • Polish spoken • Prices high • Professional discount

Museum quality 17th- and 18th-century American furniture and decorations.

SAMMY'S

484 Broome Street, New York, NY 10013 • Tel: (212) 343-2357 • Fax: (212) 343-2364 • Tue-Sat 11:00-6:00, Sun 11:00-5:00 • Gabrielle Brown • Prices medium • Major credit cards

19th- and 20th-century Americana, furniture, folk and collectibles.

DAVID A. SCHORSCH

30 East 76th Street, New York, NY 10021 • Tel: (212) 439-6100 • Fax: (212) 439-6170 • By appointment • Prices high to very high • Trade discounts

American 18th- and 19th-century furniture, folk art, paintings and decorative objects including Shaker.

⚕ WOODARD & GREENSTEIN AMERICAN ANTIQUES

506 East 74th Street, 5th floor, New York, NY 10021 • Tel: (212) 988-2906 • Fax: (212) 734-9665 • Mon-Fri 10:30-6:00 • Sat 12:00-4:00 • Thomas Woodard and Blanche Greenstein • Prices high to very high • All major credit cards

Antique quilts, country furnishings, Woodard Weave classic American rugs.

──────────── OUTSIDE MANHATTAN ────────────

SUZANNE COURCIER • ROBERT W. WILKINS

11463 Route 22, Austerlitz, NY 12017 • Telfax: (518) 392-5754 • By appointment only • Robert Wilkins • Prices medium to high

Specializing in furniture and accessories of the Shakers. Also American antique painted furniture and antique American textiles.

Antique Collectibles

General

AGES PAST

450 East 78th Street, New York, NY 10021 • Tel: (212) 628-0725 • Mon-Sat 11:00-5:00 • Richard Duchano • Prices medium to high • Trade discount • Amex

Antique Staffordshire figures, blue & white and other colors in transferware, pink lusterware. A large collection of Royal commemoratives going back to Queen Victoria, some English smalls and a few prints.

ARCHANGEL ANTIQUES

334 East 9th Street, New York, NY 10003 • Tel: (212) 260-9313 • Wed-Sun 3:00-7:00 and by appointment • Prices medium • Professional discount • Major credit cards

Specializing in 1800 to 1950 antique buttons, cuff links and eyeglasses.

BRASS ANTIQUE SHOPPE

32 Allen Street, New York, NY 10002 • Tel: (212) 925-6660 • By appointment • J. Kleinstein • Prices medium

Old New York brass candlesticks.

CAMBRIDGE ESSEX

393 Fifth Avenue, 4th floor, New York, NY 10016 • Tel: (212) 689-1142 • Fax: (212) 689-0329 • Mon-Sat 10:00-4:00 • Richard Ellis • Spanish, French and Italian spoken • All prices • Professional discount • Major credit cards

New York's "Smithsonian" of collectibles. Stamps coins and paper money, celebrity autographs, collectibles of all kinds, sports items, stocks and bonds, legal, postcards, fossils and minerals, antiquities, patent models, movie posters, travel, pre-historic artifacts. Memorabilia: presidential, civil war, aviation, automobile, Zeppelin, Olympic, historical. Huge selection of books on the decorative arts in New Jersey warehouse by appointment.

EMPORIUM ANTIQUE SHOP

20 West 64th Street, New York, NY 10023 • Telfax (212) 724-9521 • Mon-Fri 11:30-6:30, Sat-Sun 1:30-6:30 • French, German, Greek, Italian and Swedish spoken • Prices low to high • Professional discount • Major credit cards

18th century to the present: unusual objects, decorative arts, orientalia. Jensen silver, porcelain figurines and vintage jewelry.

F. H. COINS AND COLLECTIBLES

1187 Lexington Avenue, New York, NY 10028 • Tel: (212) 737-5256 • Mon-Fri 11:00-6:00, Sat 11:30-5:00 • David Heller • Prices medium to high • Professional discount

Copper, silver and gold coins from the 1700s to the present. Mainly American, some European.

RITA FORD MUSIC BOXES

19 East 65th Street, New York, NY 10021 • Tel: (212) 535-6717 • Fax: (212) 772-0992 • Mon-Sat 9:00-5:00 • Joel Gerald Wright • Prices medium to high • Major credit cards

Antique and contemporary music boxes: Swiss boxes dating from 1843, German disc boxes and some American boxes from the turn of the century. Hand-crafted carousels by New York artists and Russian lacquer boxes—all musical pieces.

THE GOLDEN TREASURY

550 Columbus Avenue, New York, NY 10024 • Tel: (212) 787-1411 •
Daily, 1:00-6:30 • Shirley Josephson • Prices low • Trade discount • All
major credit cards

**18th century through Art Deco antique collectibles and curiosities.
Lots of lamps.**

GOOD OLD TIMES

956 Madison Avenue, New York, NY 10021 • Telfax: (212) 396-3546 •
Mon-Sat 10:00-6:00 • Eric Cap and Jaro Parizek • German and Czech
spoken • Prices medium to high • Trade discounts • Major credit cards

**Fine nostalgic collectibles: juke boxes, radios, music boxes, Edison
objects, watches, clocks, cameras and more. Expert repair of pocket
and wrist watches.**

LITTLE NEST OF TREASURES, LTD.

1435 Lexington Avenue, New York, NY 10128 • Tel: (212) 996-7578 •
Mon-Sat 11:00-7:00 • Lillian Sygman • Spanish, Italian and German
spoken • Prices medium • 20% discount • Major credit cards

**Eclectic mixture of collectibles and a few antiques. Architects' mod-
els of houses, wrought iron and silver. Great browsing.**

EDWARD R. LUBIN

3 East 75th Street, New York, NY 10021 • Tel: (212) 288-4145 • Fax:
(212) 288-3041 • Mon-Fri 10:00-5:00 • French and German spoken •
Prices medium to high

**European sculpture and decorative arts, enamels, ceramics, glass,
ivories from Medieval, Renaissance and Baroque periods.**

MANHATTAN PROPS INC.

138 West 31st Street, New York, NY 10001 • Tel: (800) 866-2452 •
Fax: (212) 736-6934 • Mon-Fri 10:00-4:00, Sat by appointment • Ira
Rousso • Trade discount • Major credit cards

**Unusual offering of stuffed birds, ducks, chickens pheasants, etc.
Also a collection of natural animal skin rugs, black bear, zebra, props
for display, fossils and butterflies.**

J. GARVIN MECKING, INC.

72 East 11th Street, New York, NY 10003 • Tel: (212) 677-4316 • Mon-
Fri 10:00-5:00 • French spoken • Prices medium • Professional discount

**English Victorian decorative accessories relating to animals. Charm-
ing and whimsical.**

OLD JAPAN

382 Bleeker Street, New York, NY 10014 • Tel: (212) 633-0922 • Wed-Sun 1:00-7:00 or by appointment • Amie Belobrow • Japanese spoken • Prices medium

Old Japanese kimonos, 19th- to 20th-century Japanese Tansu chests, 100-year-old baskets, iron teapots, opium boxes, slate waterfalls for Japanese gardens.

SYLVIA PINES UNIQUITIES

1102 Lexington Avenue, New York, NY 10021 • Tel: (212) 744-5141 • Mon-Sat 10:00-6:00 • French spoken • Prices medium to high • Major credit cards

Art Nouveau, Art Deco and Victorian jewelry, objets d'art, miniature clocks, miniature paintings. Large collection of beautiful antique purses.

REGAL COLLECTION

5 West 56th Street, New York, NY 10019 • Tel: (212) 582-7696 • Fax: (212) 582-1657 • Mon-Sat 10:00-6:00 • Spanish spoken • Major credit cards

18th- to 20th-century jade and snuff bottles.

A REPEAT PERFORMANCE

156 First Avenue, New York, NY 10009 • Tel: (212) 529-0832 • Mon-Sat 12:00-8:00, Sun 2:00-8:00 • Prices medium • Professional discounts

English odds and ends, candelabra, jewelry, old leather travel kits, perfume bottles, vases, suitcases. Also some Continental and American furniture from 1900 to the 1960s.

EDWARD SHEPPARD ANTIQUES

305 East 61st Street, New York, NY 10021 • Telfax: (212) 752-3354 • By appointment • Italian, French and some German spoken • Prices medium • Trade only

European and Oriental ceramics, portrait miniatures, prints, drawings and decorative paintings.

MALVINA SOLOMON

1122 Madison Avenue, New York, NY 10028 • Tel: (212) 535-5200 • Mon-Fri 11:00-5:30, Sat 11:00-5:00 • Prices medium to high • Trade discount • All major credit cards

American art pottery: turn of the century to 1950. Vintage jewelry from the Victorian age to the 1950s in sterling and bakelite.

STACK'S RARE COINS

123 West 57th Street, New York, NY 10019 • Tel: (212) 582-2580 • Fax: (212) 245-5018 • Mon-Fri 10:00-5:00 • Harvey Stack • French and Spanish spoken • Prices medium to high

Rare coins, United States and foreign. Antique gold, copper and silver coins.

THE TUDOR ROSE ANTIQUES

28 East 10th Street, New York, NY 10003 • Tel: (212) 677-5239 • Mon-Sat 10:30-6:00 • Prices medium to high • All major credit cards

Decorative sterling silver items, picture frames, dressing table accessories, candlesticks and some Victorian sterling decorative silver.

WAVES

110 West 25th Street, 10th floor, New York, NY 10001 • Tel: (212) 989-9284 • Fax: (201) 461-7121 • Mon-Fri 12:00-6:00, Sat-Sun 10:00-6:00 • Spanish spoken • Prices medium • 10% trade discount • All major credit cards

Old wind-up phonographs, vintage radios, old television sets, microphones, advertising books, pamphlets and old neon pieces.

WORLD COLLECTIBLE CENTER

18 Vesey Street, New York, NY 10007 • Telfax: (212) 267-7100 • Mon-Fri 9:00-7:00, Sun 11:00-6:00

Buying, selling and trading in all categories; autographs, documents, maps. Collectible toys, all kinds of memorabilia, rock 'n' roll, baseball, comic books.

Art Glass

ᵾ BACCARAT

625 Madison Avenue, New York, NY 10021 • Tel: (212) 826-4100 • Fax: (212) 826-5043 • Mon-Sat 10:00-6:00 • Francois Mainetti • French, German, Italian, Spanish, Japanese spoken • Prices high • Corporate discounts • Major credit cards

One of the world's great producers of superb hand-crafted crystal since 1764. Spectacular glass sculpture.

CROSBY STUDIO

117 Crosby Street, New York, NY 10012 • Telfax: (212) 941-6863 • Mon-Fri 12:00-6:00 by appointment • Richard Weissenberger • Prices medium to high • 10-20% professional discount

Specialist in Venetian glass 1900 to 1970.

▲ DAUM BOUTIQUE

694 Madison Avenue, New York, NY 10021 • Tel: (212) 355-2060 •
Fax: (212) 355-2074 • Mon-Sat 10:00-6:00 • Evelyne Dreyfus • French
spoken • Prices medium to high • All major credit cards

Marvellous limited-edition objets d'art since 1870. Crystal, decorative accessories, stemware, barware.

DEMNER

740 Madison Avenue, New York, NY 10021 • Tel: (212) 794-3786 •
Fax: (212) 794-3923 • Mon-Sat 10:30-5:30 • Italian, French and Spanish spoken • Prices medium to high • Trade discounts • Major credit cards

Art glass; Venetian glass of the 1950s. Also, Lalique, Galle, Daum.
Wiener Werkstatte art glass of Moser, Joseph Hoffman and Hegenauer.

D.J.L. TRADING

1675 York Avenue, New York, NY 10128 • Tel: (212) 534-7802 • Fax:
(212) 534-1234 • By appointment • David Weinstein • 15% professional discount

Buying and selling of Rene Lalique glass.

▲ GALLERI ORREFORS KOSTA BODA

58 East 57th Street, New York, NY 10022 • Tel: (212) 753-1095 • Fax:
(212) 752-3705 • Mon-Fri 10:00-6:00, Sat 10:30-5:00 • Irene Shyberger
• Swedish spoken • Prices high • 20% trade discount • Major credit cards

Large selection of unique and limited edition ornamental pieces by
Orrefors and Kosta Boda artists. Stemware and giftware. Engraving.

▲ GARDNER & BARR, INC.

213 East 60th Street, New York, NY 10022 • Tel: (212) 752-0555 • Fax:
(212) 355-6031 • Mon-Sat 11:00-6:00 • Mark Scott • French spoken •
Prices medium to high • Major credit cards

One of the largest and most beautiful collections of vintage Venetian glass.

HELLER GALLERY

71 Greene Street, New York, NY 10012 • Tel: (212) 966-5948 • Fax:
(212) 966-5956 • Tue-Sat 11:00-6:00, Sun 12:00-5:00

Contemporary glass arts.

HOYA CRYSTAL GALLERY

689 Madison Avenue, New York, NY 10021 • Tel: (212) 223-6335 •
Fax: (212) 371-9129 • Mon-Sat 10:00-6:00 • Japanese spoken • Prices
high • All major credit cards

Crystal art sculpture by in-house glass artists. Stemware, barware, giftware.

LEO KAPLAN MODERN

965 Madison Avenue, New York, NY 10021 • Tel: (212) 535-2407 • Fax: (212) 535-2445 • Mon-Sat 10:00-5:30 • Scott Jacobson • Prices medium to very high • Major credit cards

Interesting collection of contemporary glass sculpture.

JEAN KARAJIAN GALLERY

250 East 60th Street, New York, NY 10022 • Tel: (212) 751-6728 • Mon-Fri 10:00-5:30 • French spoken • Prices medium to high • Trade only

French Art Deco, Rene Lalique, Daum 1920-1930. Contemporary Jean Karajian collection of chandeliers and sconces in cast bronze and alabaster.

▨ LALIQUE

680 Madison Avenue, New York, NY 10021 • Tel: (212) 355-6550 • Fax: (212) 752-0203 • Mon-Fri 10:00-6:00, Sat 10:00-5:30 • Rosalyn Hand • French spoken • Prices high • Corporate discount • Major credit cards

Remarkable art glass sculpture. Magnificent hand-crafted decorative crystal in designs unique to Lalique. Stemware, barware.

▨ MINNA ROSENBLATT LTD.

844 Madison Avenue, New York, NY 10021 • Tel: (212) 288-0257 • Mon-Sat 10:00-5:30 • A little French spoken • Prices medium to very high • Trade discount

20th-century decorative arts including original Tiffany lamps and Tiffany glass. French glass: Galle, Daum, pate de verre. Also some old Steuben glass.

▨ STEUBEN

715 Fifth Avenue, New York, NY 10022 • Tel: (212) 752-1441 • Fax: (212) 753-1354 • Mon-Sat 10:00-6:00 • Major credit cards

High quality art glass since 1903.

VENETIAN ART GALLERY

160 East 56th Street, New York, NY 10022 • Tel: (212) 980-0669 • Fax: (212) 980-6398 • Mon-Sat 10:00-6:00 • Jerome Ottiere • Italian and French spoken • Prices medium to high • 15-20% trade discounts

Venetian art glass: Venini, Barovier, Seguso. Chandeliers, lamps, antique mirrors.

WEINSTEIN GALLERIES

793 Madison Avenue, New York, NY 10021 • Tel: (212) 717-6333 • Mon-Sat 10:30-6:00 • Some French spoken • Prices medium to high • Major credit cards

Art glass: 1890 to 1940. Fine examples of Art Deco and Art Nouveau decoration. Specialties: Tiffany, Pairpoint and Handel lamps. Great collection.

Autographs

CAMBRIDGE ESSEX

393 Fifth Avenue, 4th floor, New York, NY 10016 • Tel: (212) 689-1142 • Fax: (212) 689-0329 • Mon-Sat 10:00-4:00 • Richard Ellis • Spanish, French and Italian spoken • Prices low to very high • All major credit cards

New York's "Smithsonian" of collectibles. 3 million autographs from every field, music, politics, science, the arts, sports. 20,000 square feet containing the world's largest stamp and coin collections, Pre-Columbian and African art and an amazing collection of patent models, posters, paintings, prints, manuscripts, maps.

COLLECTORS UNIVERSE

124 East 40th Street, New York, NY 10016 • Tel: (212) 922-1110 • Mon-Wed, Fri 10:00-6:30, Thu 10:00-7:30 • MC and Visa

Sports and celebrity autographs. Comic books and comic collectibles, autographed baseballs.

GARY COMBS AUTOGRAPHS

3 Sheridan Square, New York, NY 10014 • Tel: (212) 242-7209 • Fax: (212) 924-9006 • By appointment

Autographs, particularly in the fields of Americana and music.

ROGER GROSS, LTD.

225 East 57th Street, New York, NY 10022 • Tel: (212) 759-2892• Fax: (212) 835-5425

Autographed photos of singers, composers, conductors, instrumentalists. Letters and musical quotes, operatic books, memorabilia, ephemera and unsigned photographs.

CHARLES HAMILTON

166 East 63rd Street, New York, NY 10021 • Tel: (212) 888-0338 • By appointment only

Autographs bought and sold. This is one of the best in New York City.

LION HEART AUTOGRAPHS, INC.

470 Park Avenue South, New York, NY 10016 • Tel: (212) 779-7050 • Fax: (212) 779-7066 • Mon-Fri 9:00-6:00 • By appointment only

American and foreign autographs bought and sold. They do not deal in celebrities or sports figures. Their collection concentrates on the areas of art history, literature, science, music, performing arts, exploration and music.

JAMES LOWE AUTOGRAPHS, LTD.

30 East 60th Street, New York, NY 10021 • Tel: (212) 759-0775 • Fax: (212) 759-2503 • Mon-Fri 9:30-4:30

Original autographs, letters, documents and historic photography, concerning the careers of U.S. presidents, authors, famous women, scientists, composers. They also have a large collection of unsigned photographs, some from the 19th century. Specialty: the Civil War.

♛ KENNETH W. RENDELL GALLERY

989 Madison Avenue, New York, NY 10021 • Tel: (212) 717-1776 • Fax: (212) 717-1492 • Mon-Sat 10:00-6:00 and by appointment • Kenneth W. Rendell • French spoken • Branches in Boston and Beverly Hills • Amex, Visa and MC

One of the world's best known dealers in original letters and documents in all fields: Presidents, literary and historical figures, music, science, the arts. Often framed with portraits. Over 10,000 items.

DAVID SCHULSON AUTOGRAPHS

11 East 68th Street, New York, NY 10021 • Tel: (212) 517-8300 • Fax (212) 517-2014 • Mon-Fri 10:00-5:00 and by appointment

American and foreign autographs, manuscripts, documents and books. Science, literature, arts, history, cinema, photography.

TOLLET & HARMAN AUTOGRAPHS

175 West 76th Street, New York, NY 10023 • Tel: (212) 877-1566 • Fax: (212) 877-0344 • By appointment only

Autographs in various fields, signed books, vintage photographs.

Clocks and Watches

♛ FANELLI ANTIQUE TIMEPIECES LTD—NOSTALGIC TIMES

790 Madison Avenue, Suite 202, New York, NY 10021 • Tel: (212) 517-2300 • Fax: (212) 737-4774 • Mon-Fri 11:00-6:00, Sat 11:00-5:00 • Cindy Fanelli • Prices medium to high • Professional discount • Major credit cards

Antique clocks and watches. Reproduction antique advertising clocks. They are highly regarded for their repair and restoration work. Consultation available for collectors.

HUT STUDIOS

1332 Third Avenue, Suite 3C, New York, NY 10021 • Telfax: (212) 628-8377 • Mon-Fri 10:00-5:00 • Richard Hopper and Harold Gilstein • Prices medium • Professional discounts • Visa and MC

Architecturally inspired clocks and desk accessories. All pieces are handcrafted and represent architectural styles and landmarks. Their collection includes wall clocks, mantel clocks as well as card holders, pencil holders and boxes.

TIME GALLERY

1050 Second Avenue, Gallery 54, New York, NY 10022 • Tel: (212) 593-2323 • Fax: (212) 593-0111 • Mon-Sat 10:30-6:00 • Italian spoken • Prices medium to high • Professional discount

17th- through 19th-century rare and unusual clocks, mostly European.

⬥ TIME WILL TELL

962 Madison Avenue, New York, NY 10021 • Tel: (212) 861-2663 • Fax (212) 288-4069 • Mon-Sat 10:00-6:00 • Prices medium • Major credit cards

Period and contemporary wrist watches. Service for all major manufactured brands.

Decoys

GROVE DECOYS

46 Sagamore Road, Bronxville, NY 10708 • Tel: (914) 793-4824 • By appointment • William Bender

Antique waterfowl decoys. All wood. Many rare and some not so rare.

Dolls and Doll Houses

THE ANTIQUE DOLL HOSPITAL OF NEW YORK

787 Lexington Avenue, New York, NY 10021 • Tel: (212) 838-7527 • Mon-Sat 10:00-6:00 • Spanish spoken • Prices medium to high

Vintage dolls, 1890 to 1960. Repair of dolls, stuffed animals and toys.

IRIS BROWN'S VICTORIAN DOLL AND MINIATURE SHOP

253 East 57th Street, New York, NY 10022 • Tel (212) 593-2882 • Mon-Fri 11:00-5:30, Sat 12:00-5:00 • French spoken • Prices medium

Very special place. Victorian dolls and miniatures. Doll houses and miniature furniture. Miniature porcelain and silver, Victorian paper, paper dolls. Christmas ornaments. Doll repairs.

DOLL HOUSE ANTICS

1343 Madison Avenue, New York, NY 10128 • Tel: (212) 876-2288 • Mon-Fri 11:00-5:30, Sat 11:00-5:00 • All major credit cards

Miniature doll houses. Largest store of its kind that sells standard scale models, 1" to 1'. They build to order and to design. Interior decoration on order. All kinds of doll house furniture, flooring, lighting, accessories, wallpaper; some by particular, highly sought after artists.

FORTY FIFTY SIXTY

Chelsea Antiques Building, 110 West 25th Street, New York, NY 10001
• Tel (212) 463-0980 • Wed-Sun 11:00-6:00 or by appointment

Antique dolls bought, sold and repaired.

MAGIC DOLL

108 East 16th Street, New York, NY 10003 • Tel (212) 982-3655 • Fax:
(212) 673-5236 • Mon-Sat by appointment • Emma Crawford

Doll making studio classes. Antique and modern reproduction dolls
custom made. Limited edition Emma Lee porcelain dolls.

MANHATTAN DOLL HOUSE SHOP

236 Third Avenue, New York, NY 10003 • Tel (212) 253-9549 • Mon-Fri
11:00-6:00, Sat-Sun 12:00-5:00

The doll house department store. Doll houses, doll furniture, wallpapers, accessories. Also antique and new dolls.

TINY DOLL HOUSE

1146 Lexington Avenue, New York, NY 10021 • Tel (212) 744-3719 •
Mon-Fri 11-5:30, Sat 11:00-5:00 • Leslie Edelman • Prices medium to
high

Doll houses, miniatures, furniture, lighting, flooring, accessories,
building supplies and dolls for the doll houses.

Maps and Globes

W. GRAHAM ARADER III

29 East 72nd Street, New York, NY 10021 • Tel: (212) 628-3668 • Fax:
(212) 879-8714 • Mon-Sat 10:00-6:00, Sun 11:00-5:00 • Prices high
• Visa and MC

Extensive collection of antique maps, books, hand-colored natural
history engravings and antique prints, birds, views, colorplate books,
works on paper, atlases, architectural engravings.

⚏ ARGOSY BOOK STORE

116 East 59th Street, New York, NY 10019 • Tel: (212) 753-4455 • Fax
(212) 593-4784 • Mon-Fri 9:30-6:00 • Prices modest • All major credit
cards

One of New York's most interesting secondhand book shops where
unexpected treasures can turn up. Autographs, photographs, documents. Lots of maps.

▉ RICHARD B. ARKWAY

59 East 54th Street, Suite 62, New York, NY 10022 • Tel: (212) 751-8135, (800) 453-0045 • Fax: (212) 832-5389 • Mon-Fri 9:30-5:00, Sat and evenings by appointment • Paul E. Cohen • Prices medium to very high

Extraordinary collection of globes. 15th- to 19th-century museum quality maps, and atlases. Also a collection of rare historic books.

GEORGE GLAZER

28 East 72nd Street, New York, NY 10021 • Tel: (212) 535-5706 • Fax: (212) 988-3992 • Mon-Fri 10:00-5:00 • Prices medium • 20% professional discount

Antique terrestrial and celestial globes. Armillary spheres and orreries (apparatus to demonstrate to students the rotation of the earth, moon and sun). Also maps, natural history, architectural, sporting and fashion prints.

E. GREENE GALLERY

361 Bleeker Street, New York, NY 10014 • Tel: (212) 366-0645 • Fax: (201) 222-3349 • Tue-Wed 11:00-5:00, Thu 12:00-8:00, Fri-Sat 10:00-6:00 • Prices low to medium • Trade discount

Antique maps and natural history prints.

▉ MARTAYAN LAN INC.

48 East 57th Street, New York, NY 10022 • Tel: (212) 308-0018 • Fax: (212) 308-0074 • Mon-Fri 9:30-5:30 • Prices high • Trade discount

Great selection of antique maps. Free verbal appraisals.

RAND MCNALLY

150 East 52nd Street, New York, NY 10022 • Tel: (212) 758-7488 • Mon-Fri 9:00-6:00, Thu 9:00-7:00, Sat 11:00-5:00, Sun 12:00-5:00 • Cindy Solomon • Prices medium • Major credit cards

Antique finish globes, antique and contemporary stands, atlases and maps. Large collection.

Marine Collectibles

SUSAN P. MEISEL DECORATIVE ARTS

133 Prince Street, New York, NY 10014 • Tel: (212) 254-0137 • Fax: (212) 533-7340 • Tue-Sat 10:00-6:00 • French spoken • Prices medium to high • Professional discount • Major credit cards

20th-century sailboat models, liner models, nautical and scientific instruments, tools and rulers.

NORTH STAR GALLERIES

1120 Lexington Avenue, New York, NY 10021 • Telfax: (212) 794-4277
• Tue-Fri 10:00-6:00 and by appointment • Gregg K. Dietrich • French,
Italian and Spanish spoken • Prices high • Trade discount • Major credit
cards

A remarkably good collection of marine art and antiques, excellent
yacht, ship models and collectibles. Well displayed. Restoration and
custom built ship models.

♨ Musical Instruments

FRANCE MUSIQUE USA

17 West 70th Street, New York, NY 10011 • Tel: (212) 366-5466 • Fax:
(212) 633-9389 • By appointment • Yves • French spoken • Prices
high to very high

17th- and 18th-century French organs. Restoration of organs by
Yves Cabourdin who travels from France on restoration assignments.

JACQUES FRANCAIS RARE VIOLINS

200 West 57th Street, Suite 602, New York, NY 10019 • Tel: (212) 586-
2607 • Mon-Fri 10:00-5:00 • Gregory Singer

One of the world's great collection of rare violins including the works
of Amati, Bergonzi and Stradivarius. They also do certificates and
insurance appraisals.

CHRISTOPHER LANDON RARE VIOLINS, INC.

1926 Broadway, Suite 301, New York, NY 10023 • Tel: (212) 721-1716
• Fax: (212) 721-2313 • Mon-Fri 9:30-7:00 • Christopher Landon •
French, Dutch and German spoken • Prices medium • Amex

Violin and bow maker. Also restoration of antique violins. Sale of
antique French and Italian violins.

RENE A. MOREL RARE VIOLINS, INC.

250 West 54th Street, New York, NY 10019 • Tel: (212) 582-8896 •
Fax: (212) 582-7432 • French, German, Japanese and Russian spoken
• Prices very high

Sales, restoration and maintenance of rare violins, violas and cel-
los.

SAINT CYR VIOLINS

Carnegie Hall, Suite 915, 881 Seventh Avenue, New York, NY 10019 •
Tel: (212) 262-1827 • Fax: (212) 265-5074 • Mon-Fri 10:00-5:30 •
Brice Dupin de Saint Cyr • French, Italian and Spanish spoken

Luthier, violin maker, dealer, restorer, consultant on fine quality
stringed instruments and bows. Creates instruments for many leading musicians.

WURLITZER-BRUCK

60 Riverside Drive, New York, NY 10024 • Tel: (212) 787-6431 • Fax: (212) 496-6525 • By appointment • Gene Bruck and Marianne Wurlitzer • French and Italian spoken • 10% trade discount

Antique wind and brass instruments, harps, ethnic instruments: 1600 to 1920. Antiquarian books on music.

Paperweights

GEM ANTIQUES

1088 Madison Avenue, New York, NY 10028 • Tel: (212) 535-7399 • Fax: (212) 249-7267 • Mon-Sat 10:30-5:30 • Jack Feingold • Prices medium to high • Up to 25% discounts

Antique paperweights, antique and contemporary American and European decorative ceramics.

LEO KAPLAN LTD.

967 Madison Avenue, New York, NY 10021 • Tel: (212) 249-6766 • Fax: (212) 861-2674 • Mon-Sat 10:00-5:30 • French spoken • Prices medium to high • Major credit cards

Antique and contemporary French and American paperweights. 18th-century English pottery and porcelain. English and French cameo glass. Russian porcelain and enamels.

Porcelain and Ceramics

BARDITH LTD.

901 Madison Avenue, New York, NY 10021 • Tel: (212) 737-3775 • Fax: (212) 650-9388 • Mon-Fri 11:00-5:30 • Prices medium to very high • Trade discounts

Great collection of English porcelain prior to 1860. Some French and Chinese porcelain.

₩ MICHELE BEINY INC.

53 East 82nd Street, New York, NY 10028-0303 • Tel: (212) 794-9357 • Fax: (212) 772-0119 • By appointment • Michele Beiny Harkins • French, German and Spanish spoken • Prices high • Trade discounts

18th- and early 19th-century European porcelain and faience. 18th-century French furniture and decoration. French 18th-century gilt bronze objects and 18th- and 19th-century gold boxes.

FRANCOISE NUNNALLE

105 West 55th Street, New York, NY 10019 • Tel: (212) 246-4281 • By appointment • Prices high

Antique porcelain from mid-18th to mid-19th centuries. Specialist in magnificent large soup tureens. Also Chinese export, Sevres, Worcester, Derby and German Nymphenburg porcelain.

SUCHOW & SIEGEL ANTIQUES

1050 Second Avenue, New York, NY 10022 • Tel: (212) 888-3489 • Fax: (212) 758-3840 • Mon-Sat 11:00-6:00 • Sanford M. Suchow • Prices high • Trade discount • Major credit cards

18th- and early 19th-century English and Chinese export porcelain, pottery, glass and objets de vertu.

⚜ EARLE D. VANDEKAR OF KNIGHTSBRIDGE, INC.

305 East 61st Street, New York, NY 10021 • Tel: (212) 308-2022 • Fax: (212) 308-2105 • Mon-Fri 10:00-4:30 by appointment • Paul Vandekar, Elle Shushan • Prices high • Trade discount • All major credit cards

Antique porcelain and pottery, Chinese export, portrait miniatures, lighting.

Quilts

LAURA FISHER/ANTIQUE QUILTS & AMERICANA

1050 Second Avenue, New York, NY 10022 • Tel: (212) 838-2596 • Fax: (212) 355-4403 • Mon-Sat 11:00-6:00 • Laura Fisher • Some French spoken • Prices medium to high • 10-20% professional discount • Amex and Visa

American antique quilts, hooked rugs, textiles including paisley shawls, "Beacon" blankets and American folk art.

SUSAN PARRISH ANTIQUES

390 Bleeker Street, New York, NY 10014 • Telfax: (212) 645-5020 • Mon-Sat 12:00-7:00, Sun 1:00-5:00 • Some French and Spanish spoken • Prices medium

A large collection of antique quilts, American folk art, antique American furniture and weather vanes.

WOODARD & GREENSTEIN AMERICAN ANTIQUES

506 East 74th Street, 5th floor, New York, NY 10021 • Tel: (212) 988-2906 • Fax: (212) 734-9665 • Mon-Fri 10:30-6:00, Sat 12:00-4:00 or by appointment • Prices high to very high • Major credit cards
Very likely one of America's best collections of antique quilts. They also have country furnishings and the Woodard Weave classic American rugs and accessories. They have branches in major design centers in the U.S.

See also: AMERICAN ANTIQUES

Scientific Instruments

E. BUK

151 Spring Street, New York, NY 10012 • Tel: (212) 226-6891 • By appointment • Prices medium • 10 to 25% trade discounts

Very extensive fine collection of period and historical objects from the anvil to the television, specializing in scientific, mechanical, industrial, technological artifacts: machine tools, microscopes, globes, sextants, scales, telescopes. Prop rentals for film and television.

Toys and Games

BIZARRE BAZAAR LTD.

130-1/4 East 65th Street, New York, NY 10021 • Tel: (212) 517-2100 • Fax: (212) 517-2283 • Mon-Sat 11:00-6:00, appointment suggested • Mrs. Knight • Italian, French, Chinese (Cantonese) spoken • Prices medium to very high • Professional discount • Major credit cards

Museum quality transportation models: airplanes, automotive and train models. 20th-century design and antique artists' mannequins. Vintage Louis Vuitton luggage.

BURLINGTON ANTIQUE TOYS

1082 Madison Avenue, New York, NY 10028 • Tel (212) 861-9708 • Mon-Sat 11:00-6:00, Sun 12:00-5:00 • Steve Balkin • Prices medium to high • Major credit cards

The best selection of miniature toys from the turn of the century to the present, toy soldiers and die-cast car models.

CLASSIC TOYS

218 Sullivan Street, New York, NY 10012 • Tel: (212) 674-4434 • Tue-Sun 12:00-6:30 • Gideon Rettich • Prices medium • Major credit cards

Soldiers, vehicles, tin plate, stuffed toys old and new: 1890s to the present.

DARROW'S FUN ANTIQUES

1101 First Avenue, New York, NY 10021 • Tel: (212) 838-0730 • Fax: (212) 838-3617 • Mon-Fri 12:00-7:00 , Sat 12:00-4:30 and by appointment • George Darrow • Spanish spoken • Prices medium • Trade discounts • Major credit cards

Sale, rental, appraisal, purchase, of antique toys and collectibles.

GEMINI ANTIQUES

12 East 76th Street, New York, NY 10021 • Tel: (212) 734-3681 • Mon-Fri 11:00-4:30 or by appointment • Leon and Steven Weiss • Prices medium • Trade discount

Specialists in early American and European toys—1870 to 1940—and mechanical banks from 1870 to 1915.

LOVE SAVES THE DAY

119 Second Avenue, New York, NY 10003 • Tel: (212) 228-3802 •
Mon-Sun 12:00-9:00 • Prices high • Major credit cards

Collectible toys 1960s and 1970s, Barbie, Beatles, Star Wars, vintage clothing, costumes and jewelry.

SECOND CHILDHOOD

283 Bleeker Street, New York, NY 10011 • Tel: (212) 989-6140 • Mon-Sat 11:00-5:30, Sun 12:00-5:00 • Van Dexter • Prices medium • Major credit cards

Tin and cast-iron toys and soldiers 1850-1950. Iron and tin banks, doll houses, doll furniture and miniature dolls.

WORLD COLLECTIBLE CENTER

18 Vesey Street, New York, NY 10007 • Telfax: (212) 267-7100 • Sun-Fri 9:00-7:00 • Allan Shrem • Spanish, Hebrew and Japanese spoken • Prices low to medium • 25% trade discount • All major credit cards

A huge collection of vintage toys, sports, TV, rock 'n' roll, movie, political memorabilia. Also action figure parts, dolls, games, battery operated toys, parts and repairs. They've got it all.

Trains

ISLAND TRAINS

4041 Hylan Boulevard, Staten Island, NY 10308 • Tel: (718) 317-0008 • Mon-Sat 10:00-6:00 • Major credit cards

Large selection of model trains, antique and contemporary.

LLOYD RALSTON GALLERY, INC.

109 Glover Avenue, Norwalk, CT 06850 • Tel: (203) 845-0033

This is the prime auction house dealing in model trains, the source for many dealers from all over the world.

⚒ THE GOLDEN SPIKE

23 West 45th Street, New York, NY 10036 • Tel: (212) 354-7349 • Fax: (212) 768-3550 • Mon-Sat 11:00-6:00 • J. Walsh • Some French spoken • Major credit cards

One of the finest train store specializing in fine vintage model trains and accessories, 1910 to 1969.

THE RED CABOOSE

23 West 45th Street, New York, NY 10036 • Tel: (212) 575-0155 • Fax: (212) 575-0272 • Mon-Fri 11:00-7:00, Sat 11:00-6:00 • Allan Spitz • Major credit cards

A model hobby shop specializing in railroads (no stock of radio control). Absolutely everything for the model railroad; HON Scale; Marklin-Z, HO and Maxi; LGB outdoor train; plastic kits, paint, tools, video. Custom railroad layouts.

Architectural Antiques

ANTIQUARIAN TRADERS

399 Lafayette Street, New York, NY 10003 • Tel: (212) 260-1200 • Fax: (212) 529-5320 • Mon-Fri 10:00-6:00, Sat 12:00-6:00, Sun by appointment • Noelle Pugh, Manager • French and Spanish spoken • Prices high • Trade discount • Major credit cards

Large selection of architectural elements, statuary, columns, urns, stained glass and lighting fixtures. French Art Nouveau and Art Deco. Antique furniture from the American Victorian period. They specialize in restoration and custom modification of antique furniture.

BILL'S ARCHITECTURAL ANTIQUES

600 West 131st Street, New York, NY 10027 • Tel: (212) 281-0916 • By appointment only • Bill Laredo • Spanish spoken • Prices low to medium • Trade discounts

Constantly changing inventory: over 500 doors in stock; wood, wrought iron, interior, exterior, French doors, Pocket doors, entry doors, cabinets, etc., from 1850s to 1950s, staircase parts, iron work, plumbing fixtures, toilets, tubs, hardware, pier and over-mantle mirrors, mantles and over-mantles, columns, capitals, windows, tiles, stained and leaded glass. wainscotting and wall paneling, woodwork. Antique doors, fireplaces. They will also install. Specialists in restoration of row houses and brownstones.

E. BUK

151 Spring Street, New York, NY 10012 • Tel: (212) 226-6891 • By appointment • Prices medium

Architectural drawings and renderings of important 20th-century construction projects such as West Point Military Academy, Princeton University, Rockefeller Center, the Queen Mary ocean liner, etc.

IRREPLACEABLE ARTIFACTS

14 Second Avenue, New York, NY 10003 • Tel: (212) 777-2900 • Fax: (212) 780-0642 • Mon-Fri 10:00-6:00, Sat-Sun 11:00-5:00 • Evan Blum and David Callegeros • Prices medium • 10% to 20% trade discount

Two football fields of architectural and garden ornaments, statuary, fountains, gargoyles, marble and stone. From demolished buildings worldwide. Seven floors in Manhattan alone. Carved ornamental panelled rooms: English, French, Italian, Spanish in oak, walnut, pine, mahogany from 18th to 20th centuries. Restoration of architectural ornaments; paint stripping from any material and dismantling any structures or objects.

URBAN ARCHAEOLOGY

143 Franklin Street, New York, NY 10013 • Tel: (212) 431-4646 • Fax: (212) 343-2312 • Mon-Fri 8:00-6:00 • Gil Shapiro 285 Lafayette Street, New York, NY 10012 • Tel: (212) 431-6969 • Fax: (212) 941-1918 • Mon-Fri 8:00-6:00, Sat 10:00-4:00 • Steve Davenport 239 East 58th Street, New York, NY 10022 • Tel: (212) 371-4646 • Fax: (212) 371-1601 • Mon-Fri 8:00-6:00, Sat 10:00-4:00

Architectural antiques, unusual antique lighting, Victorian through the 1940s. Antique and reproduction plumbing fixtures, claw-foot tubs, faucets, showers. Vitrines and floorcases made from mahogany, bent glass and brass. Restoration through the Franklin Street store.

Asian Antiques and Art

ELEANOR ABRAHAM ASIAN ART

345 East 52nd Street, New York, NY 10022 • Telfax: (212) 688-1667 • By appointment only

Sculpture of India, Tibet and Pakistan from the 3rd to the 16th centuries. Tribal jewelry and colorful 70-year-old textiles from Afghanistan, Pakistan and India.

ANCIENT & MODERN ART GALLERY

81 Baxter Street, New York, NY 10013 • Tel: (212) 406-1131 • Mon-Sat 10:30-6:00 • Jennie Shen • Chinese spoken • Prices low to medium • Trade discounts • Visa and MC

Chinese art and antiques of the Han, Tang and Song Dynasties. Woodcarvings, ceramics, paintings, calligraphy and landscapes. Restoration of Chinese paintings. Silk mounting.

ART OF THE PAST

1242 Madison Avenue, New York, NY 10028 • Tel: (212) 860-7070 • Fax: (212) 876-5373 • By appointment

Indian, Tibetan, Nepalese and Southeast Asian paintings, sculpture, Islamic and other works of art.

D. & J. BITTKER

New York, NY • Tel: (212) 472-6227 • Fax: (212) 744-6035 • By appointment

Early Ming furniture.

BODHICITTA INC.

19 East 69th Street, 4th floor, New York, NY 10021 • Tel: (212) 639-9574 • Fax: (212) 639-9684 • Mon-Sat 10:30-6:00 • Namkha Dorjee

Art and antiques: sculpture, paintings, jewelry and some furniture from India, Nepal and Tibet. 3rd to 18th centuries.

A.R. BROOMER

1050 Second Avenue, Gallery 81, New York, NY 10022 • Tel: (212) 421-9530 • Fax: (212) 758-3840 • Mon-Sat 10:30-6:00 • Prices medium • Major credit cards

17th- and 18th-century Chinese blue and white porcelains.

RALPH M. CHAIT GALLERIES, INC.

12 East 56th Street, New York, NY 10022 • Tel: (212) 758-0937 • Fax: (212) 319-0471 • Mon-Sat 10:00-5:30 • Mrs. Marion C. Howe • Prices high • Major credit cards

Fine Chinese works of art, Neolithic to 1800 A.D. Museum quality.

ALBERTO MANUEL CHEUNG

120 East 76th Street, New York, NY 10021 • Telfax: (212) 737-5372 • By appointment • Spanish spoken • Prices medium • Trade discount • Amex

Chinese antiquities: pottery, ceramics and porcelains from Neolithic through Qing Dynasty, mainly Han and Tang.

CHINA IMPORTING CO.

28 East 10th Street, New York, NY 10003 • Tel: (212) 995-0800 • Mon-Fri 11:00-4:30 by appointment • Janice Lee • Chinese spoken • Prices medium to high

Antique Chinese porcelain and art objects.

THE CHINESE PORCELAIN COMPANY

475 Park Avenue, New York, NY 10022 • Tel: (212) 838-7744 • Fax: (212) 838-4922 • Mon-Fri 10:00-6:00, Sat 11:00-5:00 • Numerous languages spoken • MC and Visa

Asian ceramics, works of art and sculpture. European furniture and decorations.

ROGER CREELMAN FINE ARTS

399 East 72nd Street, #1011, New York, NY 10021 • Tel: (212) 734-9506 • Fax: (212) 288-1801 • By appointment

Antique Chinese ceramics and contemporary Chinese paintings.

CAROLE DAVENPORT

131 East 83rd Street, New York, NY 10028 • Telfax: (212) 734-4859 • By appointment

Asian art specializing in Japanese ceramics.

R.H. ELLSWORTH

960 Fifth Avenue, New York, NY 10021 • Tel: (212) 535-9249 • Fax: (212) 772-3404 • By appointment

Ancient Oriental art. Works with museums and collectors.

MD FLACKS LTD.

38 East 57th Street, 6th floor, New York, NY 10022 • Tel: (212) 838-4575 • Fax: (212) 838-2976 • Tue-Fri 10:00-5:00, Sat 12:00-5:00 • Marcus Flacks • Italian spoken • Prices high

16th- and 17th-century Chinese furniture, sculpture and scholars' objects.

FLYING CRANES ANTIQUES LTD.

1050 Second Avenue, Galleries 55 & 56, New York, NY 10022 • Tel: (212) 223-4600 • Fax: (212) 223-4601 • Mon-Sat 10:30-6:00 • Clifford Schaefer • Prices high • Trade discount • Major credit cards

Rare museum quality 18th- and 19th-century Japanese antiques.

⚕ E. & J. FRANKEL LTD.

1040 Madison Avenue, New York, NY 10021 • Tel: (212) 879-5733 • Fax: (212) 879-1998 • Mon-Sat 10:00-5:30 • French, Chinese, Hungarian, German and Spanish spoken • Amex, Visa and MC

Superb collection of Oriental art and antiques. Chinese and Japanese jades, porcelain, ceramics, paintings, mineral carvings and sculpture.

JOSEPH G. GERENA FINE ART

12 East 86th Street, Suite #1409, New York, NY 10028 • Tel: (212) 650-0117 • Fax: (212) 650-0118 • By appointment • French and Spanish spoken • Prices medium to high

Ancient Asian and tribal art, from Neolithic to 19th century.

CHARLES R. GRACIE & SONS, INC.

1010 Lexington Avenue, New York, NY 10021 • Tel: (212) 861-1150 • Fax: (212) 861-1944 • Mon-Fri 9:30-5:30, Sat 11:00-4:00 • Brian Gracie • French, Spanish, Chinese and Japanese spoken • Prices high • 20 to 33% trade discount • Major credit cards

Chinese and Japanese antiques, hand-painted wallpapers. Custom order screens and furniture. Clients include: White House, Blair House, Gracie Mansion, museums and top decorators.

⚕ LIZA HYDE ANTIQUE JAPANESE SCREENS

565 Park Avenue, New York, NY 10021 • Tel: (212) 752-3581 • Fax: (212) 751-6319 • Liza Hyde • By appointment • French spoken • Prices range from low to very high • 20% trade discount

Antique Japanese screens—all periods, all sizes and all prices. Specializing in fine old Japanese screen paintings and textiles.

IMPERIAL ORIENTAL ART

790 Madison Avenue, New York, NY 10021 • Tel: (212) 717-5383 • Fax: (212) 249-0333 • Mon-Sat 11:00-6:00 • Trade discount • Amex

Specialist in Chinese, Japanese and Korean ceramics and works of art from the 12th to the 20th centuries.

INTERNATIONAL JAPANESE PRINT AUCTIONEERS, INC.

20 West 64th Street, New York, NY 10023 • Telfax: (212) 787-4572 •
By appointment • Gustin Tan • Japanese and Chinese spoken • Prices
low to medium • Trade discounts • MC and Visa

Japanese woodblock prints: 18th and 19th centuries, Modern and
contemporary.

JAPAN GALLERY

1210 Lexington Avenue, New York, NY 10028 • Tel: (212) 288-2241 •
Fax: (212) 794-9497 • Ms. Ayako Abe • Japanese spoken • Trade discount • Major credit cards

18th- , 19th- and early 20th-century Japanese woodblock prints.
Museum clients.

KANG COLLECTION

9 East 82nd Street, New York, NY 10028 • Tel: (212) 734-1490 • Fax:
(212) 734-6653 • By appointment

Korean fine art and antiques.

KOKO CHINESE ANTIQUES

58 East 79th Street, New York, NY 10021 • Telfax: (212) 439-6390 •
Tue-Sat 11:00-6:00 • W.K. Ko and Marilyn Ko • Mandarin and Cantonese
spoken • Prices medium to high • Trade discount

17th- to 19th-century Chinese furniture and works of art. Pottery of
the Han, Tang and Ming dynasties.

KOREANA ART & ANTIQUES

963 Madison Avenue, New York, NY 10021 • Telfax: (212) 249-0400 •
Mon-Sat 10:00-6:00 • Moon H. Kim • Korean spoken • Prices medium
to high • Trade discount • Amex

Fine collection of Korean antiques and art; folk art and decorative
objects.

KRISHNA GALLERY OF ASIAN ARTS

153 East 57th Street, New York, NY 10022 • Tel: (212) 249-1677 • Fax:
(212) 759-6812 • By appointment

Art of Tibet, Nepal and India: 100 B.C. to 1900.

NAVIN KUMAR GALLERY

900 Park Avenue, Suite 4E, New York, NY 10021 • Tel: (212) 734-4075
• Fax: (212) 734-4076 • By appointment

Indian, Nepalese, Tibetan, Chinese and Islamic art and antiques.

J.J. LALLY & CO.

41 East 57th Street, New York, NY 10022 • Tel: (212) 371-3380 • Fax: (212) 593-4699 • Mon-Fri 9:00-5:00, Sat 10:00-4:00 • James J. Lally, President • Mandarin Chinese, French and Italian spoken • Prices high • 10% trade discount

Ancient Chinese works of art: ceramics, jades, bronzes, sculpture, tomb figures (not painting).

WILLIAM LIPTON LTD.

27 East 61st Street, New York, NY 10021 • Tel: (212) 751-8131 • Fax: (212) 751-8133 • Mon-Fri 10:00-6:00, Sat 12:00-5:00 or by appointment • Mrs. Yvonne Wong • Chinese spoken • Prices very high • Major credit cards

Marvellous early Chinese furniture and bronze lights commissioned in Paris.

LEIGHTON R. LONGHI

Box 6704, New York, NY 10028 • Tel: (212) 722-5745 • Fax: (212) 996-0721 • By appointment • German, French and Spanish spoken

Fine Oriental art specializing in Japanese screens, paintings and sculpture.

JOAN B. MIRVISS LTD

P.O. Box 1095, New York, NY 10023 • Tel: (212) 799-4021 • Fax: (212) 721-5148 • By appointment

Japanese woodblock prints, paintings, screens and decorations.

MOKOTOFF ASIAN ARTS

584 Broadway, New York, NY 10012 • Tel: (212) 941-1901 • Fax: (212) 941-1879 • Tue-Sat 12:00-6:00 • Moke Mokotoff • Chinese spoken • Prices medium to high

Buddhist art from Tibet, China, India and Nepal. Embroidered Chinese silk robes and Asian textiles.

NAGA ANTIQUES, LTD.

145 East 61st Street, New York, NY 10021 • Tel: (212) 593-2788 • Fax: (212) 308-2451 • Mon-Fri 10:00-5:00 • James Marinaccio • Prices medium to high • 20% professional discount

Fine Japanese art and antiques: painted screens, lacquerware, porcelains, bronzes, furniture, ceramics, stone sculptures and wood sculptures.

NIPPON GALLERY/NIPPON CLUB

145 West 57th Street, New York, NY 10019 • Tel: (212) 581-2223 • Fax: (212) 581-3332 • Mon-Sat 10:00-6:00 • Japanese spoken

Traditional and contemporary Japanese art.

ORIENTATIONS GALLERY

802 Madison Avenue, New York, NY 10021 • Tel: (212) 772-7705 • Fax: (212) 772-9661 • Mon-Sat 12:00-6:00 • Major credit cards

18th- and 19th-century, Edo and Meiji period, Japanese decorative arts: cloisonne enamels, bronzes, ivory and wood carvings, Satsuma, inro and netsuke.

STUART PERRIN GALLERY

80 Fourth Avenue, #4, New York, NY 10003 • Tel: (212) 533-0475 • Fax: (212) 388-0534 • By appointment • Prices medium to high • Professional discount

Specialist in fine antique Tibetan, Indian and Nepali art: bronzes, ritual objects, tankas, paintings.

RONIN GALLERY

605 Madison Avenue, New York, NY 10022 • Tel: (212) 688-0188 • Fax: (212) 593-9808 • Mon-Sat 10:30-5:30 • Japanese, French, Italian and Portuguese spoken • Major credit cards

17th- to 20th-century Japanese woodblock prints, netsuke, inro and tsuba.

SIGMA GALLERY

379 West Broadway, New York, NY 10012 • Tel: (212) 941-0014 • Fax: (212) 941-0016 • Tue-Sat 11:00-5:00 • Dolores An • Korean spoken • Trade discounts

Contemporary Asian American art with special focus on Korean and Korean American paintings, sculpture and video.

MICHAEL SIMMS

New York, NY • Tel: (212) 228-9207 • By appointment • Japanese spoken

Consultant in special areas of Japanese decorative art of the Meiji period: bronzes, ivories and matchsafes.

SINGKIANG

P.O. Box 263, Ansonia Station, New York, NY 10023 • (212) 541-9159 • By appointment • Linda Pastorino-Weiss and Norman R. Weiss • Hindi, German, French and Italian spoken • Prices medium to high • Professional discount • Amex

Ethnographic sculpture, textiles and jewelry of Indonesia, India, the Himalayas and Central Asia. Chinese pottery and porcelain from Neolithic through early Qing; European decorative arts and works on paper from late Medieval period through 18th century.

LEA SNEIDER

211 Central Park West, New York, NY 10024 • Tel: (212) 724-6171 • Fax: (212) 769-3156 • By appointment • Japanese, Korean and Chinese spoken • Prices medium

Asian Art dealer and curator specializing in Korean art and Japanese Mingei.

MICHAEL SPINDELL LTD.

163 Third Avenue, Suite 295, New York, NY 10003 • Tel: (212) 353-3666 • Fax: (212) 353-3667 • By appointment • Michael Spindel • Prices high • All major credit cards

Oriental art and antiques. Specialty in antique netsuke and contemporary netsuke by over 50 international artists.

THINGS JAPANESE

127 East 60th Street, New York, NY 10022 • Tel: (212) 371-4661 • Fax: (212) 371-1162 • Mon-Sat 11:00-5:00, Tue until 6:00 • Amex, MC and Visa

18th- to 20th-century Japanese art and antiques: woodblock prints and scrolls, porcelain, pottery, baskets, masks, screens, dolls, kimonos, netsuke, folk art and related books.

EILEEN WALTERS GALLERY

654 Madison Avenue, #1702, New York, NY 10021 • Tel: (212) 644-1414 • Fax: (212) 644-0004 • Tue-Sat 11:00-6:00 appointment recommended • Eileen Walters • French spoken • Prices low to high • Some trade discounts • Major credit cards

18th- to early 20th-century Japanese woodblock prints (Ukiyo-e through Modern).

WEISBROD CHINESE ART

36 East 57th Street, 3rd floor, New York, NY 10022 • Tel: (212) 319-1335 • Fax: (212) 319-1327 • Mon-Thu 9:30-5:30, Fri 9:30-2:30 • Spanish, French, Chinese and some Italian spoken

Chinese art and antiques from the Neolithic period to the Qing Dynasty: furniture, objects, paintings, porcelains and especially ceramics and jades.

L.J. WENDER FINE CHINESE ART

3 East 80th Street, New York, NY 10021 • Tel: (212) 734-3460 • Fax: (212) 427-4945 • Mon-Sat 10:00-5:00 • Leon and Karen Wender • Chinese spoken • Prices medium • 10-20% professional discount

Fine Chinese paintings and calligraphies. Ming Dynasty furniture and scholar table items. They can mount or restore Chinese or Japanese paintings.

⚏ DORIS WIENER

New York, NY • Tel: (212) 772-3631 • Fax: (212) 439-6626 • By appointment

Ancient Art of India, Southeast Asia and the Himalayas.

ZETTERQUIST GALLERIES

24 East 81st Street, #2B, New York, NY 10028 • Tel: (212) 988-3399 • Fax: (212) 988-2221 • By appointment • Eric J. Zetterquist • Japanese spoken • Prices high • 10% professional discount

Asian ceramics, antique and modern. Contemporary Asian art.

ARCHITECTURAL ELEMENTS

Anti-Grafitti

CLEANUP CORPORATION OF AMERICA

New York, NY 10023 • Tel: (212) 749-0710 • By appointment

An exterior building cleaning service that specializes in the removal of graffiti from all types of masonry.

HORN GRAFFITTI CONTROL CORPORATION OF AMERICA

32-45 Queens Blvd., Long Island City, NY 11101 • Tel: (718) 937-6060 • Fax: (718) 937-2226 • Mon-Fri by appointment

Restoration and cleaning of graffiti damaged surfaces.

THOMANN-HANRY, INC.

575 Madison Avenue, 25th floor, New York, NY 10022 • Tel: (212) 755-5550 • Fax: (212) 755-6385 • Mon-Fri 9:00-5:00 • Christophe S. Nissaux

This firm has a patented dry system called "Facade Gommage" for cleaning facades. The process entails gently cleaning masonry by projecting very fine powders with low pressure compressed air. No chemicals, water or detergents are used. Credits: The Louvre Museum, Paris; Tribune Tower, Chicago; and many others.

Anti-Noise

CITIQUIET INC.

218 East 81st Street, New York, NY 10028 • Tel: (212) 874-5362 • Fax: (212) 717-7354 • Mon-Fri 10:00-5:00 • David Skudin • Prices low to high • Trade discount • Major credit cards

Interior noise elimination: windows, walls, ceilings and floors. Citiquiet interior noise elimination windows, Marvin wood windows and aluminium replacement windows.

Architectural Detail

DAVID JOHNSON

42 Washington Avenue, Brooklyn, NY 11205 • Tel: (718) 875-7394 • Fax: (718) 596-0007 • Mon-Fri 9:30-5:30 • Prices medium to high • Some trade discounts

Custom architectural details in all metals. Design, fabrication to specification and installation of details in metal, etched glass, stone, light fixtures, bronze hardware, tables in stone.

Architectural Woodworking and Custom Cabinetry

ABC CABINET MAKERS AND CARPENTERS

511 West 33rd Street, New York, NY 10001 • Tel: (212) 279-5735 • Fax: (212) 279-5737 • Mon-Fri 8:30-5:00 • David Greene • Prices medium • Trade discount

Custom woodworking in a variety of hardwoods, specifically custom cabinetry for every room; design and installation; commercial and residential.

AMERICAN WOOD COLUMN

913 Grand Street, Brooklyn, NY 11211 • Tel: (718) 782-3163 • Fax: (718) 387-9099 • Mon-Fri 8:00-4:00 • Edward R. Lupo • Prices medium

Custom wood turnings: columns, balusters, finials, newels; custom wood mouldings. Extremely high quality work.

ARCHITECTURAL PANELING, INC.

979 Third Avenue (D&D), New York, NY 10022 • Tel: (212) 371-9632 • Fax: (212) 759-0276 • Mon-Fri 9:00-5:00

Top-of-the-line custom cabinetry and wall systems.

BAREWOOD ARCHITECTURAL WOODWORK

106 Ferris Street, Brooklyn, NY 11231 • Tel: (718) 875-9037 • Fax: (718) 875-3833 • Mon-Fri 8:00-5:00 • Leslie Neilson • Spanish and Polish spoken

Custom cabinets and furniture. Architectural restoration and renovation of 18th- and 19th-century elements and furniture. Specialties include: wood turning and carving, mantels, mouldings, doors and windows. References upon request.

BEECH ASSOCIATES

145 East 94th Street, New York, NY 10128 • Tel: (212) 876-6554 • Fax: (212) 410-3451 • Mon-Fri 9:00-5:00

Custom residential woodworking. Complete installations of libraries, kitchens and bathrooms. All aspects of work in wood.

PHILIPPE BESNARD INC.

171 Lincoln Avenue, Bronx, NY 10454 • Tel: (718) 402-8043 • Fax: (718) 292-5902 • Philippe Besnard • By appointment

Custom woodwork, architectural woodwork and cabinetry.

THE BUILDING BLOCK

550 West 30th Street, New York, NY 10001 • Tel: (212) 714-9333 • Fax: (212) 714-9411 • Mon-Fri 8:00-4:00 • Noah Block • Italian, Spanish and Polish spoken • Prices high

Full-service woodworking: millworking, cabinetmaking and furniture. Traditional, solid wood, woodworking including duplication for restoration and landmark work. Excellent references upon request.

THE CABINET SHOP

1583 First Avenue, New York, NY 10028 • Tel: (212) 734-1116 • Fax: (212) 628-1966 • Mon-Fri 8:00-6:00 • Prices medium to high • Major credit cards

Architectural woodworking and custom cabinetry. Installations of libraries, kitchens, bathrooms and entertainment centers. References on request.

JOHN CAMMALLERI

656 Cary Avenue, Staten Island, NY 10310 • Tel: (718) 816-6777 • Mon-Fri 7:00-4:00 • Italian and Spanish spoken

Custom cabinetry, repair of wooden chairs, antique and contemporary. Custom furniture and custom cabinetry.

CURTIS CO.

40 East 19th Street, New York, NY 10003 • Tel: (212) 673-5353 • Fax: (212) 979-9713 • Mon-Sat 10:00-6:00, Sun 12:00-6:00 • Herbert Roberts • Prices low to medium • Major credit cards

Center for solid wood furniture. Large selection in home theatre, home office, libraries. Custom and ready-made furniture. Custom architectural woodworking, custom cabinetry and installation of libraries.

FIFTY THREE RESTORATIONS, INC.

P.O. Box 2852, Church Street Station, New York, NY 10008 • Tel: (212) 566-1053 • Fax: (212) 267-4606 • By appointment • Vincent Lepre • Prices medium

Reproduction and restoration of period architectural woodwork, interior and exterior. Has an impeccable reputation for fine work on landmark buildings and museums. Oversees the entire project from the restoration of the plaster work through to the trompe l'oeil.

JACOB FROEHLICH CABINET WORKS, INC.

550-560 Barry Street, Bronx, NY 10474 • Tel: (718) 893-1300 • Fax: (718) 991-3103 • Mon-Fri 7:00-5:00 • Kristine Hannington • Italian, German and Spanish spoken • Prices high • Trade only

Very high-end residential and commercial woodworking including hard line drafting, fabrication, finishing and installation. Restoration of antique paneling and installation of all woodwork. Works for top architects and decorators.

R. GASPARRE CUSTOM FURNITURE

32-45 62nd Street, Woodside, NY 11377 • Tel: (718) 726-7348 • Fax: (212) 274-4994 • Mon-Fri 9:00-5:00 • Bruce Gasparre • Prices high

Custom architectural woodworking, custom cabinetry, wall paneling, wall units, libraries; custom kitchens; custom furniture in solid woods.

GAUGHAN CONSTRUCTION

37-26 Tenth Street, Long Island City, NY 11101 • Tel: (718) 482-1540 • Fax: (718) 482-1425 • Mon-Fri 8:00-5:00

Fabrication and installation of interior decorative architectural woodwork: mouldings, doors, floors and cabinetry.

ISLAND HOUSEWRIGHTS CORP.

6019 Amboy Road, Staten Island, NY 10309 • Telfax: (718) 948-4150 • Mon-Fri 9:00-5:00 • Russell Powell

Historic carpentry and architectural millwork. A great deal of landmark work. Credits: Historic Richmond Town and Conference House, Staten Island.

JOHN'S WOODSHOP

307 East 91st Street, New York, NY 10128 • Tel: (212) 348-1816 • By appointment • John Chernow • Spanish and Hungarian spoken • Prices medium to high

Cabinetmaker and carpenter. Custom woodworking and general contracting for kitchens, bathrooms, wall units, renovations. References on request.

OLEK LEJBZON & CO.

210 11th Avenue, New York, NY 10001 • Tel: (212) 243-3363 • Fax: (212) 243-3432 • Mon-Sat 7:30-6:00 • Peter Triestman • Many languages spoken

Architectural millwork and restoration of historic millwork. A workshop with 35 skilled European craftsmen, making cabinets to custom orders, restoring all wood elements, including furniture. Excellent references.

LICO CONTRACTING INC.

29-10 20th Avenue, Astoria, New York, 11105 • Tel: (718) 932-8300 • Fax: (718) 204-9817 • Mon-Fri 7:30-5:00 • Richard Bruno, President • Italian and Spanish spoken • Prices very high • Trade only

Superb quality millworking and cabinet construction. Finest craftsmen in all aspects of woodworking. Top references.

LITTLE WOLF CABINET SHOP

1583 First Avenue, New York, NY 10028 • Tel: (212) 734-1116 • Fax: (212) 628-1966 • Mon-Fri 8:00-6:00

Woodworking, millwork, custom cabinets and library shelving.

MANHATTAN CABINETRY

227 East 59th Street, New York, NY 10022 • Tel: (212) 750-9800 • Fax: (212) 759-0338 • James Stephens
455 Park Avenue South, New York, NY 10016 • Tel: (212) 889-8808 • 1630 Second Avenue, New York, NY 10028 • Tel: (212) 773-8870 • Mon-Thu 10:00-7:00, Fri 10:00-6:00, Sat 10:00-5:30, Sun 12:00-5:30 • Prices medium to high • Trade discount • Major credit cards

Custom cabinetry and custom-designed furniture.

MILLWORK SPECIALTIES

189 Prospect Avenue, Brooklyn, NY 11215 • Tel: (718) 768-7112 • Fax: (718) 965-3974 • Mon-Fri 8:00-4:00 • Cosmo Cotroneo

Custom mouldings for restoration and replication of 18th- , 19th- and 20th-century buildings. Raised-panel doors and double-hung sash units.

FRANK PELLITTERI

201 East 56th Street, New York, NY 10022 • Tel: (212) 486-0545 • Fax: (212) 486-0546 • By appointment • Italian spoken • Prices low to high

High-quality architectural woodworking, fine paneling, valences, cornices, shutters and custom cabinetry. Restoration of historic millwork and antique furniture restoration. French polishing.

PENSATO INDUSTRIES

1155 Manhattan Avenue, Brooklyn, NY 11222 • Tel: (718) 383-8896 • Fax: (718) 383-8289 • Mon-Fri 8:00-4:30 • Antonino Pensato • Spanish and Italian spoken • Prices medium • Trade discount

Cabinetmaking, renovation and installation.

DAVID SMOLEN/DRS INTERIORS

P.O. Box 156, Deposit, NY 13754 • Telfax: (607) 467-2572 • By appointment • Prices medium to high

High-quality custom millwork for residential and corporate spaces including built-in shelving and storage, kitchens, vanities. Custom furniture: conference tables, desks, wall panels, dining tables. Excellent references upon request.

WILLIAM SOMERVILLE, INC.

166 East 124th Street, New York, NY 10035 • Tel: (212) 534-4600 • Fax: (212) 410-0236 • Mon-Fri 9:00-5:00 • Beth Miller • French and Spanish spoken • Prices high

Excellent custom woodwork, paneling and furniture: for hotels, banks, law firms and major institutions. Clients include the Metropolitan Opera House and major hotels and banks.

SPACE CARPENTER

306 East 5th Street, Suite 23, New York, NY 10003 • Telfax: (212) 674-4237 • Mon-Fri by appointment • Kevin Rocine • French and Spanish spoken • Prices medium

Carpenter: service-oriented problem solving. Clients mainly private. References on request.

T & T WOODWORKING, INC.

37 West 20th Street, New York, NY 10011 • Tel: (212) 255-6005 • Fax: (212) 255-6006 • Mon-Sat 8:30-4:30 • Jozef Tomahatsch • Hungarian, French and Spanish spoken • Prices high

Custom woodworking, cabinetry, kitchens, bathrooms, entertainment rooms, commercial displays. Very high quality craftsmanship. Custom furniture and reproduction antique furniture. Restoration of antique furniture.

JOSEPH TEKLITS CORPORATION

345 East 104th Street, New York, NY 10029 • Tel: (212) 427-7550 • Fax: (212) 860-7129 • Mon-Fri 8:00-4:00

Woodworking shop. Specialty: very high quality wood paneling.

TRADITIONAL LINE

143 West 21st Street, New York, NY 10011 • Tel: (212) 627-3555 •
Fax: (212) 645-8158 • Mon-Fri 9:00-5:00 • James Boorstein, Anthony
Lefeber • Italian and some French spoken • Prices high

Architectural restoration primarily. Interior woodwork restoration,
antique paneling, custom work and finishing. Technical consultation for the planning and implementation of the project. Restoration
of antique furniture. Top references.

THE WORKSHOP OF ENRIQUE MARTINEZ

322 Dean Street, Brooklyn, NY 11217 • Tel: (718) 643-4003 • Mon-Fri
9:00-5:00 • Spanish spoken • Prices high • Trade discount

Custom woodwork, cabinets, entertainment centers, book units,
libraries, armoires. Custom hand-crafted furniture in solid woods,
country designs.

WOOD-O-RAMA, INC.

238 West 108th Street, New York, NY 10025 • Tel: (212) 749-6438 •
Mon-Sat 9:00-5:30 • Spanish spoken • Prices medium to high • Major
credit cards

Architectural woodworking. Specialists in mouldings with a choice
of over 700 mouldings for ceilings, doors and floors. Large stock of
hardwood mouldings. Custom cabinets and installation of ready-
made kitchen cabinets. Repair and restoration of architectural elements.

Audio Video Installations

AUDIO VIDEO CRAFTS, INC.

9-09 44th Avenue, Long Island City, NY 11101 • Tel: (718) 706-8300 •
Fax: (718) 786-0697 • Mon-Fri 9:00-5:30

Complete and expert installations of audio and video equipment.

BANG & OLUFSEN NEW YORK

952 Madison Avenue, New York, NY 10021 • Tel: (212) 879-6161 •
Fax: (212) 794-4998 • Mon-Sat 10:00-6:30, Sun 12:00-6:00 • Jeff
Yetikyel • Spanish spoken • Prices high

Very high quality audio and video systems. Full installation.

LOWELL/EDWARDS

979 Third Avenue (D&D), New York, NY 10022 • Tel: (212) 980-2862 •
Fax: (212) 980-2864 • Mon-Fri 9:00-5:00 and by appointment • Lowell
Kaps • Spanish spoken • Prices medium to high • Trade discount •
Major credit cards

Installation of complete home entertainment centers, audio and
video. Hand-crafted custom cabinetry.

LYRIC HI-FI, INC.

1221 Lexington Avenue, New York, NY 10028 • Tel: (212) 439-1900 • Fax: (212) 734-8434 • Mon-Sat 10:00-6:00 • Leonard Belleza, Barry Boris • Greek and Spanish spoken • Prices high • Major credit cards

High-end audio experts and home theatre custom installations.

ROSNER CUSTOM SOUND, INC.

11-38 31st Avenue, Long Island City, NY 11106 • Tel: (718) 726-5600 • Fax: (718) 956-7516 • 7 days by appointment • Amex

Custom sound and video installations for home, the professional and industry.

SOUND BY SINGER

18 East 16th Street, New York, NY 10003 • Tel: (212) 924-8600 • Fax: (212) 366-6350 • Mon, Wed, Fri-Sat 10:00-6:00, Tue and Thu 10:00-8:00, Sun 12:00-5:00 • Major credit cards

Expert installations of sound and television systems. Custom cabinetry.

SOUND CONTRACT, INC.

201 East 89th Street, New York, NY 10028 • Tel: (212) 831-0031 • Fax: (212) 534-3132 • By appointment

Installations of home entertainment centers.

Closets

CALIFORNIA CLOSETS

1625 York Avenue, New York, NY 10128 • Tel: (212) 517-7877 • Fax: (212) 517-3951 • Mon-Fri 10:00-6:00, Sat 10:00-3:00 • Prices medium to high • MC and Visa

Installation of closet systems, residential, office and commercial. Custom designs. Free consultation. Special order wood and melamine and wire systems.

EUROPEAN CLOSET

214 49th Street, Brooklyn, NY 11220 • Tel: (718) 567-7121 • Fax: (718) 567-8365 • Mon-Fri 9:00-5:00 • Mike Belfor • Russian spoken • Prices medium • Trade discount • Major credit cards

Closet interior organization for homes and offices. Home entertainment centers. Custom doors in wood and mirror.

NEW YORK CLOSET CO. INC.

1458 Third Avenue, New York, NY 10028 • Tel: (212) 439-9500 • Fax: (212) 439-9305 • Mon-Sat 11:00-6:00, Thu 11:00-8:00, Sun 1:00-5:00 • Prices medium to high • Major credit cards

Closet systems and all kinds of accessories and organizers for the closet.

Cork

THE CORK STORE

22 Caton Place, Brooklyn, NY 11218 • Tel: (718) 853-2300 • Fax: (718) 853-2303 • Mon-Fri 8:15-4:30 • Prices medium • Major credit cards

Cork products for architects, designers and contractors. Dry marker boards, peg boards, projection screens, cork tiles for walls and floors.

MANTON INDUSTRIAL CORK PRODUCTS, INC.

415 Oser Avenue, Haupaug, NY 11788 • Tel: (516) 273-0700 • Fax: (516) 273-0038 • Mon-Fri 8:00-4:00 • Trade only

Custom cork items to blueprint. Cork in rolls and sheets; all widths, all thicknesses.

NEW YORK BLACKBOARD, INC.

83 Rte. 22 West, Hillside, NJ 07205 • Tel: (800) 652-6273 • Fax: (201) 926-3440 • Mon-Fri 8:00-4:30 • Prices medium • Visa and MC

Cork products for the home, school and office.

Doors and Windows

ALL WINDOWS & DOOR SUPPLY

1050 Utica Avenue, Brooklyn, NY 11203 • Tel: (718) 495-9000 • Fax: 718) 445-9022 • Mon-Fri 9:00-5:00

Specialists in landmark type windows. Doors of all types, solid, panelled, carved, louvered. Parts and accessories for old windows and doors so they will be historically correct.

AMERICAN STEEL WINDOW SERVICE CO.

111 West 17th Street, New York, NY 10011 • Tel: (212) 242-8131 • Fax: (212) 924-8536 • By appointment

Restoration services for steel windows and doors.

ANTIQUARIAN TRADERS

399 Lafayette Street, New York, NY 10003 • Tel: (212) 260-1200 • Fax: (212) 529-5320 • Mon-Fri 10:00-6:00

Antique wood-panelled entry doors. American, Victorian, French, Art Nouveau, Art Deco antiques. They also have a refinishing shop.

A&S WINDOWS ASSOCIATES, INC.

88-19 76th Avenue, Glendale, NY 11385 • Tel: (718) 275-7900 • Fax: (718) 997-7683 • By appointment

Fabrication of steel windows: specialists in Tudor, Revival and Art Deco style steel casement sash windows.

PHILIPPE BESNARD, INC.

171 Lincoln Avenue, Bronx, NY 10454 • Tel: (718) 402-8043 • Fax: (718) 292-5902 • By appointment

Custom woodworking. Their specialty: clerestory windows and Gothic style doors.

B & L GROUP INC.

155 West 72nd Street, New York, NY 10023 • Tel: (212) 362-8540 • Fax: (212) 580-8409 • Mon-Fri 8:00-5:00 • Trade only

Representatives of Efco aluminum windows and Bailey steel windows. No installation.

CAL MICHAEL WOODWORKING, INC.

869 Washington Street, New York, NY 10014 • Tel: (212) 691-0992 • Fax: (212) 691-1031 • Mon-Fri 9:00-5:00 • Howard Timmins • Latvian spoken • Prices high • Trade discount

Interior millwork: specialists in doors and trim. Very high quality.

CITYPROOF CORP.

10-11 43rd Avenue, Long Island City, NY 11101 • Tel: (718) 786-1600 • Fax: (718) 786-2713 • Mon-Fri 8:00-4:30

Interior window systems in aluminum to reduce noise, drafts and pollution and to contain energy.

CONTINENTAL CUSTOM WINDOWS, INC.

255 Windsor Place, Brooklyn, NY 11218 • Tel: (718) 768-6800 • Fax: (718) 768-7580 • By appointment

Fabrication and restoration of all types of windows and doors. Restoration services.

EL-BE INSTALLATIONS, INC.

172 North Oak Street, Copiague, NY 11726 • Tel: (516) 842-0444 •
Fax: (516) 842-0493 • Mon-Fri 9:00-5:00 • Louis J. Basile • Prices high

Restoration and installation of windows. Specialists in landmark
buildings. They have worked closely with the Landmarks Commission in providing replacement windows for landmark buildings.

ENGLANDER MILLWORK CORP.

2369 Lorillard Place, Bronx, NY 10458 • Tel: (718) 364-4240/41 • Fax:
(718) 364-4780 • Mon-Fri 8:00-4:00 • Jay Winston • Spanish spoken
• Prices medium • Trade discount

Custom doors, windows and mouldings to specifications. Also replications and installation. Mortise and tenon construction. Glass and
panelled wood doors, screens. Restoration of antique doors and
old glass.

ENJO ARCHITECTURAL MILLWORK

16 Park Avenue, Staten Island, NY 10302 • Tel: (718) 447-5220/(800)
437-3656 • Fax: (718) 442-7041 • Mon-Fri 8:00-5:00, Sat by appointment

Manufacturer of architectural doors and windows and other millwork to landmark standards.

FLICKINGER GLASSWORKS

204-207 Van Dycke Street, Pier 41, Brooklyn, NY 11217 • Tel: (718)
875-1531 • Fax: (718) 875-4264

Specialty glass for door and window restoration.

GRILLION CORP.

189-93 First Street, Brooklyn, NY 11215 • Tel: (718) 875-8545 • Mon-
Fri 9:00-5:00, Sat by appointment • D. Jaffe • Spanish spoken • Trade
discount for volume

Manufacturers of room dividers and window treatments: filigree
panels, Shoji screens; set designs and backdrops.

HAHN'S WOODWORKING COMPANY

109 Aldene Road, Roselle, NJ 07203 • Tel: (908) 241-8825 • Fax: (908)
241-9293 • Mon-Fri 7:00-4:00 • Scott Hahn

Traditional and custom wooden garage door manufacturer specializing in radius top doors to match arched openings. Fabricated from
Honduras mahogany, red oak, cypress, western red cedar, redwood
and Douglas fur. Overhead operating doors with the appearance of
traditional barn doors. Other species are available.

HEIGHTS WOODWORKING CO.

630 Sackett Street, Brooklyn, NY 11217 • Tel: (718) 875-7497 • Fax: (718) 624-8890

Custom-made and landmark windows and doors, all woods and all types of glass. Mortise and tenon joinery. Restorations.

JORGENSON-CARR

111 First Street, Jersey City, NJ 07302 • Tel: (201) 792-2278 • Fax: (201) 792-1916 • Mon-Fri by appointment

Architectural woodwork: custom paneling, doors, cabinetry. Custom furniture: tables, chairs.

THE MACKENZIE GROUP, INC.

72 Reade Street, New York, NY 10007 • Tel: (212) 227-1630 • Fax: (212) 619-1885 • Mon-Fri 8:00-4:30 • Glenn Nilsen • Prices high • Trade only

Special doors for hospitals, airports, office buildings and hotels: automatic, revolving (manual and automatic) and Ellison balanced doors; as well as sliding and swinging doors. Architectural hardware: advice on compatible hardware for these specialized doors.

PANORAMA WINDOWS LTD.

767 East 132nd Street, Bronx, NY 10454 • Tel: (212) 489-6400 • Fax: (718) 402-5683 • Mon-Sat 8:00-5:00 • Douglas Simpson • Spanish spoken • Prices high

Top quality windows: aluminum, wood and steel. They work with top New York City co-ops and architects. Landmark Preservation Commission filings.

PRECISION WINDOW CO.

157 Tibbetts Road, Yonkers, NY 10705 • Tel: (914) 376-4500 • Fax: (914) 376-0144 • Mon-Fri 8:00-4:30

Repair and replacement of windows in historic buildings.

RESTORATION MANAGEMENT SERVICES, INC.

440 West 24th Street, New York, NY 10011 • Tel: (212) 929-6474 • Fax: (212) 989-0489 • Mon-Fri 8:00-5:00

Specialists in the restoration and replacement of wood windows.

SKYLINE WINDOWS

625 West 130th Street, New York, NY 10027 • Tel: (212) 491-3000 • Fax: (212) 491-5630 • Mon-Fri 8:00-5:00

Specialists in the reproduction and replacement of windows in historic buildings. The windows are wood, aluminum and steel.

WOOD WINDOW WORKSHOP

839 Broad Street, Utica, NY 13501 • Tel: (315) 724-3619 • Fax: (315) 733-0933 • Michael Kershaw • Russian spoken • Prices very high • Trade only

Custom wood windows and doors and architectural millwork.

ZELUCK ARCHITECTURAL WOOD WINDOWS & DOORS

5300 Kings Highway, Brooklyn, NY 11234 • Tel: (718) 251-8060 • Fax: (718) 531-2564 • Mon-Fri 8:00-5:00 • Roy S. Zeluck • Spanish, Polish and Chinese spoken • Prices high to very high • Trade only

Architectural custom wood windows and doors. French doors a specialty. Excellent references.

Wood Floors and Parquet Specialists

ACE FLOORS

1 Bogardus Place, New York, NY 10040 • Tel: (212) 942-8539 • Mon-Fri 7:30-5:00 • Prices medium

All types of installations, parquet, plank, strip, tongue and groove; bleaching and pickling. Also cork, tile and marble floors. 24 hour service. Bonded, insured and all work guaranteed. Free estimates.

ARCHITECTURAL FLOORING RESOURCE, INC.

151 West 28th Street, Suite 2W, New York, NY 10001 • Tel: (212) 290-0200 • Fax: (212) 290-2855 • Mon-Fri 9:00-5:00 • Spanish spoken • Prices medium to high • Trade only

Supply and installation of commercial and residential flooring materials: natural wood floors, poured epoxy and vinyl floors; all types of carpeting, residential wool carpeting, sisal and area rugs.

CARLCO FLOORS, INC.

140 Seventh Avenue, New York, NY 10011 • Tel: (212) 675-9713 • By appointment • Carlo Lanzillotti • Prices low to medium

All types of flooring for the contract market: wood, tile, carpet.

✵ CUSTOM MILLED & INLAID PARQUET, LTD.

37-11 10th Street, Long Island City, NY 11101 • Tel: (718) 472-4012 • Fax: (718) 472-2434 • Mon-Fri 8:00-6:00 and by appointment • Joseph Juhas • Hungarian, Russian and Polish spoken • Prices medium

Fine custom-milled and inlaid hardwood floor and parquet. Huge choice of custom inlay designs without any limitation. Restoration and refinishing of antique flooring. Superb craftsmanship. Top references.

EASTSIDE FLOOR SERVICE

129 East 124th Street, New York, NY 10035 • Tel: (212) 996-1800 • Fax: (212) 996-1222 • Mon-Fri 8:00-6:00

Hardwood installation, repairs and refinishing. Custom milled flooring of exotic wood species. Bleaching and pickling. Hardwood floor supplies sold.

ᴘ WILLIAM J. ERBE & CO. INC.

560 Barry Street, Bronx, NY 10474 • Tel: (212) 249-6400/(718) 991-7281 • Fax: (718) 991-4957 • Office: Mon-Fri 9:00-3:00 • David Erbe, V.P. • Prices very high

Known as the best in New York. Custom manufactured wood flooring, all species. Antique wood flooring from Europe: restored, installed and finished. Any custom design, Versailles parquet, reproduction of any antique design. Repairs and refinishing of existing wood flooring. Works for top museums and an international clientele.

FLOORMASTERS, INC.

2118 First Avenue, New York, NY 10029 • Tel: (212) 722-7111 • Fax: (212) 722-4041 • Mon-Fri 9:00-5:30 • Major credit cards

Wood, marble, vinyl, ceramic and carpet floors installed, cleaned and restored.

HOBOKEN WOOD FLOORS

979 Third Avenue (D&D), New York, NY 10022 • Tel: (212) 759-5917 • Fax: (212) 593-0263 • Mon-Fri 9:00-5:00 • Trade only • Major credit cards

One of the best known in the New York area. Complete service in wood and parquet floors.

KAMWAY

175 Lexington Avenue, New York, NY 10016 • Tel: (212) 779-1000 • Fax: (212) 779-1002 • Mon-Fri 8:30-6:00 • Prices medium to high • Trade discount • Major credit cards

All types of flooring: ceramic, marble, rubber, seamless flooring for hospitals in vinyl. Wood: parquet floating strip floors. Cork tiles and strips. Sale and installation of kitchen cabinets; bathroom installation; commercial wallpaper.

NEW YORK FLOORING

129 East 124th Street, New York, NY 10035 • Tel: (212) 427-6262 • Fax: (212) 410-1348 • Mon-Fri 9:00-5:00

Custom design and installation of all types of hardwood floors. Existing floors sanded, stained and finished, repaired and restored. Materials sold on the premises. Excellent references.

NISCO

2118 First Avenue, New York, NY 10029 • Tel: (212) 722-3333 • Fax: (212) 722-4041 • Mon-Fri 8:30-5:30 • Aury Lewis • Prices medium • Major credit cards

Installation, restoration and repairs of all floor types, except concrete.

PEISER FLOORS

21 West 100th Street, New York, NY 10025 • Tel: (212) 222-3424 • Fax: (212) 932-8955 • Mon-Fri 8:30-4:30 • Barry Peiser • French and Spanish spoken • Prices medium to high • MC and Visa

Wood flooring installation, refinishing and maintenance. All types of parquet; all types of wood. Select range of vinyl and related flooring. Excellent references.

JANOS P. SPITZER FLOORING CO., INC.

133 West 24th Street, New York, NY 10011 • Tel: (212) 627-1818 • Fax: (212) 627-7982 • Mon-Fri 8:00-4:30

Custom-designed wood floors, inlays, all styles. Restoration.

USA CONTRACTORS, INC.

140-82 34th Avenue, Flushing, NY 11354 • Tel: (212) 222-1000 • Fax: (718) 760-2549 • Available 7 days a week • Ask for Max Sotelo • French, Italian and Spanish spoken • Prices medium • 10% discount to the trade • Major credit cards

New wood floors. Repair, restoration and refinishing of existing floors. Other contract work includes custom cabinetry, closets, bath and tile work, wallpapering, kitchen cabinets marbleizing and faux finishes.

WILLIAMSBURG PARQUET FLOORING CO. INC.

576 Liberty Avenue, Brooklyn, NY 11207 • Tel: (212) 936-5004/(718) 235-5400 • Mon-Fri • 8:00-4:30 • Trade only

Installation and repair of all types of hardwood floors: residential and commercial, schools and gymnasiums. High-quality workmanship.

Marble and Stone

A & G MARBLE

132-19 34th Avenue, Flushing, NY 11354 • Tel: (718) 353-9415 • Fax: (718) 353-9701 • Mon-Fri 8:00-5:00, Sat 9:00-3:00 • Anthony Gambino • Trade discount • Major credit cards

Custom marble work: fabrication and installation.

ALCAMO MARBLE WORKS, INC.

541-543 West 22nd Street, New York, NY 10011-1161 • Tel: (212) 255-5224 • Fax: (212) 255-4060 • Mon-Fri 8:00-4:30 • Onofrio and Nino D'Angelo, Manager: Francesca D'Angelo • Italian and Spanish spoken • Prices medium • Professional discounts

Specialists in marble, granite, onyx, slate and limestone: for floors, vanity tops, columns, marble figures, bases, walls, bathrooms. Fireplaces and mantles: antique and new. Custom installation.

BARONE BROTHERS

29-05 Review Avenue, Long Island City, NY 11101 • Tel: (718) 786-9880 • Fax: (718) 482-9463 • Mon-Fri 8:00-5:00 • Joseph Barone • Trade discount

Marble, onyx, granite and tile for: walls, floors, lobbies, counter tops, fireplaces. Commercial and residential.

B & P STONE AND MARBLE SUPPLY CORP.

177-01 Liberty Avenue, Jamaica, NY 11433 • Tel: (718) 297-8400 • Fax: (718) 658-5734 • Mon-Sat 7:30-4:30 • Joseph Parlato • MC, Visa

Marble and slate for sink tops, tabletops, floors.

JOSEPH CORCORAN MARBLE, INC.

50 West Hills Road, Huntington Station, NY 11746 • Tel: (516) 423-8737 • Fax: (516) 423-8708 • Mon-Fri 7:00-5:00 • Nadine Corcoran • Spanish spoken • Prices medium • Trade discount

Very high quality limestone, slate, granite, marble, travertine, tile and slabs.

DESIGN SUPPLY/STONE SOURCE

215 Park Avenue South, New York, NY 10003 • Tel: (212) 979-6400 • Fax: (212) 979-6989 • Mon-Fri 9:00-5:00 • Jeff Green • Prices medium to high

Importers and distributors of decorative surfaces including natural stone and ceramic tile.

DIONYSIS, INC.

1189 Lexington Avenue, New York, NY 10028 • Tel: (212) 861-5616 • Fax: (212) 861-9472 • Mon-Fri 10:00-6:00, Sat 10:00-4:00 • Mike Giordas • Greek spoken • Prices medium to high • 20% trade discount • Major credit cards

Marble and ceramic tile: sales and installation. Marble fabrication and restoration. Will custom make marble fireplaces. Cast iron bases for consoles, tables and coffee tables. Restoration of vases in ceramic and marble.

D.M.S. STUDIOS

5-50 51st Avenue, Long Island City, NY 11101 • Tel: (718) 937-5648 •
Fax: (718) 937-2609 • Mon-Fri 9:00-6:00 • Daniel Sinclair • Italian spoken • Prices medium

Custom stone fabricating and carving. Custom fireplaces in limestone and marble. All areas of stone carving and sculpture.

MILLER DRUCK SPECIALTY CONTRACTING, INC./
DOMESTIC MARBLE & STONE CORP.

145 Hudson Street, New York, NY 10013 • Tel: (212) 343-3300 • Fax:
(212) 343-3301 • Mon-Fri 8:00-6:00 • Barbara Cohen • Italian, Russian
and Spanish spoken • Prices medium to high

Supply and installation of marble, granite, any natural stone and
ceramic tile. Excellent references.

EMPIRE STATE MARBLE MFG. CORP.

207 East 110th Street, New York, NY 10029 • Tel: (212) 534-2307 •
Fax: (212) 534-7795 • Mon-Fri 8:00-4:00 • Sal Migliore

Marble, slate and granite custom cut to shape and size. Marble and
stone restoration.

FORDHAM MARBLE

1931 West Farms Road, Bronx, NY 10460 • Tel: (718) 893-3380 • Fax:
(718) 893-3883 • Mon-Fri 8:00-4:30 • 421 Fairfield Avenue, Stamford,
CT 06902 • Tel: (203) 348-5088 • Fax: (203) 348-4458

A huge collection of marble, granite and limestone. Custom work.
Stairs, countertops, bathrooms, kitchens.

GENERAL STONE INDUSTRIES, INC.

Mailing: 24-16 Bridge Plaza South, Long Island City, NY 11101 • Tel:
(718) 784-4646 • Fax: (718) 784-1580 • Mon-Fri 8:00-6:00 • J. Zoli
Santo • German, Hungarian and Spanish spoken • Prices medium

Supply and installation of all types of natural building stones: engineering, investigation, consultation regarding stonework restoration, conservation, installation.

HANDWOVEN STUDIO/HWS DESIGN GROUP LTD.

838 Broadway, New York, NY 10003 • Telfax: (212) 253-8735 • Telfax:
(516) 423-9015 • Mon-Fri 9:00-6:00 • Barbara Anne Grib • Some Italian spoken • Prices very high • Trade only

Marble and stone. Specialists in hand-inlaid marble, custom made
in Italy, flooring and accessories. Custom fabrics.

IDEAL TILE OF MANHATTAN, INC.

405 East 51st Street, New York, NY 10022 • Tel: (212) 759-2339 • Fax:
(212) 826-0391 • Mon-Fri 9:00-5:00, Sat 10:00-5:00 • Some Italian
spoken • MC, Visa

Supply and installation of marble and granite.

MARBLE CREATIONS, INC.

300 East 96th Street, New York, NY 10028 • Tel: (212) 423-1222 • Fax: (212) 423-9009 • Mon-Sat 8:00-5:00 • Iqbal Shafi
1122 Washington Avenue, Bronx, NY 10456 • Tel: (718) 292-4545 • Fax: (718) 402-3010 • Mon-Sat 8:00-5:00 • Amex

Custom work in marble, granite, onyx, limestone, bluestone, slate. Marble tiles, carpets and linoleum.

MARBLE, TILE, TERRAZZO & GRANITE CORPORATION

2142 East 63rd Street, Brooklyn, NY 11234 • Tel: (718) 802-1512 • Fax: (718) 858-4673 • Mon-Sat 7:30-6:00 by appointment • Carlo Amado • Italian and some Spanish spoken • Prices medium to high • Trade discount

Fabrication and installation of marble, granite, limestone and onyx, ceramic tile. Custom-made marble tables, marble mosaic and mosaic. Countertops, bathrooms, kitchens, building lobbies. Terrazzo floors and tables. Polishing and restoration of marble, granite and all types of stone. Top quality.

MARBLE WORLD ENTERPRISES, INC.

5-28 47th Avenue, Long Island City, NY 11101 • Tel: (718) 361-6899 • Fax: (718) 361-8376 • Mon-Sat 8:30-5:00 • Costas Hagias

Marble, granite, terrazzo: interior and exterior. Fabrication and installation.

MEMO TILE CO. INC.

48 East 21st Street, New York, NY 10010 • Tel: (212) 505-0009 • Fax: (718) 291-5992 • Mon-Fri 9:30-5:30, Sat 11:00-5:00 • Ed Raker • Spanish and Italian spoken • Prices low to high • Major credit cards

Importers and distributers of ceramic tile, granite, marble, porcelain, tumbled marble; medicine cabinets, shower doors, plumbing and accessories.

METRO STONE DESIGN

1311 Travis Avenue, Staten Island, NY 10314 • Tel: (718) 370-0900 • Fax: (718) 370-0001 • Mon-Fri 9:00-6:00, Sat 10:00-3:00

Custom fabrication of counter and vanity tops, tables, bathrooms, walls, floors. Marble, granite, limestone and slate. All sizes in tiles and in all stones.

GREGORY MULLER ASSOCIATES, INC.

125 Kent Avenue, Brooklyn, NY 11211 • Tel: (718) 599-6220/(718) 599-6221 • Mon-Fri 8:30-5:00 • Harrison Muller • Italian, Spanish and Polish spoken

Italian-trained artisans who hand cut marble into tesserae for intricate old mosaic designs. Superb work.

NEW YORK MARBLE & CERAMIC INC.

430 West Fourteenth Street, New York, NY 10014 • Tel: (212) 929-1817 • Fax: (212) 929-6698 • Mon-Fri 9:00-6:00 • Maurice Laniado

Fabrication and custom installation of marble, ceramic, slate and stone work. Residential and industrial.

PUCCIO MARBLE & ONYX

661 Driggs Avenue, Brooklyn, NY 11211 • Tel: (718) 387-9778 • Fax: (718) 387-5464 • Mon-Fri 8:30-5:00, Sat by appointment • Joseph Puccio • Italian spoken • Prices high • Trade discount

Supply, manufacture and installation of marble, onyx, granite, limestone, malachite, lapis and other semi-precious stones. Kitchens, bathrooms, fireplaces, columns as well as furniture.

QUALITY TILE CORPORATION

2541 Boston Road, Bronx, NY 10467 • Tel: (718) 653-0830 • Fax: (718) 515-7927 • Mon-Fri 7:30-6:00, Sat 8:00-3:00 • Perry and Anthony Coscia • Spanish and Italian spoken • Prices medium • 25-40% professional discount • Major credit cards

Marble, granite, limestone, slate, antique stones, mosaics, mouldings, ceramic tiles, slabs: supply and installation.

STONE TECH., INC.

24-16 Bridge Plaza South, Long Island City, NY 11101 • Tel: (718) 784-4646 • Fax: (718) 784-1580 • Mon-Fri 8:00-6:00 • German, Hungarian and Spanish spoken • Prices medium

Design and engineering of stone cladding systems. Consultation on fabrication, assembly and erection technology. Controlled inspection. Failure investigation and analysis. Restoration and conservation. Top references.

TILES A REFINED SELECTION, INC.

42 West 15th Street, New York, NY 10011 • Tel: (212) 255-4450 • Fax: (212) 727-3851 • Mon-Fri 9:30-6:00, Thu 9:30-8:00, Sat 10:00-5:00 • Michael J. Weber • Spanish and French spoken • Prices medium • Trade discount

Glass, marble, granite, limestone, slate, quartzite, terra cotta, ceramic tile. Specialists in custom handmade materials. No installation.

W.D. VIRTUE CO.

160 Broad Street, Summit, NJ 07901 • Tel: (908) 273-6936 • Fax: (908) 273-8389 • Mon-Fri 8:30-5:00, Sat 10:00-4:00 • David Mozes • Prices medium to high • 15-25% trade discount • Major credit cards

Ceramic tile, marble and granite from all over the world. Sale only, no installation.

Mosaics

CHRISTINE BELFOR DESIGN LTD.

304 Hudson Street, Studio 600, New York, NY 10013 • Tel: (212) 633-6680 • Fax: (212) 645-2759 • Mon-Fri 10:00-5:00 • Prices high • Trade discount

Custom mosaics of hand-painted tile, in Byzantine style, highly rendered designs and traditional marble mosaics. Can replicate your design. Very high quality work.

PETER COLOMBO CUSTOM ARTISTIC MOSAICS

281 Phillips Avenue, South Hackensack, NJ 07601 • Tel: (201) 641-7964 • Fax: (201) 641-5884 by appointment

Custom mosaics, mostly pictorial; some decorative. Top references.

CROVATTO MOSAICS, INC.

319 First Street, Yonkers, NY 10704 • Tel: (914) 237-6210 • Fax: (914) 237-6215 • By appointment • Costante Crovatto • Price depends on intricacy of design

An Italian craftsman who deals exclusively with mosaics. He will execute mosaics to your design.

HASTINGS TILE/IL BAGNO COLLECTION

230 Park Avenue South, New York, NY 10003 • Tel: (212) 674-9700 • Fax: (212) 674-8083 • Mon-Fri 9:30-5:30, Sat 10:00-5:00 • Prices medium to high • Major credit cards

Custom mosaics for any room, any size, from a small tabletop or a floor to a swimming pool.

LODESTAR STATEMENTS IN STONE

231 East 58th Street, New York, NY 10022 • Tel: (212) 755-1818 • Fax: (212) 755-1828 • By appointment • Stewart Birtwo • Prices medium to high • Professional discount

Custom and stock design of mosaics for furniture and architectural finishes: floors, walls, ceilings, countertops. Installation, repair and restoration.

FRANZ MAYER OF MUNICH, INC.

343 Passaic Avenue, Fairfield, NJ 07004 • Tel: (201) 575-4777 • Fax: (201) 575-5588 • Dr. Gabriel Mayer • German and Italian spoken • Prices medium to high

Stained glass and mosaics. In-house designs and independent designs in all materials. Credits: Restored original mosaic fireplace designed by Frank Lloyd Wright at Charnley House in Chicago; restored mosaic interior of Lakewood Cemetery Chapel, Minneapolis, designed by Charles Lamb.

GREGORY MULLER ASSOCIATES, INC.

125 Kent Avenue, Brooklyn, NY 11211 • Tel: (718) 599-6220 • Fax: (718) 599-6221 • Mon-Fri 8:00-5:00 • Harrison Muller • Many languages spoken • Prices very high • 20% trade discount

Marble and glass mosaics, architectural stone carving, stone furniture, fireplaces, fountains. Superb craftsmanship.

PS CRAFTSMANSHIP CORPORATION

10-40 Jackson Avenue, Long Island City, NY 11101 • Tel: (718) 729-3686 • Fax: (718) 729-3781 • Mon-Fri 9:00-7:00 • Stephan Pousse • French spoken • Prices medium

Custom-designed and installed mosaics, stone marquetry, scagliola, marble work for floors and bathrooms, French limestone fireplace mantels, stone carving.

SERPENTINE/SUSAN BROWN

332 East 90th Street, Suite 5, New York, NY 10128 • Telfax: (212) 427-4232 • By appointment • Prices medium • Professional discount

Design, fabrication and installation of mosaics in all materials. Residential and commercial. References upon request.

UNICORN ART STUDIO, INC.

251 Fifth Avenue, New York, NY 10016 • Telfax: (212) 684-2644 • Mon-Fri 9:00-6:00 by appointment

Custom Florentine mosaics using classical techniques for all styles, classical and contemporary, in all materials: ceramic, stone, marble and glass. All designs from vases to walls and floors. Murals, trompe l'oeil and hand-woven tapestries.

TERRA DESIGNS TILEWORKS

241 East Blackwell Street, Dover, NJ 07801 • Tel: (201) 328-1135 • Fax: (201) 328-3624 • Mon-Fri 8:00-5:00 • Anna Salibello • Spanish and Chinese spoken • Prices high to very high • Trade only

Manufacturer of decorative and antique looking ceramic tile, specializing in stoneware mosaics, crackle glazes and custom matching of color and design. Custom replication of historic mosaic tiles, ceramic tiles and plaques. Clients: New York State Transit Authority and many others.

ZANOLIN ARTISTIC MOSAICS

RD1, Box 211C, Route 343, Dover Plains, NY 12522 • Tel: (914) 677-6011 • By appointment • Peter Zanolin • Italian spoken

Custom mosaics in Smalti glass and marble. European trained and with 30 years experience in mosaics. Repair and restoration.

Tile

ALLIED TILE MFG. CORP.

2840 Atlantic Avenue, Brooklyn, NY 11207 • Tel: (718) 647-2200 • Fax: (718) 647-2656 • Peter Gregor • Prices high • Trade only

Manufacturer of resilient vinyl floor tiles.

SHEP BROWN ASSOC.

24 Cummings Park, Woburn, MA 01801 • Tel: (617) 935-8080 • NYC Tel: (212) 265-4904 • Fax: (617) 935-2090 • By appointment • Shep Brown • Prices high to very high

Shep Brown is a legend in the tile business and makes very special custom tiles. Wide selection of stock tiles.

COUNTRY FLOORS

15 East 16th Street, New York, NY 10003 • Tel: (212) 627-8300 • Fax: (212) 627-7742 • Mon-Fri 9:00-6:00, Sat 9:00-5:00 • Lorna Catullo • French and Spanish spoken • Prices medium to very high • Major credit cards

One of New York's best sources of tile imported from all sources. Hand-crafted decorative, traditional and contemporary tiles; antiqued and tumbled marble, limestone, travertine, mosaics, majolica, terra-cotta floors, architectural elements, mouldings, sturdy floor tiles glazed to replicate the texture of cut stone and terra cotta. Quite marvellous.

ELON, INC.

150 East 58th Street, New York, NY 10155 • Tel: (212) 759-6996 • Fax: (212) 207-8023 • Mon-Fri 9:00-5:00 • Graham Barr • French and English spoken • Prices medium • 25% trade discount • MC and Visa

Handmade ceramic tiles and terra-cottas imported from Mexico and Europe. Limestone and antiqued marbles.

DAVID GARBO TILE & MARBLE

127 East 61st Street, New York, NY 10021 • Tel: (212) 223-2653 • Fax: (212) 888-3822 • Mon-Fri 9:00-5:00 • Prices medium • 25% trade discount

Fine installations of ceramic, glass and terra-cotta tiles. Also marble and stone.

HASTINGS TILE/IL BAGNO COLLECTION

230 Park Avenue South, New York, NY 10003 • Tel: (212) 674-9700 • Fax: (212) 674-8083 • Mon-Fri 9:30-5:30, Sat 10:00-5:00 • Prices medium to high • Major credit cards

Ceramic tile, marble mosaics, custom mosaics for floors, walls, tabletops and swimming pools.

IDEAL TILE OF MANHATTAN, INC.

405 East 51st Street, New York, NY 10022 • Tel: (212) 759-2339 • Fax:
(212) 826-2391 • Mon-Fri 9:00-5:00, Sat 10:00-5:00 • Amex and Visa

Tile flooring of all kinds, ceramic, marble, granite, composition.

MEMO TILE CO.

48 East 21st Street, New York, NY 10010 • Tel: (212) 505-0009 • Fax:
(718) 291-5992 • Mon-Fri 9:30-5:30, Sat 11:00-5:00 • Ed Raker •
Spanish and Italian spoken • Prices low to high • Major credit cards

Importers and distributors of ceramic tile, granite, marble, porcelain, tumbled marble. Also bathroom fixtures, cabinets and fixtures.

PARIS CERAMICS

150 East 58th Street, 7th floor, New York, NY 10155 • Tel: (212) 644-
2782 • Fax: (212) 644-2785 • Mon-Fri 9:00-5:00 • Tim Prendergast •
French, Italian and Hindi spoken • Prices high • 20% trade discount •
MC and Visa

Very high quality decorative ceramics; limestone; terrazzo; exquisite reclaimed antique limestone and terra-cotta floors.

PEDULLA CERAMIC TILES

4906 20th Avenue, Brooklyn, NY 11204 • Tel: (718) 377-7746 • Fax:
(718) 692-0317 • Mon-Fri 8:00-6:00, Thu 8:00-9:00, Sat 8:00-4:00 •
Italian, Spanish and Russian spoken • Prices medium

Ceramic tile for walls and floors, interior and exterior.

ANN SACKS TILE & STONE

5 East 16th Street, New York, NY 10003 • Tel: (212) 463-8400 • Fax:
(212) 463-0067 • Mon-Fri 9:00-6:00, Sat 11:00-4:00 • Prices medium
to high • Trade only

Wide selection of ceramic tile and stone from all over the world.
High quality.

TERRA DESIGNS TILE, BATH & STONE

49B Route 202 S., Far Hills, NJ 07931 • Tel: (908) 234-0440 • Fax:
(908) 781-1810 • Mon-Sat 10:00-6:00, Sun 12:00-4:00 • Kris Salibello
• Prices medium to very high • 25% trade discount • Major credit cards

Complete line of ceramic tile and stone at all price ranges including
upscale, unique decorative products. 5,000-square-foot showroom
with a very large selection of tile, stone, bath products and accessories.

W.D. VIRTUE CO.

160 Broad Street, Summit, NJ 07901 • Tel: (908) 273-6936 • Fax: (908)
273-8389 • Mon-Fri 8:30-5:00, Sat 10:00-4:00 • David Mozes • Prices
medium to high • 10-25% trade discount • Major credit cards

Distributor of terra-cotta tiles, terra-cotta coping balustrades, ceramic
tile, marble and granite from all over the world. No installation.

Ornamental Walls and Ceilings

A.M.R. PLASTERING CO.

3739 Paulding Avenue, Bronx, NY 10469 • Tel: (718) 994-1242 • Fax:
(718) 324-5407 • Mon-Fri 9:00-5:00 • Al Randall

Hand-crafted plaster products made from the finest quality materials
using century-old European craftsmanship. They specialize in the
restoration of decorative interior plaster work, including crown mouldings, medallions, capitals, columns and panelled ceilings. Also new
plaster walls, using two-coat and skim-coat processes.

ARCHITECTURAL SCULPTURE & RESTORATIONS, INC.

242 Lafayette Street, New York, NY 10012 • Telfax: (212) 431-5873 •
Mon-Fri 10:00-6:00, Sat 12:00-5:00 • Anna Williams • Spanish and
French spoken • Prices high

Creation of ornamental plaster for interiors: cornices, medallions,
columns, baskets. Restoration and installation.

BORO PLASTERING CORP.

1182 Broadway, New York, NY 10001 • Tel: (212) 684-3242 • Fax:
(212) 684-3243

Specialists in decorative plaster work. Credits: The New York Stock
Exchange, West End Collegiate Church and The New York Public
Theatre.

CLASSIC BUILDER'S RESOURCE, INC.

42 Madison Street, Port Washington, NY 11050 • Telfax: (516) 883-
3426 • Mon-Fri 8:00-6:00 • Tom Amato • Prices medium • Trade discount

Decorative plaster mouldings and custom hardwood mouldings. Installation. Excellent references.

HYDE PARK FINE ART OF MOULDINGS

29-16 40th Avenue, Long Island City, NY 11101 • Tel: (718) 706-0504
• Fax: (718) 706-0507 • Mon-Fri 9:00-5:00 • David Nassim and Adrian
Taylor • Prices medium • 15% trade discount

Architectural and ornamental plaster. Re-creation, custom profiles,
mouldings from architects' drawings. Credits: The Jewish Museum,
The Penn Club and Fashion Center.

LICO CONTRACTING INC.

29-10 20th Avenue, Astoria, NY 11105 • Tel: (718) 932-8300 • Fax: (718) 204-9817 • Mon-Fri 7:30-5:00 • Richard Bruno, President • Italian and Spanish spoken • Prices very high • Trade only

Any style of custom mouldings using custom-made templates that shape fresh plaster into an exact copy or create a one-of-a-kind effect. New plastering and repairs. Excellent references.

FRANK J. MANGIONE, INC.

21 John Street, Saugerties, NY 12477 • Tel: (914) 246-9863 • Mon-Fri by appointment • Frank and Henry Mangione and David Krein

Three generations, and their new partner David Krein, of specialists in historic preservation and restoration of plaster walls, ceilings and cornices. Design and implementation of new plaster finish and ornamentation. Credits: The Dakota, Henry Street Settlement, Scribner Library of Skidmore College, Rose Hill in Tivoli and the Lockwood-Matthews Mansion in Norwalk, CT.

ORNAMENTAL COMPOSITIONS

515 West End Avenue, New York, NY 10024 • Telfax: (212) 799-6337 • Mon-Fri 9:00-5:00 • Lori Hertzan and Lois Perlman • French spoken • Prices high

Design, installation and finishing of relief ornamentation and moulding used in interior architectural ornamentation. Wide selection of finishes: glazing, marbleizing, gold and silver leafing and faux bois. Thousands of designs from historic plates or photographs. All periods. Credits include the townhouse of Elsie de Wolf and great houses in Kings Point, Tuxedo Park, Old Brookville, Westhampton and Greenwich. They also worked on the main dining room in the Marymount School on Fifth Avenue.

ART GALLERIES

DIDIER AARON, INC.

32 East 67th Street • New York, NY 10021 • Tel: (212) 988-5248 • Fax: (212) 737-3513 • Mon-Fri 9:30-6:00 • Herve Aaron, President, Alan Salz • French spoken • Prices high

Old Master paintings and drawings. 18th- and 19th-century European furniture and decorative objects. Reliable expertise.

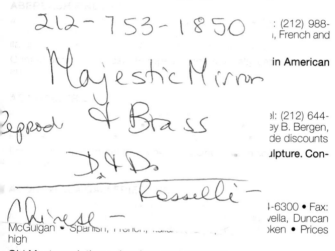

: (212) 988-, French and

in American

el: (212) 644-
ay B. Bergen,
de discounts

ulpture. Con-

I-6300 • Fax:
vella, Duncan
oken • Prices

McGuigan • Spanish, French, Italian
high

Old Master paintings, drawings and sculpture.

ADELSON GALLERIES

The Mark Hotel, 25 East 77th Street, New York, NY 10021 • Tel: (212) 439-6800 • Fax: (212) 439-6870 • Mon-Fri 9:30-5:30 • French spoken • Prices high

19th- and 20th-century American and European painting and sculpture.

RACHEL ADLER GALLERY FINE ART

41 East 57th Street, New York, NY 10022 • Tel: (212) 308-0511 • Fax: (212) 308-0516 • Mon-Fri 10:30-5:30 and by appointment • Susan Dague • Spanish and French spoken • Prices high

European art of the 1920s and 1930s, Avant-Garde art from Russia, Latin American art.

ALEXANDER GALLERY

942 Madison Avenue, New York, NY 10021 • Tel: (212) 472-1636 • Fax: (212) 734-6937 • Tue-Sat 10:00-6:00 • Alexander Acevedo • Spanish spoken • Prices medium to high • Trade discounts

18th- and 19th-century American paintings, furniture and accessories. Pre-Columbian and American Indian artifacts.

☝ AMERICAN ILLUSTRATORS GALLERY

18 East 77th Street, Suite #1A, New York, NY 10021 • Tel: (212) 744-5190 • Fax: (212) 744-0128 • Mon-Fri 2:00-5:00 and by appointment

Original artworks from American illustrators of the Golden Age: Norman Rockwell, Maxfield Parrish, Howard Pyle, N.C. Wyeth and the Brandywine School, S.C. Leyendecker, H.C. Christy and others.

ARTSHOWS AND PRODUCTS (ASAP)

18 East 77th Street, New York, NY 10021 • Tel: (212) 744-5190 • Fax: (212) 744-0128 • Mon-Fri 10:00-6:00 • Jennifer Paige

Representation of artists' estates, licensing, product development, exhibitions, publishing.

AVANTI GALLERIES

22 East 72nd Street, New York, NY 10021 • Tel: (212) 628-3377 • Fax: (212) 628-3707 • Mon-Sat 10:00-6:00 • French, Dutch, German and Italian spoken • Prices low to high • Trade discounts • All major credit cards

Modern masters and postwar European and American paintings, sculpture, works on paper and prints.

BABCOCK GALLERIES

724 Fifth Avenue, 11th floor, New York, NY 10019 • Tel: (212) 767-1852 • Fax: (212) 767-1857 • Mon-Fri 10:00-5:00 and by appointment • Michael St. Clair, Dr. John Driscoll, Jeanne Baker, Lisa Skrabek • Prices medium to high • Some trade discounts

All periods of American art, especially 19th and 20th centuries. Painting, sculpture and drawings.

ADAM BAUMGOLD FINE ART

128 East 72nd Street, New York, NY 10021 • Tel: (212) 861-7338 • Fax: (212) 288-1261 • Tue-Sat 11:00-5:00 • Prices medium to high • Trade discounts

20th century to contemporary art.

BEACON HILL FINE ART

980 Madison Avenue, New York, NY 10021 • Tel: (212) 734-3636 • Fax: (212) 734-1042 • Tue-Sat 10:00-6:00, Mon by appointment • Debra Force, Director, and Jane Egan, Ass. Dir.

19th- and early 20th-century American paintings.

WILLIAM BEADLESTON

980 Madison Avenue, New York, NY 10021 • Tel: (212) 327-4094 • Fax: (212) 327-4195 • Mon-Fri 10:00-6:00, appointment suggested • William Beadleston, President • French, Italian and most languages spoken

Impressionists and 20th-century masters.

ARLENE BERMAN FINE ART

111 East 81st Street, New York, NY 10028 • Tel: (212) 472-3108 • Fax: (212) 472-1665 • By appointment • Prices medium • Trade discounts

American decorative paintings, primarily from the 1930s and 1940s.

BERRY-HILL GALLERIES

11 East 70th Street • New York, NY 10021 • Tel: (212) 744-2300 • Fax: (212) 744-2838 • Mon-Fri 9:30-5:30, Sat 10:00-5:30 • Frederick D. Hill and James Berry-Hill • Prices very high

18th- , 19th- and 20th-century American and European paintings and sculpture. Specialists in the 19th-century art of the China trade. Contemporary paintings and sculpture.

☙ MARY BOONE GALLERY

745 Fifth Avenue, 4th floor, New York, NY 10151 • Tel: (212) 752-2929 • Fax: (212) 752-3939 • Tue-Sat 10:00-6:00 • Mary Boone • Spanish and some French spoken • Prices high

American contemporary painting, sculpture and drawings.

J. HAMILTON BUCK, INC.

111 East 80th Street, #9C, New York, NY 10021 • Tel: (212) 439-9000 • Fax: (212) 439-9088 • By appointment • Joan Menken • French, German and some Italian spoken • Prices high to very high

Art dealer specializing in European and American masters. Exclusive representation of private collectors wishing to buy or sell.

BYRON GALLERY

25 East 83rd Street, New York, NY 10028 • Tel: (212) 249-0348 • Fax: (212) 517-3004 • By appointment • Charles A. Byron, Owner • French spoken

Modern masters and surrealists.

CADE

1045 Madison Avenue, New York, NY 10021 • Tel: (212) 734-3670 • Fax: (212) 737-7206 • Tue-Sat 11:00-6:00 • French spoken

Modern and contemporary artists: abstract and figurative, specializing in European artists of the 1950s.

CDS GALLERY

76 East 79th Street, New York, NY 10021 • Tel: (212) 772-9555 • Fax: (212) 772-9542 • Tue-Sat 10:00-5:30 • Clara Diament Sujo • Spanish and French spoken

Contemporary art of Europe, the Americas and Australia.

CHINOH ART GALLERY

575 Fifth Avenue, New York, NY 10017 • Telfax: (212) 986-2420 • Mon-Fri 10:30-7:00, Sat-Sun 11:00-6:30 • Hiroko Takeda • Japanese spoken • Prices medium • Major credit cards

Contemporary Japanese and American paintings and prints.

COHEN GALLERY

1018 Madison Avenue, 4th floor, New York, NY 10021 • Tel: (212) 628-0303 • Fax: (212) 628-9560 • Mon-Fri 10:00-6:00, Sat 10:00-5:30 • Michel Cohen • French spoken • Prices high

French Impressionism: European Modern masters including Calder, Chagall, Dubuffet, Gris, Matisse, Miro, Moore, Picasso. Very important contemporary art: de Kooning, Diebenkorn, Francis and Rothko.

THOMAS COLVILLE FINE ART

1000 Madison Avenue, New York, NY 10021 • Tel: (212) 879-9259/ (203) 787-2816 • By appointment only • German spoken • Prices medium to high

19th-century American and French Barbizon School paintings, watercolors and drawings.

MAXWELL DAVIDSON GALLERY

41 East 57th Street, New York, NY 10022 • Tel: (212) 759-7555 • Fax: (212) 759-5824 • Mon-Sat 10:00-5:30 • Maxwell and Mary Davidson • French spoken • Prices medium to high

20th-century Modern and contemporary masters: paintings, drawings and sculpture.

DAVIS & LANGDALE COMPANY, INC.

231 East 60th Street, New York, NY 10022 • Tel: (212) 838-0333 • Fax: (212) 752-7764 • Tue-Sat 10:00-5:00 • Michelle Martin

Specialists in 19th- and 20th-century American art. 18th- , 19th- and 20th-century British drawings and watercolors. Contemporary art. APF frame showroom on premises.

WILLIAM R. DAVIS FINE ARTS

737 Park Avenue, New York, NY 10021 • Tel: (212) 988-4886 • Fax: (212) 988-4676 • By appointment • German spoken

Late 19th- and early 20th-century works on paper, especially by Toulouse-Lautrec and Egon Schiele.

DAVLYN GALLERY

975 Madison Avenue, New York, NY 10021 • Tel: (212) 879-2075 • Tue-Sat 10:00-5:30 • Berta Katz • French and Italian spoken

19th- and 20th-century European paintings and sculpture.

MARISA DEL RE GALLERY

41 East 57th Street, New York, NY 10022 • Tel: (212) 688-1843 • Fax: (212) 688-7019 • Tue-Sat 10:00-5:30 • Italian, French and Spanish spoken

American and European Modern and contemporary paintings, drawings and sculpture.

PAUL DREY GALLERY

11 East 57th Street, New York, NY 10022 • Tel: (212) 753-2551 • Fax: (212) 838-0339 • Mon-Fri 10:00-5:00 • Margot Drey Catherwood, John A. Catherwood

European Old Master and 19th-century drawings.

THE ELKON GALLERY

18 East 81st Street, New York, NY 10028 • Tel: (212) 535-3940 • Fax: (212) 737-8479 • Mon-Fri 10:00-5:30 • Dorothea McKenna Elkon, President • French, Spanish and German spoken • Prices medium to high

Modern and contemporary American, European and Latin American masters. Paintings, drawings and sculpture.

ANDRE EMMERICH GALLERY

41 East 57th Street, New York, NY 10022 • Tel: (212) 752-0124 • Fax: (212) 371-7345 • Tue-Sat 10:00-5:30 • Andre Emmerich, Donald McKinney, James Yohe, Louise Eliasof • French spoken • Prices very high • MC and Visa

Modern and contemporary Masters including: Pierre Alechinsky, Al Held, David Hockney and the Estates of Josef Albers, Milton Avery, Friedel Dzubas, Sam Francis, Keith Haring, Hans Hofmann, Morris Louis, John McLaughlin, Jack Tworkov.

LYNN G. EPSTEEN

New York, NY 10021 • Tel: (212) 753-2408 • Fax: (212) 249-3898 • By appointment • Lynn G. Epsteen, Michele Sauer • French, Spanish and Portuguese spoken

19th- and 20th-century European and American paintings, drawings, sculpture and prints.

MARGO FEIDEN GALLERIES

699 Madison Avenue, New York, NY 10021 • Tel: (212) 677-5330 • Fax: (212) 688-1593 • Daily 10:00-6:00 • Lynn Surry • Prices medium • 15% trade discount • Major credit cards

Al Hirshfeld pen and ink drawings, limited editions of lithographs and etchings.

⚑ RICHARD L. FEIGEN & CO.

49 East 68th Street, New York, NY 10021 • Tel: (212) 628-0700 • Fax: (212) 249-4574 • Mon-Fri 10:00-5:00 • Italian and French spoken

15th- to 20th-century paintings, drawings and watercolors.

DAVID FINDLAY GALLERIES

984 Madison Avenue, New York, NY 10021 • Tel: (212) 249-2909 • Fax: (212) 249-2912 • Mon-Sat 10:00-5:00 • Lindsay Findlay, Rebecca Senior, Philip B. Smith

19th- and 20th-century European paintings, sculpture and graphics.

DAVID FINDLAY, JR. FINE ART

41 East 57th Street, #1115, New York, NY 10022 • Tel: (212) 486-7660 • Fax: (212) 980-2650 • Tue-Sat 10:00-5:30, Mon by appointment • David and Lee Findlay • French spoken

19th- and early 20th-century American paintings and sculpture. 1800 to 1940.

PETER FINDLAY GALLERY

41 East 57th Street, #310, New York, NY 10022 • Tel: (212) 644-4433 • Fax: (212) 644-1675 • Tue-Sat 10:00-6:00 • French, Italian and German spoken

French Impressionist and 20th-century paintings. French and American 20th-century graphics. American contemporary paintings.

⚑ WALLY FINDLAY GALLERIES

14 East 60th Street, New York, NY 10022 • Tel: (212) 421-5390 • Fax: (212) 838-2460 • Mon-Fri 9:30-5:30, Sat 9:30-5:00 • French spoken

Post-Impressionist paintings. American and European contemporary art.

FORUM GALLERY

745 Fifth Avenue, 5th floor, New York NY 10151 • Tel: (212) 355-4545 • Fax: (212) 355-4547 • Tue-Sat 10:00-5:30 • Robert S. Fishko, Thomas Holman • French spoken • Major credit cards

20th-century Realism. American Modernist paintings, drawings and sculpture. Contemporary figurative art.

FRENCH & CO.

17 East 65th Street, New York, NY 10021 • Tel: (212) 535-3330 • Fax: (212) 772-1756 • Mon-Fri 9:00-5:00 • Martin Zimet • French and Italian spoken • Prices medium to high

Old Masters to 19th-century European paintings.

BARRY FRIEDMAN LTD.

32 East 67th Street, New York, NY 10021 • Tel: (212) 794-8950 • Fax: (212) 794-8889 • Tue-Sat 10:00-6:00, Mon by appointment • Scott Cook, Director • French, German, Italian and Spanish spoken • Prices high

Early European 20th-century Avant-Garde art and design. 20th-century decorative arts, French furniture and accessories of the late 19th century through 1950.

GAGOSIAN GALLERY

980 Madison Avenue, New York, NY 10021 • Tel: (212) 744-2313 • Fax: (212) 772-7962 • Tue-Sat 10:00-6:00 • Larry Gagosian • German and French spoken • Prices medium to high

American and European Modern and contemporary paintings and sculpture.

GALLERY 71

974 Lexington Avenue, New York, NY 10021 Tel: (212) 744-7779 • Mon-Thu 10:00-7:00, Fri-Sat 10:00-6:00 • Alfred Gonzalez • Spanish spoken • Major credit cards

Contemporary works of art specializing in scenes of New York, mezzo-tints, lithographs and watercolors.

JANOS GAT GALLERY

1100 Madison Avenue, New York, NY 10028 • Tel: (212) 327-0441 • Fax: (212) 327-0442 • Tues-Sat 11:00-6:00 and by appointment • Janos Gat • 6 languages spoken • Prices low to high

20th-century Hungarian art. Contemporary American art specializing in the 1950s and 1960s: Knox Martin and Julian Beck.

♛ HILDE GERST GALLERY, INC.

987 Madison Avenue, New York, NY 10021 • Tel: (212) 288-3400 • Fax: (212) 288-7878 • Mon-Sat 11:00-5:000 • Hilde W. Gerst • French, Spanish, German, Italian and Polish spoken • Prices medium to very high • 10% trade discounts

Fine Impressionist and Post-Impressionist paintings and contemporary sculpture.

GODEL & CO.

39A East 72nd Street, New York, NY 10021 • Tel: (212) 288-7272 • Fax: (212) 772-0304 • Mon-Fri 10:00-6:00, Sat 10:00-5:00

19th- and 20th-century American art. Antique frames.

JAMES GOODMAN GALLERY

41 East 57th Street, New York, NY 10022 • Tel: (212) 593-3737 • Fax: (212) 980-0195 • Tue-Sat 10:00-6:00, Mon by appointment • James Neil Goodman and Katherine K. Goodman • Spanish spoken

19th- and 20th-century European and American Modern and contemporary paintings, sculpture and drawings.

JAMES GRAHAM & SONS, INC.

1014 Madison Avenue, New York, NY 10021 • Tel: (212) 535-5767 • Fax: (212) 794-2454 • Tue-Sat 9:30-5:30 • Robert C. Graham, Jr. President, Cameron M. Shay, Vice President, Virginia D. Tobeason

19th- and 20th-century American paintings. 19th- and 20th-century American and European sculpture. Western art. Contemporary art. British ceramics.

♛ BOB P. HABOLDT & CO.

22 East 80th Street, 3rd floor, New York, NY 10021 • Tel: (212) 249-1183 • Fax: (212) 472-2413 • Mon-Fri 9:30-6:00, Sat 11:00-5:00 • Bob Haboldt • Dutch, French and German spoken • Prices very high

Remarkable collection of Old Master paintings and drawings. Also an excellent gallery on the Faubourg-Saint-Honore, Paris.

BEN ALI HAGGIN

East 78th Street, New York, NY 10021 • Tel: (212) 988-0871 • By appointment • French spoken

American paintings and drawings of the 19th and early 20th centuries.

STEPHEN HAHN

9 East 79th Street, New York, NY 10021 • Tel: (212) 570-0020 • Fax: (212) 288-7511 • By appointment • Stephen Hahn, President, Cary Lochtenberg, Director • French spoken

19th- and 20th-century European works of art.

NOHRA HAIME GALLERY

41 East 57th Street, New York, NY 10022 • Tel: (212) 888-3550 • Fax: (212) 888-7869 • Mon-Sat 10:00-6:00 • Nohra Haime, President, Joel Magnani • French and Spanish spoken

Contemporary European, American and Latin American paintings and sculpture.

HALL & KNIGHT

21 East 67th Street, New York, NY 10021 • Tel: (212) 737-2266 • Fax: (212) 737-8325 • Mon-Fri 10:00-5:30, preferably by appointment • French and Italian spoken

Old Masters through 19th-century European Modern and Modern masters. Paintings and drawings.

MICHAEL HALL FINE ARTS

49 East 82nd Street, New York, NY 10028 • Tel: (212) 249-5053 • Fax: (212) 249-5735 • By appointment • French and Italian spoken

Renaissance to early 20th-century sculpture.

LILLIAN HEIDENBERG

45 East 66th Street, New York, NY 10021 • Tel: (212) 628-6110 • Fax: (212) 628-4958 • Mon-Fri 10:00-5:30, Sat-Sun by appointment • French, German and Italian spoken • Prices medium to high • Trade discounts

Art dealer specializing in master works: 19th- and 20th-century paintings, sculpture and works on paper.

HEXTON GALLERY

41 East 78th Street, New York, NY 10022 • Tel: (212) 570-9335 • Fax: (212) 570-6543 • Tue-Sat 10:00-6:00

Representational art: Frederick Hart and Robert Kipniss.

HILL-STONE, INC.

Box 278, Gracie Station, (Park Avenue/eighties), New York, NY 10028 • Tel: (212) 249-1397 • Fax: (212) 861-4513 • By appointment • Alan N. Stone and D. Lesley Hill • French, German and Italian spoken • Prices very high • 10% professional discount

Old Master prints and drawings: Renaissance to the 19th century.

HIRSCHL & ADLER GALLERIES

21 East 70th Street, New York, NY 10021 • Tel: (212) 535-8810 • Fax: (212) 772-7237 • Tue-Fri 9:30-5:15, Sat 9:30-4:45 • Stuart Feld • French and Spanish spoken • Prices high

18th- to mid-20th-century American and European paintings, sculpture, prints, works on paper.

HIRSCHL & ADLER MODERN

21 East 70th Street, New York, NY 10021 • Tel: (212) 535-8810 • Fax: (212) 772-7237 • Tue-Fri 9:30-5:15, Sat 9:30-4:45 • Frank del Deo, Betty Cunningham • French and Spanish spoken • Prices high

Contemporary American and European paintings, drawings and sculpture.

JEM HOM FINE ART

118 East 60th Street, New York, NY 10022 • Tel: (212) 688-1772 • Fax: (212) 688-2329 • By appointment • Jem Hom, Director, and Betty Hom • Chinese spoken

19th- and 20th-century European and American prints and works on paper.

HOORN-ASHBY GALLERY

766 Madison Avenue, New York, NY 10021 • Tel: (212) 628-3199 • Fax: • (212) 861-8162 • Mon-Sat 10:00-6:00 • Mary-Claire Barton • French spoken

Contemporary American and European Realism featuring Donald Jurney and Janet Rickus.

VIVIAN HORAN FINE ART

35 East 67th Street, New York, NY 10021 • Tel: (212) 517-9410 • Fax: (212) 772-6107 • Mon-Sat 10:00-6:00 • Vivian Horan • French spoken

20th-century European and American paintings, drawings and sculpture.

HUBERT GALLERY

1046 Madison Avenue, New York, NY 10021 • Tel: (212) 628-2922 • Fax: (212) 794-3889 • Tue-Sat 11:00-6:00 and by appointment • Some French and Spanish spoken

19th- and 20th-century works on paper. Contemporary Realist paintings.

‖ LEONARD HUTTON GALLERIES

41 East 57th Street, New York, NY 10022 • Tel: (212) 751-7373 • Fax: (212) 832-2261 • Tue-Sat 10:00-5:30 • Ingrid Hutton, Margaret Ann Cawley • German spoken

20th-century masterworks. Special focus on German Expressionism, Russian Avant-Garde, Cubism and Italian Futurism.

ISSELBACHER GALLERY

64 East 86th Street, New York, NY 10028 • Tel: (212) 472-1766 • Fax: (212) 472-3078 • By appointment • Alfred Isselbacher, Director

Late 19th-century and 20th-century up to 1970 prints and drawings.

JARO FINE ARTS

756 Madison Avenue, New York, NY 10021 • Telfax: (212) 396-3547 •
Mon-Sat 10:00-6:00 • Jaro Parizek • German, Croation and Czech spoken • Prices medium • Trade discounts • Major credit cards

Original oil and acrylic paintings, fine Naive art and a large collection of art glass.

JENSEN FINE ARTS

4 East 77th Street, New York, NY 10021 • Telfax: (212) 861-6008 •
Tue-Sat 11:00-5:00 • Diane Jensen • Some French spoken • Major credit cards

Late 19th- and early 20th-century American paintings: Boston School, Hudson River School and American Impressionists.

JORDAN-VOLPE GALLERY

958 Madison Avenue, New York, NY 10021 • Tel: (212) 570-9500 •
Fax: (212) 737-1611 • Mon-Fri 10:30-5:30, Sat by appointment

19th- and 20th-century American paintings.

KAHAN GALLERY

922 Madison Avenue, New York, NY 10021 • Tel: (212) 737-4230/861-3682 • Fax: (212) 744-1569 • Tue-Sat 11:00-5:00 • Alexander Kahan • German and French spoken • Prices medium to very high • Trade discounts

Post-Impressionist and School of Paris paintings.

JANE KAHAN GALLERY

922 Madison Avenue, New York, NY 10021 • Tel: (212) 744-1490 •
Fax: (212) 744-1598 • Tue-Sat 10:00-6:00, Mon by appointment •
Charles Mathes • Spanish and French spoken • Prices medium to very high • Trade discounts • MC and Visa

Modern European and American masters. Paintings, graphics, sculpture, ceramics and tapestries.

KENNEDY GALLERIES

730 Fifth Avenue, #206, New York, NY 10019-4105 • Tel: (212) 541-9600 • Fax: (212) 977-3833 • Tue-Sat 10:00-6:00 • Lawrence A. Fleischman and Martha J. Fleischman

American paintings, sculpture and prints from the 18th, 19th and 20th centuries.

JACK KILGORE & CO.

154 East 71st Street, New York, NY 10021 • Tel: (212) 650-1149 • Fax: (212) 650-1389 • By appointment only • Mireille Mosler • Dutch, German and French spoken

Dutch and Flemish Old Master paintings.

⚐ KNOEDLER M. & COMPANY

19 East 70th Street, New York, NY 10021 • Tel: (212) 794-0550 • Fax: (212) 772-6932 • Tue-Fri 9:30-5:30, Sat 10:00-5:30 • Ann Freedman, President • Some Spanish spoken • Amex

Contemporary paintings, sculpture and drawings, primarily American.

KOUROS GALLERY

23 East 73rd Street, New York, NY 10021 • Tel: (212) 288-5888 • Fax: (212) 794-9397 • Tue-Sat 10:30-6:00 • Greek, Portuguese and French spoken

Impressionist, Modern and contemporary paintings and sculpture.

KRAUSHAAR GALLERIES

724 Fifth Avenue, New York, NY 10019 • Tel: (212) 307-5730 • Tue-Fri 9:30-5:30, Sat 10:00-5:00 • Carole M. Pesner, Katherine Kaplan

Paintings, drawings and sculpture by 20th-century American artists.

JAN KRUGIER GALLERY

41 East 57th Street, New York, NY 10022 • Tel: (212) 755-7288 • Fax: (212) 980-6079 • Tue-Sat 10:00-5:30 • Tzila Krugier, Emmanuel Benador, Director of Graphics • French spoken

19th- and 20th-century Modern masters. Exclusive agent for the Marina Picasso collection of works by Pablo Picasso. Original Picasso graphics.

JANIE LEE MASTER DRAWINGS

P.O. Box Q., Gracie Station, New York, NY 10028 • Tel: (212) 988-3663 • Fax: (212) 737-6099 • By appointment • Sarah Buttrick

20th-century European and American drawings.

DANIEL E. LEWITT GALLERY

16 East 79th Street, New York, NY 10021 • Tel: (212) 628-0918 • Thu-Sat 12:00-5:00 and by appointment

Modern art; WPA artists.

LITTLEJOHN CONTEMPORARY

41 East 57th Street, New York, NY 10022 • Tel: (212) 980-2323 • Fax: (212) 980-2346 • Tue-Sat 10:00-5:30 • Jacquie Littlejohn • Prices medium

Monthly exhibitions by the contemporary artists represented by the gallery. Among these are: Rene Pierre Allain, Anne Appleby, Christian Haub, Julie Heffernan, John Kindness, Gwenn Thomas.

L.M. FINE ART

16 East 71st Street, New York, NY 10021 • Tel: (212) 517-5656 • Fax: (212) 517-9189 • Mon-Fri 10:00-5:30 • Max Lang • German, French and Italian spoken • Some trade discounts

20th-century paintings, sculpture and original works on paper. European Modern masters and American contemporary.

JEFFREY H. LORIA & CO.

19 East 72nd Street, New York, NY 10021 • Tel: (212) 249-2526 • Fax: (212) 472-3044 • By appointment • Jeffrey H. Loria • French spoken

19th- and 20th-century European and American master paintings, sculpture and works on paper.

KENNETH LUX GALLERY

851 Madison Avenue, 2nd floor, New York, NY 10021 • Tel: (212) 861-6839 • Fax: (212) 861-6866 • By appointment

Late 19th- and early 20th-century American paintings.

MAGIDSON FINE ART

1070 Madison Avenue, New York, NY 10028 • Tel: (212) 288-0666 • Fax: (212) 288-6050 • Mon-Fri 10:30-6:00, Sat 11:00-6:00, Sun afternoon • Melton & Denise Magidson • Some French spoken

Modern and contemporary European and American art. American Pop Art.

MARBELLA GALLERY

28 East 72nd Street, New York, NY 10021 • Tel: (212) 288-7809 • Tue-Sat 11:00-5:30

19th- and early 20th-century American art.

MATTHEW MARKS GALLERY

1018 Madison Avenue, New York, NY 10021 • Tel: (212) 861-9455 • Fax: (212) 861-9382 • Tue-Sat 10:00-5:30 • Some French spoken • Major credit cards

International contemporary art: paintings, drawings, sculpture, photograpy.

MARY-ANNE MARTIN/FINE ART

23 East 73rd Street, New York, NY 10021 • Tel: (212) 288-2213 • Fax: (212) 861-7656 • Tue-Sat 11:00-5:00, Mon by appointment • Mary-Anne Martin and Matthew M. Rembe • Spanish spoken • Prices low to very high • Trade discounts

Modern and contemporary Latin American paintings.

BARBARA MATHES GALLERY

41 East 57th Street, 3rd floor, New York, NY 10022 • Tel: (212) 752-5135 • Fax: (212) 752-5145 • Tue-Sat 9:30-5:30 • Barbara Mathes, Laurence Shopmaker • French spoken

Modern and contemporary American and European paintings and drawings. Contemporary photography.

PAUL MCCARRON/SUSAN SCHULMAN

1014 Madison Avenue, New York, NY 10021 • Tel: (212) 772-1181 • Fax: (212) 472-2497 • Mon-Sat 9:30-6:00 • German spoken • Prices low to high

Selling and buying original prints and drawings from the late 15th to the early 20th centuries.

JASON MCCOY, INC.

41 East 57th Street, New York, NY 10022 • Tel: (212) 319-1996 • Fax: (212) 319-4799 • Tue-Sat 10:00-5:30 • Jason McCoy • Some French spoken

American and European Modern and contemporary paintings and sculpture.

MCKEE GALLERY

745 Fifth Avenue, New York, NY 10151 • Tel: (212) 688-5951 • Fax: (212) 752-5638 • Tue-Sat 10:00-6:00 • David McKee, Renee Conforte McKee

American and European contemporary paintings and sculpture.

ROBERT MILLER GALLERY

41 East 57th Street, New York, NY 10022 • Tel: (212) 980-5454 • Fax: (212) 935-3350 • Tue-Sat 10:00-6:00 • Robert Miller • French and Italian spoken

Modern and contemporary paintings, sculpture and photography.

ACHIM MOELLER FINE ART

167 East 73rd Street, New York, NY 10021 • Tel: (212) 988-8483 • Fax: (212) 988-8480 • Mon-Sat 10:00-5:00 • French and German spoken

19th- and 20th-century European art; 20th-century American art. Paintings, drawings and sculpture.

DC MOORE GALLERY

724 Fifth Avenue, New York, NY 10019 • Tel: (212) 247-2111 • Fax: (212) 247-2119 • Tue-Sat 10:00-5:30 • Bridget Moore, President, Edward De Luca, Director • Italian spoken

Modern and contemporary American and European art.

DONALD MORRIS GALLERY

32 East 76th Street, New York, NY 10021 • Tel: (212) 570-1567 • Fax: (212) 517-6479 • By appointment • Donald, Florence and Steven Morris

20th-century American and European art. African art.

MARK MURRAY FINE PAINTINGS

529 East 85th Street, New York, NY 10028 • Tel: (212) 472-6836 • Fax: (212) 794-0265 • By appointment • Mark Murray • Prices medium to high • 10 to 15% trade discount

19th- and early 20th-century European and American paintings. Landscapes, still lifes, interiors, Orientalists, sporting, marines.

EDWARD TYLER NAHEM

56 East 66th Street, New York, NY 10021 • Tel: (212) 517-2453 • Fax: (212) 861-3566 • Mon-Fri 9:30-5:30 • French, Spanish and Norwegian spoken

19th- and 20th-century European and American masters.

OTTO NAUMANN, LTD.

22 East 80th Street, New York, NY 10021 • Tel: (212) 734-4443 • Fax: (212) 535-0617 • Mon-Fri 10:00-5:30, Sat by appointment • Otto Naumann • German and Dutch spoken

Old Master paintings specializing in 17th-century Flemish and Dutch paintings and drawings.

NEUHOFF GALLERY

41 East 57th Street, New York, NY 10022 • Tel: (212) 838-1122 • Fax: (212) 838-1250 • Tue-Sat 10:00-6:00 • Heidi Neuhoff • Portuguese and French spoken

Contemporary Russian and Brazilian paintings, sculpture and drawings.

JILL NEWHOUSE DRAWINGS

12 East 86th Street, New York, NY 10028 • Tel: (212) 249-9216 • Fax: (212) 734-4098 • By appointment • French spoken

Old Master and 19th-century European and American drawings and watercolors.

NEWHOUSE GALLERIES

19 East 66th Street, New York, NY 10021 • Tel: (212) 879-2700 • Fax: (212) 517-2680 • Mon-Fri 9:30-5:00 • Meg Newhouse, Director; Adam Williams, Stuart Kirkpatrick

Old Masters and sporting paintings.

ODYSSIA GALLERY

305 East 61st Street, New York, NY 10021 • Tel: (212) 486-7338 • Fax: (212) 486-7396 • By appointment • Odyssia Skouras • French and Italian spoken • Prices medium to high • Trade discount

Representative of the works by Jess. Selections of works by other American artists.

O'HARA GALLERY

41 East 57th Street, #1302, New York, NY 10022 • Tel: (212) 355-3330 • Fax: (212) 355-3361 • Tue-Sat 10:00-5:30, Mon by appointment • Ruth O'Hara, Director; Jonathan O'Hara, Steven O'Hara, Associates

Impressionist, Modern and contemporary masters.

PACE WILDENSTEIN

32 East 57th Street, New York, NY 10022 • Tel: (212) 421-3292 • Fax: (212) 421-0835 • Tue-Fri 9:30-6:00, Sat 10:00-6:00 • Arnold B. Glimcher, Chairman; Douglas Baxter, Peter Boris, Susan Dunne, Marc Glimcher, Bernice Rose, Anthony Grant

Modern and contemporary European and American paintings, sculpture and drawings.

FLORIAN PAPP

962 Madison Avenue, New York, NY 10021 • Tel: (212) 288-6770 • Fax: (212) 517-6965 • Mon-Fri 9:00-5:30, Sat 10:00-5:00 • Spanish spoken • Prices high

Extraordinary gallery with 18th- and 19th-century European and English paintings, furniture and decorations.

PARRISH & REINISH

25 East 73rd Street, New York, NY 10021 • Tel: (212) 734-7332 • Mon-Fri 9:30-5:30 by appointment • Martha Parrish and James Reinish • French spoken • Prices medium

19th- and 20th-century American and European paintings, sculpture and works on paper.

MARILYN PEARL GALLERY

710 Park Avenue, New York, NY 10021 • Tel: (212) 734-7421 • Fax: (212) 734-7244 • By appointment

Modern and contemporary paintings and sculpture. European and American works of the 1930s and 1940s.

GERALD PETERS GALLERY

177 East 78th Street, New York, NY 10021 • Tel: (212) 628-9760 • Fax: (212) 628-9635 • Mon-Fri 9:00-5:00 and by appointment • Reagan Upshaw • Prices high • 10 to 20% trade discount

19th- and 20th-century American paintings and sculpture. Hudson River School, Classic Western, American Impressionists, The Eight, The Taos Society, the O'Keeffe-Stieglitz Circle.

PRAXIS INTERNATIONAL ART

25 East 73rd Street, New York, NY 10021 Tel: (212) 772-9478 • Fax: (212) 772-0949 • Tue-Sat 11:00-6:00, Mon by appointment • Spanish and German spoken • Amex

Contemporary Latin American art.

RAYDON GALLERY

1091 Madison Avenue, New York, NY 10028 • Tel: (212) 288-3555 • Mon-Sat 10:00-6:00 and by appointment • Alexander R. Raydon • French, German, Russian, Polish and Spanish spoken • Prices medium • 10% trade discounts

Paintings, sculpture, prints and drawings from the Renaissance to the present. Emphasis on the American art of the 19th and early 20th centuries. Conservation and fine framing.

HAROLD REED GALLERY

New York, NY 10021 • Tel: (212) 861-6362 • By appointment

20th-century European and American masters.

GALERIE RIENZO

922 Madison Avenue, New York, NY 10021 • Tel: (212) 288-2226 • Fax: (212) 988-1539 • Tue-Sat 10:30-5:00 and by appointment • Robert Rienzo • Some Spanish spoken

Impressionist, Post-Impressionist and Modern French paintings and works on paper.

CHRISTOPHER J. ROBINSON

157 East 74th Street, PH-A, New York, NY 10021 • Tel: (212) 734-2939 • Fax: (212) 734-0019 • By appointment • French and Italian spoken • Prices low to high • Trade discounts

Old Master and 19th-century paintings and drawings.

ALEX ROSENBERG FINE ART

3 East 69th Street, New York, NY 10021 • Tel: (212) 628-0606 • Fax: (212) 628-4969 • By appointment • French spoken

Contemporary American, European and Cuban paintings, sculpture, drawings and graphics.

PAUL ROSENBERG & CO.

20 East 79th Street, New York, NY 10021 • Telfax: (212) 472-1134 • By appointment • French spoken

Renaissance to 20th-century European paintings, drawings and sculpture.

⚏ ROSENBERG & STIEBEL

32 East 57th Street, New York, NY 10022 • Tel: (212) 753-4368 • Fax: (212) 935-5736 • Mon-Fri 10:00-5:00 • Eric Stiebel, Gerald C. Stiebel, Penelope Hunter-Stiebel • French and German spoken

Old Master paintings, sculpture and drawings.

ROSENFELD FINE ART

303 East 57th Street, New York, NY 10022 • Tel: (212) 888-7935 • Fax: (212) 888-7923 • By appointment only • Samuel Rosenfeld

20th-century American art, especially WPA, 1930s and 1940s Realists and Modernists.

MICHELLE ROSENFELD GALLERY

16 East 79th Street, New York, NY 10021 • Tel: (212) 734-0900 • Fax: (201) 327-1794 • Mon-Sat 10:00-6:00 • Michelle and Herbert Rosenfeld • French and German spoken

Impressionist and Modern masters: paintings, drawings and sculpture.

SAIDENBERG GALLERY

1018 Madison Avenue, New York, NY 10021 • Tel: (212) 288-3387/8 • Tue-Fri 11:00-5:00 and by appointment • Eleonore Saidenberg • French, German and Spanish spoken • Prices high • Trade discounts

Early 20th-century European masters: paintings, drawings, sculpture and prints.

⚏ SALANDER-O'REILLY GALLERIES

20 East 79th Street, New York, NY 10021 • Tel: (212) 879-6606 • Fax: (212) 744-0655 • Mon-Sat 9:30-5:30 • Leigh A. Morse, Director • Italian and French spoken

Old Master to 19th-century French, English and American Modernists and contemporary paintings, sculpture and works on paper.

SCHILLAY FINE ART

161 East 71st Street, New York, NY 10021 • Tel: (212) 861-8353 • Fax: (212) 772-3758 • By appointment • Richard Schillay

British, Continental and American paintings of the 19th and 20th centuries including some important French Impressionists and Post-Impressionists.

GALLERY SCHLESINGER

24 East 73rd Street, New York, NY 10021 • Tel: (212) 734-3600 • Fax: (212) 472-6519 • Mon-Fri 11:00-5:00, Sat 12:00-4:00 • Some German spoken

20th-century and contemporary European and American art. American abstract painters of 1930 to 1960.

SCHMIDT-BINGHAM GALLERY

41 East 57th Street, New York, NY 10022 • Tel: (212) 888-1122 • Fax: (212) 754-1863 • Tue-Sat 10:00-5:30

Contemporary American art.

70 ART GALLERY

130 East 70th Street, New York, NY 10021 • Tel: (212) 472-2234 • Fax: (212) 472-2368 • Mon-Fri 10:00-6:00, Sat 12:00-5:00 • Juan Rodriguez • Spanish spoken • Prices medium to high • Visa and MC

Contemporary works in all media. Art restoration and framing.

ANITA SHAPOLSKY GALLERY

152 East 65th Street, Patio level, New York, NY 10021 • Tel: (212) 452-0930 • Fax: (212) 452-0926 • Wed-Sat 11:00-6:00, Tue by appointment • Spanish and French spoken • Prices medium • Trade discount • Amex

Painting, sculpture and works on paper in the abstract expressionist tradition.

SHEPHERD GALLERY

21 East 84th Street, New York, NY 10028 • Tel: (212) 861-4050 • Tue-Sat 10:00-6:00 • Robert Kashey and Martin L. H. Reymert • Prices medium to high

Paintings, sculpture and drawings by French, German, Austrian and Russians who lived in Paris in the great years of 1780 to 1920.

H. SHICKMAN GALLERY

980 Madison Avenue, New York, NY 10021 • Tel: (212) 249-3800 • Fax: (212) 472-1178 • By appointment

Old Master paintings and drawings. 19th-century French paintings.

SINDIN GALLERY

956 Madison Avenue, New York, NY 10021 • Tel: (212) 288-7902 • Fax: (212) 288-7895 • Tue-Sat 10:00-6:00 • Bernita Mirisola • Prices very high

Sculpture, paintings, drawings and graphics by Modern and contemporary masters. 19th- to 20th-century prints; Latin American paintings, graphics and sculpture.

PER SKARSTEDT FINE ART

42 East 76th Street, New York, NY 10021 • Tel: (212) 737-2060 • Fax: (212) 737-4171 • By appointment • Swedish spoken

European and American contemporary art.

SOLOMON & CO. FINE ART

959 Madison Avenue, New York, NY 10021 • Tel: (212) 737-8200 • Mon-Sat 10:30-5:30 • Gerald and Sally Solomon

American and European Modern masters.

SOMA GALLERIES

829 Madison Avenue, New York, NY 10021 • Tel: (212) 535-3950 • Fax: (212) 535-3980 • Mon-Fri 11:00-4:00 • Marina Elli • Prices medium to high • 15% trade discount • Visa and MC

Eclectic European 18th- and 19th-century art as well as early 20th-century decorative art.

SOUFER GALLERY

1015 Madison Avenue, New York, NY 10021 • Tel: (212) 628-3225 • Fax: (212) 628-3752 • Tue-Sat 10:00-5:00 • Mrs. Mahboubeh Soufer • Prices medium • 20% trade discount

Paintings and sculpture featuring in particular French Post-Impressionists and German Expressionists.

☙ SPANIERMAN GALLERY

45 East 58th Street, New York, NY 10022 • Tel: (212) 832-0208 • Fax: (212) 832-8114 • Mon-Sat 9:30-5:30 • Ira Spanierman and Gavin Spanierman • Prices low to high

19th- and early 20th-century American paintings including Hudson River School, American Impressionism and early Modernists.

☙ STAIR SAINTY MATTHIESEN

22 East 80th Street, New York, NY 10021 • Tel: (212) 288-1088 • Fax: (212) 628-2449 • Mon-Fri 9:00-6:00, Sat by appointment • Guy Stair Sainty, Elizabeth Frost Sainty • French, Italian and Spanish spoken • Prices very high • Trade discounts

French paintings 1600 to 1870. Italian and Spanish paintings from the 17th and 18th centuries. Dutch paintings from the 17th century.

ALAN STONE GALLERY

113 East 90th Street, New York, NY 10128 • Tel: (212) 987-4997 • Fax: (212) 987-1655 • Tue-Fri 10:00-6:00, Sat 10:00-5:00 • Claudia Stone

Contemporary paintings and sculpture, Abstract Expressionism and tribal arts.

HOLLIS TAGGART GALLERIES

48 East 73rd Street, New York, NY 10021 • Tel: (212) 628-4000 • Fax: (212) 717-4119 • Mon-Sat 10:30-5:00 • Hollis C. Taggart • Spanish and French spoken

19th- and 20th-century American paintings including Impressionism, Ashcan, Hudson River School and contemporary Realism. Appraisals.

LEILA TAGHINIA-MILANI GALLERY

1080 Madison Avenue, New York, NY 10028 • Tel: (212) 570-6173 • Fax: (212) 744-6523 • By appointment • Leila Taghinia-Milani, Daniel Hamparsumyan • French spoken • Prices medium to high

Private fine arts dealer in 19th- and 20th-century European, American and Latin American paintings, sculpture and works on paper.

E.V. THAW., INC.

726 Park Avenue, New York, NY 10021 • Tel: (212) 535-6333 • Fax: (212) 535-1465 • By appointment • Eugene Thaw, President, Patricia P. Tang • French spoken

Paintings and drawings of all periods.

THROCKMORTON FINE ART, INC.

153 East 61st Street, 4th floor, New York, NY 10021 • Tel: (212) 223-1059 • Fax: (212) 223-1937 • Tue-Sat 11:00-5:00 • Yona Backer • Spanish, French, German and Dutch spoken • Prices low to high • Some trade discounts

Ancient art: Egyptian, Chinese and African ceramica and stone sculpture. Colonial Latin American paintings. Contemporary and vintage Latin American photography and works on paper. Large collection of Pre-Columbian art by appointment only.

DAVID TUNICK, INC.

12 East 81st Street, New York, NY 10028 • Tel: (212) 570-0090 • Fax: (212) 744-8931 • Appointment suggested • Walton H. Boring Shannon Timms, Elizabeth Tunick, David P. Tunick

Old Master and Modern prints and drawings.

UBU GALLERY

16 East 78th Street, New York, NY 10021 • Tel: (212) 794-4444 • Fax: (212) 794-4289 • Tue-Sat 11:00-6:00 • Jack Banning, Adam Boxer, Rosa Esman • French and Spanish spoken

20th-century Avant-Garde exhibitions specializing in Dada, Bauhaus, Russian revolutionary works, Surrealism, contemporary photographs, drawings.

EARLE D. VANDEKAR OF KNIGHTSBRIDGE INC.

305 East 61st Street, New York, NY 10021 • Tel: (212) 308-2022 • Fax: (212) 308-2105 • By appointment • Elle Shushan • Prices medium • 20% professional discount • Major credit cards

18th- and 19th-century portrait miniatures, ceramics and furniture.

VANDERWOUDE TANANBAUM GALLERY

128 East 72nd Street, New York, NY 10021 • Tel: (212) 879-8200 • Fax: (212) 879-0785 • Tues-Sat by appointment • Suzanne Vanderwoude and Dorothy Tananbaum • Some French spoken • Trade discounts

20th-century Modernism to Abstract Expressionism.

⚇ WEINTRAUB GALLERY

965 Madison Avenue, New York, NY 10021 • Tel: (212) 879-1195/1132 • Fax: (212) 570-4192 • Tue-Sat 10:00-5:00 • Jacob D. Weintraub • Prices high • Trade discounts

20th-century master sculptors: Botero, Moore, Marini, Manzu, Calder.

MICHAEL WERNER

21 East 67th Street, New York, NY 10021 • Tel: (212) 988-1623 • Fax: (212) 988-1774 • Mon-Sat 10:00-6:00 • Gordon VeneKlasen, • Spanish and French spoken

Modern and contemporary European and American paintings, sculpture and drawings. Specialist in German contemporary art.

WIDING & PECK FINE ART

47 East 66th Street, New York, NY 10021 • Tel: (212) 472-1455 • Fax: (212) 472-1239 • Mon-Sat 10:00-5:30 by appointment • Eric Widing and Glann Peck • German and Italian spoken • Prices medium to high • Trade discounts

19th- and early 20th-century American and European art.

D. WIGMORE FINE ART

22 East 76th Street, New York, NY 10021 • Tel: (212) 794-2128 • Mon-Sat 9:30-5:30 • Deedee Wigmore • Some French and German spoken

Hudson River School, American Impressionism and 1930s to 1940s Realism.

⚇ WILDENSTEIN & CO.

19 East 64th Street, New York, NY 10021 • Tel: (212) 879-0500 • Fax: (212) 517-4715 • Mon-Fri 10:00-5:00 • Many languages spoken

Old and Modern Master paintings, drawings and sculpture.

WINSTON WACHTER FINE ART

111 East 65th Street, #2B, New York, NY 10021 • Tel: (212) 327-2526 • Fax: (212) 327-2529 • Mon-Fri 10:00-6:00, Sat 11:00-5:00 • Stacey Winston and Christine Wächter • French, German and Italian spoken • Prices medium • Major credit cards

Contemporary paintings, photography, works on paper. Art tours.

THE WRIGHT GALLERY

41 East 57th Street, 11th floor, New York, NY 10022 • Tel: (212) 702-0132 • Fax: (212) 759-7476 • Tue-Sat 10:00-6:00

Contemporary American art.

DAVID AND CONSTANCE YATES

P.O. Box 580, Lenox Hill Station, New York, NY 10021 • Tel: (212) 879-7758 • Fax: (212) 794-4680 • By appointment

European drawings and sculpture.

RICHARD YORK GALLERY

21 East 65th Street, New York, NY 10021 • Tel: (212) 772-9155 • Fax: (212) 288-0410 • Mon-Fri 10:00-5:30 • Richard T. York • French spoken

American art from 1750 to 1950. Paintings, sculpture, drawings and watercolors.

ZABRISKIE GALLERY

41 East 57th Street, New York, NY 10022 • Tel: (212) 752-1223 • Fax: (212) 752-1224 • Tue-Sat 10:00-5:30 • Christoph Gerozissis • French, German, Spanish and Portuguese spoken

19th- and 20th-century photography. 20th-century and contemporary paintings, drawings and sculpture.

————————— THE UPPER WEST SIDE OF MANHATTAN —————————

GEORGE ADAMS GALLERY

41 West 57th Street, 7th floor, New York, NY 10019 • Tel: (212) 644-5665 • Fax: (212) 644-5666 • Tue-Fri 10:00-6:00, Sat 10:00-5:00 • Spanish spoken • Prices medium to high

Contemporary American art. Latin American art.

AGNEWS, INC.

15 West 53rd Street • New York, NY 10019 • Tel: (212) 317-1871 • Fax: (212) 317-1872 • Julian Agnew • Prices medium to high

All periods in British paintings, Old Master paintings and drawings.

⛩ ASSOCIATED AMERICAN ARTISTS

20 West 57th Street • New York, NY 10019 • Tel: (212) 399-5510 • Fax: (212) 582-9697 • Tue-Sat 10:00-6:00 • Emilio Steinberger • French, Spanish and Italian spoken • Prices medium to high • Major credit cards

Modern and contemporary paintings and works on paper.

BARON/BOISANTE EDITIONS

50 West 57th Street, New York, NY 10019 • Tel: (212) 581-9191 • Fax: (212) 581-9291 • Tue-Sat 10:00-6:00 • Elise Boisante • French and Japanese spoken • Prices low • 20-25% trade discounts and 40% on editions

Prints, drawings and sculpture by young contemporary artists.

⛩ J.N. BARTFIELD

30 West 57th Street, 3rd floor, New York, NY 10019 • Tel: 245-8890 • Fax: (212) 541-4860 • Mon-Fri 9:30-5:00, Sat 10:30-2:30

19th- and 20th-century American, Western and Sporting art: oils, bronzes and watercolors by the masters of the American West. Works by The Taos Society.

BLUM HELMAN GALLERY

20 West 57th Street, New York, NY 10019 • Tel: (212) 245-2888 • Fax: (212) 265-4592 • Joseph Helma, Irving Blum, Christine Wächter • Prices medium to high

Modern and contemporary European and American paintings, drawings and sculpture.

BREWSTER ARTS

41 West 57th Street, New York, NY 10019 • Tel: (212) 980-5373 • Fax: (212) 980-5997 • Tue-Sat 10:00-5:30 • German, French and Spanish spoken • Prices medium to high • Trade discounts • Major credit cards

Latin American, with special focus on Mexico and Cuba, and European paintings, drawings and sculpture.

GARTH CLARK GALLERY

24 West 57th Street, Suite 305, New York, NY 10019 • Tel: (212) 246-2205 • Fax: (212) 489-5168 • Tue-Sat 10:00-5:30 • Mark Del Velcchio • French Portuguese and Spanish spoken • Prices medium

Modern and contemporary ceramics.

SYLVAN COLE GALLERY

101 West 57th Street, New York, NY 10019 • Tel: (212) 333-7760 • By appointment

American prints and drawings. Works by American artists.

TIBOR DE NAGY GALLERY

724 Fifth Avenue, New York, NY 10019 • Tel: (212) 421-3780 • Fax: (212) 421-3731 • Tue-Sat 10:00-5:30 • Andrew H. Arnot, Eric Brown • Prices modest to high • Trade discounts

Contemporary European and American paintings, sculpture and works on paper. Current artists include: Fairfield Porter, Edwin Dickinson, Rudy Burckhardt.

FISCHBACH GALLERY

24 West 57th Street, New York, NY 10019 • Tel: (212) 759-2345 • Fax: (212) 757-0202 • Tue-Sat 10:00-5:30 • Lawrence L. DeCarlo, Beverly M. Zagor, Marilyn C. Fischbach • French spoken • Trade discounts

American contemporary Realism.

SHERRY FRENCH GALLERY

24 West 57th Street, New York, NY 10019 • Tel: (212) 247-2457 • Fax: (212) 247-2810 • Tue-Sat 10:00-6:00 • Sherry French • Prices medium

Paintings and sculpture by American contemporary Realist artists.

GALLERY AT LINCOLN CENTER

136 West 65th Street, New York, NY 10023 • Tel: (212) 580-4673 • Mon-Sat 10:00-8:00 • Major credit cards

The List Collection of prints and posters on permanent exhibition. Six other exhibits per year relating to music and the performing arts.

GALLERY 84

50 West 57th Street, New York, NY 10019 • Tel: (212) 581-6000 • Tue-Sat 11:00-5:00 • Joe Bascom • Many languages spoken • Trade discounts

Contemporary abstract and realistic art: paintings, drawings, graphics, prints, colored-pencil drawings, watercolors. Photography.

MARIAN GOODMAN GALLERY AND MULTIPLES

24 West 57th Street, New York, NY 10019 • Tel: (212) 977-7160 • Fax: (212) 581-5187 • Tue-Sat 10:00-6:00 • Marian Goodman, Jill Sussman • French spoken • Prices low to high • Trade discounts • Major credit cards

Contemporary paintings, sculpture, prints and photography.

HAMMER GALLERIES

33 West 57th Street, New York, NY 10019 • Tel: (212) 644-4400 • Fax: (212) 832-3763 • Mon-Fri 9:30-5:30 • French and Spanish spoken • Major credit cards accepted for certain items

19th- and 20th-century American and European paintings. Contemporary realist art.

JOSEPH HELMAN GALLERY

20 West 57th Street, New York, NY 10019 • Tel: (212) 245-2888 • Fax: (212) 265-4592 • Tue-Sat 10:00-6:00 • Paris Murray • French spoken • Prices medium to high

Modern and contemporary American and European paintings and sculpture.

JANIS GALLERY

110 West 57th Street, New York, NY 10019 • Tel: (212) 586-0110 • Fax: (212) 262-0525 • Tue-Sat 10:00-5:30 • Carroll Janis and David Janis • French spoken

Masters from the entire 20th century: paintings, sculpture, photography.

GALERIE LELONG

20 West 57th Street, New York, NY 10019 • Tel: (212) 315-0470 • Fax: (212) 262-0624 • Tue-Sat 10:00-5:30 • Mary Sabbatino, Director; Cecile Panzieri, Ass. Dir. • French and German spoken • Prices medium to high

Modern and contemporary paintings and sculpture from the United States, Europe and Latin America. Modern and contemporary prints, photography and works on paper.

LUNN, LTD.

P.O. Box 826, Radio City Station, New York, NY 10101-0826 • Tel: (212) 765-2269 • Fax: (212) 664-0975 • By appointment • Harry H. Lunn, Jr.

19th- and 20th-century prints and photographs.

WALTER MAIBAUM FINE ARTS

50 West 57th Street, New York, NY 10019 • Tel: (212) 541-5000 • Fax: (212) 541-5238

20th-century Cubist paintings, Surrealism, American Modernism and some Russian Avant-Garde art.

MARLBOROUGH GALLERY

40 West 57th Street, New York, NY 10019 • Tel: (212) 541-4900 • Fax: (212) 541-4948 • Mon-Sat 10:00-5:30 • Pierre Levai • French spoken • Prices medium to high

A leading gallery in American and European Modern and contemporary paintings and sculpture.

PARK SOUTH GALLERY

885 Seventh Avenue, New York, NY 10019 • Tel: (212) 246-5900 • Fax: (212) 541-5716 • Tue-Sat 10:00-6:00 • French spoken • Prices low to high • Some trade discounts • Major credit cards

Turn-of-the-century stone lithographs: Toulouse-Lautrec, Mucha, Steinlen.

MICHAEL ROSENFELD GALLERY

24 West 57th Street, New York, NY 10019 • Tel: (212) 247-0082 • Fax: (212) 247-0402 • Tue-Sat 10:00-6:00

American art 1910-1950.

MARY RYAN GALLERY

24 West 57th Street, New York, NY 10019 • Tel: (212) 397-0669 • Fax: (212) 397-0766 • Tue-Sat 10:00-5:00 • Mary Ryan • French, German and Italian spoken • Prices medium to high • Visa and MC

American and British paintings, prints and works on paper—1920s to contemporary.

SACKS FINE ART

171 West 57th Street, New York, NY 10019 • Tel: (212) 333-7755 • Fax: (212) 541-6065 • By appointment • Beverly and Ray Sacks

American paintings and African American paintings.

GALERIE ST. ETIENNE

24 West 57th Street, Room 802, New York, NY 10019 • Tel: (212) 245-6734 • Fax: (212) 765-8493 • Tue-Sat 11:00-5:00 • Jane Kallir and Hildegard Bachert • German and Italian spoken • All ranges of prices • Some discounts

German and Austrian Expressionism and self-taught art. 19th- and 20th-century Naive art.

SUSAN SHEEHAN GALLERY

20 West 57th Street, 7th floor, New York, NY 10019 • Tel: (212) 888-1122 • Fax: (212) 888-0497 • Tue-Sat 10:00-6:00 and by appointment • Susan Sheehan • Some Spanish and French spoken • Amex and Visa

19th- and 20th-century American and European paintings and works on paper.

TATISTCHEFF & CO.

50 West 57th Street, New York, NY 10019 • Tel: (212) 664-0907 • Fax: (212) 541-8814 • Tue-Sat 10:00-6:00 • Peter Tatistcheff and Carol Craven, Director • French and Russian spoken

Contemporary American paintings and drawings.

VIRIDIAN GALLERY

24 West 57th Street, New York, NY 10019 • Tel: (212) 245-2882 • Tue-Sat 10:30-6:00 • Prices medium to high

Contemporary prints, paintings, sculpture and photos.

JOAN T. WASHBURN

20 West 57th Street, New York, NY 10019 • Tel: (212) 397-6780 • Fax: (212) 397-4853 • Tue-Sat 10:00-6:00 • Joan T. and Alan Washburn

19th- and 20th-century American paintings, sculpture, photographs, drawings and prints.

WEYHE GALLERY

101 West 57th Street, New York, NY 10019 • Tel: (212) 333-7610 • By appointment • Gertrude Weyhe Dennis

American prints and drawings, 1920 to 1950.

WRIGHT

42 East 57th Street, New York, NY 10019 • Tel: (212) 702-0132 • Fax: (212) 759-7476 • Tue-Sat 10:00-6:00

Contemporary American art.

GERALD WUNDERLICH & CO.

50 West 57th Street, New York, NY 10019 • Tel: (212) 974-8444 • Fax: (212) 956-0553 • Tue-Sat 10:00-5:30, Mon by appointment • Christine Anerealla • Prices medium to high • Trade discounts

Traditional American art. American contemporary Realism.

——————— THE LOWER EAST SIDE OF MANHATTAN ———————

PARK SLOPE GALLERY

559 Tenth Street, Brooklyn, NY 11215 • Tel: (718) 768-4883 • Fax: (212) 965-4199 • By appointment • Phyllis Wrynn • French spoken • Prices medium • 15-20% professional discount

Represents WPA artists (Leon Bibel); contemporary black & white photographer George Forss; mid-20th-century American art: all media; folk art: all media; advertising; textiles.

SALAMAGUNDI CLUB GALLERIES

47 Fifth Avenue, New York, NY 10003 • Tel: (212) 255-7740 • Fax: (212) 229-0172 • Daily 1:00-5:00

Contemporary paintings, watercolors and drawings. Exhibitions change approximately every two weeks.

——————— THE LOWER WEST SIDE OF MANHATTAN ———————

ACTUAL ART FOUNDATION/FULCRUM GALLERY

480 Broome Street, New York, NY 10013 • Tel: (212) 966-6848 • Tue-Sat 11:00-6:00, Sun 1:00-6:00 • Valerie Shakespeare • French and some German spoken • Prices low to medium • Major credit cards

Specializes in Actual Art: art that evolves and changes materially over time.

BROOKE ALEXANDER/BROOKE ALEXANDER EDITIONS

59 Wooster Street, 2nd floor, New York, NY 10012 • Tel: (212) 925-4338 • Fax: (212) 941-9565 • Wed-Sat 12:00-6:00 • Carolina Nitsch-Jones • German and Spanish spoken • Prices medium • Amex accepted

Contemporary paintings, drawings and sculpture.

MITCHELL ALGUS GALLERY

25 Thompson Street, New York, NY 10012 • Tel: (212) 966-1758 • Tue-Fri 3:00-7:00, Sat 11:00-6:00 • Prices medium • Trade discount

Contemporary art specializing in the 50s, 60s and 70s. Edward Avedisian, Larry Zox, Leonid Robert Mallary, Voy Fangor.

AMBASSADOR GALLERIES

137 Spring Street, New York, NY 10012 • Tel: (212) 431-9431 • Fax: (212) 431-8123 • Mon-Fri 10:00-5:00, Sat 12:00-5:00

Contemporary established and emerging artists.

AMERICAN FINE ARTS CO.

22 Wooster Street, New York, NY 10013 • Tel: (212) 941-0401 • Fax: (212) 274-8706 • Tue-Sat 11:00-6:00 • Christine Tsvetanov • German and French spoken • Prices low • Trade discounts • Major credit cards

Contemporary art. Photography, video, collage, paintings, installations.

ART IN GENERAL

79 Walker Street, New York, NY 10013 • Tel: (212) 219-0473 • Fax: (212) 219-0511 • Tue-Sat 12:00-6:00 • Major credit cards

Nonprofit exhibition space for artists. Paintings, sculpture, drawings, photography, mixed media, video. Contemporary art.

ATLANTIC GALLERY

475 Broome Street, New York, NY 10013 • Tel: (212) 219-3183 • Tue-Sun 12:00-6:00

Cooperative gallery with 30 member artists. Among these are Michael Hayes, Nancy Kearing, Ragnar Naess, Patricia Quinn, Sjogren Rowe, Susan Schott, Bryna Silbert. Paintings, sculpture and works on paper.

ATMOSPHERE

81 Greene Street, New York, NY 10012 • Telfax: (212) 343-9115 • Mon-Sat 11:00-6:30, closed Wed, Sun 12:30-6:00 • Kevin and Robin Platt • Prices high • Trade discount • Major credit cards

Contemporary decorative arts: paintings, objects, furniture, painted tables by IKERU and the works of 80 international artists.

PAOLO BALDACCI GALLERY

521 West 21st Street, New York, NY 10011 • Tel: (212) 463-0919 • Fax: (212) 463-0940 • Tue-Sat 10:00-5:30 • Neal Guma • German and Italian spoken

Italian Modern and international contemporary art: paintings, sculpture and works on paper.

BASILICO FINE ARTS

26 Wooster Street, New York, NY 10013 • Tel: (212) 966-1831 • Fax: (212) 334-5187 • Tue-Sat 10:30-6:00

Contemporary art: paintings, sculpture, photography, video and installations.

BENEDETTI GALLERY

52 Prince Street, New York, NY 10012 • Tel: (212) 226-2238 • Fax: (212) 431-8106 • Daily 11:00-5:00 • Charles Huller • Italian and Spanish spoken • Prices very high • Trade discount • Major credit cards

Specializes in art work by Erte. Acrylics by Hart and Wilkinson. Bronzes by Felix de Weldon, creator of the Iwo Jima War Memorial. Paintings of Anthony Quinn.

DENISE BIBRO FINE ART

584 Broadway, New York, NY 10012 • Telfax: (212) 941-1734 • Tue-Sat 11:00-5:00 • Prices medium

Contemporary paintings, sculpture, works on paper, photography of established and emerging artists.

BOESKY & CALLERY FINE ARTS

51 Greene Street, New York, NY 10013 • Tel: (212) 941-9888 • Fax: (212) 343-7903 • Tue-Sat 10:00-6:00 • Marianne Boesky and Patrick Callery • French spoken • Prices medium to very high

Contemporary art, primarily emerging artists.

BONINO GALLERY

48 Great Jones Street, New York, NY 10012 • Tel: (212) 598-4262 • Fax: (212) 982-2842 • By appointment only • Fernanda Bonino speaks Spanish, Portuguese, French and Italian

Contemporary Italian and Latin American paintings and sculpture.

⚏ CALDWELL SNYDER GALLERY

451 West Broadway, New York, NY 10012 • Tel: (212) 387-0208 • Fax: (212) 387-0717 • Mon-Sat 11:00-7:00, Sun 11:00-6:30 • Joni Binder • Spanish, Italian and some French spoken • Prices medium • Trade discounts • Major credit cards

Contemporary paintings, graphics and sculpture of emerging artists. Among these are: Regina Saura, Piotr Strelnik, Gilles Marrey, Thomas Pradzynski, Manel Anoro, Claire Klarewicz-Okser.

CLAUDIA CARR GALLERY—WORKS ON PAPER

478 West Broadway, New York, NY 10012 • Tel: (212) 673-5518 • Fax: (212) 673-0123 • Wed-Sat 11:00-5:30, Tue by appointment • Some French spoken • Prices low to medium • Trade discount

All aspects of contemporary works on paper and photography.

CAST IRON GALLERY

159 Mercer Street, New York, NY 10012 • Tel: (212) 274-8624 • Fax: (212) 925-0342 • Tue-Sun 11:00-6:00 • Japanese spoken • Prices low to medium • Trade discounts • Major credit cards

Contemporary art: 70% Japanese artists and 30% international artists. New exhibits every 3 weeks.

LEO CASTELLI

420 West Broadway, New York, NY 10012 • Tel: (212) 431-5160 • Fax: (212) 431-5361
578 Broadway, New York, NY 10012 • Tel: (212) 941-6279 • Fax: (212) 431-0093 • Tue-Sat 10:00-6:00 • Leo Castelli, Susan Brundage, Patricia Brundage • Italian and French spoken

European and American contemporary paintings, drawings and sculpture.

CFM GALLERY

112 Greene Street, New York, NY 10012 • Tel: (212) 966-3864 • Fax: (212) 226-1041 • Tue-Sun 12:00-6:00 • Prices medium to high

Contemporary realist art. European and American figurative artists. Originals and graphics.

CLEMENTINE

526 West 26th Street, 2nd floor, New York, NY 10001 • Tel: (212) 243-5937 • Fax: (212) 243-3927 • Thu-Fri 12:00-8:00, Sat 10:00-6:00, Sun 12:00-6:00 • Abby Messitte and Elizabeth Burke • French spoken

Contemporary emerging artists in all media.

CHARLES COWLES GALLERY

420 West Broadway, New York, NY 10012 • Tel: (212) 925-3500 • Fax: (212) 925-3501 • Tue-Sat 10:00-6:00 • Charles Cowles, Bill Carroll

Modern and contemporary art.

PAULA COOPER GALLERY

534 West 21st Street, New York, NY 10011 • Tel: (212) 255-1105 • Fax: (212) 255-5156 • Tue-Sat 10:00-6:00 • Paula Cooper • French and German spoken

Contemporary sculpture, paintings, drawings, prints, photography and video.

D'AMELIO-TERRAS GALLERY

525 West 22nd Street, New York, NY 10011 • Tel: (212) 352-9460 • Fax: (212) 352-9464 • Wed-Sun 11:00-6:00 • Christopher D'Amelio and Lucien Terras • French spoken • Prices low to high

International contemporary art: paintings, sculpture, video, photography, installation. Gallery artists include: Tony Feher, Joe Scanlan, Donald Judd, Robert Gober, Bruce Naumann.

NICHOLAS DAVIES GALLERY

23 Commerce Street, New York, NY 10014 • Tel: (212) 243-6840 • Fax: (212) 243-6842 • Tue-Sat 11:00-6:00 • French and Spanish spoken • Prices medium • Major credit cards

Wide range of work by emerging contemporary artists from all over the world. All media, drawings and paintings. Also rare, out-of-print books on design, fashion 1915 to 1960s.

EDITION SCHELLMANN

50 Greene Street, New York, NY 10013 • Tel: (212) 219-1821 • Fax: (212) 941-9206 • Tue-Sat 12:00-6:00 and by appointment • Meg Malloy • Prices medium to high • Trade discounts

Contemporary and conceptual minimal prints and multiples. Gallery and publisher.

G.W. EINSTEIN CO.

591 Broadway, New York, NY 10012 • Tel: (212) 226-1414 • Fax: (212) 941-9561 • Thu-Sat 11:00-6:00 and by appointment • Italian and Japanese spoken • Trade discounts

20th-century American paintings and works on paper.

RONALD FELDMAN FINE ARTS

31 Mercer Street, New York, NY 10013 • Tel: (212) 226-3232 • Fax: (212) 941-1536 • Tue-Sat 10:00-6:00 • Ronald Feldman, Freyda Feldman

Contemporary paintings, sculpture, installations, drawings and video.

FOTOUHI CRAMER GALLERY

560 Broadway, Suite 205, New York, NY 10012 • Tel: (212) 431-1304 • Fax: (212) 432-0472 • Tue-Sat 10:00-6:00 • Renee Fotouhi • Prices medium • Trade discounts • Major credit cards

Contemporary paintings, drawings, watercolors, sculpture, all media, photography.

JESSICA FREDERICKS GALLERY

504 West 22nd Street, New York, NY 10011 • Tel: (212) 633-6555 •
Fax: (212) 367-9502 • Wed-Sun 11:00-6:00 • Jessica Fredericks and
Andrew Freiser • Some Japanese spoken • Prices low to medium

Young, emerging and established contemporary artists from New
York and Los Angeles.

GAGOSIAN GALLERY

136 Wooster Street, New York, NY 10012 • Tel: (212) 228-2828 • Fax:
(212) 228-2878 • Tue-Sat 10:00-6:00 • Larry Gagosian • German and
French spoken • Prices medium to high

Modern and contemporary paintings and sculpture.

BARBARA GLADSTONE GALLERY

515 West 24th Street, New York, NY 10011 • Tel: (212) 206-9300 •
Fax: (212) 206-9301 • Tue-Sat 10:00-6:00 • Italian, Dutch and French
spoken

Contemporary art of all media.

GREENE NAFTALI

526 West 26th Street, New York, NY 10001 • Tel: (212) 463-7770 •
Wed-Sat 10:00-6:00, Sun 12:00-6:00 • Carol Greene, Director • Japanese, German, French and Italian spoken • Prices very low to high

Contemporary art, painting, video, sculpture, photography and installations.

STEPHEN HALLER GALLERY

560 Broadway, New York, NY 10012 • Tel: (212) 219-2500 • Fax: (212)
219-3246 • Tue-Sat 10:00-6:00 • Stephen Haller

Gestural Minimalism, paintings, sculpture and works on paper. Mid-
career and emerging artists: many in museum collections.

O.K. HARRIS WORKS OF ART

383 West Broadway, New York, NY 10012 • Tel: (212) 431-3600 • Fax:
(212) 925-4797 • Tue-Sat 10:00-6:00 • Ivan C. Karp • French and
Spanish spoken • Prices high • 20% trade discount • Amex

20th-century paintings, sculpture, drawings, watercolors, photography, collectibles, antiques.

PAT HEARN GALLERY

530 West 22nd Street, New York, NY 10011 • Tel: (212) 727-7366 •
Fax: (212) 727-7467 • Wed-Sun 11:00-6:00 • Pat Hearn and Leslie
Nolen • Visa

Young and emerging contemporary art from Europe and America.

GALLERY HENOCH

80 Wooster Street, New York, NY 10012 • Tel: (212) 966-6360 • Fax: (212) 966-6362 • Tue-Sat 10:30-6:00 • George Henoch Shechtman • Spanish spoken • Prices medium • 10 to 15% discount

Contemporary American and European Realist paintings and sculpture.

NANCY HOFFMAN GALLERY

429 West Broadway, New York, NY 10012 • Tel: (212) 966-6676 • Fax: (212) 334-5078 • Tue-Sat 10:00-6:00 • Nancy Hoffman, Sique Spence, Christopher Watson • French and Spanish spoken • Major credit cards

Contemporary paintings, sculpture, drawings, watercolors and prints.

ILLUSTRATION HOUSE, INC.

96 Spring Street, 7th floor, New York, NY 10012-3923 • Tel: (212) 966-9444 • Fax: (212) 966-9425 • Tue-Sat 10:30-5:30 • Roger T. Reed • Prices medium • Visa and MC

Illustrative paintings and drawings of the past 100 years including Norman Rockwell, Charles Addams, N.C. Wyeth and Dr. Seuss. Appraisals and twice-annual auctions.

IN KHAN

415 West Broadway, New York, NY 10012 • Tel: (212) 226-6484 • Fax: (212) 226-6494 • Tue-Sat 10:00-6:00 • Korean spoken

Contemporary paintings, drawings, sculpture, photography, installations.

JUNE KELLY GALLERY

591 Broadway, New York, NY 10012 • Tel: (212) 226-1660 • Fax: (212) 226-2433 • Tue-Sat 11:00-6:00 • Spanish and some French spoken • Prices high to very high • Trade discount

Contemporary paintings, sculpture and photography representing more than 20 emerging, mid-career and established artists.

JIM KEMPNER FINE ART

225 Lafayette Street, Suite 811, New York, NY 10012 • Tel: (212) 966-2688 • Fax: (212) 966-2595 • Wed-Sat 10:00-6:00

Prints and works on paper by contemporary masters: Rauschenberg, Jasper Johns.

KENT

67 Prince Street, New York, NY 10012 • Tel: (212) 966-4500 • Fax: (212) 966-2820 • Tue-Sat 12:00-6:00 • Douglas Walla

Modern and contemporary paintings, drawings and sculpture.

PHYLLIS KIND GALLERY

136 Greene Street, New York, NY 10012 • Tel: (212) 925-1200 • Fax: (212) 941-7841 • Tue-Sat 10:00-6:00 • Phyllis Kind, Ron Jagger

Contemporary American and Russian paintings, sculpture and works on paper. Also self-taught and European art brut.

LINDA KIRKLAND GALLERY

504 West 22nd Street, New York, NY 10011 • Tel: (212) 627-3930 • Fax: (212) 255-2647 • Wed-Sat 11:00-6:00, Sun 12:00-5:00 • Spanish spoken

Emerging artists showing work that has a conceptual bent with a visual sensuality.

MONIQUE KNOWLTON GALLERY

568 Broadway, Suite 102, New York, NY 10012 • Tel: (212) 966-2625 • Fax: (212) 966-2093 • Tue-Fri 10:00-6:00, Sat 11:00-6:00 • Kimberly Marrero • German, French and Italian spoken • Prices medium • 15 to 20% professional discount

Contemporary paintings, sculpture and photography.

KREPS

580 Broadway, New York, NY 10012 • Tel: (212) 965-1911 • Fax: (212) 965-9675 • Tue-Sat 11:00-6:00

Contemporary works by emerging younger artists: abstract, figurative, minimalist and videos.

KUSTERA

41 Wooster Street, New York, NY 10012 • Tel: (212) 965-1527 • Fax: (212) 965-1529 • Tue-Sat 10:00-6:00 • Anna Kustera • Some Italian and French spoken

Contemporary emerging and mid-career artists: abstract, figurative, surrealist, minimalist.

XAVIER LA BOULBENNE GALLERY

504 West 22nd Street, New York, NY 10011 • Tel: (212) 462-4111 • Fax: (212) 645-7656 • Wed-Sun 11:00-6:00 • French, Spanish and German spoken

Contemporary art—emerging multimedia international artists.

BRUCE B. LEWIN GALLERY

136 Prince Street, New York, NY 10012 • Tel: (212) 431-4750 • Fax: (212) 431-5012 • Tue-Sat 10:00-6:00 • Bruce Lewin • Prices medium • Trade discounts • Major credit cards

Photo-realistic and pop paintings and figurative sculpture.

STUART LEVY FINE ART

588 Broadway, Suite 303, New York, NY 10012 • Tel: (212) 941-0009 • Fax: (212) 941-7987 • Tue-Sat 12:00-6:00 and by appointment • Stuart Levy, Director • French and Spanish spoken • 10-20% professional discount

Specializes in 19th- and 20th-century European and American figurative, narrative and abstract painting, photography, sculpture, works on paper and mixed media. Strong focus on contemporary, cutting-edge photography.

LUHRING AUGUSTINE

130 Prince Street, New York, NY 10012 • Tel: (212) 219-9600 • Fax: (212) 966-1891 • Tue-Sat 10:00-6:00 • Roland Augustine, Lawrence Luhring

Contemporary and Modern paintings, drawings, sculpture and photography. All media.

CURT MARCUS GALLERY

578 Broadway, New York, NY 10012 • Tel: (212) 226-3200 • Fax: (212) 941-6365 • Tue-Sat 10:00-6:00 • Anastasia Aukeman • French spoken • Major credit cards

Contemporary American and European paintings, sculpture, drawings, watercolors, photography, video, installations.

NANCY MARGOLIS GALLERY

560 Brodway, Suite 302, New York, NY 10012 • Tel: (212) 343-9523 • Fax: (212) 343-9524 • Tue-Sat 10:00-5:30 • Nancy Margolis • Italian spoken • Prices medium to high • Major credit cards

Contemporary American and European ceramics; works on paper.

MATTHEW MARKS GALLERY

523 West 24th Street, New York, NY 10011 • (212) 243-0200 • Fax: (212) 243-0047 • Tue-Sat 10:00-6:00 • Prices medium to high

International contemporary art: paintings, drawings, sculpture, photography. Works in all media.

MATTHEW MARKS GALLERY

522 West 22nd Street, New York, NY 10011 • Tel: (212) 243-1650 • Fax: (212) 243-2503 • Wed-Sat 12:00-6:00 • Prices medium to high

International contemporary art: paintings, drawings, sculpture, photography. Works in all media.

BILL MAYNES CONTEMPORARY ART

225 Lafayette Street, Room 302, New York, NY 10012 • Telfax: (212) 431-3952 • Tue-Sat 11:00-6:00 • Bill Maynes • German spoken • Prices low • Trade discounts

Paintings and sculpture by promising emerging artists.

MILES STUDIO GALLERY

118 West 27th Street, New York, NY 10001 • Telfax: (212) 691-7094 •
Matthew Albert Miles • By appointment only • Albanian spoken • Prices
medium to high

Artist's own studio: contemporary impressionist paintings.

MONTSERRAT GALLERY

584 Broadway, New York, NY 10012 • Tel: (212) 941-8899 • Fax: (212)
274-1717 • Tue-Sat 12:00-6:00 • Major credit cards

Contemporary paintings, sculpture and watercolors.

MORRIS-HEALY GALLERY

530 West 22nd Street, New York, NY 10011 • Tel: (212) 243-3753 •
Fax: (212) 243-3668 • Wed-Sun 11:00-6:00 • Paul Morris, Tom Healy •
Prices low to high • Major credit cards

Exhibitions of emerging artists.

MICHELE MOSKO MILLER FINE ART

354 Broome Street, New York, NY 10013 • Tel: (212) 226-0166 • Fax:
(212) 226-0215 • Wed-Fri 1:00-6:00

Contemporary American paintings, sculpture, photography, limited
edition prints and screens.

NOLAN-ECKMAN GALLERY

560 Broadway, Room 604, New York, NY 10012 • Tel: (212) 925-6190
• Fax: (212) 334-9139 • Tue-Fri 10:00-6:00, Sat 11:00-6:00 • David
Nolan, Carol Eckman, Susan Graage • German and Spanish spoken

European and American drawings and works on paper.

ANNINA NOSEI GALLERY

530 West 22nd Street, New York, NY 10011 • Tel: (212) 741-8695 •
Fax: (212) 741-2379 • Tue-Sat 11:00-6:00 • Jason Prohaska • Italian,
Spanish and French spoken • Prices medium to very high • Trade dis-
counts

Contemporary American and European art: sculpture, painting and
photography.

PACE WILDENSTEIN

142 Greene Street, New York, NY 10012 • Tel: (212) 431-9224 • Fax:
(212) 431-9280 • Tue-Sat 10:00-6:00 • Susan Dunne

The greats in contemporary art.

KATHERINA RICH PERLOW GALLERY

560 Broadway, 3rd floor, New York, NY 10012 • Tel: (212) 941-1220 •
Fax: (212) 274-9834 • Tue-Sat 10:00-6:00 • German and Spanish spoken • Prices medium • 15 to 20% professional discount

Contemporary painting, sculpture and photography.

PERRY ART GALLERY

472 Broome Street, New York, NY 10013 • Tel: (212) 925-6796 • Fax: (212) 925-0849 • Mon-Fri 10:00-6:00, Sat-Sun 11:00-6:00 • Hebrew spoken • Prices low to high • Major credit cards

International contemporary art: all media.

MAX PROTETCH GALLERY

525 West 22nd Street, New York, NY 10011 • Tel: (212) 633-6999 • Tue-Sat 10:00-6:00 • Spanish spoken

Contemporary sculpture and paintings; architects' drawings and works in clay.

QUARTET EDITIONS

568 Broadway, Suite 104A, New York, NY 10012 • Tel: (212) 219-2819 • Fax: (212) 219-2875 • Tue-Fri 10:00-5:00, Sat 12:00-5:00 • French spoken • Prices medium • Trade discounts • Amex and Visa

Publishers of contemporary prints: Christo, Sol Lewitt, Joan Snyder, Kara Walker.

GALLERY REVEL

96 Spring Street, New York, NY 10012 • Tel: (212) 925-0600 • Fax: (212) 431-6270 • Mon-Fri 10:00-6:00, Sun 12:00-5:00 • Marvin Carson • Some Spanish spoken • Prices medium • Some trade discounts • Major credit cards

Contemporary representational painters and sculptors.

BARRY ROSEN & JAAP VAN LIERE MODERN AND CONTEMPORARY ART

362 West Broadway, New York, NY 10013 • Tel: (212) 925-5425 • Fax: (212) 925-0726 • By appointment only • Trade discounts

American and European art of the 20th century and exhibitions of contemporary art.

SHAFRAZI

119 Wooster Street, New York, NY 10012 • Tel: (212) 274-9300 • Fax: (212) 334-9499 • Tue-Sat 10:00-6:00 • Japanese spoken

Contemporary paintings, drawings and sculpture.

JACK SHAINMAN GALLERY

560 Broadway, 2nd floor, New York, NY 10012 • Tel: (212) 966-3866 • Fax: (212) 334-8453 • Tue-Sat 10:00-6:00 • Jack Shainman

American and European contemporary art, sculpture, paintings, photography and video.

ANITA SHAPOLSKY GALLERY

99 Spring Street, New York, NY 10012 • Tel: (212) 334-9755 • Fax: (212) 334-6817 • Wed-Sat 11:00-6:00, Tue by appointment

Focus on 1st, 2nd and 3rd generations of the New York School of Abstract Expressionism.

HOLLY SOLOMON GALLERY

172 Mercer Street, New York, NY 10012 • Tel: (212) 941-5777 • Fax: (212) 226-4990 • Tue-Sat 10:00-6:00 • Holly Solomon, Tom Farmer.

Contemporary American and European paintings, sculpture, photography and performance art.

SONNABEND GALLERY

420 West Broadway, New York, NY 10012 • Tel: (212) 966-6160 • Fax: (212) 941-9218 • Tue-Sat 10:00-6:00 • Ileana Sonnabend, Antonio Homem • French, Spanish, Italian and Portuguese spoken

Contemporary American and European art: paintings, sculpture and photography.

SPERONE WESTWATER

142 Greene Street, New York, NY 10012 • Tel: (212) 431-3685 • Fax: (212) 941-1030 • Tue-Sat 10:00-6:00 • David Leiber, Director • Italian and French spoken • Prices medium to high

Contemporary American and European paintings and sculpture.

SRAGOW GALLERY

73 Spring Street, New York, NY 10012 • Tel: (212) 219-1793 • Mon-Sat, call for hours • Ellen Sragow • Prices low to medium

Works by African American artists. Abstract Impressionist prints, 1960s Mexican prints and prints of the 1930s and 1940s.

STARK GALLERY

113 Crosby Street, New York, NY 10012 • Tel: (212) 925-4484 • Fax: (212) 274-9525 • Tue-Sat 10:00-5:00 • Eric Stark • Some French and Spanish spoken • Prices medium • Some trade discounts

The work of established and emerging artists from Europe and the Americas.

STEINBAUM KRAUSS GALLERY

132 Greene Street, New York, NY 10012 • Tel: (212) 431-4224 • Fax: (212) 431-3252 • Tue-Sat 10:00-6:00 • Bernice Steinbaum and Judith Krauss • Spanish spoken

American contemporary art, paintings, sculpture, works on paper and photography.

STEFAN STUX GALLERY

535 West 20th Street, New York, NY 10011 • Tel: (212) 352-1600 •
Fax: (212) 352-0302 • Wed-Sun 11:00-6:00 • Prices medium

International contemporary paintings, sculpture and photography.

TEAM GALLERY

527 West 26th Street, New York, NY 10001 • Tel: (212) 279-9219 • Fri-
Sun 11:00-8:00 • Spanish and German spoken • Prices low to medium

Installation work and video art.

SUSAN TELLER GALLERY

568 Broadway, #103A, New York, NY 10012 • Tel: (212) 941-7335 •
Tue-Sat 11:00-6:00 • Some French spoken • Prices medium

American works on paper and paintings 1930-1950.

EDWARD THORP GALLERY

103 Prince Street, New York, NY 10012 • Tel: (212) 431-6880 • Fax:
(212) 219-0881 • Tue-Sat 10:00-6:00 • Edward Thorp and Elizabeth
Heskin

Contemporary American and European painters and sculptors.

303 GALLERY

525 West 22nd Street, New York, NY 10011 • Tel: (212) 255-1121 •
Fax: (212) 255-0024 • Wed-Sun 10:00-6:00 • Nora Tobbe • Prices
medium • Some trade discounts

European and American contemporary art: emerging artists.

JACK TILTON GALLERY

49 Greene Street, New York, NY 10013 • Tel: (212) 941-1775 • Fax:
(212) 941-1812 • Tue-Sat 10:00-6:00 • Jack Tilton and Susan Hort,
Owners; Annabella Johnson, Director • Italian spoken

International contemporary art: paintings, sculpture, photography.
Installations.

THE TIME IS ALWAYS NOW

476 Broome Street, New York, NY 10013 • Tel: (212) 343-2424 • Fax:
(212) 966-2408 • Tue-Sun 12:00-6:00 • Peter T. Tunney • Swedish
and French spoken • Amex

Original contemporary works including photography, works on paper, collages, oils on canvas, limited edition George Rodrigue's "Blue
Dog" silk screens. Exclusive representative of Peter Beard.

JOHN WEBER GALLERY

142 Greene Street, New York, NY 10012 • Tel: (212) 966-6115 • Fax: (212) 941-8727 • Tue-Sat 10:00-6:00 • John Weber, Joyce Nereaux • Italian and German spoken

Contemporary art of Europe, America and South America: paintings, sculpture and photography. Australian Aboriginal art: The Papunya Tula Group. Among the 29 artists represented by the gallery are: Alice Aycock, Daniel Buren, Victor Burgin, Joana Rosa, Hamish Fulton.

WOODWARD GALLERY

476 Broome Street, 5th floor, New York, NY 10013 • Tel: (212) 966-3411 • Fax: (212) 966-3491 • Tue-Sat 11:00-6:00, Thu 11:00-8:00 • John and Christine Woodward • Spanish and Italian spoken • Prices medium • 10 to 20% trade discount • MC and Visa

Contemporary established and emerging artists.

WOOSTER GARDENS

558 Broadway, New York, NY 10012 • Tel: (212) 941-6210 • Fax: (212) 941-5480 • Tue-Sat 11:00-6:00 • Prices low to high • Trade discount

International contemporary art, 19th- and 20th-century photography. Some limited editions.

Special Categories of Art

♕ American Art

J.N. BARTFIELD GALLERIES AND FINE BOOKS

30 West 57th Street, New York, NY 10019 • Tel: (212) 245-8890 • Fax: 541-4860 • Mon-Fri 10:00-5:00, Sat 10:00-3:00 • George Murray • Prices medium to high.

Specialist in the "masters of the west", the artists of Taos and 19th- and 20th-century American paintings and sculpture. A truly remarkable collection.

THOMAS COLVILLE FINE ART

1000 Madison Avenue, New York, NY 10021 • Tel: (212) 879-9259 • By appointment only

19th- and 20th-century American and French Barbizon School paintings, watercolors and drawings.

HIRSCHL & ADLER GALLERIES, INC.

21 East 70th Street, New York, NY 10021 • Tel: (212) 535-8810 • Fax: (212) 772-7237

American and European fine and decorative arts of the 18th to the 20th century.

GERALD PETERS GALLERY

177 East 78th Street, New York, NY 10021 • Tel: (212) 628-9760 • Fax: (212) 628-9635

American paintings; classic Western, Hudson River School, Impressionism, the Eight, The Taos Society and The O'Keeffe-Steiglitz Circle.

American Folk Art

AMERICAN PRIMITIVE GALLERY

594 Broadway, #205, New York, NY 10012 • Tel: (212) 966-1530 • Fax: (212) 343-0272 • Mon-Sat 11:00-6:00 • Aarne Anton • Estonian, Czech and Rumanian spoken • Prices medium • 10-20% trade discount • Major credit cards

American folk, outsider and self-taught art; paintings and sculpture. Bases and mounting for sculpture, ethnographic art and antiquities.

COMING TO AMERICA

276 Lafayette Street, New York, NY 10012 • Tel: (212) 343-2968 • 7 days 11:00-6:00 • Jim Cole • Italian spoken • Trade discount • Major credit cards

American folk art items, painted furniture, weathervanes, 1930s revival upholstered furniture designed by Cole.

ALLAN L. DANIEL

230 Central Park West, New York, NY 10024 • Tel: (212) 799-0825 • Fax: (201) 930-9765 • By appointment • Prices medium to high

Early American folk art, including paintings, carvings, weathervanes and furniture and decorative objects.

WILLIAM GREENSPON WORKS OF ART

465 West End Avenue, New York, NY 10024 • Tel: (212) 787-2727 • By appointment

Extraordinary folk art collection with an emphasis on sculpture. Some American Indian art mainly from the Northwest coast.

FRANK J. MIELE GALLERY

1086 Madison Avenue, New York, NY 10028 • Tel: (212) 249-7250 •
Fax: (212) 249-7267 • Mon-Fri 10:00-6:00, Sat 10:00-5:00, Sun 12:00-
5:00 • Prices medium • Trade discount • Major credit cards

Contemporary American folk art, including paintings, sculpture, ceramics and furniture.

STEVE MILLER-AMERICAN FOLK ART

17 East 96th Street, New York, NY 10128 • Tel: (212) 348-5219 • Fax:
(212) 427-4278 • Mon-Sat 12:30-6:00 • Steve Miller • Some Spanish
spoken • Prices low to medium • 20% professional discount

Investment quality American folk art, weathervanes, cigar store figures, American Primitive paintings: all 19th century.

MARK MILLIKEN GALLERY

1200 Madison Avenue, New York, NY 10128 • Tel: (212) 534-8802 •
Mon-Sat 10:00-6:00 • Justin Coster • Prices medium • 15% trade discount • Major credit cards

Handmade American crafts; blown glass, ceramics, silver and wood.
Custom work available.

RICCO/MARESCA GALLERY

152 Wooster Street, New York, NY 10012 • Tel: (212) 780-0071 • Fax:
(212) 780-0076 • Tue-Sat 11:00-6:00 • French spoken • Prices medium to high • Trade discount • Amex

Outsider self-taught folk art and contemporary photography.

TUCKER ROBBINS

366 West 15th Street, 5th floor, New York, NY 10011 • Tel: (212) 366-
4427 • Fax: (212) 366-6697 • Mon-Fri 10:00-4:30 or by appointment •
Tucker and Mexx • Spanish and French spoken • Prices medium • Trade
discount

International folk art and antiques from Southeast Asia, Africa, Latin
America; unique handcrafts, woven items, baskets and handmade
furniture. Special source.

THE AMERICAN FOLK ART GALLERY

374 Bleeker Street, New York, NY 10014 • Tel: (212) 366-6566 • Fax:
(212) 366-6599 • Mon-Sat 12:00-7:00, Sun 12:00-5:00 • Adam J.
Weitsman • Prices medium • 10% trade discount • Major credit cards

18th- , 19th- and 20th-century Primitives, furniture and Americana,
including tramp art and textiles.

See also: AMERICAN ANTIQUES

American Indian Art

ALASKA ON MADISON

937 Madison Avenue, New York, NY 10021 • Tel: (212) 879-1782 • Tue-Sat 11:30-6:00 • Jack Bryan • Prices medium to high • 10% trade discount • Major credit cards

The art of the Alaskan and Canadian Eskimo. Objects from the Northwest as well. From antiquity to contemporary. Splendid.

AMERICAN INDIAN COMMUNITY HOUSE GALLERY AND MUSEUM

708 Broadway, 2nd floor, New York, NY 10003 • Tel: (212) 598-0100 • Fax: (212) 598-4909 • Tue-Sat 12:00-6:00 • Rosemary Richmond, Curator, and Joanna Osborne Big Feather

American Indian and Canadian Indian contemporary painting, sculpture, photography, installations and prints.

THE COMMON GROUND, INC.

19 Greenwich Avenue, New York, NY 10014 • Tel: (212) 989-4178 • Fax: (212) 989-0573 • Mon-Fri 12:00-7:00, Sat 11:30-6:30, Sun 12:00-6:00 • Prices medium to high • Dealer discount • Major credit cards

Antique and contemporary arts of the American Indian.

THE COMMON GROUND GALLERY

55 West 16th Street, New York, NY 10011 • Tel: (212) 620-3122 • Fax: (212) 989-4178 • Tue-Sat 1:00-7:00 • Prices medium to high

Exhibitions and sale of American Indian art and artifacts.

Ancient Art and Antiquities

⚑ ACANTHUS

22 East 80th Street, New York, NY 10021 • Tel: (212) 570-6670 • Fax: (212) 570-5173 • By appointment • Brian T. Aitken • French and Italian spoken • Prices high

Greek and Roman art.

ALEX GALLERY

41 East 57th Street, New York, NY 10022 • Tel: (212) 486-3434 • Fax: (212) 223-4409 • Mon-Fri 10:00-5:00 • Richard Aryeh • Persian spoken • Prices medium to very high

Specialists in rare Islamic and Persian art. Miniature paintings, paintings, sculpture, lacquer work, manuscripts, enamels, ceramics, Russian and Swiss objets de vertu and antiquities.

ANAVIAN GALLERY

298 Fifth Avenue, New York, NY 10001 • Tel: (212) 594-3833 • Fax: (212) 594-6373 • By appointment • Persian spoken

Ancient Near Eastern and Islamic artifacts and archaeology.

✙ ANTIQUARIUM FINE ANCIENT ARTS GALLERY, LTD.

948 Madison Avenue, New York, NY 10021 • Tel: (212) 734-9776 • Fax: (212) 879-9362 • Tue-Fri 10:00-5:30, Sat 11:00-5:00 • Robin F. Beningson • French spoken • Prices medium to very high • Trade discount • All major credit cards

Museum quality Classical, Egyptian and Near Eastern antiquities, ancient jewelry and ancient glass.

✙ ARIADNE GALLERIES

970 Madison Avenue, New York, 10021 • Tel: (212) 772-3388 • Fax: (212) 517-7562 • Mon-Sat 10:00-6:00 • French and Chinese spoken • Prices high • Amex

Greek and Roman antiquities, Byzantine art, objects and jewelry. One of the best.

FORTUNA FINE ARTS GALLERY

984 Madison Avenue, New York, NY 10021 • Tel: (212) 794-7272 • Fax: (212) 794-7275 • Mon-Sat 10:00-6:00 • German and French spoken • Prices medium to high • All major credit cards

Classical Greek, Roman, Near Eastern, Egyptian and Byzantine antiquities.

ROBERT HABER ASSOCIATES, INC.

16 West 23rd Street, New York, NY 10003 • Tel: (212) 243-3656 • Fax: (212) 727-9669 • By appointment • Prices medium to high • Some French, German and Modern Greek spoken

Gallery of Greek, Roman, Egyptian and Byzantine antiquities.

HJB ANCIENT & TRIBAL ART

21 East 65th Street, New York, NY 10021 • Tel: (212) 535-9118 • Fax: (212) 861-9893 • Mon-Fri 10:00-5:00, appointment suggested • Harmer Johnson

Antiquities and tribal art objects: Greek, Roman, Egyptian, Pre-Columbian cultures and Oceanic cultures.

✙ THE MERRIN GALLERY

724 Fifth Avenue, New York, NY 10019 • Tel: (212) 757-2884 • Fax: (212) 757-3904 • Tue-Sat 10:00-6:00 • Samuel and Edward Merrin • Prices high

Egyptian, Greek, Roman, Etruscan and Near Eastern antiquities.

ROYAL-ATHENA GALLERIES

153 East 57th Street, New York, NY 10022 • Tel: (212) 355-2034 • Fax: (212) 688-0412 • Mon-Sat 10:00-6:00 • Dr. Jerome M. Eisenberg, Director • French, Spanish and Rumanian spoken • Prices high • Most major credit cards

Greek, Roman, Etruscan, Egyptian and Near Eastern Classical antiquities.

SADIGH GALLERY ANCIENT ART

303 Fifth Avenue, Suite 1603, New York, NY 10016 • Tel: (212) 725-7537 • Fax: (212) 545-7612 • Mon-Fri 10:00-8:00, Sun by appointment • Mehrdad Sadigh • Persian and Hebrew spoken • Prices medium • Professional discount • Major credit cards

Ancient Roman, Greek, Egyptian, Near Eastern and Pre-Columbian art and coins. 4,000 square feet of collectibles from antiquity to the Civil War.

SAFANI GALLERY

980 Madison Avenue, New York, NY 10021 • Tel: (212) 570-6360 • Fax: (212) 861-4136 • By appointment only

Roman, Greek, Egyptian and Near Eastern ancient and Islamic art.

FREDERICK SCHULTZ ANCIENT ART

41 East 57th Street, 11th floor, New York, NY 10022 • Tel: (212) 758-6007 • Fax: (212) 832-0448 • Tue-Sat 10:00-6:00 • Blake Woodruff • French, Italian and German spoken • Prices very high

Ancient Egyptian, Classical, Near Eastern, early European and archaic Eskimo works of art.

THROCKMORTON FINE ART, INC.

153 East 61st Street, 4th floor, New York, NY 10021 • Tel: (212) 223-1059 • Fax: (212) 223-1937 • Tue-Sat 11:00-5:00 • Yona Backer • Spanish, French, German and Dutch spoken • Prices low to high • Some trade discounts

Ancient art: Egyptian, Chinese and African ceramics and stone sculpture. Colonial Latin American paintings; contemporary and vintage Latin American photography and works on paper. Large collection of Pre-Columbian art, by appointment.

WARD & CO. WORKS OF ART INC.

962 Park Avenue, New York, NY 10028 • Tel: (212) 327-4400 • Fax: (212) 327-3851 • By appointment • Stark Ward, Theodore Padovano • German, French and Italian spoken

Prehistoric, ancient and medieval art.

Animal Art

WILLIAM SECORD GALLERY

52 East 76th Street, New York, NY 10021 • Tel: (212) 247-0075 • Fax: (212) 288-1939 • Mon-Sat 10:00-5:00 • William Secord • French and Japanese spoken • Prices medium to high • 10% trade discount • Major credit cards

17th-century animal art, specializing in dog paintings, including works by Maud Earl, John Emms, Arthur Wardle and Edwin Landseer.

Animation Art

ANIMAZING GALLERY

415 West Broadway, 2nd floor, New York, NY 10012 • Tel: (212) 226-7374 • Fax: (212) 226-7428 • Mon-Sat 11:00-7:00, Sun 12:00-6:00 • Nick Leone and Alan D. Makowski • Prices low to very high • Trade discount • Major credit cards

Original vintage and contemporary cells and drawings from all major animation studios, Disney, Warner Bros., Hanna-Barbera, MGM.

Architectual Art

E. BUK

151 Spring Street, New York, NY 10012 • Tel: (212) 226-6891 • By appointment • Prices medium • Trade discount

Architectural drawings and renderings including important 20th-century American projects such as: Princeton University, West Point Academy, Rockefeller Center, Queen Mary ocean liner and many more.

MICHAEL INGBAR GALLERY OF ARCHITECTURAL ART

568 Broadway, New York, NY 10012 • Tel: (212) 334-1100 • Fax: (212) 334-9214 • Tue-Sat 12:00-6:00 • Michael Ingbar • Prices medium • Trade discounts • Major credit cards

All media of fine art depicting, primarily, New York City buildings and structures.

Children's Art

KENDRA KRIENKE

230 Central Park West, New York, NY 10024 • Tel: (212) 580-6516 • Fax: (201) 930-9765 • By appointment • Kendra Krienke • Prices low to medium • 10% professional discount

Oil paintings, watercolors, drawings: original vintage art by illustrators for children and fantasy.

Ethnic and Tribal Art

AFRICAN HEMINGWAY GALLERY

1050 Second Avenue, #96, New York, NY 10022 • Telfax: (212) 838-3650 • Mon-Sat 10:30-6:00, Sun 12:00-6:00 • Brian Gaisford • Spanish and French spoken • Prices low • Visa and Amex

African art: sculptures in wood and stone, paintings. African photographic safaris arranged.

APN TRADING CORP.

1527 Agate Street, Bay Shore, NY 11706 • Telfax: (516) 968-8874 • By appointment only • Alex/Poppy Najoan • German and Dutch spoken • Prices medium to high • Major credit cards.

Ethnographic, tribal, primitive and ancient art.

CINQUE GALLERY, INC.

560 Broadway, Suite 504, New York, NY 10012 • Telfax: (212) 966-3464 • Tue-Sat 1:00-6:00 • Ruth Jett, Director • Prices negotiated with artists on exhibition.

Nonprofit gallery space showcasing the work of African American artists primarily.

KENKELEBA GALLERY

214 East Second Street, New York, NY 10009 • Tel: (212) 674-3939 • Fax: (212) 505-5080 • Wed-Sat 11:00-6:00 • Corrine Jennings • MC, Visa, Discover

African American art and the art of the African Diaspora. Exhibition catalogues, forums, archives.

MARIPOSA—ART FROM THE AMERICAS

140 West End Avenue, New York, NY 10023 • Tel: (212) 799-5929 • Fax: (212) 724-5627 • By appointment • Beate Echols • Spanish and German spoken • Prices medium • Some trade discounts

Ethnic and folk art and antiques from Latin America, including textiles. From colonial times to contemporary.

PACE PRIMITIVE

32 East 57th Street, New York, NY 10022 • Tel: (212) 421-3688 • Fax: (212) 751-7280 • Tue-Fri 9:30-5:30, Sat 10:00-6:00 • Italian, Norwegian and some French spoken • Prices medium to very high • Trade discount

African art and Himalayan masks.

MICHAEL RHODES/AFRICAN ART

453 West 43rd Street, New York, NY 10036 • Tel: (212) 246-2204 • Michael Rhodes • Prices medium to high • Professional discount

Antique traditional African sculpture, specializing in west and central African sculpture.

ERIC ROBERTSON AFRICAN ART GALLERY

36 West 22nd Street, New York, NY 10010 • Tel: (212) 675-4045 • Fax: (212) 366-0718 • Mon-Sat 11:00-6:00 or by appointment • French spoken • Prices medium to high • Discounts to collectors and museums

Collector quality traditional African art.

MERTON D. SIMPSON GALLERY

1063 Madison Avenue, New York, NY 10028 • Tel: (212) 988-6290 • Fax: (212) 988-3041 • Tue-Sat 10:30-5:30 • French and German spoken

Tribal and modern art specializing in African art.

PAUL STEINHACKER—PRIMITIVE AND ASIATIC ART

151 East 71st Street, New York, NY 10021 • Tel: (212) 879-1245 • By appointment

Antique African, American Indian, Eskimo, Oceanic and Tibetan arts.

TAMBARAN GALLERY

5 East 82nd Street, New York, NY 10028 • Tel: (212) 570-0655 • Fax: (212) 628-1547 • Mon-Fri 11:00-6:00

Tribal arts of South America, Africa, Oceania. Pre-Columbian art.

TAWA AFRICAN ART

594 Broadway, Suite 407, New York, NY 10012 • Telfax: (212) 219-1313 • Mon-Fri 11:00-5:00, Sat 12:00-6:00 and by appointment • Farid Tawa • French and Spanish spoken • Prices low to high • Trade discount

African tribal art. Restoration of sculpture and mounting of sculpture.

Marine Art

NORTH STAR GALLERIES

1120 Lexington Avenue, New York, NY 10021 • Telfax: (212) 794-4277 • Tue-Fri 10:00-6:00 and by appointment • Gregg K. Dietrich • French, Spanish and Italian spoken • Prices high • Trade discounts • Major credit cards

A remarkable collection of fine marine art, antiques, excellent yacht and ship models and marine collectibles. Restoration and custom-built ship models.

SMITH GALLERY

P.O. Box 20385, New York, NY 10011 • Tel: (212) 744-6171 • Fax: (212) 647-0562 • By appointment

19th- and 20th-century American marine paintings, drawings and watercolors.

Photo Art

BONNI BENRUBI GALLERY

52 East 76th Street, New York, NY 10021 • Tel: (212) 517-3766 • Fax: (212) 288-7815 • Tue-Sat 11:00-6:00 • Bonni Benrubi • Prices low to high • Trade discount

20th-century and contemporary photography.

JANET BORDEN GALLERY

560 Broadway, New York, NY 10012 • Tel: (212) 431-0166 • Fax: (212) 274-1679 • Tue-Sat 11:00-5:00 • Prices medium

Contemporary photography.

JAMES DANZIGER GALLERY

130 Prince Street, New York, NY 10012 • Tel: (212) 226-0056 • Fax: (212) 226-2565 • Wed-Sat 11:00-6:00, Tue by appointment • Prices medium

Photo art from the 20th century. Some rare collectible pictures.

GALLERY 292

120 Wooster Street, New York, NY 10012 • Tel: (212) 431-0292 • Fax: (212) 941-7479 • Tue-Sat 11:00-6:00 • Tom Gitterman • Prices low to high • Trade discount • MC and Visa

Vintage and 20th-century photography, photography books and portfolios.

HOWARD GREENBERG GALLERY

120 Wooster Street, New York, NY 10012 • Tel: (212) 334-0010 • Fax: (212) 941-7479 • Tue-Sat 11:00-6:00 • Howard Greenberg • Spanish spoken • Prices low to high • Trade discount • Visa

20th-century classic American photography, specializing in fine vintage and contemporary photographs.

HOUK FRIEDMAN

851 Madison Avenue, New York, NY 10021 • Tel: (212) 628-5300 • Fax: (212) 861-1030 • Tue-Sat 11:00-6:00 • Amex

Vintage and 20th-century photographic art.

ROBERT MANN GALLERY

42 East 76th Street, New York, NY 10021 • Tel: (212) 570-1223 • Fax: (212) 570-1699 • Tue-Sat 11:00-6:00 • MC and Visa

Fine vintage and contemporary photography.

LAURENCE MILLER GALLERY

138 Spring Street, New York, NY 10012 • Tel: (2112) 226-1220 • Fax: (212) 226-2343 • Tue-Fri 10:00-6:00, Sat 11:00-6:00 • Vicki Harris • Trade discount • Amex

Vintage and contemporary fine art photography.

PACE WILDENSTEIN MCGILL

32 East 57th Street, New York, NY 10022 • Tel: (212) 759-7999 • Fax: (212) 759-8964 • Tue-Fri 9:30-5:30, Sat 10:00-6:00 • Some French spoken • Trade discounts

20th-century photography.

PHOTOCOLLECT

740 West End Avenue, New York, NY 10025 • Tel: (212) 222-7381 • Fax: (212) 222-7506 • By appointment

19th- and 20th-century photography.

YANCEY RICHARDSON GALLERY

560 Broadway, Suite 503, New York, NY 10012 • Tel: (212) 343-1255 • Fax: (212) 343-0839 • Tue-Sat 11:00-6:00 • Yancey Richardson • Some French spoken • Prices medium • 15% trade discount • Major credit cards

20th-century and contemporary photography.

SOHO PHOTO GALLERY

15 White Street, New York, NY 10013 • Tel: (212) 226-8571 • Tue 6:00-8:00, Fri-Sat-Sun 1:00-6:00

Contemporary photography.

STALEY-WISE GALLERY

560 Broadway, New York, NY 10012 • Tel: (212) 966-6223 • Fax: (212) 966-6293 • Tue-Sat 11:00-5:00 • French and German spoken • Prices low • Trade discount • Major credit cards

20th-century photography.

THE WITKIN GALLERY

415 West Broadway, New York, NY 10012 • Tel: (212) 925-5510 • Fax: (212) 925-5648 • Tue-Sat 11:00-6:00 • French spoken • Major credit cards

Photography: 19th century to the present.

Posters

ALPHAVILLE

226 West Houston Street, New York, NY 10014 • Tel: (212) 675-6850 • Fax: (212) 741-2609 • Mon-Thu 12:00-8:00, Fri-Sat 12:00-9:00, Sun 1:00-7:00 • Spanish spoken • Prices medium • Trade discounts • Major credit cards

Vintage posters from movies, science fiction and horror. Also an incredible collection of antique toys.

NICOLAS BAILLY POSTERS & GRAPHICS

55 West 17th Street, 6th floor, New York, NY 10011 • Tel: (212) 627-4398 • Fax: (212) 929-6398 • Tue-Sat 12:00-6:00 and by appointment • Nicolas Bailly • French spoken • Prices low to high • Some trade discounts

Original vintage posters: 1890s to 1960s and contemporary European.

CERUTTI MILLER GALLERY

42 West 17th Street, 2nd floor, New York, NY 10011 • Tel: (212) 645-0808 • Fax: (212) 924-7978 • Tue-Sat 11:00-6:00 • Ruth Miller • French spoken • Major credit cards

Original posters specializing in posters of the 1900s to 1950s.

CHISHOLM GALLERY

55 West 17th Street, 6th floor, New York, NY 10011 • Tel: (212) 243-8834 • Fax: (212) 929-6398 • Tue-Fri 12:00-5:00, Sat 12:00-6:00 • Gail Chisholm • French and Spanish spoken • Prices medium • Some trade discounts • Major credit cards

Original vintage advertising posters from turn of the century to 1960s: wine, food, liquor, travel: specializing in French posters of the 1920s and 1930s. Framing available.

DRYDEN GALLERY

127 Fourth Avenue, New York, NY 10003 • Tel: (212) 420-1690 • Fax: (212) 674-9036 • Mon-Sat 11:00-7:00, Sun 11:00-6:00 • Donald and Mary Dryden • French spoken

Antique posters and custom framing.

J. FIELDS GALLERY

55 West 17th Street, New York, NY 10011 • Tel: (212) 989-4520 • Mon-Sat 9:00-5:00

Specialists in original European and American movie posters. They do linen mounting of posters and framing.

LA BELLE EPOQUE VINTAGE POSTERS, INC.

280 Columbus Avenue, New York, NY 10023 • Tel: (212) 362-1770 • Fax: (212) 362-1843 • Mon-Sat 11:00-7:00, Sun 12:00-6:00 • Linda Tarasak • Some trade discounts • Major credit cards

Original vintage lithographic advertising posters 1880s through 1945. Specialists in Art Nouveau and Art Deco. Conservation, restoration and custom framing.

METROPOLIS COMICS AND COLLECTIBLES

873 Broadway, Suite 201, New York, NY 10003 • Tel: (212) 627-9691 • Fax: (212) 260-4304 • By appointment • Prices medium • Major credit cards

Vintage posters, comics, especially movie posters. Mail-order service.

MFI ART CO. INC.

568 Broadway, New York, NY 10012 • Tel: (212) 334-1100 • (212) 334-9214 • Mon-Fri 9:30-6:00 • Michael Ingbar • Italian and some Spanish and French spoken • Trade discount • Major credit cards

Posters for offices their specialty. They claim to have the largest collection of posters in the U.S. Large selection of prints and paintings. They will make house calls.

MISTINGUETTE

548 Broadway, 3rd floor, New York, NY 10012 • Tel: (212) 941-8552 • Fax: (212) 941-9139 • Mon-Wed 9:00-5:30, Thu 9:00-7:00, Fri 9:00-4:00 • David Benrimon • French, Hebrew and Spanish spoken • Prices medium • MC and Visa

Conservation mounting of posters, dry mounting, 100% rag mat boards, French matting, natural wood frames, 22ct gold leaf frames, Art Deco and European mouldings, chop and join services. French and European posters.

MOTION PICTURE ARTS GALLERY

133 East 58th Street, 10th floor, New York, NY 10022 • Tel: (212) 223-1009 • Fax: (212) 371-0809 • Tue-Fri 12:00-5:00 • Joe Burtis • French, Spanish and Italian spoken • Prices medium • 10% trade discount • All credit cards

Huge collection of American and European motion picture posters, from the silent screen era to the present day. For sale or for rent.

MOVIE STAR NEWS

134 West 18th Street, New York, NY 10011 • Tel: (212) 620-8160 • Fax: (212) 727-0634 • Mon-Fri 10:00-6:00, Sat 11:00-6:00 • Prices medium • Trade discounts • Major credit cards

Posters and photographs from new release movies. Old photos of movie stars.

PARIS IMAGES

170 Bleeker Street, New York, NY 10012 • Tel: (212) 473-7552 • Fax: (212) 505-0582 • Daily 10:00-01:00 AM • French and Spanish spoken • Prices medium • Trade discounts • Major credit cards

Posters of the City of Paris of all periods. Artists' posters from the Renaissance to the 20th century and advertising posters.

PARK SOUTH GALLERY

885 Seventh Avenue, New York, NY 10019 • Tel: (212) 246-5900 • Fax: (212) 541-5716 • Tue-Sat 10:00-6:30 • Ruth Gold • French spoken • Prices low to high • Some trade discounts • Major credit cards

Antique posters, especially from the period 1890 to 1930. Some Art Deco posters and some stone lithographs. Toulouse-Lautrec, Mucha, Steinlen, Cheret; posters from France, Germany, Switzerland and America.

POSTER AMERICA

138 West 18th Street, New York, NY 10011-5403 • Tel: (212) 206-0499 • Fax: (212) 727-2495 • Tues-Sat 11:00-6:00, Sun 12:00-5:00 • Louis Bixenman and Kermit Johns • Prices medium • 10% discount • Major credit cards

Original advertising posters from 1890 to 1980; Art Deco, Art Nouveau, World Wars I and II, entertainment posters, 20th-century Avant-Garde design movements, travel and transportation. American 1890s; European 1920-1965; Japanese 1950-1980. Custom framing.

POSTER AUCTIONS INTERNATIONAL

601 West 26th Street, New York, NY 10001 • Tel: (212) 604-9443 • Fax: (212) 604-9175 • Mon-Fri 9:00-5:00 by appointment • French spoken

Twice-yearly auctions in May and November of original advertising posters. All countries and periods, specializing in French Belle Epoque, Art Nouveau and Art Deco.

POSTERMAT, INC.

37 West 8th Street, New York, NY 10003 • Tel: (212) 228-4027 • Fax: (212) 995-8287 • Mon-Sat 10:00-8:00, Sun 11:00-8:00 • Prices medium • Trade discounts • Major credit cards

Over 5,000 movie posters from all periods, all nations. Posters of rock groups and artists' reproductions. An original Greenwich Village hangout.

POSTER PORTFOLIO LTD.

401 Lafayette Street, 5th floor, New York, NY 10003 • Tel: (212) 777-7716 • Mon-Fri 10:00-6:00, Sat 10:00-2:00 by appointment • Prices medium • Trade discounts

Exhibition and entertainment posters.

POSTERS PLEASE INC.

601 West 26th Street, 13th floor, New York, NY 10001 • Tel: (212) 787-4000 • Fax: 604-9175 • Mon-Fri 9:00-5:00 • Terry Shargel • French spoken • Prices high • Major credit cards

Antique advertising posters.

PSYCHEDELIC SOLUTION

33 West 8th Street, New York, NY 10003 • Tel: (212) 529-2462 • Tue-Sat 12:00-8:00, Ring bell • Prices medium

Posters: the gallery name hints at their specialty. Posters of rock groups and psychedelic graphics.

REINHOLD-BROWN GALLERY

26 East 78th Street, New York, NY 10021 • Tel: (212) 734-7999 • Fax: (212) 734-7044 • Tues-Sat 10:30-5:00 • Robert Brown and Susan Reinhold, owners • French spoken • Prices medium to very high • 10% trade discount

Rare original posters from 1900 to 1965. Important 20th-century graphic design and multiples from the 1950s to the present. Some stone lithos.

ST. LIFER ART EXCHANGE

11 Hanover Square, #703, New York, NY 10005 • Tel: (212) 825-2059 • By appointment only • French spoken • Prices medium to high • Trade discounts

20th-century paintings, prints, exhibition posters, catalogues raisonnés and illustrated art books.

TRITON GALLERY

323 West 45th Street, New York, NY 10036 • Tel: (212) 765-2472 • Fax: (212) 956-6179 • Mon-Sat 10:00-6:00 • Prices medium • Trade discounts • Major credit cards

Contemporary posters from Broadway theatres.

MARK WEINBAUM

2211 Broadway, New York, NY 10024 • Tel: (212) 873-1893 • Fax: (212) 769-9348 • By appointment • French, Italian and Russian spoken • Prices low to high • Trade discount

Fine vintage posters 1890-1980 and illustrated color-plate books.

PHILIP WILLIAMS POSTERS

60 Grand Street, New York, NY 10013 • Tel: (212) 226-7830 • Mon-Sun 11:00-7:00 • Philip Williams • Italian and some French spoken • Prices low to very high

Original posters from 1880 to 1950.

Pre-Columbian Art

ANCIENT ART OF THE NEW WORLD, INC.

42 East 76th Street, New York, NY 10021 • Tel: (212) 737-3766 • Fax: (212) 772-0702 • By appointment • Claudia Giangola and John Menser • Some French, Italian and Spanish spoken

Important Pre-Columbian works of art.

DAVID BERNSTEIN PRE-COLUMBIAN ART

737 Park Avenue, New York, NY 10021 • Tel: (212) 794-0389 • Fax: (212) 861-8728 • By appointment • Spanish spoken • Visa

A stunning collection of Pre-Columbian gold, textiles and ceramics.

LANDS BEYOND

1218 Lexington Avenue, New York, NY 10028 • Tel: (212) 249-6275 • Tue-Sat 11:30-6:00 • Barbara A. Bower • Spanish spoken • Prices low to high • Some trade discounts

Superb collection of Pre-Columbian art: all periods and cultures.

DAVID M. LANTZ

22 East 21st Street, New York, NY 10010 • Telfax: (212) 598-0426 •

By appointment

Works of art of The Americas, Asia and Africa. Pre-Columbian textiles and ceramics; African sculpture and textiles; Asian textiles.

LOVEED FINE ARTS

575 Madison Avenue, 10th floor, New York, NY 10022 • Tel: (212) 605-0591 • Fax: (212) 605-0592 • By appointment • Edward Roberts, Daniel Hamparsumyan and Ronald Kuchta • French and Spanish spoken • Prices medium to high

Private dealers in Pre-Columbian art, contemporary ceramic sculpture and Modern and contemporary European paintings.

THROCKMORTON FINE ART, INC.

153 East 61st Street, 4th floor, New York, NY 10021 • Tel: (212) 223-1059 • Fax: (212) 223-1937 • Tues-Sat 11:00-5:00 • Yona Backer • Spanish, French, German and Dutch spoken • Prices low to high • Some trade discounts

Large and very special collection of Pre-Columbian art, by appointment only. The gallery's regular hours are for the Ancient Art collection and the Latin American Colonial paintings and contemporary and vintage Latin American photography and works on paper.

Prints

W. GRAHAM ARADER III

29 East 72nd Street, New York, NY 10021 • Tel: (212) 628-3668 • Fax: (212) 879-8714 • Mon-Sat 10:00-6:00 • Prices high • Some trade discounts

Antique prints: birds, botanicals, maps, views, architectural engravings; watercolors and color-plate books and atlases.

G.W. EINSTEIN CO.

591 Broadway, New York, NY 10012 • Tel: (212) 226-1414 • Fax: (212) 941-9561 • Thu-Sat 11:00-6:00 or by appointment

20th-century American prints and drawings. Some paintings.

FITCH-FEBVREL GALLERY

5 East 57th Street, New York, NY 10022 • Tel: (212) 688-8522 • Fax: (212) 207-8065 • Tue-Sat 11:00-5:30 • Andrew Fitch • French spoken • Prices low to high • Trade discount

European and some American 19th- and 20th-century prints and drawings: Redon, Max Klinger. Belle Epoque artists: LeGrand, Robbe, Helleu Tissot. 20th-century artists: Pascin and Braque.

FRANCIS FROST GALLERY

50 West 57th Street, New York, NY 10019 • Tel: (212) 459-1950 • Fax: (212) 459-1951 • Tue-Sat 10:30-5:30 • Some French spoken • Trade discounts

19th- and 20th-century prints and paintings; European and American.

ISSELBACHER GALLERY

64 East 86th Street, New York, NY 10028 • Tel: (212) 472-1766 • Fax: (212) 472-3078 • By appointment • Alfred Isselbacher

Prints from the late 19th century and up to 1970.

JEM HOM FINE ART

118 East 60th Street, New York, NY 10022 • Tel: (212) 688-1772 • Fax: (212) 688-2329 • By appointment • Jem Hom, Director, and Betty Hom • Chinese spoken

19th- and 20th-century European and American prints and works on paper.

JIM KEMPNER FINE ART

225 Lafayette Street, New York, NY 10012 • Tel: (212) 966-2688 • Fax: (212) 966-2595 • Wed-Sat 10:00-6:00 and by appointment • Rebecca Lax • Prices low to high • 10 to 40% trade discounts

A fine collection of contemporary prints.

PAUL McCARRON/SUSAN SCHULMAN

1014 Madison Avenue, New York, NY 10021 • Tel: (212) 772-1181 • Fax: (212) 472-2497 • Mon-Sat 9:30-6:00 • Prices low to high

Selling and buying original prints and drawings from the late 15th century to the early 20th century.

MARCKLE MYERS, LTD

1030A Lexington Avenue, New York, NY 10021 • Telfax: (212) 288-3288 • Mon-Fri 11:00-6:00, Sat 12:00-5:00 • Marckle Myers • Prices low to high • Trade discount • Amex

French and Italian 18th- and 19th-century prints.

OLD PRINT CENTER OF PHYLLIS LUCAS

981 Second Avenue, New York, NY 10022 • Tel: (212) 755-1516 • Fax: (212) 753-1441 • Tue-Sat 9:30-7:00, Sat 9:30-6:00 • Peter Lucas • Spanish spoken • Prices medium

Old prints: sports, golf, birds, flowers, Audubon, Currier & Ives. Posters, maps and signed graphics by major artists: Leroy Neiman. Publisher of Dali graphics.

THE OLD PRINT SHOP

150 Lexington Avenue, New York, NY 10016 • Tel: (212) 683-3950 • Fax: (212) 779-8040 • Tue-Fri 9:00-5:00, Sat 9:00-4:00 • Kenneth, Robert and Harry Newman • Prices low to high

American prints, drawings, watercolors and paintings: 1700-1950. Decorative prints and maps. Correct framing.

PACE PRINTS

32 East 57th Street, New York, NY 10022 • Tel: (212) 421-3237 • Fax: (212) 832-5162 • Tue-Fri 9:30-5:30, Sat 10:00-6:00 • Kristin Heming • Italian, Norwegian and some French spoken • Prices low to high • Trade discounts

Old Master, Modern and contemporary prints. One of New York's best sources for prints of all periods.

JEFFREY RUESCH FINE ART

134 Spring Street, New York, NY 10012 • Tel: (212) 925-1137 • Fax: (212) 226-8070 • Mon-Fri 11:00-6:00 • Some French and Italian spoken • Prices medium • Trade discounts • Major credit cards

Contemporary prints and Art Nouveau and Art Deco posters.

WILLIAM H. SCHAB MASTER PRINTS & DRAWINGS, INC.

1594 York Avenue, Box #20, New York, NY 10028 • Tel: (212) 410-2366 • Fax: (212) 427-1138 • By appointment • French, German and Italian spoken • Trade discounts

Old Master and Modern prints and drawings.

SEE GALLERY

100 West 81st Street, New York, NY 10024 • Telfax: (212) 362-7300 • By appointment • Kenn Donnellon • Prices low to high • Some trade discounts • Major credit cards

Vintage and contemporary works on paper and sculpture. Art installation.

MARTIN SUMERS GRAPHICS

50 West 57th Street, New York, NY 10019 • Tel: (212) 541-8336 • Tue-Sat 10:00-5:00 • Prices medium • Trade discounts

20th-century prints and drawings from America, England and Europe.

JOHN SZOKE GRAPHICS

164 Mercer Street, New York, NY 10012 • Tel: (212) 219-8300 • Fax: (212) 966-3064 • Tue-Fri 11:00-5:00 • Prices medium

Contemporary prints.

DAVID TUNICK, INC.

12 East 81st Street, New York, NY 10028 • Tel: (212) 570-0090 • Fax: (212) 744-8931 • Mon-Fri 10:00-5:30, appointment suggested • French and some German spoken • Prices medium to high • Trade discounts

Old Master and Modern prints and drawings.

Sporting Art

J.M. BARTFIELD GALLERIES, INC.

30 West 57th Street, New York, NY 10019 • Tel: (212) 245-8890 • Fax: (212) 541-4860 • Mon-Fri 10:00-5:00, Sat 10:00-3:00 and by appointment • Michael Frost, Director • Prices medium to very high

American paintings of gentlemen's sports, hunting and fishing, from 1819 to the present, by masters such as Carl Rungius, Odgen Pleissner, A.B. Frost and the remarkable contemporary artist Arthur Shilstone; some European sporting paintings. Original sculptures relating to sport by Frederic Remington and Charles Russell. Paintings by Bierstadt and paintings and sculpture by all the most noted artists who portrayed the life and times of the American Wild West. Prestigious contemporary western and wildlife artists: Michael Coleman, William Acheff.

NEWHOUSE GALLERIES

19 East 66th Street, New York, NY 10021 • Tel: (212) 879-2700 • Fax: (212) 517-2680 • Mon-Fri 9:30-5:00 • Meg Newhouse, Director; Adam Williams and Stuart Kirkpatrick • Prices high

Old Master and sporting paintings.

IAN PECK FINE PAINTINGS

980 Madison Avenue, New York, NY 10021 • Tel: (212) 980-4545 • Fax: (212) 980-4584 • Mon-Fri 10:00-6:00, Sat by appointment

British and American sporting art: paintings and bronzes.

ART NOUVEAU / ART DECO

L'ART DE VIVRE, INC.

978 Lexington Avenue, New York, NY 10021 • Tel: (212) 734-3510 •
Mon-Fri 10:00-7:00, Sat 11:00-6:00 • Charles Fuller • French spoken •
Prices medium

One of New York's largest collections of early 20th-century French
furniture, lighting and decorative objects. Concentration on the
1920s, 1930s and 1940s.

ARTISAN ANTIQUES

81 University Place, New York, NY 10003 • Tel: (212) 751-5214 • Fax:
(212) 353-3970 • Mon-Fri 10:00-6:00 • Prices medium to high

Art Deco and Art Nouveau furniture and objects.

BELGIS-FREIDEL GALLERY

77 Mercer Street, New York, NY 10012 • Tel: (212) 941-8715 • Fax:
(212) 941-8569 • Mon-Sat 10:00-6:00 • Prices medium to high

Art Deco and Art Nouveau prints and posters. Also 19th century
through Modern and contemporary.

BENEDETTI GALLERY

52 Prince Street, New York, NY 10012 • Tel: (212) 226-2238 • Fax:
(212) 431-8106 • Mon-Fri 10:00-6:00 • Prices medium

Art Deco and Art Nouveau as well as contemporary art.

DECO DELUXE

993 Lexington Avenue, New York, NY 10021 • Tel: (212) 472-7222 •
Mon-Sat 11:00-6:00, Sun by appointment

Art Deco furniture, lighting, accessories, art and jewelry.

⌧ DELORENZO

958 Madison Avenue, New York, NY 10021 • Tel: (212) 249-7575 •
Mon-Fri 9:30-6:00 • Anthony DeLorenzo

Table lamps, floor lamps and torchères by the great masters of Art
Deco and Art Nouveau.

D.J.L. TRADING

1675 York Avenue, New York, NY 10128 • Tel: (212) 534-7802 • Fax:
(212) 534-1234 • By appointment only

Art Nouveau Lalique glass and Art Deco glass.

J. ALASTAIR DUNCAN

1435 Lexington Avenue, New York, NY 10128 • Tel: (212) 348-7829 •
Fax: (212) 289-3482 • By appointment only

Late 19th- and early 20th-century decorative arts.

LEONARD FOX LTD.

790 Madison Avenue, New York, NY 10021 • Tel: (212) 879-7077 •
Fax: (212) 772-7692 • Mon-Fri 9:30-5:00 or by appointment • French
spoken • Prices high • 10% professional discount • Amex

Rare illustrated books from the Art Deco, Art Nouveau and Modern
periods.

BARRY FRIEDMAN LTD.

32 East 67th Street, New York, NY 10021 • Tel: (212) 794-8950 • Fax:
(212) 794-8889 • Tue-Sat 10:00-6:00, Mon by appointment • Scott
Cook, Director • French, German, Italian and Spanish spoken • Prices
high

Early European 20th-century design and decorative arts. French
furniture and accessories of the late 19th century through the 1950s.

ROBERT GINGOLD

95 East 10th Street, New York, NY 10003 • Tel: (212) 475-4008 • By
appointment • French and German spoken • Prices medium to high

Excellent quality Art Deco furniture, silver and art objects.

LEO KAPLAN MODERN

965 Madison Avenue, New York, NY 10021 • Tel: (212) 535-2407 •
Fax: (212) 535-2495 • Mon-Sat 10:00-5:30 • Scott Jacobson • Prices
medium • Major credit cards

Art Deco furniture and contemporary glass sculpture.

JEAN KARAJIAN GALLERY

250 East 60th Street, New York, NY 10021 • Tel: (212) 751-6728 •
Mon-Fri 10:00-5:30 • French spoken • Prices medium to high • Trade
only

French Art Deco, Renè Lalique, Daum 1920s and 1930s. Chandeliers, sconces, bronzes and alabaster.

KARL KEMP & ASSOCIATES ANTIQUES

29 East 10th Street, New York, NY 10003 • Tel: (212) 254-1877 • Fax:
(212) 228-1236 • Mon-Fri 10:00-5:30, Sat 12:00-5:00 • French, German and Spanish spoken • Prices medium to high • 20% professional
discount

French Art Deco furniture. Neoclassic antiques, especially
Biedermeier.

EILEEN LANE ANTIQUES

150 Thompson Street, New York, NY 10012 • Tel: (212) 474-2988 • Fax: (212) 673-8669 • 7 days 11:00-7:00 • Bo Lindstrad • French, German and Swedish spoken • Prices medium • 10 to 20% professional discount • Major credit cards

Extraordinary collection of alabaster light fixtures of the 1900s, all custom wired. Specialists in 1830-1930 blonde wood furniture from Scandinavia and Austria. Custom refinishing and reupholstery.

LEE'S STUDIO, INC.

1755 Broadway, New York, NY 10019 • Tel: (212) 581-4400 • Fax: (212) 581-7023 • Mon-Sat 10:00-6:30 • Mitchell Steinberg • French and Spanish spoken • Prices high • Professional discount • All major credit cards

Art Deco furniture, accessories and contemporary lighting.

◾ MACKLOWE GALLERY

667 Madison Avenue, New York, NY 10021 • Tel: (212) 644-6400 • Fax: (212) 755-6143 • Mon-Fri 10:30-6:00, Sat 10:30-5:00 • Prices high

Superb Art Nouveau and Art Deco furniture, art objects from France, lamps, glass, lighting, prints, ceramics, bronzes, glass; antique and estate jewelry.

MAISON GERARD

124 East 10th Street, New York, NY 10003 • Tel: (212) 674-7611 • Fax: (212) 475-6314 • Mon-Fri 11:00-6:00 or by appointment • Gerard Widdershoven • French, German, Italian, Dutch and Flemish spoken • Prices high • 20% professional discount • All major credit cards

French and American Art Deco furniture, carpets, lighting and art objects.

MALMAISON

253 East 74th Street, New York, NY 10021 • Tel: (212) 288-7569 • Fax: (212) 517-7652 • Mon-Fri 9:00-5:00 • Roger Prigent • French spoken • Prices high

1930s and 1940s Art Deco furniture. Early 19th-century French and Russian antiques, paintings, sculpture and accessories.

MOOD INDIGO

181 Prince Street, New York, NY 10012 • Tel: (212) 254-1176 • Tue-Sat 12:00-7:00, Sun 1:00-6:00 • Diane Petipas • Prices medium to high

Art Deco accessories, Fiestaware, bakelite jewelry. 1939 World's Fair items, cocktail shakers, smoking accessories and a large selection of Russel Wright dinnerware.

♔ LILLIAN NASSAU, LTD.

220 East 57th Street, New York, NY 10022 • Tel: (212) 759-6062 • Fax: (212) 842-9493 • Mon-Sat 10:30-4:30 • Paul Nassau, Harry Wallace, Arlie Sulka • Prices high • Professional discounts

Original works by Louis Comfort Tiffany, including lamps, glass, paintings, pottery, decorative objects and furniture of the Art Deco and Art Nouveau periods. American sculpture.

NEWEL ART GALLERIES

425 East 53rd Street, New York, NY 10022 • Tel: (212) 758-1970 • Fax: (212) 371-0166 • Mon-Fri 9:00-5:00 • Spanish spoken • Prices medium to very high

French and English Art Deco furniture and decorations. Extraordinary.

POLLARO CUSTOM FURNITURE INC.

356 Glenwood Avenue, East Orange, NJ 07017 • Tel: (201) 748-5353 • Fax: (201) 675-7778 • Mon-Fri 8:00-6:00 and by appointment • Frank Pollaro • Prices very high

Fabricator of museum quality handmade furniture specializing in French Art Deco, particularly the work of Ruhlmann. Restoration and replication.

PRIMAVERA GALLERY

808 Madison Avenue, New York, NY 10021 • Tel: (212) 288-1569 • Fax: (212) 288-2102 • Mon-Sat 11:00-6:00 • Audrey Friedman, Haim Manishevitz • Prices medium to high • All major credit cards

Art Deco furniture and glass; silver; paintings; Wiener Werkstätte jewelry.

RENEE ANTIQUES

8 East 12th Street, New York, NY 10003 • Tel: (212) 929-6870 • Mon-Fri 9:30-6:00, Sat 9:30-3:00 • Italian, German, Spanish, French and Russian spoken • Prices medium to high

Art Deco, Art Nouveau, art glass, lighting, porcelain, furniture, bronzes.

RETRO-MODERN STUDIO

58 East 11th Street, New York, NY 10003 • Tel: (212) 674-0530 • By appointment

French and American Art Deco furniture, light fixtures and art objects.

♔ MINNA ROSENBLATT GALLERY

844 Madison Avenue, New York, NY 10021 • Tel: (212) 288-0257 • Fax: (212) 288-0250 • Mon-Sat 10:00-5:30 • French spoken • Prices high • Professional discount

Extraordinary collection of 20th-century decorative arts, including original Tiffany lamps, Tiffany glass, French glass including Galle, Daum and pâte de verre. Some old Steuben glass.

JEFFREY RUESCH FINE ART

134 Spring Street, New York, NY 10012 • Tel: (212) 925-1137 • Fax: (212) 226-8070 • Mon-Fri 11:00-6:00 • Some French and Italian spoken • Prices medium • Trade discounts • Major credit cards

Art Nouveau and Art Deco posters and contemporary prints.

SAPHO GALLERY INC.

1037 Second Avenue, New York, NY 10022 • Tel: (212) 308-0880 • Fax: (212) 750-4797 • Mon-Fri 10:30-6:00 • Shelley Cohen • French, Hebrew and German • Prices medium • All major credit cards

French Art Deco furniture, lighting, sculpture and decorations.

JEROME SPILLER

110 West 25th Street, New York, NY 10001 • Tel: (212) 989-3414 • Sat-Sun 10:00-5:00 and by appointment

Art Deco and Art Nouveau glass.

UPLIFT LIGHTING

506 Hudson Street, New York, NY 10014 • Tel: (212) 929-3632 • Fax: (212) 255-1439 • Seven days 12:00-8:00 • Randy Wicker • Prices medium • Major credit cards

They claim to have the world's largest collection of Art Deco chandeliers and wall sconces as well as a full line of original and reproduction Art Deco table lamps.

MARK J. WEINBAUM

220 Broadway, New York, NY 10024 • Tel: (212) 873-1893 • Fax: (212) 769-9348 • By appointment • French, Italian and Russian spoken • 10% trade discount

Art Deco and Art Nouveau decorative objects, small furniture, posters and prints.

WEINSTEIN GALLERIES

793 Madison Avenue, New York, NY 10021 • Tel: (212) 712-6333 • Mon-Sat 10:30-6:00 • French spoken • Prices medium to high • All major credit cards

Fine examples of Art Nouveau and Art Deco decoration. They specialize in Tiffany, Pairpoint and Handel lamps. Turn-of-the-century American art glass and some paintings.

WOOSTER GALLERY

86 Wooster Street, New York, NY 10012 • Tel: (212) 683-3159 • Fax: (212) 941-6678 • Seven days 10:30-6:30 • Ralph Beatrice • Prices medium

Art Deco furniture and furnishings.

ART REPRODUCTIONS

M.J. DURRANT

157 East 74th Street, New York, NY 10021 • Tel: (212) 288-5798 • Fax: (212) 288-3135 • By appointment • Minnie Durrant • Prices medium • 20% trade discount

A large selection of fine reproduction prints and antique prints from England, beautifully framed. Animal prints, shells, cartoon prints, heraldic crests and botanicals.

FABULOUS FORGERIES

119 West 40th Street, New York, NY 10018 • Tel: (212) 840-2248 • Mon-Fri 10:00-6:30 • Spanish and some German spoken • Prices medium • All major credit cards

Copies of famous paintings, oils on canvas. Creates sculptures, columns and pedestals.

TROUBETSKOY PAINTINGS, LTD.

979 Third Avenue (D&D), New York, NY 10022 • Tel: (212) 688-6544 • Fax: (212) 688-6225 • Mon-Fri 10:00-5:00 • Christopher Moore • French spoken • Trade and retail • Prices high • 25% discounts • Amex

Custom paintings from originals. Custom frames and gold leafing studio. Restoration of frames. Their paintings have been used in movies such as "The Age of Innocence" and others. Rentals for movies.

Portraits to Order

HOME PORTRAITS

25 Alexander Avenue, White Plains, NY 10606 • Telfax: (914) 682-3771 • 7 days 8:00-6:00 • Susan Stillman • Prices medium

Commissioned acrylic paintings of people's homes. 3 formats available. Beautiful work.

PORTRAITS, INC.

985 Park Avenue, New York, NY 10028 • Tel: (212) 879-5560 • Fax: (212) 988-3755 • Mon-Fri 10:00-5:00, Sat 11:00-4:00 • Marian MacKinney • Prices medium to very high • Trade discount

Representative of 125 portrait artists and sculptors. Professional assistance available with every aspect of commissioned work.

ARTISANS AND CRAFTSMEN

The wealth of any city is not measured by money nor by its elegant shops and tall buildings. The true riches of any city reside in its people. New York is truly blessed in that regard. Streams of immigrants have brought in their skills: from Europe, from the Middle East, from Asia, from Africa and from Latin America.

Look behind the door of any workshop in any part of town and you will find a marvellous mingling of cultures, languages and an enormous diversity of skills.

Search hard enough and you will find the best there is, and it could have come from anywhere in the world. The patrimony of many nations has enriched all of us and will continue to flourish, becoming the patrimony we are privileged to leave for future generations.

Art Foundries

BEDI MAKKY ART FOUNDRY INC.

227 India Street, Brooklyn, NY 11222 • Tel: (718) 383-4191 • Mon-Fri 7:00-4:30 • Steve Makky and Peter Maurer • Hungarian, some German and Rumanian spoken

Sculpture casting, French sand casting, lost wax process, architectural castings, repairs and restorations.

JOEL MEISNER & CO. LTD.

115 Schmidt Boulevard, Farmingdale, NY 11735 • Tel: (516) 249-0680 • Fax: (516) 249-0697 • By appointment

Full-service art casting. Bronze and silver repairs. Model making and enlarging. Miniatures to monument.

MODERN ART FOUNDRY INC.

18-70 41st Street, Long Island City, NY 11105 • Tel: (718) 728-2030 • Fax: (718) 267-0819 • Mary Jo Bursige, Manager

All casting, small to large.

M. OSBORNE

16 East 18th Street, New York, NY 10003 • Tel: (212) 675-4505 • Mon-Fri 9:00-6:00 • Italian spoken • Prices according to size

Art foundry, casting, enlarging, all metals.

PIETRASANTA FINE ARTS INC.

49 Bleeker Street, New York, NY 10012 • Tel: (212) 477-6989 • Fax: (212) 477-1523 • Mon-Fri 10:00-8:00, Sat by appointment • Gino Giannaccinini • Spanish, Italian, German, French and Dutch spoken

Sculpture casting studio and art gallery. Professional casting in wax, bronze, plaster and bonded metals. Specialists in mould making. Custom sculpture enlargements. Patina processing and restoration.

CHRISTINE ROUSSEL, INC.

177 South Fourth Street, Brooklyn, NY 11211 • Tel: (718) 388-9633 • Fax: (718) 388-9613 • By appointment • Mark or Christine Roussel

Sculpture restoration and conservation. Museum work.

SCULPTURE HOUSE CASTING, INC.

155 West 26th Street, New York, NY 10001 • Tel: (212) 645-9430 • Fax: (212) 645-3717 • Mon-Fri 8:00-6:00, Sat 10:00-4:00 • Salvatore Perrotta • Italian spoken

Complete sculpture casting service. Enlarging, reducing, model making. Sculpture tools and supplies on site.

Basket Maker

DEBORAH SMITH

37 Market Street, Red Hook, NY 12571 • Tel: (914) 758-0327 • By appointment • Prices medium to high

Reproductions of antique baskets and basket sculpture. Unusual work.

Caning and Restoration of Cane

BERGEN UPHOLSTERY & FURNITURE CO., INC.

283 Main Street, Hackensack, NJ 07601 • Tel: (201) 489-0555 • Mon-Sat 9:30-5:30 • Thu 9:30-8:30 • Stan Sinowitz • Spanish spoken • Prices medium to high • Major credit cards

Caning and repairs of cane seating.

OLEK LEJBZON & CO.

210 11th Avenue, 11th floor, New York, NY 10001 • Tel: (212) 243-3363 • Fax: (212) 243-3432 • Mon-Sat 7:30-6:00 • Peter Triestman • Most languages spoken

Expert caning in all styles.

WESTSIDE CHAIR CANING & REPAIR INC.

371 Amsterdam Avenue, 2nd floor, New York, NY 10024 • Tel: (212) 724-4408 • Wed-Sat 11:00-7:00, Sun 1:00-5:00 • Jeffrey Weiss • Prices medium • Trade discount

Fine hand and machine caning: rush, splint, Danish seat cord, wicker restoration, re-glueing and repairs. Occasional sale of unclaimed chairs.

YORK END CANING

454 East 84th Street, New York, NY 10028 • Tel: (212) 288-6843 • Mon-Fri 9:00-6:00, Sat 10:00-5:00 • Jack Hubsmith • Prices medium

Re-caning and repair of broken chairs. Hand caning, machine caning, all styles, splint, rush, etc. Free local pickup and delivery.

Decorative Painting and Trompe l'Oeil

A&A ART-PAINTING STUDIOS

1569 Ocean Avenue, Brooklyn, NY 11230 • Telfax: (718) 252-7660 • 7 days by appointment • Russian and Turkish spoken

Decorative painting, faux finishes, trompe l'oeil in realistic architectural styles. Murals and restoration of murals. Custom mosaics in Smalti glass. Commercial and residential work.

COLLEEN BABINGTON

300 West 12th Street, New York, NY 10014 • Telfax: (212) 924-4868 • Mon-Fri by appointment • Prices medium

All styles of decorative painting. Specialties include custom stenciling for floors and ceilings. Also gilded, rubbed or washed finishes for walls, furniture and objects.

ARLENE BERMAN FINE ARTS

111 East 81st Street, New York, NY 10028 • Tel: (212) 472-3108 • Fax: (212) 472-0115 • By appointment • Prices medium

Decorative painting with emphasis on the American 1930s and 1940s.

ROBERT J. BRAUN

104 West 87th Street, New York, NY 10024 • Tel: (212) 799-6282 • By appointment • Prices high

High-quality decorative painting, trompe l'oeil and murals on canvas and furniture.

WYLENE COMMANDER ART AND DECORATION STUDIO

64 East 86th Street, New York, NY 10028 • Telfax: (212) 744-9878 • Studio: (212) 639-9006 • Office Mon-Fri 8:00-8:00 • Studio Mon-Fri 9:00-5:00 • Prices medium

Decorative painting, faux finishes, murals and fine screens. Specialty: glazing, faux bois, marbleizing. Large murals and representational painting.

ELIZABETH DOW LTD.

580 Broadway, Suite 1206, New York, NY 10012 • Tel: (212) 219-8822 • Fax: (212) 941-1331 • Mon-Fri 9:00-5:00 • Mark Sheppill • Trade discount

Hand-painted wallcoverings and decorative painting.

EVA ART & DESIGN, INC.

37 Northfield Road, Glen Cove, NY 11542 • Tel: (800) 843-8382 • Beeper (917) 247-6431 • Fax: (212) 422-0979 • Prices high

Faux finishes, trompe l'oeil paintings, gilding. Creates stained, sandblasted, carved glass works. Top references.

EVERGREENE PAINTING STUDIOS

635 West 23rd Street, 4th floor, New York, NY 10011 • Tel: (212) 727-9500 • Fax: (212) 727-9538 • By appointment

Restoration of painted and gilded walls and ceilings, replication of wood graining to match old decorative paint schemes, stenciling and hand-painting. International assignments.

PIERRE FINKELSTEIN—GRAND ILLUSION DECORATIVE PAINTING

20 West 20th Street, #1009, New York, NY 10011 • Telfax: (212) 675-2286 • Mon-Sat 8:00-6:00 • French spoken • Prices high

Masterly decorative painting: fine marble and wood graining, new glaze finishes and trompe l'oeil, painted ornaments and complicated stencils over gold leaf. Graduate of the Van Der Kellen Superior Institute of Brussels. Awarded the prestigious "Meilleur Ouvrier de France". Author of two books on the subject.

BILL GIBBONS

368 Broadway, #203, New York, NY 10013 • Tel: (212) 227-0039 • By appointment • French spoken • Prices medium to high

Creates murals and trompe l'oeil in historic styles. Very good references.

ANNE HARRIS STUDIO

333 Park Avenue South, New York, NY 10010 • Mon-Fri 9:00-5:00 by appointment

Decorative painter specializing in murals, all periods and styles, from Old Master styles through the 20th century. Distressing and ageing. Works for dealers, designers and private individuals.

CHUCK HETTINGER DECORATIVE PAINTING

208 East 13th Street, New York, NY 10003 • Telfax: (212) 614-9848 • By appointment • Prices high

Decorative painting specializing in surface work: special glazes, stripes, classic finishes such as wood graining, marbleizing. Special finishes in collaboration with client. Color consultations.

HORAN, INC. DECORATIVE PAINTING

55 Central Park West, New York, NY 10023 • Tel: (212) 873-1373 • Fax: (212) 877-0987 • Leslie Horan Simon • By appointment • Prices high to very high

Murals, decorative painting and paintings; large damask stenciling and wallpapers, etc. International clients.

MAER-MURPHY, INC.

420 West 49th Street, New York, NY 10019 • Tel: (212) 265-3460 • Fax: (212) 582-9358 • Mon-Fri 9:00-5:00 • Duane Nathman • Prices high

Painting, plastering, gilding, murals, decorative finishes of any kind. Historic stencil patterns. Mural recovery.

MICHAEL TYSON MURPHY STUDIO

346 West 56th Street, No. 5D, New York, NY 10019 • Tel: (212) 757-2737 • Fax: (212) 977-7740 • Mon-Fri 10:00-5:00 by appointment • Italian and French spoken • Prices high • Trade only

Decorative painting for all surfaces: walls, floors, ceilings, furniture. All unique, custom designed and hand finished. Works for well-known designers.

TOBY NUTTALL

300 West 23rd Street, #12A, New York, NY 10011 • Tel: (212) 206-9730 • By appointment • Some French spoken

Decorative painter specializing in wood graining. All finishes. Gilding and restoration. Works for well-known personalities all over the U.S.

INGE E. PETERS

31 East 79th Street, New York, NY 10021 • Tel: (212) 288-4056 • Fax: (212) 535-4838 • Mon-Fri 9:00-5:00 • German, French and Spanish spoken • Prices high

Intricate painted finishes: tortoise, shagreen, croco, rice grain, lacquer, gilding on furniture and objects. Wall glazing. References on request.

ELIZABETH SADOFF ASSOCIATES

26th Street, Suite 303, New York, NY 10001 • Tel: (212) 924-5404 • Fax: (212) 741-8825 • Mon-Sat by appointment • Some French spoken • Prices medium to high

Custom murals, painted finishes, plaster relief, decorative painting on furniture. Will design custom furniture pieces. Residential and commercial work. Excellent references.

▮ JOE STALLONE

75 Riverside Drive, #2R, New York, NY 10024 • Tel: (212) 787-2011 • Fax: (212) 787-2027 • Mon-Fri by appointment • Prices medium to high

Faux painting; specializing in super-realistic faux bois, faux marble for all interior surfaces, walls, furniture, floors. Trained at top New York schools and the Institut Superieur de Peinture, Brussels. 30 years experience and a client list that reads like Who's Who.

EMMA TAPLEY

417 Grand Street, Brooklyn, NY 11211 • Tel: (718) 599-5896 • Mon-Fri by appointment

Decorative painter specializing in wall finishes: faux bois, trompe l'oeil, gilding, stenciling, marbleizing and Swedish plaster. References upon request.

ANDREW TEDESCO STUDIOS

214 East 31st Street, New York, NY 10016 • Telfax: (212) 689-0173 • 7 days by appointment • Prices medium

Hand-painted decorative art work, murals, fine art, reproductions of paintings, trompe l'oeil. Residential and commercial work. Client references available on request.

SIME VANJAK

14 35th Street, #31, Astoria, NY 11106 • Tel: (718) 956-3707 • By appointment • Croatian spoken

Decorative finishing: marbleizing, wood graining, lacquering, Venetian stucco. Interiors and exteriors.

\

VON VERWER STUDIO

336 East 13th Street, #C5, New York, NY 10003 • Tel: (212) 674-5015 • Fax: (212) 674-5494 • By appointment • Dutch spoken • Prices medium

Murals: contemporary and period. Faux finishes, glazing and gilding. Interiors, theatre and films. High-quality work.

LISA WASSONG-DOMINIQUE LANGE STUDIO

150 East 69th Street, #17G, New York, NY 10021 • Tel: (212) 288-1316 • Fax: (212) 772-8562 • Mon-Fri 8:00-6:00 • French, Spanish and Italian spoken • Prices medium

Decorative painting: glazing, marbleizing, faux bois, lapis, malachite, trompe l'oeil, stenciling. Top references.

☗ WATHERSTON ASSOCIATES, INC.

249 East 48th Street, New York, NY 10017 • Tel: (212) 751-9658 • Fax: (212) 593-2726 • By appointment • Margaret Watherston

Conservation and restoration of murals. Easel paintings. Clients are museums, public buildings and individuals.

☗ KAREN YAGER FINE ART CONSERVATION

211 West 106th Street, #2C, New York, NY 10025 • Telfax: (212) 864-3687 • By appointment

Painting conservation and wall painting. Mural conservation and restoration. Works for museums, galleries, collectors, artists.

Gilders

☗ ANTIQUARIATO

150 East 28th Street, #1605, New York, NY 10001 • Tel: (212) 727-0733 • Mon-Fri 9:00-5:00 • Hicham Ghandour • Italian and French spoken • Prices medium • Professional discount

High-quality gilding, polychrome, French polishing for top antique dealers, major art museums and renowned interior designers.

FINE ART CONSERVATION SERVICES

419 Third Avenue, New York, NY 10016 • Tel: (212) 889-8173 • Fax: (212) 683-1550 • Mon-Sat 10:00-6:00 • Robert Hammerquist • Spanish and Chinese spoken • Prices medium to high • Trade discount • Major credit cards

Gilding of sculptured and inlaid wood frames. Clients are museums, galleries and collectors.

FITZKAPLAN RESTORATION, INC.

131 Varick Street, 10th floor, New York, NY 10013 • Tel: (212) 989-8779 • Fax: (212) 989-8794 • Diane Fitzgerald, Eve Kaplan • Prices on estimate

Gilding, Oriental lacquering, japanning and painted finishes on furniture. Work for antique dealers, designers and private clients.

JOULE, INC.

344 West 38th Street, New York, NY 10018 • Tel: (212) 947-8143 • Fax: (212) 563-5370 • Mon-Fri 8:00-5:00 • Melanie Denby • Prices high to very high • Trade only

Gilding of furniture, objects, frames, mirrors, drapery hardware: poles and finials. Restoration and French polishing. Works for well-known designers.

LOWY

223 East 80th Street, New York, NY 10021 • Tel: (212) 861-8585 • Fax: (212) 988-0443 • Mon-Fri 9:00-5:30 • Larry Shar • Spanish, Italian, French and Chinese spoken • Prices medium to very high • Major credit cards

Gilding and restoration of antique frames and antique wood furniture. A New York institution. Works for all the museums, collectors and the great galleries.

PASCALE PATRIS

202 Dean Street, Brooklyn, NY 11217 • Tel: (718) 935-0822/(212) 570-3858 • By appointment only • Pascale Patris • French spoken • Prices medium to high • Professional discount

Gilding and polychrome on wood support: fine furniture, panels, sculpture, terra cotta and plaster. Superb work and in demand by the major museums.

SHEELIN WILSON GILDING STUDIO

315 East 91st Street, New York, NY 10128 • Tel: (212) 722-2089 • Mon-Fri 9:00-5:00 by appointment • Sheelin Wilson • Prices low to medium

Restoration and conservation of gilded and painted surfaces. Interior and exterior architectural gilding. Water/oil gilding, polychrome and lacquer finishes, antique giltwood furniture, objets d'art. Modern gilded finishes and gilding on stone, metal, wood and plaster. Works with major museums, antique dealers, designers and private clients.

JEFFREY WIRSING

66 West 10th Street, New York, NY 10011 • Telfax: (212) 673-1762 • By appointment • Italian spoken • Prices high • Trade discounts

Gilding and restoration of furniture and objets d'art for illustrious clients.

Glass Carver

NEW YORK CARVED ARTS

115 Grand Street, New York, NY 10013 • Tel: (212) 966-5924 • By appointment • Jean-Claude Fevrier • Trade discount

Glass carver. Custom carved glass, i.e., carved glass panels, doors, tabletops and much more. Credits include museums, hotels, restaurants, Seaman's Chapel, La Côte Basque.

Ornamental Iron Craftsmen

LA FORGE FRANCAISE

36 Hampton Road, Southampton 11968 • Tel: (516) 283-2883 • Fax: (516) 287-3405 • Thu-Mon 11:00-5:00 • Malou Humbert • French and German spoken • Prices high • 20% trade discount • Visa

Custom metal furniture, traditional styles and unique signed pieces in wrought iron.

THE GARDEN ROOM

1179 Lexington Avenue, New York, NY 10028 • Telfax: (212) 879-1179 • Mon-Sat 10:00-6:00 • Mark McCarty

Wrought iron architectural elements, railings, tables and furniture.

LAKE CONSTRUCTION

150 King Street, Brooklyn, NY 11231 • Tel: (718) 852-7700 • Fax: (718) 522-2059 • Mon-Fri 6:00-5:00 • George Lucey

Installation and restoration of ornamental iron. Wrought iron fences and railings.

☖ LES METALLIERS CHAMPENOIS CORP. (LMC CORP.)

77 Second Avenue, Paterson, NJ 07514 • Tel: (201) 279-3573 • Fax: (201) 881-0235 • Mon-Fri 7:30-6:00, Sat by appointment • Jean Wiart • French spoken • Prices very high

Design, fabrication and installation of fine metalwork: gates, stair railings, balconies, etc. Their work is in the finest French master craftsman tradition. Excellent references upon request.

ROMA ORNAMENTAL IRON WORKS

737 39th Street, Brooklyn, NY 11232 • Tel: (718) 972-4188 • Fax: (718) 948-7588 • Mon-Fri 9:00-4:30 • Tony • Italian spoken • Trade discounts

All types of ornamental and structural iron works, balconies, railings, gates, window guards.

STAR METAL INC.

74 Bayard Street, Brooklyn, NY 11222 • Tel: (718) 384-2766 • Fax: (718) 384-5180 • Mon-Fri 9:00-6:00 • David Maurice • French and Spanish spoken • Prices high

Custom forged metal works: architectural stairs, railings and furniture. Master craftsman.

TREITEL-GRATZ CO., INC.

13-06 Queens Plaza South, Long Island City, NY 11101 • Tel: (718) 361-7774 • Fax: (718) 392-8281 • Mon-Fri 8:00-5:00 • Donald S. Gratz • Prices very high

Custom metal fabrication: furniture, sculpture (not cast), metal components for sculptors.

TRIBORO IRON WORKS, INC.

38-30 31st Street, Long Island City, NY 11101 • Tel: (718) 361-9600 • Fax: (718) 361-5422 • Mon-Fri 8:00-5:00 • Italian and Spanish spoken • Prices medium

Balconies, railings, ornamental and structural iron work, gates, window guards.

Art Quilter

MARILYN HENRION

505 Laguardia Place, #23D, New York, NY 10012 • Tel: (212) 982-8949 • Studio Tel: (717) 775-6471 • 7 days by appointment • Trade discount

Original one-of-a-kind contemporary art quilts for residential or corporate interiors. Designed, crafted and hand-quilted by artist with international reputation.

Stained Glass Window Artists

ALBERT STAINED GLASS

57 Front Street, Brooklyn, NY 11201 • Tel: (718) 625-6464 • Fax: (718) 625-5380 • Mon-Fri 9:00-6:00, Sat 11:00-5:00 • Al Husted • Spanish and French spoken • Prices medium • MC and Visa

Restoration and creation of stained glass. Replication of Gothic, Nouveau, Deco, Glasgow and Prairie. Worked on Grand Central, churches, schools, hotels and for private clients.

ART GLASS STUDIO, INC.

543 Union Street, Brooklyn, NY 11215 • Tel: (718) 596-4553 • By appointment • Ernest Porcelli

Glass artist in all facets of glass, stained, leaded, beveled, acid edged, sand blasting, fusing. Custom tiles and custom design shop. Expert restoration. High-end private clients and institutions.

CLERKIN HIGGINS STAINED GLASS, INC.

21 Stuyvesant Oval, #2D, New York, NY 10009 • Tel: (718) 486-5652 • Fax: (212) 253-8913 • By appointment • Mary C. Higgins • Prices medium to high

Stained glass creation and conservation. Works for museums, public institutions and private homes.

FEMENELLA & ASSOCIATES, INC.

3 Brighton Court, Annandale, NJ 08801 • Tel: (908) 735-6840 • Fax: (908) 713-1771 • By appointment • Arthur J. Femenella, President • Spanish spoken • Prices medium to high

Stained glass restoration, specializing in plated, opalescent windows. Clients are museums, churches and private collectors.

⊞ ATELIER FOUCAULT

114 Montgomery Avenue, Staten Island, NY 10301 • Telfax: (718) 727-3122 • Quarter Circle Bell Ranch, 41348 Road 29, Elizabeth, CO 80107 • Tel: (303) 646-4784 • Fax: (303) 646-4765 • By appointment • Marie-Pascale Foucault • French spoken

Stained glass conservation. Museum standard. Glass designer, glass painter. First-quality copies of stained glass, covering periods from 11th to 16th centuries.

LAMB STUDIOS

P.O. Box 291, Philmont, NY 12565 • Tel: (888) 672-7267 • Fax: (518) 672-7597 • Mon-Fri 9:00-5:00 • Donald Samick • Prices medium • Trade only

Restoration and creation of stained glass. Studio has worked continuously since 1857. Clients include state and government agencies, churches, institutions and private individuals.

VICTOR ROTHMAN FOR STAINED GLASS

1468 Middland Avenue, #5A, Bronxville, NY 10708 • Tel: (914) 776-1617 • Fax: (914) 237-2032 • Mon-Fri 9:00-5:00
Studio: 161 Varick Street, New York, NY 10011 • Tel: (212) 255-2551 • By appointment

Stained glass fabrication and restoration. Residential, commercial, museum and ecclesiastic stained glass windows.

VENTURELLA STUDIO

32 Union Square East, Suite 1110, New York, NY 10003 • Tel: (212) 228-4252 • Fax: (212) 979-6679 • By appointment • Thomas Venturella • Some French spoken • Prices high to very high

Museum quality restoration, conservation and creation of stained and leaded glass. References upon request.

Straw Marquetry

SANDRINE VIOLLET

Atelier Viollet, 505 Driggs Avenue, Brooklyn, NY 11211 • Tel: (718) 782-1727 • Fax: (718) 782-1602 • Mon-Fri 7:30-6:00 • French spoken • Prices high

Custom design and marquetry work in straw on objects and pieces of furniture. This work can be done on walls, small objects such as boxes, coffee tables, consoles, armoires. Impossible to duplicate by machine, this work is quite extraordinary. Excellent references.

Wood Carvers

AMERICAN WOOD COLUMN

913 Grand Street, Brooklyn, NY 11211 • Tel: (718) 782-3163 • Fax: (718) 387-9099

Manufacturer of wood columns, turnings and cabinets. Reproductions of original designs.

BAREWOOD ARCHITECTURAL WOODWORK

106 Ferris Street, Brooklyn, NY 11231 • Tel: (718) 875-9037 • Fax: (718) 875-3833 • Mon-Fri 8:00-5:00 • Leslie Neilson • Spanish and Polish spoken • Prices medium

Custom cabinets, furniture and architectural restoration. Specialist in 18th- and 19th-century renovation, including wood turning and carving, mantels, mouldings, doors and windows. Clients include the New York City Landmarks Conservancy and the Central Park Conservancy.

DELACRUZ WOOD TURNING CO.

554 West 142nd Street, New York, NY 10031 • Tel: (212) 862-3496 • Spanish spoken

Wood turning to order.

DEUTSCH & CIFARELLI WOODTURNING AND TWISTING, INC.

599 11th Avenue, New York, NY 10036 • Tel: (212) 581-5238 • Mon-Fri 8:00-5:00 • Prices medium to high

Wood carving and wood turning: table legs and finials. Machine carving and hand turning for table legs, finials and anything that needs to be turned.

₩ CAROLE HALLE WOODCARVING STUDIO

1205 Manhattan Avenue, 2nd floor, Brooklyn, NY 11222 • Tel: (718) 383-4727 • Fax: (718) 383-1915 • By appointment • French and Italian spoken • Prices medium to high • 10% trade discount

Custom wood carving: frames, decorative and architectural elements. Also restoration of antique furniture. Works for museums, galleries and individuals.

LEGS UNLIMITED

129 West 29th Street, 2nd floor, New York, NY 10001 • Tel: (212) 629-5630 • Fax: (212) 268-4577 • Mon-Fri 9:00-5:00 • Joseph Biunno • Spanish, Russian, Italian and other languages • Price medium to very high • Major credit cards

Carved and turned custom legs for sofas, chairs, beds, ottomans, tables, benches, desks.

A. ROBINWOOD MANUFACTURING

1 Knickerbocker Avenue, Brooklyn, NY 11237 • Tel: (718) 456-4870 • Fax: (718) 456-1367 • Mon-Fri 8:00-4:00 • Mel Alvarez

Wood parts to your specifications. Hand wood turning, lamp bases.

RON WIENER, WOOD CARVER

54 Cottage Street, Jersey City, NJ 07306 • Telfax: (201) 659-5666 • Mon-Fri by appointment • Prices high

Hand-carved ornamentation and components for cabinetmakers and builders. Historically correct hand-carved elements for embellishment of architectural details. Works from sketches, photos and original designs.

Restorers

⚜ Antique Conservation and Restoration Workshops

ALEXANDERS SCULPTURAL SERVICE

117 East 39th Street, New York, NY 10016 • Tel: (212) 867-8866 • By appointment • Italian spoken

Restoration of sculpture.

ARC & BORIS EXPERT RESTORATION

110 West 25th Street, #707, New York, NY 10001 • Tel: (212) 633-6286 • Daily 10:30-5:30 • Boris Kuznetsov • Prices medium • Trade discount • Major credit cards

Restoration of ancient art, murals, antique furniture. Very good references upon request.

ARCHITECTURAL SCULPTURE AND RESTORATION

242 Lafayette Street, New York, NY 10012 • Tel: (212) 431-5873 • Fax: (212) 334-4230 • Mon-Fri 10:00-6:00, Sat 12:00-5:00

Architectural sculptural elements: fabrication and restoration. Work for architects, designers and private clients.

ARK RESTORATION   252 W. 37   17th fl.

~~350 Seventh Avenue, 10th~~ floor, New York, NY 10001 • Tel: (212) 244-1028 • Fax: (212) 244-1319 • Mon-Fri 10:00-6:00 by appointment • Russian and Ukrainian spoken • Prices according to the work

One of the few places in the world where you can have rare Limoges and other enamels restored. They also restore porcelain, faience, ceramics, art glass and semi-precious stone carvings.

glass   732-583-5873
Tony Joshec (N.J.)

CHRISTINE BELFOR

304 Hudson Street, New York, NY 10013 • Tel: (212) 633-6680 • Fax: 645-2759 • Mon-Fri 10:00-5:00 • Prices high • 25% trade discount • Major credit cards

Tile murals, tile paintings, decorative tile, marble mosaics, hand-painted Byzantine mosaics, hand-painted basins and hand-painted dinnerware.

CENTER ART STUDIO

250 West 54th Street, #901, New York, NY 10019 • Tel: (212) 247-3550 • Fax: (212) 586-4045 • Mon-Fri 9:00-6:00 • Lansing Moore • Italian and Spanish spoken • Prices medium • Major credit cards

Restoration of porcelain, glass, stone, frames, marble sculptures, some furniture. The studio also designs and fabricates custom display bases and cases.

CLASSICAL RESTORATION AND DESIGN, INC.

150 West 28th Street, #1502, New York, NY 10001 • Tel: (212) 989-4540 • Fax: (212) 691-0052 • Mon-Fri 9:00-7:00 • Guintaras Miachkaouskas • Lithuanian, Russian, Ukrainian and Polish spoken • Prices medium to high

Professional restoration and conservation of porcelain, marble, alabaster, glass, bronze, ivory, stained glass windows.

FITZKAPLAN RESTORATION, INC.

131 Varick Street, 10th floor, New York, NY 10013 • Tel: (212) 989-8779 • Fax: (212) 989-8794 • Mon-Fri 9:00-5:00 • Diane Fitzgerald, Eve Kaplan • Some French and Spanish spoken • Prices medium

Restoration of antique furniture and objets d'art: water gilding, oriental lacquer, antique painted finishes. Serves top antique dealers, auction houses, designers and individuals.

FLICKINGER GLASSWORKS

204-207 Van Dyke Street, Brooklyn, NY 11217 • Tel: (718) 875-1531 • Fax: (718) 875-4264

Restoration of glass: will bend, cut, fuse glass for glass restoration projects.

GLASS RESTORATIONS

1597 York Avenue, New York, NY 10028 • Tel: (212) 517-3287 • Mon-Fri 9:30-5:00 • Augustine Jochac • Hungarian spoken

Restoration of crystal and glass of any kind; stemware, dishes, candlesticks, vases, bowls.

CHARLES R. GRACIE & SONS, INC.

121 West 19th Street, New York, NY 10011 • Tel: (212) 861-1150 • Fax: (212) 861-1944 • Brian Gracie • French, Spanish, Chinese and Japanese spoken • Prices high • 20% trade discount • Major credit cards

Custom order murals, furniture and screens, restoration of Oriental screens, furniture, lacquer, paintings and wallpaper.

MATTHEW HANLON RESTORATIONS

146 Avenue of the Americas, Suite 602, New York, NY 10013 • Tel: (212) 242-7589 • Fax: (212) 337-1021 • Mon-Fri 9:30-5:30 • Prices high

Conservation and restoration of art objects, especially ceramics, bronzes, marble, ivory and terra cotta.

JERARD STUDIO

131 Union Street, Brooklyn, NY 11231 • Tel: (718) 852-4128 • Fax: (718) 852-2408 • Mon-Sat 9:00-6:00 • John Jerard

Design, fabricate, install and restore furniture, painting, sculpture and back-painted glass.

HALINA MCCORMACK

5 White Street, New York, NY 10013 • Tel: (718) 448-0262 • By appointment • Polish spoken

Conservation of icons, medieval paintings on wood or canvas. Also ceramics, specializing in majolica.

MOORLAND STUDIOS, INC.

25 South Main Street, Stockton, NJ 08559 • Tel: (609) 397-8983 • Fax: (609) 397-0886 • David Cann and Constance Bassett • Prices high

Conservation and restoration of sculpture and metal objects.

PS CRAFTSMANSHIP CORPORATION

10-40 Jackson Avenue, Long Island City, NY 11101 • Tel: (718) 729-3686 • Fax: (718) 729-3781 • Mon-Fri 9:00-7:00 • Stephan Pousse • French spoken • Prices medium • Trade discount

Restoration of stone; etched glass work; stone marquetry; scagliola; marble work for gallery floors and bathrooms; French limestone fireplace mantels; stone carving and mosaics.

RESTORATION & DESIGN STUDIO

249 East 77th Street, New York, NY 10021 • Tel: (212) 517-9742 • Mon-Fri 10:00-5:00, Wed 1:00-5:00 • Paul Karner

Restoration of antiques and fine metal art: silver, gold, copper and brass plating; soft soldering, polishing, lacquering. Restoration of silver, bronzes, lighting fixtures. Restoration of ivory sculpture and ivory insulators for coffee pots. Flatware blades replaced or reset. Combs or brushes replaced.

RESTORATION WORKS

368 Broadway, #502, New York, NY 10013 • Tel: (212) 732-2959 • Mon-Fri by appointment • Amy Kalina and Monica Yus • Spanish and Italian spoken • Prices medium to high • Trade discount

Object restoration and conservation: porcelain, ceramics, ivory, stone, alabaster and jade. They teach at FIT and mentor interns.

CHRISTINE ROUSSEL, INC.

177 South Fourth Street, Brooklyn, NY 11211 • Tel: (718) 388-9633 • Fax: (718) 388-9613 • By appointment

Restoration and conservation of sculpture. Mould making, model making, all foundry techniques. They restored the Columbus monument on Columbus Circle.

SANO STUDIO

767 Lexington Avenue, New York, NY 10021 • Tel: (212) 759-6131 •
Mon-Fri 10:00-5:00 • Polish spoken

Restoration of ceramics, porcelain and pottery. Display pieces only.

SERVICE PLATING CO.

154 North Seventh Street, New York, NY 11211 • Tel: (718) 388-9360
• Fax: (718) 388-2584 • Mon-Fri 7:00-4:00 • Ruben A. Mirensky •
Spanish, Hebrew, Arabic and French spoken • Prices medium • Trade
discount • Major credit cards

Metal finishing: refurbishing of hardware, bathroom fixtures, lamps.

IVAN VALTCHEV

469 West 57th Street, New York, NY 10019 • Tel: (212) 757-0096 • By
appointment • Russian, French, German, Polish, Italian and Bulgarian
spoken • All work on pre-estimate

Restoration workshop specializing in the restoration of marble and
stone sculpture, stucco, sgraffito, bronze sculpture, fine paintings,
canvas panels and icons. References include major museums in
Europe and America. The White House and Vanderbilt Mansions.

♔ Antique Furniture Restoration

ANTIQUE CONSERVATION INCORPORATED

129 West 29th Street, 11th floor, New York, NY 10001 • Tel: (212) 947-
6946 • Fax: (212) 947-0752 • Mon-Fri 9:00-5:00 • Maryalice Huggins
• French and Polish spoken • Prices high

Restoration of 18th-century furniture, gilding, cabinet work, painted
furniture, finishing. Antique shop in studio. Works for auction houses
and top designers.

ATELIER ANTIQUES/ATELIER

465 Broome Street, New York, NY 10013 • Tel: (212) 925-3820 • Mon-
Fri 11:00-7:00, Sat 12:00-6:00 • Jiri Novak • Prices medium • Professional discount • Amex

Restoration of antique furniture and makers of custom furniture.
Atelier Antiques sells 18th- and 19th-century furniture.

BAGGOTT FRANK CONSERVATION

430 Broome Street, 2nd floor, New York, NY 10013 • Tel: (212) 226-
6244 • Fax: (212) 431-3962 • Mon-Fri 9:00-5:00 • Thomas W. Frank •
Italian spoken • Prices high • Repeat customers pay less

Restoration and conservation of joined wooden objects. High-quality
restoration of 18th- and 19th-century furniture. Excellent references
upon request.

BLATT BILLIARD CORP.

809 Broadway, New York, NY 10003 • Tel: (212) 674-8855 • Fax: (212) 598-4514 (800) 252-8855 • Mon-Fri 9:00-6:00, Sat 10:00-4:00 • Ron Blatt • Spanish spoken • Prices low to high • Professional discounts

Restoration of antique billiard tables and other game tables.

CARLTON HOUSE RESTORATION

245 West 29th Street, Suite 802, New York, NY 10001 • Telfax: (212) 239-6635 • Mon-Fri 8:30-5:30 • Kenneth Dell • Prices medium

Restoration and conservation of fine antique furniture specializing in 18th- and 19th-century French and English furniture. High-quality work for professional and private clients. Excellent references.

CENTER ART STUDIO

250 West 54th Street, Suite 901, New York, NY 10019 • Tel: (212) 247-3550 • Fax: (212) 586-4045 • Mon-Fri 9:00-6:00 • Lansing Moore • Italian and Spanish spoken • Prices medium to high • Major credit cards

Restoration of furniture, porcelain, glass, frames, stone and marble sculpture. Custom furniture, pedestals, display bases and cases made to order. Works for leading auction houses.

DIDIER COGEN ANTIQUE RESTORATION

114 Bogert Street, Teaneck, NJ 07666 • Telfax: (201) 837-8027 • Mon-Fri 8:00-6:00 • French spoken • Prices medium to high • Trade discount

Restoration of 17th- and 18th-century furniture: marquetry, veneer, polishing. Restoration of wall panels. Works often in Manhattan. Excellent references upon request.

THE FURNITURE RESTORATION WORKSHOP, INC.

1550 Richmond Terrace, Staten Island, NY 10310 • Tel: (718) 442-3781 • Fax: (718) 273-2239 • Mon-Fri 8:00-5:00, Sat 9:00-1:00 • Matthew M. Long • Spanish spoken • Prices medium to high • Discounts for volume

Comprehensive wood restoration, refinishing, maintenance, upholstery. On-site shop. Touch-ups and repairs. References upon request.

CHARLES R. GRACIE & SONS, INC.

121 West 19th Street, New York, NY 10011 • Tel: (212) 861-1150 • Fax: (212) 861-1944 • Mon-Fri 8:00-4:00 • Brian Gracie • French, Spanish, Chinese and Japanese spoken • Prices high • 20% trade discount • Major credit cards

Restoration of Oriental screens, furniture, lacquer and paintings. Antique wallpaper restoration. Custom order murals, furniture and screens. Clients include The White House, Blair House, Gracie Mansion, major museums and top designers.

JOULE INC.

344 West 38th Street, New York, NY 10018 • Tel: (212) 947-8143 • Fax: (212) 563-5370 • Mon-Fri 8:00-5:00 • Melanie Denby • Prices high to very high • Trade only

Gilding, restoration and French polishing: furniture, objects, mirrors and frames. Gilding of drapery hardware: pole and finials. Works for top designers.

MICHAEL LAZA ANTIQUE RESTORATION

547 West 27th Street, 5th floor, New York, NY 10001 • Tel: (212) 279-0629 • Mon-Fri 8:00-4:00 • Michael Laza speaks Hungarian • Prices medium • 15% professional discount

Repair and refinishing of fine antique furniture. Clients are antique dealers and private customers.

OLEK LEJBZON & CO.

210 Eleventh Avenue, 11th floor, New York, NY 10001 • Tel: (212) 243-3363 • Fax: (212) 243-3432 • Mon-Sat 7:30-6:00 • Peter Triestman • Most languages spoken • Prices medium to high

Restoration of antique furniture and objects. French polishing, gilding; antique reproductions, architectural millwork. 35 European craftsmen on staff including cabinetmakers, upholsterers, artists, stone masons, metal machinists, carpenters and others.

LES 2 ILES

104 West 27th Street, New York, NY 10001 • Tel: (212) 604-9743 • Fax: (212) 604-9341 • Mon-Fri 8:00-6:00 or by appointment • Eric Demeret • French, Russian, Spanish and Chinese spoken • Prices low to medium • Trade discount

Many years of experience in European quality restoration and conservation of fine antique furniture, specializing in veneer, marquetry, French polishing, gold leafing. Excellent references. Antique furniture and reproduction of 18th-century Russian furniture available for sale.

DAVID LINKER EBENISTE

216 West 18th Street, Suite 803, New York, NY 10011 • Tel: (212) 337-3272 • Fax: (212) 337-3202 • Mon-Fri 9:00-5:00 • French and Dutch spoken • Works to estimate

Antique furniture restoration. Specialization: 17th- and 18th-century French furniture, including marquetry and Boulle. 15 years study and apprenticeship in Amsterdam and Paris, including 3 years at the Cour de Varenne and the Ecole Boulle. One of the very best. Gallery with eclectic mix of furniture from Alsatian armoires of the 1630s to 19th-century American commodes and tables. The gallery also represents the extraordinary French contemporary artist Jules-Franck Mondoloni. Bronze repair and replacement. Mercury gilding.

MARY ANN MILES

226 East 70th Street, New York, NY 10021 • Tel: (212) 988-6691 • By appointment • Prices medium • Trade discount

Restoration of antique and non-antique furniture. References upon request.

D. MILLER RESTORERS, INC.

166 East 124th Street, New York, NY 10035 • Tel: (212) 876-1861 • Fax: (212) 410-0236 • Mon-Fri 9:00-5:00 • Robin Miller

Antique furniture restoration, mountings for sculpture. Works for top museums, auction houses and well-known dealers.

ANGELO MONTAPERTO

216 West 18th Street, New York, NY 10011 • Tel: (212) 691-5006 • Mon-Fri 9:00-5:00 • Spanish, Italian and some French spoken • Prices medium to high

Restoration and conservation of 18th- and 19th-century American and Continental furniture. Specialty: marquetry; French polishing. Top museum work and private clients.

NINO WOODCRAFT CORP.

95 Montgomery Avenue, Staten Island, NY 10301 • Tel: (718) 442-7491 • Mon-Fri 8:00-5:00 • Nino Lo Savio • Italian and Spanish spoken • Prices medium • Trade discount

Finishing and restoration of all kinds of woods: doors, furniture, everything in wood except floors. Private clients and decorators.

OXFORD ANTIQUE RESTORERS

942 Madison Avenue, New York, NY 10021 • Tel: (212) 517-4400 • Fax: (212) 737-4751 • Mon-Fri 7:30-3:00 • John Grande • Prices medium

Restoration of antique furniture, gilding, mirror replacement, leather lining, marquetry cutting. Top references.

FRANK PELLITTERI, INC.

201 East 56th Street, New York, NY 10022 • Tel: (212) 486-0545 • Fax: (212) 486-0546 • Frank Pellitteri • By appointment • Italian spoken • Prices low to high

Fine antique furniture restoration and repair. French polishing. References provided.

JUAN ANGEL POGONZA/FURNITURE RESTORATION

526 West 26th Street, Studio #915, New York, NY 10001 • Telfax: (212) 691-6251 • Mon-Fri 9:00-5:00 • Spanish, Italian and Swedish spoken • Prices medium

Restoration of 18th- and 19th-century French and Continental furniture: French polishing, inlays, marquetry, gilding. Restoration of furniture bronzes.

TIMOTHY RIORDAN, INC.

111 Cedar Street, New Rochelle, NY 10801-5219 • Tel: (212) 360-1246, (914) 235-6424 • Mon-Sat 10:00-6:00 • Prices medium • Some trade discounts

Restoration and conservation of 18th- to early 19th-century American, English and Continental furniture. Polishing, gilding and Oriental lacquer. Works on site and in situ. References from top auction houses and galleries.

ELI C. RIOS

515 West 29th Street, New York, NY 10001 • Tel: (212) 643-0388 • Fax: (212) 643-0566 • Mon-Fri 9:00-4:30 by appointment • French, Spanish, Portuguese, German and Chinese spoken • Free estimates

Restoration and conservation of fine antique furniture: 18th- and 19th-centuries. Marquetry, inlays, gilding, wood carving, Chinese lacquer and japanning. Restoration of painted surfaces; all hand-rubbed shellacked finishes and French polishing. Replacement of leather for desks. One of the finest in New York, Mr. Rios gives restoration classes.

MIGUEL SACO RESTORATION

37 East 18th Street, 6th floor, New York, NY 10003 • Tel: (212) 254-2855 • Fax: (212) 254-2852 • Mon-Fri 8:30-5:30 • Rafael Rovira • Spanish, French and some Portuguese spoken • Prices high • Trade discount

Complete services of conservation and restoration of antique and fine furniture—ultimate museum quality—from Renaissance to contemporary. World renowned. Top references.

LAZLO SALLAY

37 West 20th Street, Suite 601, New York, NY 10011 • Telfax: (212) 866-0112 • Mobile (917) 783-5717 • Mon-Fri by appointment • Hungarian and German spoken • Prices medium • Trade discounts

Restoration of antique furniture and French polishing. Excellent references.

SAN LORENZO RESTORATION WORKSHOP, LTD.

526 West 26th Street, Suite 304, New York, NY 10001 • Tel: (212) 766-4770 • Fax: (212) 766-4797 • Tue-Sat 11:00-6:00 and by appointment • Catherine Weinstock speaks French, Italian and German • Prices medium to high • Trade discount

Antique furniture restoration: structural; all types of finishes, English and French polishing; decorative finishes; water gilding with gold leaf and oil gilding. Upholstery.

SOTHEBY'S RESTORATION

400 East 111th Street, New York, NY 10028 • Tel: (212) 860-5446 • Fax: (212) 876-1064 • Mon-Fri 8:00-4:00 • President: Alastair Colin Stair, Brian D. Stair • Spanish and Italian spoken • Prices high • Trade discount

Restoration of antique furniture and fine art. All periods and all styles.

OLAF UNSOELD

Studio: 68 Jay Street, Unit 303, Brooklyn, NY 11201 • Telfax: (718) 802-1659 • Mon-Fri 9:30-5:30 by appointment • German and Dutch spoken • Prices high

Conservation of fine antique furniture and wood artifacts. Works for major museums. Other references upon request.

Bronze Restoration and Metal Finishing

BIAGGI PLATING

6913 18th Avenue, Brooklyn, NY 11204 • Tel: (718) 236-2687 • By appointment • Frankie Biaggi

High-quality plating of all types of metal specializing in church work: electroplated gold, brass, bronze, silver. Caters to all metal needs for individuals and decorators.

MICHAEL DOTZEL & SON, INC.

402 East 63rd Street, New York, NY 10021 • Tel: (212) 838-2890 • Fax: (212) 371-4839 • Mon-Fri 8:00-5:00 • Prices medium to high

Expert metal craftsman. Repairing and refinishing of antique bronze items: casting duplicate parts, polishing, rewiring, gold plating.

EMPIRE METAL FINISHING

15-09 129th Street, College Point, NY 11356 • Tel: (718) 358-8100 • Fax: (718) 358-0037 • Mon-Fri 8:00-5:00, Closed 12:30-1:30 • Spanish spoken • Prices medium to high

Plating and polishing of all metals: gold, silver, brass, nickel, copper and oxidized finishes. Antiques, lighting and architectural hardware.

EXCALIBUR BRONZE SCULPTURE FOUNDRY

85 Adams Street, Brooklyn, NY 11201 • Tel: (718) 522-3330 • Fax: (718) 522-0812 • Mon-Sat 8:00-4:30 • William Gold • French, Spanish and Russian spoken • Prices high • Trade discount • Major credit cards

Fabrication and restoration of bronze furniture and lighting. Historical restoration of all bronze from monumental to a door knob. Gold plating.

HYGRADE PLATING

22-07 41st Avenue, Long Island City, NY 11101 • Tel: (718) 392-4082
• Fax: (718) 472-4117 • Mon-Thu 7:00-4:00, Fri-Sat 7:00-12:00 • Ed
Byers • Spanish spoken • Prices medium to high • Trade discount •
Major credit cards

Custom plating of all metal finishes: chrome, nickel, 24ct gold, copper, black nickel (smoked chrome), pewter (light and dark), oil rubbed
bronze. Restoration of all metal objects and finishes.

NEXTON INDUSTRY

51 South First Street, Brooklyn, NY 11211 • Tel: (718) 599-3837 • Fax:
(718) 599-4177 • Mon-Fri 8:00-5:00 • Peter Swoboda, Leon Krivulin •
Several languages • Prices medium • Trade discount

Refinishing and restoration of brass antique pieces. Custom work
in brass and bronze and stainless steel. Manufacture brass decorative hardware and bathroom accessories (parts for railings).

ERIC S. TURNER & CO., INC.

33-35 Centre Avenue, New Rochelle, NY 10802 • Tel: (914) 235-7114
• Fax: (914) 235-7196 • Mon-Thu 7:00-5:30, Fri 7:00-3:00 • Kenneth
E. Turner • Spanish spoken • Prices high to very high

Metal finishing including grinding and polishing: bright nickel and
chrome, satin nickel and chrome electroplating.

WOODSIDE METAL FINISHERS

12 Technology Drive, Suite 14, East Setauket, NY 11733 • Telfax: (516)
689-6424 • Mon-Thu 8:30-5:30, Fri 9:00-5:00 • James Rethorn • Prices
medium to high • Trade discount

Restoration and metal finishing: chrome, nickel, oil rubbed bronze,
brass, 24ct gold Greek tone, copper, verdigris. Specialists in architectural hardware: boating, plumbing.

⚑ Restoration of Carpets, Tapestries, Textiles and Embroidery

BEAUVAIS CARPETS, INC.

201 East 57th Street, New York, NY 10022 • Tel: (212) 688-2265 • Fax:
(212) 688-2384 • Mon-Fri 9:00-5:30 • David Amini • French spoken •
Prices high to very high

Expert restoration of carpets and tapestries of the 15th to the 19th
centuries. Clients and museums and private individuals.

RESTORATION BY COSTIKYAN LTD.

28-13 14th Street, Long Island City, New York 11102 • Tel: (718) 726-1090 • Fax: (212) 726-1887 • Mon-Fri 8:30-5:00 • Spanish spoken • Prices high • Trade discount • MC and Visa

Cleaning and restoration of carpets (hand-knotted, tapestry weave and hand-tufted) of different countries of origin. Impeccable references.

F.J. HAKIMIAN

136 East 57th Street, New York, NY 10022 • Tel: (212) 371-6900 • Fax: (212) 753-0277 • Mon-Fri 9:30-5:30 • F. Joseph Hakimian • Prices high

Restoration and conservation of antique European and Oriental rugs and tapestries.

SILK SKIES RESTORATION

351 East 61st Street, New York, NY 10021 • Tel: (212) 759-9661 • Fax: (212) 371-5452 • Tue-Sat 10:00-6:00 • Suzan J. Mati • Hungarian spoken • Prices medium

Restoration of antique tapestries, Aubusson, needlepoint, hooked rugs, embroidery. Clients include museums, antique dealers, auction houses and individuals.

Restoration and Repair of Clocks

ANTIQUARIAN HOROLOGISTS

87 Nassau Street, Room 509, New York, NY 10038 • Tel: (212) 587-3715 • By appointment only • John D. Metcalf

Specialist in restoration of long case clocks, French clocks and all mechanical clocks. He is called the "Flying Clock Doctor" for collectors who have emergencies. Top references.

ARCADIAN CLOCK COMPANY

154 East 55th Street, New York, NY 10022 • Tel: (212) 446-9083 • By appointment • David M. Munro

Antique clock restoration, all mechanical clocks. First-class references.

LUIGI CERAMI RESTORATION OF ANTIQUE TIMEPIECES

320 East 52nd Street, New York, NY 10022 • Tel: (212) 750-0556 • Fax: (212) 644-8048 • By appointment

Repair and restoration of antique clocks. The more complicated the mechanism, the better.

CLOCK HUTT

255-02 Northern Boulevard, Little Neck, NY 11363 • Tel: (718) 428-8531 • Tue-Fri 10:00-4:30, Sat 11:00-4:30

Restoration of 18th- and 19th-century European and American clocks.

FANELLI ANTIQUE TIMEPIECES LTD.

790 Madison Avenue, New York, NY 10021 • Tel: (212) 517-2300 • Fax: (212) 737-4774 • Mon-Fri 11:00-6:00, Sat 11:00-5:00 • Cindy Fanelli • Prices medium to high • Major credit cards

Expert restoration of antique clocks and watches.

FOSSNER TIMEPIECES CLOCK SHOP INC.

1057 Second Avenue, New York, NY 10022 • Tel: (212) 249-2600 • Fax: (212) 935-0339 • Mon-Fri 10:00-5:30, Sat 11:00-4:00 • Slovak languages spoken • Prices medium to high • Trade discount • Major credit cards

Repair of grandfather clocks, vintage clocks and watches.

GALLERIA PER TUTTI LTD.

50 Central Park South, New York, NY 10019 • Tel: (212) 888-5176 • Fax: (212) 421-6175 • Mon-Sun 9:30-7:00 • George Motta

Clock repair and restoration: grandfathers, grandmothers, wall clocks, cuckoo clocks, mantel and shelf clocks. Antique to contemporary.

S. GUTMAN & SONS

5702 14th Avenue, Brooklyn, NY 11219 • Tel: (718) 851-5443 • Mon-Fri 9:30-5:00

Restoration of antique clocks and barometers. Works for private collectors and dealers.

SUTTON CLOCK SHOP

139 East 61st Street, New York, NY 10021 • Tel: (212) 758-2260 • Fax: (212) 688-3694 • Mon-Fri 11:00-4:00 • Knud Sutton • French and German spoken

Restoration of clocks: all mechanisms.

Restoration of Enamels

ARK RESTORATION

350 Seventh Avenue, 10th floor, New York, NY 10001 • Tel: (212) 244-1028 • Fax: (212) 244-1319 • Mon-Fri 10:00-6:00 by appointment • Russian and Ukrainian spoken • Prices according to the work

One of the few places in the world where you can have rare Limoges and other enamels restored. They also restore porcelain, faience, ceramics, art glass and semi-precious stone carvings.

Restoration of Icons

ALBERTO MANUEL CHEUNG

120 East 76th Street, New York, NY 10021 • Telfax: (212) 737-5372 •
By appointment • Alberto Cheung • Spanish spoken • Prices medium •
10-15% trade discount • Amex accepted

Restoration of Greek and Russian icons. Painting and gilding of
icons.

HALINA MCCORMACK

5 White Street, New York, NY 10013 • Tel: (718) 448-0262 • By appointment • Polish spoken

Conservation of paintings on wood and canvas: icons and Medieval paintings.

IVAN VALTCHEV

469 West 57th Street, New York, NY 10019 • Tel: (212) 757-0096 • By
appointment • Russian, French, German, Polish, Italian and Bulgarian
spoken • All work on pre-estimate

Restoration of icons as well as paintings, canvas panels, re-lining
of large canvas portraits, restoration of sculpture in marble, stone
and sculpture to order. He has worked for the major museums in
the United States and Europe and several of New York's private
clubs.

Manuscript Illuminations

GABRIEL GUILD

6 North Pearl Street, Suite 404E, Portchester, NY 10573 • Telfax: (914)
935-9362 • Mon-Fri 10:00-5:00 • Patricia Miranda • Prices vary

Manuscript illuminations. Also gives classes at the Metropolitan
Museum and at Baggott Leaf Company.

Restoration of Marble and Stone

A. ADAMI CONTRACTING CORP.

197 Waverly Avenue, Brooklyn, NY 11205 • Tel: (718) 875-0477 • Fax:
(718) 875-0491

Stone renovation of all kinds, brownstone, limestone facades.

ARTISAN RESTORATION GROUP

12-02 Astoria Boulevard, Long Island City, NY 11102 • Tel: (718) 267-1777 • Fax: (718) 267-1789

Restoration of the structural integrity of buildings, restorations of stone work, cleaning and brick repairing.

B & H ART-IN-ARCHITECTURE, LTD.

201 Allen Street, New York, NY 10002 • Tel: (212) 420-1584 • Fax: (212) 475-3489

Creation, fabrication and carving of replacement architectural ornmentation in all materials.

CRAFTWORKS

340 East Sixth Street, New York, NY 10003 • Tel: (212) 388-0983

Repair and replacement of all kinds of stone work.

D.M.S. STUDIO

5-50 51st Avenue, Long Island City, NY 11101 • Tel: (718) 937-5648 • Fax: (718) 937-2609

Restoration or replication of architectural and artistic stone details. Reproduction of statues, portraits in stone, ornaments and complex mouldings in marble, limestone or bronze.

GATTI & LOPEZ, INC.

350 West 52nd Street, New York, NY 10019 • Tel: (718) 589-5320 • Fax: (718) 991-8398

Restoration of brownstone and limestone facades, mouldings, sidewalks.

KENTEC

1437 Basset Avenue, Bronx, NY 10465 • Tel: (800) 677-7921 • Fax: (718) 824-8260

Masonry conservation, stone restoration, waterproofing.

LAZARIAN CARPET & MARBLE CARE

P.O. Box 3105, Ridgefield, NJ 07657 • Tel: (201) 941-2650 • Fax: (201) 945-1974 • 9:00 to flexible • John Lazarian • Armenian, Turkish and Arabic spoken • Prices high • Trade and retail • 10% professional discount

Marble and granite restoration, water damage restoration. Maintenance for natural stone floors, table and countertops and other surfaces.

MARBLELITE

255 Fifth Avenue, 3rd floor, New York, NY 10016 • Tel: (212) 779-8305 • Fax: (212) 725-2562 • Mon-Fri 9:00-5:00 • Kobe Jack

Marble restoration. Diamond disks to sand and hone, powder to polish.

MASTERCRAFT MARBLE

147-27 19th Avenue, 2nd floor, New York, NY 11357 • Tel: (718) 767-5589

Restoration and repair of marble, terrazzo and stone. Residential and commercial.

PORT MORRIS MARBLE & METAL RESTORATION & MAINTE-NANCE CORP.

1285 Oak Point Avenue, Bronx, NY 10474 • Tel: (718) 378-6100 • Fax: (718) 328-1074

Specialists in all types of stone and metal repair, restoration and maintenance.

RESTORATION CONCEPTS CORPORATION

432 Austin Place, Bronx, NY 10455 • Tel: (718) 402-3400 • Fax: (718) 402-4039

A complete range of services for the exterior maintenance and restoration of all types of masonry.

SKODA DESIGN, INC.

126 East 12th Street, New York, NY 10003 • Tel: (212) 505-3195 • Fax: (212) 475-2174

Stone carvings in all stone materials. Preservation and restorations as well as replications.

STERLING SERVICES CO.

636 West 43rd Street, New York, NY 10036 • Tel: (212) 643-8888 • Mon-Fri 9:00-5:00 • Ned Gargiulo • Prices medium

Restoration of marble, stone, metal.

STONE TECH, INC.

24-16 Bridge Plaza South, Long Island City, NY 11101 • Tel: (718) 784-4646 • Fax: (718) 784-1580

Restoration of natural stone and related structural elements in buildings and statues.

Restoration of Paintings

ALVAREZ FINE ART SERVICES, INC.

524 Broadway, New York, NY 10012 • Tel: (212) 219-3724 • Fax: (212) 274-9520 • Mon-Fri 9:00-5:00 • Scott Crawitz • Spanish spoken • Prices medium • Trade discount

Specialist in the conservation and restoration of fine art works on paper. Matting and framing. Top references.

ALAN M. FARANCZ PAINTING CONSERVATION STUDIOS

361 West 36th Street, New York, NY 10018 • Tel: (212) 563-5550 • Fax: (212) 947-1186 • Mon-Fri by appointment

Conservation of paintings and painted surfaces, including painted sculpture. Private clients and public institutions.

FINE ART CONSERVATION SERVICES

419 Third Avenue, New York, NY 10016 • Tel: (212) 889-8173 • Fax: (212) 683-1550 • Mon-Sat 10:00-6:00 • Robert Hammerquist • Spanish and Chinese spoken

Fine art restoration and preservation. Museum and gallery clients.

J.K. FLYNN COMPANY

525 Fifth Street, Brooklyn, NY 11215 • Tel: (212) 768-4726 • Fax: (718) 768-1726 • By appointment

Restoration of American and European paintings. Cleaning, lining, re-lining and varnishing. References available.

LOWY

223 East 80th Street, New York, NY 10021 • Tel: (212) 861-8585 • Fax: (212) 988-0443 • Mon-Fri 9:00-5:30 • Larry Shar • Spanish, Italian, French and Chinese spoken • Prices medium to very high • Major credit cards

Restoration of paintings on canvas and wood panels.

NEW YORK CONSERVATION CENTER, INC.

519 West 26th Street, New York, NY 10001 • Tel: (212) 714-0620 • Fax: (212) 714-0149 • By appointment • John Scott • Prices high

Art and architecture conservation, consulting and restoration services.

CAROLINE RIEGER FINE ART CONSERVATION

12 East 86th Street, New York, NY 10028 • Telfax: (212) 472-2739 • Mon-Sat by appointment • Some French spoken • Prices medium

Fine art conservation, specialist in works on paper. Museums, auction houses, galleries and private collectors.

RIVERDALE GALLERY AND CONSERVATORS

4601 Henry Hudson Parkway, Studio #A on 247th Street, Riverdale, NY 10471 • Telfax: (718) 549-3800 • Mon-Sat 10:00-6:00 and by appointment • Helmut E. Zitzwitz • German spoken • Prices low • Trade discount

Oil painting restoration with "Beva" materials and methods. Archival work, custom framing, paper restoration. Top references.

STONELEDGE CONSERVATION AND MASTER FRAMING

5 East 67th Street, New York, NY 10021 • Tel: (212) 772-6942 • Fax: (201) 361-6574 • Mon-Fri 10:00-5:00 • References available

Restoration and conservation of works of art: paintings, works on paper, sculpture and art objects.

TANYA ART RESTORATION

1378 York Avenue, New York, NY 10021 • Tel: (212) 472-8286 • By appointment • Russian spoken

Restoration of 19th- and early 20th-century oil paintings. Excellent references upon request.

FELIX VOLTSINGER

57 Front Street, Brooklyn, NY 11201 • Tel: (718) 802-1966 • Fax: (718) 643-9132

Restoration of paintings.

WATHERSTON ASSOCIATES INC.

249 East 48th Street, New York, NY 10017 • Tel: (212) 751-9658 • Fax: (212) 593-2726 • By appointment • Margaret Watherston

Restoration and conservation of paintings and murals. Top references.

KAREN YAGER FINE ART CONSERVATION

211 West 106th Street, #2C, New York, NY 10025 • Telfax: (212) 864-3687 • By appointment

Painting conservation, wall painting and mural conservation and restoration. Museums, public institutions. Author of six books on preservation and conservation.

JOEL AND TERESA ZAKOW ART RESTORATION

149 Wooster Street, New York, NY 10012 • Tel: (212) 477-5457 • Mon-Fri 9:00-5:00 • Jan Jarecki • French, Polish, Russian and Cantonese spoken

Restoration and conservation of paintings and polychrome. References from museums, galleries, auction houses and private collectors.

Restoration of Porcelain, Ceramics, Faience and Pottery

ARK RESTORATION

350 Seventh Avenue, 10th floor, New York, NY 10001 • Tel: (212) 244-1028 • Fax: (212) 244-1319 • Mon-Fri 10:00-6:00 by appointment • Russian and Ukrainian spoken • Prices vary

Restoration of porcelain, faience, enamels, ceramics, art glass, carved semi-precious stone carving

CENTER ART STUDIO

250 West 54th Street, #901, New York, NY 10019 • Tel: (212) 247-3550 • Fax: (212) 586-4045 • Mon-Fri 9:00-6:00 • Lansing Moore • Italian and Spanish spoken • Prices medium • Major credit cards

Restoration of porcelain, glass, stone, frames, marble sculptures, some furniture. The studio also designs and fabricates custom display bases and cases.

CLASSICAL RESTORATION AND DESIGN, INC.

150 West 28th Street, #1502, New York, NY 10001 • Tel: (212) 989-4540 • Fax: (212) 691-0052 • Mon-Fri 9:00-7:00 • Guintaras Miachkaouskas • Lithuanian, Russian, Ukrainian and Polish spoken • Prices medium to high

Professional restoration and conservation of porcelain, marble, alabaster, glass, bronze, ivory, stained glass windows.

RESTORATION WORKS

368 Broadway, #502, New York, NY 10013 • Tel: (212) 732-2959 • Mon-Fri 10:00-5:00 • Amy Kalina and Monica Yus • Spanish and Italian spoken • Prices medium to high

Restoration and conservation of all kinds of ceramics, stone, ivory and small wooden objects.

SANO STUDIO

767 Lexington Avenue, New York, NY 10021 • Tel: (212) 759-6131 • Mon-Fri 10:00-5:00 • Polish spoken

Restoration of ceramics, porcelain and pottery. Display pieces only.

Restoration of Posters

PHILIP WILLIAMS POSTERS, INC.

60 Grand Street, New York, NY 10013 • Tel: (212) 226-7830 • Fax: (212) 226-0712 • 7 days 11:00-7:00 • French, Italian and Spanish spoken • Prices low, medium, high • Major credit cards

The one great place in New York to restore damaged posters. They also do linen backing. The establishment has one of the largest poster collections in America.

Restoration of Antique Quilts

PIE GALINAT—ANTIQUE QUILT RESTORATION

4783 Michael Lane, Ponce Inlet, FL 32127-7140 • Tel: (904) 756-7085 • Fax: (904) 322-5839 • By appointment and by UPS • Prices medium • Bank check or money order

Antique quilt restoration and conservation. Custom stretchers for quilts and hooked rugs. Rag carpets can be sewn together for area rugs with custom color binding. Clients are museums all over the U.S., top antique dealers and private collectors.

Restoration Contractors

ALLSTRIP, INC.

71 Third Street, Brooklyn, NY 11231 • Tel: (718) 596-7823 • Fax: (718) 596-1493 • Mon-Fri 9:00-5:00 • Hal Peller • French spoken • Prices medium to high

A restoration company specializing in restoring prewar buildings in New York City: ornamental and flat plaster restoration, carpentry, cabinets and millwork; hardware restoration; tile and marble; electrical and plumbing; floors (wood, tile, marble, troweled seamless quartzite, epoxy composition, terrazzo); all kinds of painting and wall coatings; special techniques for stripping and re-finishing. Credits: Cooper-Hewitt Museum, Ellis Island National Monument and many others.

AOI RESTORATION, INC.

649 Morgan Avenue, Brooklyn, NY 11222 • Tel: (718) 388-0900 • Fax: (718) 388-5795

Complete exterior restorations of terra cotta, brick, marble, ornamental copper cornice, slate and tile roof. Credits: Munson Building and private homes.

APOLLON WATERPROOFING AND RESTORATION CORP.

24-37 46th Street, Astoria, NY 11103 • Tel: (718) 728-8000 • Fax: (718) 728-2565

Restoration and waterproofing of exteriors, pointing, restoration of metalwork, masonry repair, repair of metal and wood windows and replacement of slate roofs. Credits: American Museum of Natural History, Harlem Courthouse and other public institutions.

APPLE RESTORATION AND WATERPROOFING, INC.

132 Bedford Avenue, Brooklyn, NY 11211 • Tel: (718) 599-5055 • Fax: (718) 599-3588

Restoration in all aspects, including cleaning, replications, repair of painted wood windows and doors. Credits: U.S. Post Office, Freeport; Kreisel Building and New Amsterdam Theatre.

ARROW RESTORATION, INC.

37-15 Hunters Point Avenue, Long Island City, NY 11101 • Tel: (718) 729-0411 • Fax: (718) 361-0048

Specialists in masonry repair, waterproofing and structural maintenance of commercial and civic buildings and residences. Credits: Singer Building, Hempstead House, New York State Capitol.

ASHWOOD RESTORATION COMPANY

92 Sunnyside Avenue, Tarrytown, NY 10591 • Telfax: (914) 631-9226

Restoration of 18th- and 19th-century buildings, everything from drawings through specifications to woodworking restoration. Credits: The Peter Jay House, Rye and the Peter Jay Munro House, Larchmont.

ASTRO WATERPROOFING & RESTORATION CORP.

128-19 22nd Avenue, College Point, New York, NY 11356 • Tel: (718) 762-3765 • Fax: (718) 762-3757

Maintenance and restoration of the entire building envelope. Restoration of exterior limestone and brownstone, wooden windows, cast iron, copper ornamental finials, terra cotta and brick. Credits: Flushing Town Hall, the Flatiron Building.

THE BELLET COMPANY, INC.

3160 Webster Avenue, Bronx, NY 10467 • Tel: (718) 798-9181 • Fax: (718) 798-0671

Complete exterior building restoration and maintenance, roofing, waterproofing and quarry-tile decking. Credits: Beacon Hotel, Nicholas Roerich Museum.

BELLVALE CONSTRUCTION, INC.

P.O. Box 127, Bellvale, NY 10912 • Tel: (914) 986-5107 • Fax: (914) 986-6709

Specialists in slate and copper roofing and restorations. Credits: Horton Hall, Middletown; Church of St. Luke and St. Matthew, Brooklyn; Bear Mountain Bridge Administration Building.

BRISK WATERPROOFING COMPANY

720 Grand Avenue, Ridgefield, NJ 07657 • Tel: (201) 945-0210 • Fax: (201) 945-7841

Full-service restoration providing repairs and replacements from the building roof to its foundations. Credits: Trinity Church and U.S. Customs House.

BURDA CONSTRUCTION CORP.

888 Fifth Avenue, Brooklyn, NY 11232 • Tel: (718) 853-9700 • Fax: (718) 854-3806

Specialists in masonry, wood, roof and metalwork repairs, especially brownstone facades, cornices and stoops. Credits: Grace Episcopal Church, Brooklyn, and Church of Holy Apostles, New York.

CLARK & WILKINS

1871 Park Avenue, New York, NY 10035 • Tel: (212) 534-5110 • Fax: (212) 534-6799

Restoration of structural and ornamental metalwork, masonry, waterproofing, fencing and security enclosures.

CRACOVIA GENERAL CONTRACTORS, INC.

115 Dobbin Street, Brooklyn, NY 11222 • Tel: (718) 349-1866 • Fax: (718) 349-1767

Restoration of masonry, wood, stone facades and exterior and interior architectural woodworking. Credits: The Metropolitan Club; Penn Residence, Kings Point.

CRYSTAL RESTORATION ENTERPRISES, INC.

109 South Regent Street, Port Chester, NY 10573 • Tel: (914) 937-0500 • Fax: (914) 937-7582

Specialists in the cleaning and restoration of building interiors damaged by fire or flooding. Credits: Church of Our Savior, Rye, and many private residences.

DEERPATH CONSTRUCTION, INC.

37 Progress Street, Union, NJ 07083 • Tel: (908) 964-0408 • Fax: (908) 687-6749

Exterior masonry reconstruction, pointing, caulking replacement, structural steel replacement and rehabilitation, concrete repairs and resurfacing. Credits: Ellis Island National Monument, Church of the Incarnation, Newark Museum.

EDSON CONSTRUCTION CORP

255 First Street, Brooklyn, NY 11215 • Tel: (718) 768-3476 • Fax: (718) 768-9452

All types of masonry repair and restoration. Credits: Private homes.

FIFTY THREE RESTORATIONS, INC.

P.O. Box 2852, Church Street Station, New York, NY 10008 • Tel: (212) 566-1053 • Fax: (212) 267-4606

Restoration of historic sites, sacred sites and some private residences. Specialists in woodworking and all facets of building restoration. Credits: Church of the Holy Apostles, Gould Foundation.

FRANDAL CONSTRUCTION CORPORATION

5266 Arthur Kill Road, Staten Island, NY 10307 • Tel: (718) 317-8963 • Fax: (718) 317-9639

Full-service restoration company, window replacements, plaster restoration, restoration of Caen stone, marble, terra cotta. Credits: Grand Central Station, Boat House Cafe.

DEMETRIUS GARDELIS

78 St. Mark's Avenue, Brooklyn, NY 11217 • Tel: (718) 783-4868

Specialist in reproducing and repairing ornamental plaster, custom painting, wood refinishing and installation of wall coverings. Credits: St. Constantine and Helen Cathedral, public buildings and private homes.

GOLDEN RULE CONSTRUCTION CORP.

270 Lafayette Street, New York, NY 10012 • Tel: (212) 966-4555 • Fax: (212) 966-4647

All aspects of historic preservation and restoration. Credits: Kosiuszko Foundation House, Arisman House.

THE GRENADIER CORPORATION

1590 East 233rd Street, Bronx, NY 10466 • Tel: (718) 324-3700 • Fax: (718) 994-6477

Specialist in exterior masonry restoration. Credits: Convent of the Sacred Heart, Church of St. Thomas More, Polytechnic University of New York.

E.W. HOWELL CO., INC.

2 Seaview Boulevard, Port Washington, NY 11050 • Tel: (516) 621-1100 • Fax: (516) 621-1192

General contractor for exterior restorations. Credits: Polo/Ralph Lauren Store (formerly Rhinelander Mansion), Schermerhorn Row.

INTEGRATED CONSERVATION CONTRACTING, INC.

247 West 30th Street, New York, NY 10001 • Tel: (212) 947-0066 •
Fax: (212) 947-7766

This contractor has a focus on historic buildings and monuments.
A full range of services. Exterior and interior conservation, all trades.
Credits: Grace Church, Morris Jumel Mansion, Oxford University
Press.

JAMES A. JENNINGS CO., INC.

689 Mamaroneck Avenue, Mamaroneck, NY 10543 • Tel: (914) 381-
5300 • Fax: (914) 381-5812

Full-service contractor with an emphasis on commercial, industrial
and institutional buildings. Credits: Ellis Island National Monument,
Seton Center, Louise LeGras Hall, Bronx.

LEHRER MCGOVERN BOVIS, INC.

Preservation Division, 200 Park Avenue, New York, NY 10166 • Tel:
(212) 592-6700 • Fax: (212) 592-6788

The preservation division of this large contractor is dedicated to
the restoration and preservation of historic buildings and the mod-
ernization and re-positioning of older buildings. All trades, all disci-
plines. Credits: Statue of Liberty, Ellis Island National Monument,
Pocantico Historic Area.

OLEK LEJBZON & CO.

210 11th Avenue, 11th floor, New York, NY 10001 • Tel: (212) 243-
3363 • Fax: (212) 243-3432 • Peter Triestman

This workshop has a staff of 35 skilled on-staff European craftsmen. Their specialties are: preservation of historic buildings, architectural millwork, fabrication of historic millwork, masonry. Restoration of marble, stone and metal. Restoration of antique objects
and furniture. French polishing, gilding, decorative painting, marquetry, wood turning. Coromandel restoration, leather restoration,
upholstering. Credits: Oak Lounge, Jules Bistro Restaurant and
many private residences.

MILLWORK SPECIALTIES

189 Prospect Avenue, Brooklyn, NY 11215 • Tel: (718) 768-7112 •
Fax: (718) 965-3974

They manufacture or replicate wood windows and doors, mouldings for 18th-, 19th- and early 20th-century buildings. Credits: Farm
Museum, the Metropolitan Club and many more.

PSATY WATERPROOFING CORP.

108-18 Queens Boulevard, Forest Hills, NY 11375 • Tel: (718) 544-
8545 • Fax: (718) 520-8175

All aspects of exterior construction and restoration. Credits: First
National Savings Bank, Swiss Center.

REMCO

500 Tenth Avenue, New York, NY 10018 • Tel: (212) 695-4000 • Fax: (212) 967-7342

One of the largest contractors in New York offering every aspect of restoration and exterior renovation. Specialists in facade restoration, building cleaning, waterproofing, architectural metal and marble refinishing. Credits: Dakota Apartments, the Century Association, Fred F. French Building.

F.J. SCIAME CONSTRUCTION CO.

247 Water Street, New York, NY 10038 • Tel: (212) 964-9800 • Fax: (212) 964-9854

All the trades involved in the rehabilitation and restoration of historic buildings. Credits: Victory Theater, 243 Water Street at South Street Seaport.

STUART-DEAN CO.

366 Tenth Avenue, New York, NY 10001 • Tel: (212) 695-3180 • Fax: (212) 967-0988

Specialists in the restoration of marble: repairing, sanding, repointing, cleaning and polishing. Restoration of bronzework and sandstone. Credit: Chrysler Building.

TRADITIONAL LINE, LTD.

143 West 21st Street, New York, NY 10011 • Tel: (212) 627-3555 • Fax: (212) 645-8158 • James Boorstein & Anthony Lefeber

Architectural restoration and furniture restoration. Comprehensive interior restoration services with special emphasis on refinishing and restoring wood, reproduction of 17th- and 18th-century wood paneling. Also hardware repair and reproduction and elevator cab restoration. Credits: Museums, public buildings and private residences.

URBAN D.C., INC.

970 Grand Street, Brooklyn, NY 11211 • Tel: (718) 599-4000 • Fax: (718) 599-4099

Custom fabrication in masonry, cast stone, metals, fiberglass and wood. Installations. Credits: Riverside Church; New York Studio School of Drawing, Painting and Sculpture; Price and McRory Building.

WEST NEW YORK RESTORATION, INC.

1049 Lowell Street, Bronx, NY 10459 • Tel: (718) 617-2504

Full-service contractor specializing in the restoration of masonry facades of stone, brick, terra cotta and stucco, standing and batten seam copper roofing and other types of roofing. Credits: St. Jean Baptiste Church, 475 Tenth Avenue, 780 West End Avenue.

YATES GROUP

36 Bruckner Boulevard, Bronx, NY 10454 • Tel: (718) 993-5700 • Fax: (718) 665-1571

Specialists in exterior restoration, including roofing, waterproofing, ornamental metal terraces and masonry. Credits: One-Five Coenties Slip, 138-140 Prince Street, 272 Alexander Avenue.

ZIPCO BUILDERS

2727 Throop Avenue, Bronx, NY 10469 • Tel: (718) 798-2020

Full-service restoration contractor providing all trades including ornamental plastering, flat work, architectural decorative wood details and door and window replications. Credits: Midtown Community Court; Whitby Mansion, Rye.

ARTIST AND ARTISAN SUPPLIES

A.I. FRIEDMAN

44 West 18th Street, New York, NY 10011 • Tel: (212) 243-9000 • Fax: (212) 925-7230 • Mon-Fri 9:00-7:00, Sat 10:00-6:00, Sun 12:00-5:00 • Major credit cards

Full line of artist supplies.

GRACE BAGGOTT/BAGGOTT LEAF CO.

430 Broome Street, 2nd floor, New York, NY 10013 • Tel: (212) 431-GOLD • Fax: (212) 431-3962 • Mon-Fri 10:00-6:00, Sat 10:00-2:00 • Prices medium • Major credit cards

Gold leaf, traditional and exotic finishing materials for artisans and the hobbyist. Supplies for leafing in 100 different types of metal finishes. Tools for leafing.

ARTHUR BROWN & BROTHERS

2 West 46th Street, New York, NY 10036 • Tel: (212) 575-5555 • Fax: (212) 575-5865 • Mon-Fri 9:00-6:30, Sat 10:00-6:00 • All major credit cards

Wholesale and retail artist materials, airbrush supplies, stretchers. Studio and school accounts welcomed.

CHARRETTE

215 Lexington Avenue, New York, NY 10016 • Tel: (212) 683-8822 • Fax: (212) 683-5787 • Mon-Fri 8:30-7:00, Sat 10:00-5:00, Sun 12:00-5:00 • Major credit cards

Supplies and furniture for the design professional. They also do a large telephone and fax-order business.

EMPIRE ARTISTS MATERIALS, INC.

851 Lexington Avenue, New York, NY 10021 • Tel: (212) 737-5002 • Mon-Fri 8:30-6:00, Sat 9:00-5:00 • Hazel, Jeffrey and Evan J. Scheier • Prices medium • Major credit cards

Brand-name artist materials, oils, watercolors, gouaches, paper, canvas, brushes, boards, drawing pens, easels, drafting supplies, drawing tables. Custom matting and framing.

SAM FLAX

12 West 20th Street, New York, NY 10011 • Tel: (212) 620-3038 • Fax: (212) 633-1082 • Mon-Fri 8:30-6:30, Sat 10:00-6:00, Sun 12:00-5:00 • Major credit cards
425 Park Avenue, New York, NY 10022 • Tel: (212) 620-3060 • Fax: (212) 644-0138 • Mon-Fri 8:30-7:00, Sat 10:00-6:00 • Major credit cards

Material for the fine arts, graphic supplies, presentation materials, art books, picture frames.

GREENTEX UPHOLSTERY SUPPLIES

236 West 26th Street, New York, NY • Tel: (212) 206-8585 • Fax: (212) 206-6671 • Mon-Thu 8:00-4:00, Fri 8:00-1:30 • Major credit cards

Everything for the upholsterer of walls and furniture, upholsterers' tools and drapery hardware.

GUERRA PAINT & PIGMENT

510 East 13th Street, New York, NY 10009 • Tel: (212) 529-0628 • Fax: (212) 777-5688 • Mon-Sat 10:00-6:00, Sun 2:00-6:00 • Art Guerra • Spanish and some French spoken • Major credit cards

Very special and large stock of unusual paints and pigments. 180 liquid pigments and 250 dry ones. Additives include metallics to glass beads, glitter, powdered recycled tires.

JANOVIC PLAZA

1150 Third Avenue, New York, NY 10021 • Tel: (212) 772-1400 • Central order department Tel: (718) 786-4444 • Mon-Sat 9:00-6:00, Sun 10:00-4:00 • Major credit cards

Paints, varnishes, brushes, painters supplies, drapery hardware, architectural mouldings, tiles, blinds, fabrics and other artisans' supplies. Call their central order department for other outlets.

KATE'S PAPERIE

561 Broadway, New York, NY 10003 • Tel: (212) 941-9816 • Mon-Fri 10:00-7:00, Sat 10:00-6:00, Sun 12:00-6:00
8 West 13th Street, New York, NY 10011 • Tel: (212) 633-0570 • Mon-Fri 10:00-7:00, Sat 10:00-6:00 • Prices medium to high

Marvellous collection of fine arts papers from all over the world and an extraordinary selection of ribbons, ropes and cords.

KENSEAL CONSTRUCTION PRODUCTS CORPORATION

34-10 Borden Avenue, Long Island City, NY 11101 • Tel: (718) 937-5490 • Fax: (718) 392-1283 • Mon-Fri 7:00-5:00 • Ken Lippman, Jr. • Spanish spoken • Prices medium • Major credit cards

Repair, restoration and waterproofing products for metal, masonry and other various substrates for contractors and restorers.

LEE'S ART SHOP

220 West 57th Street, New York, NY 11019 • Tel: (212) 247-0110 • Fax: (212) 247-0507 • Mon-Fri 9:00-7:00, Sat 9:30-6:30, Sun 12:00-5:00 • Mike Stone • French, Spanish, German and Italian spoken • Prices medium to high • Trade discounts • Major credit cards

Very large selection of artist and artisan supplies, graphics supplies, custom framing, drafting supplies and a large airbrush department. Extensive paper department. Drafting furniture and seating.

NEW YORK CENTRAL ART SUPPLY

62 Third Avenue, New York, NY 10003 • Tel: (212) 473-7705 • Fax: (212) 475-2542 • Mon-Sat 8:30-6:30 • All major credit cards

Commercial and fine art supplies, pigments, stretchers, linen and cotton canvases, faux finish and gold leafing supplies, airbrush materials, textile design, fabric paints and supplies.

PEARL PAINT CO.

308 Canal Street, New York, NY 10013 • Tel: (212) 431-7932 • Fax: (212) 274-8290 • (800) 221-6845 • Mon-Wed, Fri-Sat 9:00-6:00, Thu 9:00-7:00, Sun 9:00-5:30 • All major credit cards

Ten floors laden chock-a-block with everything the artist and artisan can want. Silk screen materials, gold leaf, all too numerous to mention. See it for yourself.

T.J. RONAN PAINT CORP.

749 East 135th Street, Bronx, NY 10454 • Tel: (718) 292-1100 • Fax: (718) 292-0406 • Mon-Fri 8:30-5:00

Paints for the decorative painter and the trompe l'oeil artist.

SCULPTORS SUPPLY CO.

242 Elizabeth Street, New York, NY 10012 • Tel: (212) 673-3500 • Mon-Fri 9:00-5:00, Sat 10:00-3:00 • Major credit cards

Sculptors' supplies and tools. Material for the sculptor: wood, stone, clay and wax.

SCULPTURE HOUSE CASTING, INC.

155 West 26th Street, New York, NY 10001 • Tel: (212) 645-9430 • Fax: (212) 645-3717 • Mon-Fri 8:00-6:00, Sat 10:00-4:00 • Major credit cards

Supplies and services for the sculptor; mould making, casting, restoration.

SEPP LEAF PRODUCTS, INC.

381 Park Avenue South, New York, NY 10016 • Tel: (212) 683-2840 •
Fax: (212) 725-0308 • Mon-Fri 9:00-5:00 • Ines Sepp • Many languages
spoken • Prices high • Major credit cards

Wholesale supply of gold leaf and gilding products.

M. SWIFT & SONS, INC.

10 Love Lane, Hartford, CT 06112 • Tel: (203) 522-1181 • (800) 628-
0380 • Fax: (860) 249-5934 • Mon-Fri 8:00-4:30 • Major credit cards

Gold leaf surface, glass, patent roll gold and many other metal leaf
products.

UTRECHT ART AND DRAFTING SUPPLIES

111 Fourth Avenue, New York, NY 10003 • Tel: (212) 777-5353 • Fax:
(212) 420-9632 • Mon-Sat 9:00-6:00, Sun 12:00-5:00 • Spanish spoken • Major credit cards

All fine art materials: paints, brushes, canvases, papers, sketch
books, clay. Artists' and architects' tables and chairs.

Needlepoint Supplies

JOAN'S NEEDLECRAFT STUDIO, INC.

240 East 29th Street, New York, NY 10016 • Tel: (212) 532-7129 •
Tue-Fri 11:00-7:00, Sat 11:00-6:00

Large selection of hand-painted canvases; full line of patterns;
needlepoint and embroidery supplies; kits for cross-stitch and latch
hook rugs; pillow finishing and custom framing.

WALLIS MAYERS NEEDLEWORKS, INC.

30 East 68th Street, New York, NY 10021 • Tel: (212) 861-5318 • Tue-
Fri 11:40-6:30, Sat 11:40-5:30 • Prices medium to high • Major credit
cards

Beautiful hand-painted canvases, yarns, kits. Complete supplies.
Pillow and rug finishing.

RITA'S NEEDLEPOINT

150 East 79th Street, New York, NY 10021 • Tel: (212) 737-8613 •
Tue-Fri 10:30-6:00, Sat 10:30-5:00 • Prices medium to high

Hand-painted needlepoint canvases, full line of fibers: wool, cotton, hand-dyed threads, metallics. Supplies for counted cross-stitch:
patterns, fabrics and cotton fibers.

STITCHES EAST

55 East 52nd Street, New York, NY 10022 • Tel: (212) 421-0112 • Mon-Sat 10:00-6:00

A remarkable selection of yarns, patterns, needles and canvases. Expert instruction. All supplies for knitting and needlepoint.

WOOLWORKS, INC.

1260 Third Avenue, New York, NY 10021 • Tel: (212) 861-8700 • Mon-Fri 9:00-4:30 • Mr. Inman Cook • Prices high

Hand-painted needlepoint designs; mounting of pillows, rugs, chairs, screens, etc.

AUCTION HOUSES

CHRISTIE'S

502 Park Avenue at 59th Street, New York, NY 10019 • Tel: (212) 546-1000 • Fax: (212) 759-7204 • Mon-Sat 10:00-5:00 • Christopher Burge, Chairman and Principal Auctioneer; Patricia Hambrecht, Managing Director • Most languages spoken

One of the world's best-known auction houses. Paintings, jewelry, antiques, antiquities, collectibles, fine art and art objects. Weekly auctions except in the summer.

CHRISTIE'S (EAST)

219 East 67th Street, New York, NY 10021 • Tel: (212) 606-0400 • Fax: (212) 737-6076 • Mon-Sat 10:00-5:00, Mon exhibition hours 12:00-7:00 • Most languages spoken

Lower lot value than the main auction room, but handles the same things as their parent: paintings, jewelry, antiques, art objects, film and television memorabilia, Hollywood posters, toys. Good place to learn how auctions work.

WILLIAM DOYLE GALLERIES, INC.

175 East 87th Street, New York, NY 10028 • Tel: 427-2730 • Fax: (212) 369-0892 • Call for exhibition hours • Principal Auctioneer, Rodney Lang • Spanish, Italian and French spoken • All price levels

Antique furniture, paintings, silver, porcelain, art objects, collectibles. Many specialty sales: couture, toys, Lalique and others. Auctions every two weeks.

GUERNSEY'S AUCTION

108 East 73rd Street, New York, NY 10021 • Tel: (212) 794-2280 • Fax: (212) 744-3638 • Mon-Fri 9:00 to 5:00 • Principal Auctioneer, Arlan Ettinger • Prices medium to very high • Major credit cards

Many multi-day events. Leader in auctioning specialized commodities of the 20th century, from carousel horses to movie posters and racing cars. Six events a year.

H.R. HARMER, INC.

3 East 28th Street, New York, NY 10016 • Tel: (212) 532-3700 • Fax: (212) 447-5625 • Call for exhibition hours

Auction sales of autographs, rare manuscripts and letters.

IVY & MADER PHILATELIC AUCTIONS

32 East 57th Street, New York, NY 10022 • Tel: (212) 486-1222 • Fax: (212) 486-0676 • Mon-Fri 9:00-5:00, Sat by appointment • Walter Mader, President

Four auctions a year of rare stamps and covers from all over the world.

METROPOLITAN BOOK AUCTIONS

123 West 18th Street, 4th floor, New York, NY 10011 • Tel: (212) 929-4488 • Fax: (212) 463-7099 • Call for schedule • Visa and MC

Eight to ten auctions per year of rare books, prints, maps, ephemera and photographs.

PHILLIPS FINE ART AUCTIONEERS & APPRAISERS

406 East 79th Street, New York, NY 10021 • Tel: (212) 570-4830 • Fax: (212) 570-2207 • Mon-Fri 9:00-5:00 • Call for exhibition dates • Prices medium to very high

Fine paintings, prints, jewelry, antique furniture, stamps, antique silver, coins and medals.

POSTER AUCTIONS INTERNATIONAL

601 West 26th Street, New York, NY 10001 • Tel: (212) 604-9443 • Fax: (212) 604-9175 • Mon-Fri 9:00-5:00 by appointment • French spoken

Twice-yearly auctions in May and November. Original advertising posters. All countries and periods specializing in French Belle Epoch, Art Nouveau and Art Deco.

ROBERT A. SIEGEL AUCTION GALLERIES, INC.

65 East 55th Street, New York, NY 10022 • Tel: (212) 753-6421 • Fax: (212) 753-6429 • Mon-Fri 9:30-5:30 • Scott Trepel, President and Auctioneer

10 auctions per year of stamps, postal history, autographs and manuscripts.

SOTHEBY'S

1334 York Avenue, New York, NY 10021 • Tel: (212) 606-7000 • 24 hour information (212) 606-7425 • Fax: (212) 606-7107 • Mon-Fri 9:00-5:00 • Diana D. Brooks, President and CEO

The world's best-known auctioneers. Weekly sales of fine art, antiques, art objects, collectibles, coins, stamps, silver, antiquities. Everything.

STACK'S COIN CO.

123 West 57th Street, New York, NY 10019 • Tel: (212) 582-2580 • Fax: (212) 245-5018 • Mon-Fri 10:00-5:00 • Harvey Stack

America's oldest and largest dealers in rare coins. 10 auctions per year.

SWANN GALLERIES, INC.

104 East 25th Street, New York, NY 10010 • Tel: (212) 254-4710 • Mon-Fri 9:00-6:00

Weekly auctions of rare books, autographs, maps, prints, drawings, photographs, posters.

TEPPER GALLERIES

110 East 25th Street, New York, NY 10010 • Tel: (212) 677-5300 • Fax: (212) 673-3686 • Adam Hutter • Prices medium to high

Sales every other Friday and Saturday. Sales at 10:00 and Preview at 9:00. Antique furniture, bronzes, paintings, porcelains, carpets, jewelry, silver, tapestries, art objects. Good reproductions.

VILLA GRISEBACH AUCTIONS

120 East 56th Street, New York, NY 10022 • Tel: (212) 308-0762 • Fax: (212) 308-0655 • Mon-Fri 9:00-5:00 • Call for schedule

19th- and 20th-century German art.

BATHROOMS

AF SUPPLY CORP.

21 West 21st Street, New York, NY 10010 • Tel: (212) 243-5400 • Fax: (212) 243-2403 • Mon-Fri 8:00-5:00 • Bennett Friedman • Gaelic and French spoken • Prices medium to very high • Trade discount • Major credit cards

Distributors of fine bath fixtures and hardware.

♯ CHRISTINE BELFOR DESIGN LTD.

304 Hudson Street, Studio 600, New York, NY 10013 • Tel: (212) 633-6680 • Fax: (212) 645-2759 • Mon-Fri 10:00-5:00 • Prices high • 25% trade discount • Major credit cards

Hand-painted tile, mosaics and hand-decorated sinks. Superb.

THE BRASS CENTER

248 East 58th Street, New York, NY 10022 • Tel: (212) 421-0090 • Fax: (212) 371-7088 • Mon-Fri 8:30-5:00 • Spanish and French spoken • Prices medium to high • 25% trade discount • Major credit cards

Bath accessories, plumbing fixtures and fittings, shower enclosures, large choice of towel warmers. Decorative door and window hardware.

COLLECTANIA

49 Greenwich Avenue, New York, NY 10014 • Tel: (212) 727-9160 • Mon-Sat 12:00-7:30, Sun 12:00-6:00 • Sharon Rossano • French spoken • Prices medium to high • 15% trade discount on antiques • Major credit cards

Charming choice of collectibles and decorative accessories for the bath and other rooms.

CROSSTOWN CUSTOM SHADE & GLASS INC.

200 West 86th Street, New York, NY 10024 • Tel: (212) 787-8040 • Fax: (212) 787-8467
115 West 10th Street, New York, NY 10011 • Tel: (212) 647-1519 • Fax: (212) 647-1500 • Tue-Thu 8:30-7:00, Wed & Fri 8:30-5:00, Sat 9:30-4:00 • Prices medium • MC, Visa and Discover

Shower and tub enclosures; radiator enclosures in wood and metal; glass and mirror work.

DAVIS & WARSHOW, INC.

150 East 58th Street, 1st floor, New York, NY 10155 • Tel: (212) 688-5990, (212) 593-0435 • Fax: (212) 593-0446 • Mon-Fri 8:00-5:30 • Sheldon Malc • Prices low to very high • 25% professional discount • Major credit cards

Bathroom fixtures, faucets, accessories, mirrors, shower heads, shower stalls, sinks, toilets, tubs, urinals, water closet toilets and flush valve, whirlpools. Kohler, American Standard, Dorbracht, Kallista, Cherry Creek plumbing products.

DESIGN SOURCE BY DAVE SANDERS

115 The Bowery, New York, NY 10022 • Tel: (212) 274-0022 • Fax: (212) 274-0627 • Mon-Fri 8:00-5:00 • Sheik Anif • Spanish spoken • Prices medium to high • Major credit cards

Bathroom toilets, tubs, kitchen sinks, medicine cabinets and a full line of decorative bath accessories including faucets, towel bars. A full line of decorative hardware, door, window and cabinetry, plumbing fixtures and fittings.

ELGOT

937 Lexington Avenue, New York, NY 10021 • Tel: (212) 879-1200 • Fax: (212) 794-9228 • Mon-Fri 9:30-5:30, Sat 10:00-4:00 • Spanish spoken • Prices medium to high • MC and Visa

Custom bathrooms and kitchens. Bath renovation, custom cabinetry and installation.

HASTINGS TILE/IL BAGNO COLLECTION

230 Park Avenue South, New York, NY 10003 • Tel: (212) 674-9700 • Fax: (212) 674-8083 • Mon-Fri 9:30-5:30, Sat 10:00-5:00 • Prices medium to high • Trade discount • MC, Visa and Discover

Bathroom furniture and accessories: contemporary European styles. Vanities, sinks, toilets, bathtubs and bathtub enclosures, shower doors, mirrors, medicine cabinets, cabinets and towel bars. Installation of shower doors and bathtub enclosures. Ceramic tile, marble mosaics, custom mosaics.

HOWARD KAPLAN BATH SHOP

47 East 12th Street, New York, NY 10003 • Tel: (212) 674-1000 • Fax: (212) 228-7204 • Mon-Fri 9:00-5:00 • Crawford Bray • Prices high • Visa and MC

Antique and reproduction bathroom furniture, lighting, fixtures and accessories. Custom vanities, lighting and mirrors. Design assistance. Very special source.

KRAFT

306 East 61st Street, New York, NY 10021 • Tel (212) 838-2214 • Fax: (212) 644-9254 • Mon-Fri 9:00-5:00 • Jack Randolph • Prices medium to high • 25% trade discount • Visa and MC

Wide variety of bathroom fixtures, lighting and decorative hardware for the kitchen and bath. Architectural door hardware available in a variety of finishes.

KRUPS KITCHENS & BATH LTD.

11 West 18th Street, New York, NY 10011 • Tel: (212) 243-5787 • Fax: (212) 243-3205 • Mon-Fri 9:00-6:00, Sat 9:00-5:00 • Prices medium • Professional discount • Major credit cards

Collection of kitchen and bath appliances, fixtures, custom cabinetry and countertops. Elements to furnish bathroom: toilets, sinks, bathtubs, vanities, faucets, towel bars, cabinetry and countertops.

LINCOLN PLUMBING & HEATING SUPPLY INC.

35 Giffords Glen, Staten Island, New York, NY 10309 • Tel: (718) 984-5500 • Fax: (718) 984-6022 • Mon-Fri 9:00-5:00, Thu 9:00-8:00, Sat 9:00-4:00 • Prices medium

Bathroom fittings and fixtures.

MELGA SALES CORP.

1616 Coney Island Avenue, Brooklyn, NY 11230 • Tel: (718) 258-9292 • Fax: (718) 252-0997 • Mon-Fri 8:00-5:30, Sun 10:00-2:00 • Gabi Shabtai • Prices high

Bathtub reglazing. Bathroom fixtures: showerheads and faucets, bathtubs, basins, toilet bowls, shower doors, medicine cabinets, vanities. Shower enclosures. Reglazing of floors and walls.

NEW YORK REPLACEMENT PARTS CORP.

Showroom: 1464 Lexington Avenue, New York, NY 10128 • Mon-Fri 9:00-5:00
Store: 1456 Lexington Avenue, New York, NY 10128 • Tel: (212) 534-0818 • Fax: (212) 410-5783 • Mon-Fri 6:45-6:00, Sat 8:00-12:00 • Prices medium to high • Trade discount • Major credit cards

Everything for the bathroom: all fixtures, fittings and accessories. Spare parts and faucets. No installation.

POGGENPOHL U.S. INC.

230 Park Avenue South, New York, NY 10003 • Tel: (212) 228-3334 • Fax: (212) 358-9893 • Mon-Fri 9:30-5:30, Sat 10:00-5:00 • Michael K. Storms • Spanish and German spoken • Prices high to very high • Trade discount • Major credit cards

Cabinetry and accessories for the kitchen and bath: bath fixtures, bathtubs, shower enclosures, countertops with complete installation. Custom cabinetry.

RUTT OF NEW YORK CITY

150 East 58th Street, 9th floor, New York, NY 10022 • Tel: (212) 752-7888 • Fax: (212) 644-2086 • Mon-Fri 9:00-5:00

Custom-made bathroom cabinets.

☗ SHERLE WAGNER INTERNATIONAL, INC.

60 East 57th Street, New York, NY 10022 • Tel: (212) 758-3300 • Fax: (212) 207-8010 • Mon-Fri 9:00-5:00 • Chinese and Spanish spoken • Prices high to very high

One of the best in the country for bathroom fixtures and accessories. Hand-chased decorative hardware for the entire home.

SIMON'S HARDWARE & BATH

421 Third Avenue, New York, NY 10016 • Tel: (212) 532-9220 • Fax: (212) 481-0564 • Mon-Fri 8:00-5:30, Thu 8:00-7:00, Sat 10:00-6:00 • Walter Ress and Charles Fishman • Spanish and French spoken • Prices medium to high • 20% to 25% trade discount • Major credit cards

Extensive bath department including fixtures, accessories, marble, granite, stone, slate, tile and solid surface materials. Excellent choice of decorative hardware.

SMALLBONE

150 East 58th Street, 9th floor, New York, NY 10155 • Tel: (212) 838-4884 • Fax: (212) 838-4936 • Mon-Fri 9:00-6:00 • Robert Hughes • French, Spanish spoken • Prices very high • Amex

Handmade English bathrooms, bathroom furniture and cabinetry. Planning, design and installation. Kitchens and bedrooms as well.

SMOLKA CO. INC.

231 East 33rd Street, New York, NY 10016 • Tel: (212) 686-2300 • Fax: (212) 779-0652 • Mon-Sat 7:00-6:00 • John Bonsignore • Italian and Spanish spoken • Prices medium • 25% professional discount • MC and Visa

A wide variety of bath and kitchen fixtures, fittings and accessories. High quality since 1904.

URBAN ARCHAEOLOGY

43 Franklin Street, New York, NY 10013 • Tel: (212) 431-4646 • Fax: (212) 343-9312 • Mon-Fri 8:00-6:00 • Gil Shapiro
285 Lafayette Street, New York, NY 10012 • Tel: (212) 431-6969 • Fax: (212) 941-1918 • Mon-Fri 8:00-6:00, Sat 10:00-4:00 • Steve Davenport
239 East 58th Street, New York, NY 10022 • Tel: (212) 371-4646 • Fax: (212) 371-1601 • Mon-Fri 8:00-6:00 • 10% trade discount • MC and Visa

An extensive line of reproduction and antique bath fixtures and accessories, including medicine and dental cabinets, tile, sinks, tubs and a great selection of lighting.

WATERWORKS

469 Broome Street, New York, NY 10013 • Tel: (212) 966-0605 • Fax: (212) 966-6747 • Mon-Sat 10:00-5:00 • Davi Abramson
237 East 58th Street, New York, NY 10022 • Tel: (212) 371-9266 • Fax: (212) 371-9263 • Mon-Fri 10:00-5:00 • William Singer • Prices high to very high • MC and Visa

French, English and German bath and kitchen fixtures including Czech and Speake. Handmade ceramic tile, mosaics and stone. Everything for the bath and kitchen: shower and basin sets, faucets and accessories.

BILLIARDS

⛾ BLATT BOWLING & BILLIARD CORPORATION

809 Broadway, New York, NY 10001 • Tel: (212) 674-8855 • Fax: (212) 598-4514 • Mon-Fri 9:00-6:00, Sat 10:00-4:00 • Ron Blatt • Spanish spoken • Prices medium to very high • Major credit cards

Antique late 19th- and early 20th-century billiard tables, Victorian through Art Deco. Many styles available, some with heavy inlays. They also sell all billiard supplies: cloth, cues, balls, chalk. Also some high-quality game tables and supplies. They will custom make billiard tables.

V. LORIA & SONS

178 Bowery, New York, NY 10012 • Tel: (212) 925-0300 • Fax: (212) 925-0305 • Mon-Fri 10:30-6:00, Sat 10:30-4:00 • Spanish spoken • Prices medium to high

Antique and reproduction billiard tables in styles ranging from the 1890s to the 1930s: European and American. Billiard tables for the professional and for the home. Also new and used tables bought and sold.

HENRY W.T. MALI & CO.

257 Park Avenue South, New York, NY 10010 • Tel: (212) 475-4960 • Fax: (212) 533-8169 • Mon-Fri 9:00-5:00 • Fred Mali • Prices medium • Trade only

The largest and oldest manufacturer of pool and billiard cloth. Huge selection of grades and colors available. Manufacturer of two-piece pool cues.

BOOKS

BOOKBINDING AND RESTORATION

A BOOKBINDING COMPANY

315 East 86th Street, New York, NY 10028 • Tel: (212) 987-9286 •
Mon-Fri 9:00-5:30 • Prices medium

Bookbinding and restoration. Gold stamping. Work for libraries, universities and rare book collectors.

ALLIED BOOK BINDING AND GOLD STAMPING

150 West 28th Street, New York, NY 10001 • Tel: (212) 229-1493 •
Pager (917) 641-6441 • Prices medium to high

Binding, expert gold stamping, library bindings in cloth or leather.

ALPHA PAVIA BOOKBINDING CO.

601 West 26th Street, New York, NY 10001 • Tel: (212) 929-5430 •
Mon-Fri 9:00-6:00 • Prices medium to high

Custom binding and gold stamping, leather or cloth; restorations.

ASSOCIATED BINDERY INC.

405 East 70th Street, New York, NY 10021 • Tel: (212) 879-5080 •
Mon-Fri 9:00-5:30

Fine leather and cloth binding. Repairs and restoration. Gold stamping and hand binding.

J.N. BARTFIELD GALLERIES AND FINE BOOKS

30 West 57th Street, New York, NY 10019 • Tel: (212) 245-8890 • Fax:
(212) 541-4860 • Mon-Fri 10:00-5:00, Sat 10:00-3:00 • George Murray
• Prices high • All credit cards

Superb bookbinding. Also a collection of rare books in fine bindings and some of the best Western American art.

BOOKBINDERS DELUXE

121 Bennett Avenue, New York, NY 10033 • Tel: (212) 740-9388 • Fax:
(212) 740-1099 • Mon-Fri 9:00-6:30, Sat 9:00-2:30 • Prices medium
to high

Binding of books and periodicals. Expert restoration and handmade boxes.

BOOKS & BINDING

33 West 17th Street, New York, NY 10011 • Tel: (212) 229-0004 •
Mon-Fri 9:00-5:00 • Prices medium to high

All bindings, including custom, hand-crafted work: leather, gold
stamping.

CLASSIC BINDING CO.

150 Nassau Street, New York, NY 10003 • Tel: (212) 619-2091 • Mon-
Fri 9:00-5:00 • Prices medium to high

Good quality bookbinding.

DE RAY BRAUN BOOKBINDERS, INC.

37 West 26th Street, New York, NY 10001 • Tel: (212) 685-2255 •
Mon-Fri 8:30-6:00 • Prices medium to high

Good quality bookbinding and hand stamping.

DISTINCTIVE BOOKBINDING, INC.

155 East 31st Street, New York, NY 10016 • Tel: (212) 685-4004 • By
appointment

Fine leather bindings. Specialist in elegant menus, custom hand-
marbleized papers.

GINESTA EUDALDO

264 West 40th Street, New York, NY 10018 • Tel: (212) 302-0303

Expert binding and repair of rare books and bibles. For libraries
and collectors. In leather or cloth.

HARWITT BINDERY

121 Bennet Avenue, New York, NY 10033 • Tel: (212) 923-4112

Expert bookbinding for libraries and collectors.

IMPERIAL FINE BOOKS, INC.

790 Madison Avenue, New York, NY 10021 • Tel: (212) 861-6620 •
Fax: (212) 249-0333 • Mon-Fri 9:00-5:00 • Prices high to very high

Complete restoration and bookbinding of damaged and aged books.
Fine leather bindings, beautiful sets, vintage children's books.

CHARLES A. STRATTON

233 Spring Street, New York, NY 10013 • Tel: (212) 229-2859 • Fax:
(212) 229-2842 • Mon-Fri 8:00-5:00

Custom-made books for libraries and collectors of rare books. Pen
ruling, Smythe sewing, numbering. Repairs and restoration.

WEITZ, WEITZ & COLEMAN

1377 Lexington Avenue, New York, NY 10128 • Tel: (212) 832-2213 •
Mon-Thu 9:00-7:00, Fri 9:00-5:00, Sat 12:00-5:00 • Herbert Weita and
Elspeth Coleman • Prices high to very high

Fine bookbinding. They specialize in binding manuscripts for authors and scripts for film and stage stars. Fine leathers and excellent papers. They also restore fine books and bindings and deal in
rare books.

BOOKSELLERS

The City of New York is, without doubt, the capital of the publishing world. No other great city in the world produces the same volume of printed words. Books, magazines, advertising, catalogs, data and statistics are distributed by the multi-millions every day.

Booksellers can be found in every part of the city. Some even have shops or kiosks on the streets. *All New York* can help you find those dealers who have the best selections of the specialty you are looking for, whether it be a book on eighteenth-century furniture or a work on children's collectible toys.

One should not overlook the great museums of New York. All of them, without exception, have book shops offering excellent selections of hard-to-find books on fine art, interior design, antiques, gardening, architecture and collectibles. They also feature and sell reproductions of treasures in their own collections.

Then, not to be missed, is one of life's great pleasures: a visit to one of the book superstores. Drop in to a Barnes and Noble or Borders store and enjoy a cappuccino while browsing.

For reference and research, the resources of New York are hard to beat. The New York Public Library and its many branches are user-friendly, and their new computer center on Lexington Avenue at East 34th Street is state-of-the-art.

For specific material on the arts, *All New York* recommends the library in the Metropolitan Museum, The Frick Art Library, The New-York Historical Society and the New York Genealogical Society.

Remember, the "Big Apple" is a treasure trove. This guide may help you find your way. Information is listed by bookshop specialty.

Antique and Rare

APPELFELD GALLERY

1372 York Avenue, New York, NY 10021 • Tel: (212) 988-7835 • Fax: (212) 876-8915 • Mon-Fri 10:00-5:00 • Louis Appelfeld, Owner

Rare books. Fine bindings. Subject specialties: illustrated books, children's books, history of America in the 19th century, American literature, travel, British literature and history, autographs and manuscripts. 25,000 volumes. Book appraisals. Catalogs.

W. GRAHAM ARADER III

29 East 72nd Street, New York, NY 10021 • Tel: (212) 628-3668 • Fax: (212) 879-8714 • Mon-Fri 10:00-6:00, Sat-Sun 10:00-6:00 • W. Graham Arader III, Owner

Antiquarian, illustrated books, Americana, bibliography, reference, maps and travel, prints, drawings, cartography, facsimile editions, imports.

ARGOSY BOOK STORE

116 East 59th Street, New York, NY 10022 • Tel: (212) 753-4455 • Fax: (212) 593-4784 • Mon-Fri 9:00-6:00, Sat 10:00-5:00 • Naomi Hample and Judith Lowry

Used and antiquarian, hardcover out-of-print books. Subject specialties: art-general, medicine, maps, atlases, prints, drawings. 500,000 volumes. Appraisals. Catalogs ten times per year.

RICHARD B. ARKWAY

59 East 54th Street, New York, NY 10022 • Tel: (212) 751-8138 • (800) 453-0045 • Fax: (212) 832-5389 • Mon-Fri 9:00-5:00 • Richard Arkway, Paul Cohen

Antiquarian bookseller. Subjects: exploration, voyages, illustrated books, travel, science, medicine, antique and rare maps, globes and atlases.

⚐ J.N. BARTFIELD

30 West 57th Street, 3rd Floor, New York, NY 10019 • Tel: (212) 245-8890 • Fax: (212) 541-4860 • Mon-Fri 10:00-5:00, Sat 10:00-3:00

Excellent antiquarian, hardcover books. Fine bindings, fore-edge paintings, illustrated books, Western Americana, atlases and maps, colorplate books, Americana, Canadiana, discovery and exploration, natural history, sports, autographs, manuscripts, prints, sporting books, leatherbound sets and singles. 375,000 volumes. Appraise library collections, original art. Catalogs.

BAUMAN RARE BOOKS

301 Park Avenue, New York, NY 10022 • Tel: (212) 759-8300 • Fax: (212) 759-8350 • Mon-Sat 10:00-7:00 • David L. Bauman, Natalie Bauman

Rare and out-of-print books. Subject specialties: General literature, autographs, manuscripts, signed editions, Americana, law, science, travel, history, economics, Judaica, children's books. 3,000 volumes. Three to four catalogs per year.

BLACK SUN BOOKS

157 East 57th Street, New York, NY 10022 • Tel: (212) 688-6622 • Fax: (212) 751-6529 • Mon-Fri 9:00-5:00 • By appointment • Harvey Tucker, Linda Tucker

Antiquarian bookseller. Illustrated books, fine printing, autographs, manuscripts, prints, drawings, British literature, American literature, Livres d'artistes, appraisals. Original art for books. Catalogs.

BOOKLEAVES

304 West Fourth Street, New York, NY 10014 • Tel: (212) 924-5638 • Tue-Sun 12:00-8:00 • Arthur Farrier

Used, antiquarian, hardcover and paperback, out-of-print books. Art, literature, cinema, performing arts, photography. 3,000 volumes.

BOOKS OF WONDER

16 West 18th Street, New York, NY 10011 • Tel: (212) 989-3270 • (800) 835-4315 • Fax: (212) 645-3038 • Mon-Sat 11:00-7:00, Sun 12:00-6:00 • Peter Glassman

New, used and rare hardback and paperback. Children's, folklore, mythology. Books related to the Wizard of Oz and Baumiana. 15,000 volumes. Greeting cards, toys, original illustrations. Monthly newsletter (free), catalog of collectible children's books, Oz collector catalog twice per year.

JAMES F. CARR

227 East 81st Street, New York, NY 10028 • Tel: (212) 535-8110 • Mon-Fri 1:00-4:00

Antiquarian, hardcover. Americana, fine bindings. Mari Sandos, Christmas keepsake books autographs. 40,000 volumes.

CHRISTIE'S-BOOK AND MANUSCRIPT DEPT.

502 Park Avenue, New York, NY 10022 • Tel: (212) 546-1195 • Fax: (212) 980-8163 • Mon-Fri 10:00-5:00 • Stephen Massey

Auctions of the finest rare books, manuscripts and autographs.

CHRISTIE'S EAST BOOK AND MANUSCRIPT DEPT.

219 East 67th Street, New York, NY 10021 • Tel: (212) 606-0400 • Fax: (212) 737-6076 • Mon-Fri 10:00-5:00 • Francis Wahlgret

On consignments: books, autographs, maps, decorative graphics.

CRAWFORD DOYLE BOOKSELLERS

1082 Madison Avenue, New York, NY 10028 • Tel: (212) 288-6300 • Fax: (212) 517-8002 • Mon-Wed, Fri-Sat 10:00-6:00, Thu 10:00-9:00, Sun 12:00-5:00 • John K. Doyle • Dutch, French, German and Irish spoken

New and rare, out-of-print books. Staff has 50 years experience advising on books.

JAMES CUMMINS BOOKSELLER

699 Madison Avenue, 7th Floor, New York, NY 10021 • Tel: (212) 688-6441 • Fax: (212) 688-6192 • Mon-Sat 10:00-6:00 • James B. Cummins

Old and rare books. British, American, literature and illustrated books, travel, sports, fishing. Appraise library collections, books purchased. 50,000 volumes.

WILLIAM DOYLE GALLERIES

175 East 87th Street, New York, NY 10128 • Tel: (212) 427-2730 • Mon-Fri 8:00-5:00 • Brendan Cahill, Book Specialist

Auction house which has occasional estate auctions of books and private library collections.

DONALD A. HEALD RARE BOOKS AND FINE ART

124 East 74th Street, New York, NY 10021 • Tel: (212) 744-3505 • Fax: (212) 628-7847 • By appointment • Donald A. Heald

Old and rare books. Natural history, exploration, voyages, illustrated books, colorplate books, prints and drawings, watercolors, first editions, sporting, maps, manuscripts, prints. 2,000 volumes. Appraisals.

GLENN HOROWITZ BOOKSELLER

19 East 76th Street, New York, NY 10021 • Tel: (212) 557-1381 • Fax: (212) 557-2976 • Mon-Fri 10:00-5:00 • Glenn Horowitz

Old and rare books: poetry, history, literature, limited editions, historical fiction. Autographs, manuscripts, letters. Catalogs 3-4 times per year.

IDEAL BOOKSTORE

547 West 110th Street, New York, NY 10025 • Tel: (212) 662-1909 • Fax: (212) 662-1640 • Mon-Fri 10:00-6:00, Sat 11:00-4:00 • Aaron Lutwak

Out-of-print, remainders. Humanities, social sciences, cultural history, philosophy, Judaica, history. 45,000 volumes. 4 catalogs per year.

IMPERIAL FINE BOOKS

790 Madison Avenue, New York, NY 10021 • Tel: (212) 861-6620 • Fax: (212) 249-0333 • Mon-Sat 10:30-5:30 • Bibi T. Mohamed

Rare, old hardcover books: history, poetry, children's, literature, fine bindings, fore-edge paintings, first editions, sets, leatherbound books. 5,000 volumes. Search service. Appraisals of library collections, bookbinding, restoration. Annual catalog.

H.P. KRAUS RARE BOOKS AND MANUSCRIPTS

16 East 46th Street, New York, NY 10017 • Tel: (212) 687-4808 • Fax: (212) 983-4790 • Mon-Fri 9:30-5:00

Old books, incunabula, Americana, science, books about books, bibliography, illuminated manuscripts. 10,000 volumes, 3-4 catalogs per year.

THE LAW BOOK EXCHANGE

135 West 29th Street, New York, NY 10001 • Tel: (212) 594-4341 • (800) 422-6686 • Fax: (212) 465-8178 • Mon-Fri 9:30-5:30 • Roland C. Hill, Gregory F. Talbot

Old and rare, out-of-print books on law. 35,000 volumes. Appraisals of library collections, prints, legal prints. Catalog.

MARTAYAN LAN

48 East 57th Street, 4th floor, New York, NY 10022 • Tel: (212) 308-0018 • Fax: (212) 308-0074 • Mon-Fri 9:30-5:30 • Richard Lan, Seyla Martayan

Antiquarian bookseller: medicine, architecture, Americana, travel, maps, atlases, science, technology, early printed books, fine bindings. Catalogs.

MONOGRAPHS LTD.

124 West 25th Street, New York, NY 10001 • Tel: (212) 604-9510 • Fax: (212) 604-0959 • Tue-Sun 12:00-6:00 • Lawrence Lesman • Major credit cards

Rare and out-of-print 19th- and 20th-century photography books. Worldwide search service and mail order. Catalog.

NEW YORK BOUND BOOKSHOP

50 Rockefeller Plaza, New York, NY 10020 • Tel: (212) 245-8503 • Mon-Fri 10:00-5:00, Sat 12:00-4:00 • Barbara L. Cohen, Judith Stonehill

New, used and antiquarian bookseller, old and rare books on New York City and State. 4,000 volumes. Catalog.

PHILLIPS AUCTIONEERS

406 East 79th Street, New York, NY 10021 • Tel: (800) 825-ARTI • Fax: (212) 570-2207 • Mon-Fri 9:00-5:00 • Claudia Florian, Elizabeth Merry

Auction house: Books: European 1600-1900. 20th-century American autographs, manuscripts, philately.

KENNETH W. RENDELL GALLERY

989 Madison Avenue, New York, NY 10021 • Tel: (212) 717-1776 • (800) 447-1007 • Fax: (212) 717-1492 • Mon-Sat 10:00-6:00 • Kenneth W. Rendell

Superb collection of antiquarian books, autographs and manuscripts, illuminated manuscripts. Appraisals. Catalogs nine times per year.

WILLIAM H. SCHAB GALLERY

24 West 57th Street, New York, NY 10019 • Tel: (212) 410-2366 • Fax: (212) 974-0339 • Tue-Sat 9:30-5:30 • Frederick G. Schab

Antiquarian hardcover books: incunabula, illustrated books, ancient history and literature, humanities, history of science, art history. Sidelines: manuscripts, prints, drawings. Annual catalog.

DAVID SCHULSON

11 East 68th Street, New York, NY 10021 • Tel: (212) 517-8300 • Fax: (212) 517-2014 • Mon-Fri 10:00-5:00 • David Schulson, Claudia Strauss Schulson

Antiquarian bookseller specializing in literature, science, art, music and European and American history. Catalogs.

R.M. SMYTHE AND CO.

26 Broadway, Suite 271, New York, NY 10004 • Tel: (212) 943-1880 • Fax: (212) 908-4047

Auction house with frequent sales of rare books.

SOTHEBY'S BOOK AND MANUSCRIPTS DEPT.

1334 York Avenue, New York, NY 10021 • Tel: (212) 606-7385 / (212) 606-7000 • Fax: (212) 606-7041 • Mon-Fri 9:00-5:30 • David N. Redden

Book auctions: hardcover, Americana, autographs and manuscripts, colorplate books, early printed books, fine bindings, first editions, illuminated manuscripts, maps and atlases, fine printing, illustrated books, incunabula. Appraisals.

STUBBS BOOKS AND PRINTS

330 East 59th Street, 6th floor, New York, NY 10022 • Tel: (212) 772-3120 • Fax: (212) 794-9071 • Mon-Sat 10:00-6:00 • John H. Stubbs, Jane K. Stubbs

Old and rare books in all fields. Sidelines and services: original art, architectural drawings. 2,500 volumes.

SWANN GALLERIES

104 East 25th Street, New York, NY 10010 • Tel: (212) 254-4710 • Fax: (212) 979-1017 • Mon-Fri 9:00-6:00 • George S. Lowry

Auction house. Autographs/manuscripts, Judaica, photography, maps and atlases, Americana, literature, early printed books. Works of art on paper, appraisals. Catalogs 35 times per year, quarterly newsletter.

URSUS ART BOOKS IN SOHO

375 West Broadway, 3rd floor, New York, NY 10012 • Tel: (212) 226-7858 • Fax: (212) 226-7955 • Mon-Fri 10:00-6:00, Sat 11:00-5:00, Sun 10:00-6:00 • Peter Kraus

One of the best in New York City. Antiquarian bookseller. Fine arts, decorative arts, performing arts, prints and drawings, architecture, modern art, illustrated books, natural history. Branch of Ursus Books located at 981 Madison Avenue.

⚐ URSUS BOOKS AND PRINTS

981 Madison Avenue, 2nd floor, New York, NY 10021 • Tel: (212) 772-8787 • Fax: (212) 737-9306 • Mon-Fri 10:00-6:00, Sat 11:00-5:00 • Evelyn L. Kraus, Thomas Peter Kraus • French, German and Italian spoken • Prices medium to high • Major credit cards

An excellent source for new and antiquarian books on art, fine arts, architecture and natural history; illustrated books and fine bindings. Book binding to order and conservation. Mail order and exhibition catalogs.

VLE-VIEUX LIVRES D'EUROPE

16 East 65th Street, 5th Floor, New York, NY 10021 • Tel: (212) 861-5694 • Fax: (212) 861-1434 • By appointment

Antiquarian bookseller. France, French language and literature, 18th century France.

WEITZ, WEITZ & COLEMAN

1377 Lexington Avenue, New York, NY 10128 • Tel: (212) 831-2213 • Mon-Fri 9:00-7:00, Sat 12:00-5:00

Rare, out of print. Americana, the arts, books about books, bibliography, history. Fine bindings, colorplates. Services: bookbinding, book restoration.

XIMENES RARE BOOKS, INC.

19 East 69th Street, New York, NY 10021 • Tel: (212) 744-0226 • Fax: (212) 472-8075 • Mon-Fri 10:00-5:30 • Stephen Weissman

Antiquarian first editions, imports, old and rare books. Americana, exploration and voyages, British literature, American literature, science, medicine, economics. Autographs and manuscripts. Catalogs.

Architecture, Fine Arts and Decoration

ACANTHUS BOOKS

54 West 21st Street, New York, NY 10010 • Tel: (212) 463-07
50 • Fax: (212) 463-0752 • Mon-Fri 9:00-5:30 • Barry Cenower • Spanish and French spoken • Visa and MC

Antiquarian bookseller: architecture, antiques, collectibles, decorative arts, design, landscape architecture. 2,000 volumes.

ARCADE BOOKS

P.O. Box 5176, FDR Station, New York, NY 10150 • Tel: (212) 724-5371 • By appointment • Michael T. Sillerman

Used, hardcover and imports: architecture, engineering, decorative arts, design, New York City and State reference works on environment, Modern art, urban planning. 5,000 volumes.

✠ ARCHIVIA: THE DECORATIVE ARTS BOOK SHOP

944 Madison Avenue, New York, NY 10021 • Tel: (212) 439-9194 • Fax: (212) 744-1626 • Mon-Fri 10:00-6:00, Sat 11:00-5:00 • Joan Gers and Cynthia Conigliaro • Italian, Spanish, French and Korean spoken • Prices medium • Major credit cards

One of the best in the field. Books in-print, out-of-print, foreign titles in architecture, furniture, interior design, gardens, decorative arts. Search service. Two catalogs per year.

ARTE PRIMITIVO INC.

3 East 65th Street, New York, NY 10021 • Tel: (212) 570-0393 • Mon-Fri 11:30-5:00 • Mildred Kaplan

Very good selection of books on American art, South American art, archaeology, Pre-Columbian, Meso-American archaeology.

RICK BARANDES

41 North Moore Street, Room 6, New York, NY 10013 • Tel: (212) 673-7851 • Mon-Sat 10:00-6:00 by appointment • Rick Barandes

Antiquarian bookseller: design, decorative arts, glass, ceramics; magazines, journals, newspapers; books on engineering, fashion, costume, graphic arts. 3,000 volumes, 40,000 periodicals.

BOOKS AND BINDING

33 West 17th Street, New York, NY 10011 • Tel: (212) 229-0004 • Fax: (212) 229-0044 • Mon-Thu 9:00-9:00, Fri 9:00-8:00, Sat 10:00-7:00, Sun 11:00-5:00 • Joe Landau

New, used, antiquarian books. Art, dictionaries and encyclopedia. Fine bindings, photography, architecture. Bookbinding. Catalog.

CFM GALLERY

112 Greene Street, New York, NY 10012 • Tel: (212) 966-3864 • Fax: (212) 226-1041 • Mon-Fri 12:00-6:00 • Neil P. Zukerman

New and used books in French. Fine bindings, first editions, illustrated books, limited editions, out-of-print books. Art books on the Symbolists, Modern Symbolists, Surrealists. 1,000 volumes. Specialist in books on Salvador Dali and Leonor Fini.

COOPER-HEWITT MUSEUM SHOP BOOK DEPT.

2 East 91st Street, New York, NY 10128 • Tel: (212) 860-6878 / (212) 860-6931 • Fax: (212) 860-6909 • Tue 10:00-8:45, Wed-Sat 10:00-4:45, Sun 12:00-4:45

New and used, mail order, hardcover and paperback, facsimile editions, imports, children's books. Books on textiles, history, design, architecture, decorative arts, 2,300 titles. One catalog per year. Sidelines: greeting cards, gifts, reproductions, stationery, toys, jewelry, posters.

EX LIBRIS

160A East 70th Street, New York, NY 10021 • Tel: (212) 249-2618 • Fax: (212) 249-1465 • Mon-Fri by appointment • Elaine Lustig Cohen

First editions, illustrated books, foreign language books, limited editions, out of print. Books on art: Russian Avant-Garde, Surrealism, Dada, Bauhaus, Futurism. Design. 5,000 volumes. Catalog 3 times per year.

FASHION DESIGN BOOKS

234 West 27th Street, New York, NY 10001 • Tel: (212) 633-9646 • Fax: (212) 633-0807 • Mon-Thu 8:30-8:00, Fri 9:00-5:00, Sat 10:00-4:00

New hardcover and paperback. Books on fashion, costume design, clothing. Art supplies, sewing supplies and magazines.

FASHION INSTITUTE OF TECHNOLOGY BOOKSTORE

Branch of Barnes & Noble
227 West 27th Street, New York, NY 10001 • Tel: (212) 564-4275 • Mon-Thu 8:30-7:00, Fri 8:30-5:00, Sat 10:00-2:00

New hardcover and paperback, remainders, used books on fashion, costume. Children's books.

LEONARD FOX LTD.

790 Madison Avenue, Suite 204, New York, NY 10021 • Tel: (212) 879-7077 • Fax: (212) 772-9692 • Mon-Fri 9:30-5:00 or by appointment • Leonard Fox

Illustrated books. Art Deco, Art Nouveau, Modern art, prints, drawings, livres d'artistes, watercolors. 500 volumes.

FRICK COLLECTION-BOOK SHOP

1 East 70th Street, New York, NY 10021 • Tel: (212) 288-0700 • Tues-Sat 10:00-5:45, Sun 12:00-5:45

Hardcover and paperback books on art. European art, 1600-1900.

A.I. FRIEDMAN

44 West 18th Street, New York, NY 10011 • Tel: (212) 243-9000 • Fax: (212) 242-1238 • Mon-Fri 9:00-6:00, Sat 12:00-7:00 • Jim White
44 West 45th Street, New York, NY 10036 • Tel: (212) 337-8619 • Mon-Fri 9:00-5:30

Hardcover and paperback books on fine art, graphic arts, photography, computers, advertising, typography, art magazines. 500 titles. Annual catalog. Art supplies, prints, posters.

DEY GOSSE

1150 Fifth Avenue, New York, NY 10128 •Tel: (212) 996-4629 • By appointment • Dey Gosse

Antiquarian books on architecture, fine arts, decorative arts, art history, Middle Eastern art, South American art, illustrated books, Horace Walpole and his contemporaries. Catalog.

SOLOMON R. GUGGENHEIM MUSEUM BOOKSTORE

1071 Fifth Avenue, New York, NY 10128 • Tel: (212) 423-3615 • Sun-Wed 10:00-6:00, Thu 10:00-4:00, Fri-Sat 10:00-8:00

Hardcover and paperback books on art, Modern art.

☒ HACKER ART BOOKS

45 West 57th Street, 5th floor New York, NY 10019 • Tel: (212) 688-7600 • Fax: (212) 754-2554 • Mon-Sat 9:30-6:00 • Pierre H. Colas, Manager

A superb collection of art books. New, antiquarian, mail-order service. Fine arts, art in general, applied arts, prints and drawings, architecture and design. 1,000,000 volumes, 50,000 titles. Catalogs 4 times per year.

J.N. HERLIN

40 Harrison Street, Apartment 25D, New York, NY 10013 • Tel: (212) 732-1086 • By appointment • Jean-Noel Herlin

Antiquarian, out-of-print books on Modern art. 5,000 volumes.

INTERNATIONAL CENTER OF PHOTOGRAPHY

1150 Fifth Avenue, New York, NY 10128 • Tel: (212) 860-1751 • Fax: (212) 360-6490 • Tue 11:00-8:00, Wed-Sun 11:00-6:00
1133 Avenue of the Americas, New York, NY 10036 • Tel: (212) 768-4684 • Tue 11:00-8:00, Wed-Sun 11:00-6:00

New hardcover and paperbacks on photography.

HARMER JOHNSON BOOKS

21 East 65th Street, New York, NY 10021 • Tel: (212) 535-9118 • Fax: (212) 861-9893 • Mon-Fri 10:30-5:00 • Harmer Johnson, Peter Sharrer

In-print and out-of-print books and periodicals: archaeology and tribal art; art history, colorplate books, ancient and classical art, African art, American Indian art, Pre-Columbian art, art of Oceania, history of Australia, Native Americans. 10,000 volumes.

THE LIMITED EDITIONS CLUB

980 Madison Avenue, New York, NY 10021 • Tel: (212) 737-7600 • Fax: (212) 249-3939 • By appointment • Sidney Shiff • Prices very high • Major credit cards

Ligne d'artiste books and print portfolios.

METROPOLITAN MUSEUM OF ART BOOKSHOP

1000 Fifth Avenue, New York, NY 10028 • Tel: (212) 650-2911 • Fax: (212) 650-2170 • Sun, Tue-Thu 9:30-5:15, Fri-Sat 9:30-8:45, Closed Mon

One of the best selections of art books in New York. New hard-cover, paperback. Mail order. Classical studies, art, architecture, arms and armour, fashion, photography, textiles, history. 11,000 volumes. Magazines, prints, art reproductions, stationery, musical instruments.

METROPOLITAN MUSEUM OF ART BOOKSHOP-CLOISTERS BRANCH

Fort Tryon Park, New York, NY 10040 • Tel: (212) 923-3700 • Tue-Sat 9:30-5:15

New hardcover and paperback books: Medieval and Renaissance history and art. Especially books on tapestries.

METROPOLITAN MUSEUM OF ART BOOKSHOP-AT ROCKEFELLER CENTER

15 West 49th Street, New York, NY 10020 • Tel: (212) 332-1360 • Fax: (212) 332-1390 • Mon-Sat 9:30-8:00, Sun 11:00-8:00

Hardcover and paperback books on art, decoration, architecture, art history.

MORTON BOOKS: THE INTERIOR DESIGN BOOKSHOP

989 Third Avenue, New York, NY 10022 • Tel: (212) 421-9025 • Mon-Sat 11:00-6:00 • Mark West, Manager • Amex, MC and Visa

A large collection of interior design books including architecture, antique furniture, great homes, guides, gardens. Practically next door to the Design and Decoration Building at 979 Third Avenue. A great resource for the professional and the budding designer.

MUSEUM OF AMERICAN FOLK ART-MUSEUM SHOP

52 West 50th Street, New York, NY 10020 • Tel: (212) 247-5611 •
Mon-Fri 10:30-6:00, Sat 10:30-5:30
2 Lincoln Square, New York, NY 10023 • Tel: (212) 496-2966 • Mon
11:00-6:00, Tue & Thu 11:00-7:30, Fri-Sat 11:00-7:00, Sun 12:00-
6:00

Hardcover and paperback children's books on folk art, American
art.

MUSEUM OF MODERN ART BOOKSTORE

11 West 53rd Street, New York, NY 10019 • Tel: (212) 708-9700 •
Mon-Tue, Sat-Sun 11:00-5:45, Thu-Fri 11:00-8:45

Hardcover, paperback books: Modern art, design, photography, architecture, cinema. 3,500 titles.

MUSEUM OF THE CITY OF NEW YORK-MUSEUM SHOP

1220 Fifth Avenue, New York, NY 10029 • Tel: (212) 534-1672 (ext.
230) • Fax: (212) 423-0758 • Wed-Sat 10:00-5:00, Sun 1:00-5:00

Hardback and paperback. Subjects include New York City, fashion,
theatre, and the decorative arts, children's books, prints, toys including antique replicas, posters, postcards, dolls, stationery, videotapes.

⚏ NATIONAL ACADEMY OF DESIGN-BOOKSHOP

1083 Fifth Avenue, New York, NY 10128 • Tel: (212) 369-4880 • Wed-
Thurs 10:00-5:00, Fri 12:00-8:00, Sat-Sun 12:00-5:00

New books: good collection of books on Impressionism, Modern,
contemporary art and design.

THE NEW MUSEUM OF CONTEMPORARY ART BOOKSHOP

583 Broadway, New York, NY 10012 • Tel: (212) 219-1222 • Tue-Sun
12:00-6:00

New, hardcover, paperback books: Modern and Postmodern art.

A PHOTOGRAPHERS PLACE

133 Mercer Street, New York, NY 10012 • Tel: (212) 431-9358 • Fax:
(212) 941-7920 • Mon-Sat 11:00-8:00, Sun 12:00-6:00 • Harvey S.
Zucker

New, used, hardcover, paperback, imports, remainders, out-of-print
books on 19th-century photography. 9,000 volumes, 4,000 titles.

PIERPONT MORGAN LIBRARY BOOKSHOP

29 East 36th Street, New York, NY 10016 • Tel: (212) 685-0008 (Ext. 358) • (800) 861-0001 • Fax: (212)481-3484 • Tue-Sat 10:30-5:00, Sun 1:00-5:00 • John Frazier

New, hardcover, imports, paperback, children's books. European, 1600-1900 art, Medieval and Renaissance art, master drawings, history, illuminated manuscripts, books about books, bibliography, literature, early printed books, autographs, manuscripts. 2,000 volumes. Gifts, note cards, postcards, posters. Annual Christmas catalog.

PRINTED MATTER AT DIA

77 Wooster Street, New York, NY 10012 • Tel: (212) 925-0325 • Fax: (212) 925-0464 • Tue-Fri 10:00-6:00, Sat 11:00-7:00 • David Dean

New, mail order, hardcover, paperback books: art, livres d'artistes.

RIZZOLI BOOKSTORE

31 West 57th Street, New York, NY 10019 • Tel: (212) 759-2424 • (800) 52-BOOKS • Mon-Sat 9:00-8:00, Sun 11:00-7:00
3 World Financial Center, New York, NY 10281 • Tel: (212) 385-1400 • Fax: (212) 608-7905 • Mon-Thurs 10:00-9:00, Fri-Sun 10:00-7:00

RIZZOLI BOOKSTORE AND ART BOUTIQUE

454 West Broadway, New York, NY 10012 • Tel: (212) 674-1616 • (800) 52-BOOKS • Fax: (212) 979-9504 • Mon 11:00-10:00, Fri-Sat 11:00-12:00, Sun 12:00-8:00

Good collection of books on the arts, imports. Books on architecture, art, design, graphic arts, Italian language and literature, photography, fashion, business management and a large selection of children's books. Catalogs twice a year.

SCHOOL OF VISUAL ARTS

Branch of Barnes & Noble
207 East 23rd Street, New York, NY 10010 • Tel: (212) 685-7140 • Mon-Thu 9:00-7:00, Fri 9:00-5:00, Sat 10:00-2:00

Excellent collection of books on the graphic arts.

STRAND BOOKSTORE

828 Broadway, New York, NY 10003 • Tel: (212) 473-1452 • Fax: (212) 473-2591 • Mon-Sat 9:30-9:30, Sun 11:00-9:30

Marvellous shop with used books, art, architecture, photography. Good rare book department. Many review copies of recent works in all fields at great prices.

THE STRAND ANNEX

950 Fulton Street, New York, NY 10038 • Tel: (212) 732-6670 • Mon-Fri 8:30-8:00, Sat-Sun 11:00-8:00

New, used, antiquarian, hardcover and paperback, children's, imports and review copies. Many works on Americana, architecture, art, occasional first editions, history, humanities, literature, performing arts, photography. Broadway location contains 2,500,000 volumes. Catalogs. One of New York's best book sources.

STUDIO MUSEUM IN HARLEM BOOKSHOP

144 West 125th Street, New York, NY 10027 • Tel: (212) 864-4500 • Fax: (212) 666-5753 • Wed-Fri 10:00-5:00, Sat-Sun 1:00-6:00

New books on American and African art, African American studies, the African diaspora.

URBAN CENTER BOOKS

457 Madison Avenue, New York, NY 10022 • Tel: (212) 935-3592 • Fax: (212) 223-2887 • Mon-Thu 10:00-7:00, Fri 10:00-6:00, Sat 10:00-5:30

Hardcover and paperback, imports, children's books, books on architecture, design, history of preservation, urban planning, landscape architecture. 16,000 titles. Magazines (current and back issues), search service. Annual catalog. Mail-order service.

Arms and Military

THE COMPLEAT STRATEGIST

11 East 33rd Street, New York, NY 10016 • Tel: (212) 685-3880 • Mon-Wed, Fri-Sat 10:30-6:00, Thu 10:30-9:00
342 West 57th Street, New York, NY 10019 • Tel: (212) 582-1272 • Mon-Sat 11:00-8:00, Sun 12:00-5:00
630 Fifth Avenue, New York, NY 10111 • Tel: (212) 265-7449 • Mon-Fri 10:30-5:30

New hardcover and paperbacks. Many British imports. Military, war, war games, fiction, science fiction, fantasy and horror. Games, maps, posters, computer software. 3,000 volumes.

Cartoons and Comic Strips

ACTION COMICS

1551 Second Avenue, New York, NY 10028 • Tel: (212) 639-1976 •
Fax: (212) 639-1977 • Mon-Sat 11:00-8:00, Sun 12:00-6:00 • Stephen
Passarelli

New and used mail-order bookseller. Children's comic books. 100,000
volumes. Additional specialties: sports and other trading cards; magic
cards. Sidelines and services: restoration and evaluation.

COMIC ART GALLERY

118 East 59th Street, 2nd floor, New York, NY 10022 • Tel: (212) 759-
6255 • Mon-Fri 11:30-7:00, Sat 12:00-6:00 • Joseph Lihach

New and old periodicals, mail-order bookseller. Hardcover, paperback, imports, children's books. Subject specialties: comic books,
graphic arts, humor, prints, drawings, magazines, journals, newspapers. Additional specialties: signed editions, toys. Comic art,
collectibles, japanimation. Science fiction and horror.

JIM HANLEY'S UNIVERSE

14 West 33nd Street, New York, NY 10001 • Tel: (212) 268-7088 •
Fax: (212) 268-7728 • Mon-Fri 8:00-10:00, Sat, Sun 10:30-9:30

New hardcover and paperbacks, children's imports. Subject specialties: comic books, illustrated books, literature, pop culture, west-
erns, fantasy, horror. 100,000 volumes. Sidelines and services: videotapes, toys, games, comic book supplies, trading cards.

MANHATTAN COMIC AND CARDS

228 West 23rd Street, New York, NY 10011 • Tel: (212) 243-9349 •
Mon-Wed 10:00-9:00, Thu 10:00-9:00, Fri 10:00-9:30, Sat 10:00-7:30,
Sun 12:30-5:30

Comic books, collectibles, card collectibles, trade paperbacks and
action figures.

METROPOLIS COMICS AND COLLECTIBLES

873 Broadway, #201, New York, NY 10003 • Tel: (212) 260-4147 •
Fax: (212) 260-4304 • Mon-Fri 10:00-6:00

Mail-order comic books. Cinema posters. 60,000 volumes. Two
catalogs per year.

SAINT MARK'S COMICS

11 St. Mark's Place, New York, NY 10003 • Tel: (212) 598-9439 • Fax:
(212) 477-1294 • Mon 10:00-11:00, Tue-Sat 10:00-1:00, Sun 11:00-
11:00

Children's books, comic books, magazines, science fiction, toys,
graphic illustration comic books for adults.

VILLAGE COMICS

214 Sullivan Street, New York, NY 10012 • Tel: (212) 777-2770 • • Fax: (212) 475-9727 • Mon-Tue 10:30-7:30, Wed-Sat 10:00-9:00, Sun 11:00-7:00 • Joseph Lihach • French and Spanish spoken • 20-30% trade discount

Complete selection of comics, reserve services, model kits, posters. New and old comic books, children's books, periodicals, signed editions, posters, prints and drawings.

Cinema and Theatre

ANIMATION ART GUILD

330 West 45th Street, Suite 9D, New York, NY 10036 • Tel: (212) 765-3030 • Fax: (212) 765-2727 • Mon-Fri 10:00-6:00 • Pamela Scoville

Animation art, books on films. Walt Disney memorabilia is their specialty. Mail-order for books only.

APPLAUSE THEATRE & CINEMA BOOKS

211 West 71st Street, New York, NY 10023 • Tel: (212) 496-7511 • Fax: (212) 721-2856 • Mon-Sat 10:00-8:00, Sun 12:00-6:00 • Glenn Young

New books on the performing arts, theatre, cinema, radio and television. Specialty: books on acting, directing, technical aspects, criticism. 60,000 volumes. Mail order, many books imported from Britain. One catalog per year.

ASSOCIATION OF INDEPENDENT VIDEO AND FILM MAKERS

304 Hudson Street, 6th floor North, New York, NY, 10013 • Tel: (212) 807-1400 • Fax: (212) 663-8519 • Mon-Fri 9:00-6:00

New books on cinema and video production. Information services, magazines, seminars.

BOOKLEAVES

304 West 4th Street, New York, NY 10014 • Tel: (212) 924-5638 • Tue-Sun 12:00-8:00 • Arthur Farrier

Used and out-of-print books: literature, the arts and general non-fiction.

DRAMA BOOK SHOP

723 Seventh Avenue, New York, NY 10019 • Tel: (212) 944-0595/(800) 322-0595 • Fax: (212) 921-2013 • Mon-Tue, Thu-Fri 9:30-7:00, Wed 9:30-8:00, Sat 10:30-5:30, Sun 12:00-5:00 • Arthur and Rozanne Seelen

One of New York's best sources for books on theatre, dance, films, radio and television. 50,000 volumes. Periodicals, music scores, vocal selections, play scripts.

SAMUEL FRENCH BOOKSHOP

45 East 25th Street, 2nd floor, New York, NY 10010 • Tel: (212) 206-8990 • Mon-Fri 9:00-5:00

The professional actors, producers and directors resource for books dealing with theatre, drama, music. Enormous collection of play scripts.

JULLIARD SCHOOL BOOKS

60 Lincoln Center Plaza, New York, NY 10023 • Tel: (212) 799-5000 Ext. 237 • Fax: (212) 724-0469 • Mon-Thu 9:30-7:30, Fri 9:30-6:00, Sat 10:00-6:00

A large selection of books on dance, music, opera, theatre. 15,000 volumes. CDs and videos.

METROPOLITAN OPERA SHOP

Lincoln Center, 136 West 65th Street (Columbus Avenue at 63rd Street, inside the lobby of Metropolitan Opera House), New York, NY 10023 • Tel: (212) 580-4090 • Mon-Sat 10:00-9:30, Sun 12:00-6:00

Excellent choice of books on opera. Annual catalog.

MUSEUM OF TELEVISION AND RADIO GIFT SHOP

25 West 52nd Street, New York, NY 10019 • Tel: (212) 621-6880 • Tue-Wed 12:00-6:00, Thu 12:00-8:00, Fri 12:00-9:00, Sat-Sun 12:00-6:00

New hardcover and paperback books on radio, television and video. 700 volumes. Videotapes, audio cassettes, TV and radio memorabilia.

JOSEPH PATELSON MUSIC HOUSE, LTD.

160 West 56th Street, New York, NY 10019 • Tel: (212) 757-5587 • Fax: (212) 246-5633 • Mon-Sat 9:00-6:00

New and used hardcover, paperback and textbooks on music, opera, biography, autobiography, performing arts. Music theory, sheet music, metronomes, music stands, tuning forks, composers' portraits, batons. 7,500 volumes (2,000 titles). Two catalogs per year.

PERFORMING ARTS SHOP

Metropolitan Opera House, Lincoln Center, 136 West 65th Street, Concourse level, New York, NY 10023 • Tel: (212) 580-4356 • Mon-Sat 10:00-8:00

Excellent selection of books, CDs and videos on all the performing arts, opera, music, theatre, dance and even the circus.

RICHARD STODDARD PERFORMING ARTS BOOKS

18 East 16th Street, Room 305, New York, NY 10003 • Tel: (212) 645-9576 • Mon-Tue, Thu-Sat 11:00-6:00

Antiquarian book seller. Hardcover, paperback, first editions, limited-edition books. Subject specialties: performing arts, circus, dance, films, music, theatre, autographs, manuscripts, ephemera. 8,000 volumes. Playbills (12,000 in stock).

WURLITZER-BRUCK

60 Riverside Drive, New York, NY 10024 • Tel: (212) 787-6431 • Fax: (212) 496-6525 • By appointment

Antiquarian books on music, autographs, manuscripts, opera, prints, illuminated manuscripts. Prints and paintings of musicians.

Gastronomy and Oenology

KITCHEN ARTS AND LETTERS

1435 Lexington Avenue, New York, NY 10128 • Tel: (212) 876-5550 • Mon 1:00-6:00, Tue-Fri 10:00-6:30, Sat 11:00-6:00 • Nahum Waxman, Owner

New and out-of-print American and imported books. Foreign language books are largely from France. Cooking, wine, health and nutrition, agriculture.

History

AMERICAN MUSEUM OF NATURAL HISTORY

79th Street and Central Park West, New York, NY 10024 • Tel: (212) 769-5150 • Mon-Thu 10:00-5:45 • Fri-Sat 10:00-8:00

Books on natural history and children's books. 2,100 volumes, video rentals.

BLACK BOOKS PLUS

702 Amsterdam Avenue, New York, NY 10025 • Tel: (212) 749-9632 • Tue-Fri 11:00-6:00, Sat 11:00-5:00 • Glenderlyn Johnson

New and used hardcover, paperback, children's, out-of-print books. Books relating to African American history, art, literature and politics. 3,000 titles. Mail order.

FRAUNCES TAVERN MUSEUM STORE

54 Pearl Street, New York, NY 10004 • Tel: (212) 425-1778 • Fax: (212) 509-3467 • Mon-Fri 10:00-4:45, Sat-Sun 12:00-4:00

History of America, colonial times and the American Revolution, history of New York City, American art, decorative arts.

GENERAL GRANT NATIONAL MEMORIAL-BOOKSTORE

Riverside Drive and West 122nd Street, New York, NY 10027 • Tel: (212) 666-1640 • 7 days 9:00-4:30

Books on the history of America and the Civil War, particularly Ulysses Grant.

OAN-OCEANIE AFRIQUE NOIRE BOOKS

15 West 39th Street, New York, NY 10018 • Tel: (212) 840-8844 • Fax: (212) 840-3304 • Mon-Fri 10:00-5:30

New and used, rare, hardcover and paperback books. Subjects include the history of Africa, African literature, history and literature of Australia and Oceania, history of Native Americans, ethnic studies, Southeast Asia.

THEODORE ROOSEVELT BIRTHPLACE NATIONAL HISTORIC SITE-BOOKSTORE

28 East 20th Street, New York, NY 10003 • Tel: (212) 260-1616/(212) 260-0536 • Wed-Sun 9:00-5:00 • Kathryn Gross

American history 19th and 20th century, Theodore Roosevelt, antiques and collectibles, architecture, biography, autobiography.

Judaica

BLOCH PUBLISHING

37 West 26th Street, New York, NY 10010 • Tel: (212) 532-3977 • Fax: (212) 779-9169 • Mon-Fri 9:30-3:30 • Charles E. Bloch

New Israeli and British imports, textbooks, children's books, out of print, remainders; all on Judaica.

CENTRAL YIDDISH CULTURE ORGANIZATION

25 East 21st Street, New York, NY 10010 • Tel: (212) 505-8305 • Tue, Thu 10:00-3:00

Used books and imports. Poetry, Judaica, Yiddish literature. 9,000 volumes.

JEWISH BOOK CENTER OF THE WORKMAN'S CIRCLE

45 East 33rd Street, New York, NY 10016 • Tel: (212) 889-6800 • (800) 922-2558 • Fax: (212) 532-7518 • Mon-Thu 9:00-6:00, Fri 9:00-4:30, Sun 11:00-3:00

New mail-order books: Judaica and Yiddish writings. 1,000 titles. Videotapes, CDs, literary magazines, search service.

JEWISH MUSEUM SHOP

1109 Fifth Avenue, New York, NY 10128 • Tel: (212) 423-3211 • Fax: (212) 423-3232 • Sun, Mon, Wed, Thu 11:00-5:45, Fri 11:00-3:00

New and mail-order paperback and hardcover books on Judaica, women's studies, children's books and cooking.

COLLEGIATE BOOKSTORE AT YESHIVA UNIVERSITY

2539 Amsterdam Avenue at West 186th Street, New York, NY 10033 • Tel: (212) 923-5782 • Mon-Thu 10:30-4:15

New hardcover and paperback textbooks, Judaica.

YESHIVA UNIVERSITY MUSEUM-GIFT SHOP

2520 Amsterdam Avenue at West 185th Street, New York, NY 10033 • Tel: (212) 960-5390 • Tue, Thu 11:00-5:00, Wed 12:00-6:00, Sun 12:00-6:00

New hardcover Israeli imports. Books in Hebrew. Judaica.

Orientalism

AMERICA EAST BOOK CO.

46 Bowery Street, New York, NY 10013 • Tel: (212) 233-4926 • Mon-Sun 10:00-8:00

New books on China including Chinese language and literature.

ASAHIYA BOOKSTORES OF NEW YORK, INC.

52 Vanderbilt Avenue, New York, NY 10017 • Tel: (212) 883-0011 • Fax: (212) 883-1011 • Mon-Sun 10:00-8:00

New hardcover and paperbacks on Japan including Japanese language and literature. 95% of the books are in Japanese, 5% are in English. 110,000 volumes.

THE ASIA SOCIETY BOOKSTORE

725 Park Avenue, New York, NY 10021 • Tel: (212) 288-6400 • Mon-Fri 10:00-6:30, Sat 11:00-6:00, Sun 12:00-5:00

New hardcover imports. Children's books, juvenile books, paperbacks, remainders. Asian studies. 30,000 volumes. Catalogs.

ASIAN RARE BOOKS

175 West 93rd Street, Suite 16-D, New York, NY 10025 • Tel: (212) 316-5334 • Fax: (212) 316-3408 • Mon-Sat 9:00-5:00 by appointment • Stephen Feldman

Antiquarian books on Asian studies, China, Chinese language and literature, Japan, Japanese language and literature, Orient, Asian art. 3,000 volumes.

KINOKUNIYA BOOKSTORE

10 West 49th Street, New York, NY 10020 • Tel: (212) 765-1461 • Fax: (212) 541-9335 • 7 days 10:00-7:30

The New York branch of the huge Japanese superstore. New Japanese imports. Japanese language and literature.

Sciences

HAYDEN PLANETARIUM-BOOKSTORE

79th Street and Central Park West, New York, NY 10024 • Tel: (212) 769-5910 • Mon-Fri 9:00-5:00, Sat-Sun 10:00-5:30

New hardcover and paperback books on astronomy, space exploration. Children's books.

JONATHON A. HILL BOOKSELLER

325 West End Avenue, New York, NY 10023 • Tel: (212) 496-7856 • Fax: (212) 496-9182 • By appointment • Jonathon A. Hill

Antiquarian books on science, medicine and books about books, bibliography. 2,000 volumes.

BRUCE J. RAMER, EXPERIMENTA OLD AND RARE BOOKS

401 East 80th Street, Suite 24-J, New York, NY 10021 • Tel: (212) 772-6211 / (212) 772-6212 • Fax: (212) 650-9032 • By appointment

Antiquarian old and rare books. Medicine, mathematics, natural history, science, early printed books, astronomy, occult, mysticism. 2,000 volumes.

Sports

DOWN EAST ENTERPRISES

50 Spring Street, 5th floor, New York, NY 10012 • Tel: (212) 925-2632 • Mon-Fri 11:00-6:00 • Leon R. Greenman, Owner

New books: travel, skiing, hiking, camping, canoeing, guides to mountainous areas of U.S., Canada, South America, Europe, Asia, and Africa. 5,000 volumes. Maps and books on repairing and modifying outdoor equipment, National Park maps of U.S. Geological Surveys.

EASTERN MOUNTAIN SPORTS-MANHATTAN I

20 West 61st Street, New York, NY 10023 • Tel: (212) 397-4860 •
Mon-Fri 10:00-9:00, Sat 10:00-6:00, Sun 12:00-6:00

EASTERN MOUNTAIN SPORTS-MANHATTAN II

611 Broadway, New York, NY 10012 • Tel: (212) 505-9860 • Mon-Fri
10:00-9:00, Sat 10:00-6:00, Sun 12:00-9:00

New books on sports, hiking, mountaineering, travel.

MILLERS

117 East 24th Street, New York, NY 10010 • Tel: (212) 673-1400 •
Mon, Tue, Wed, Fri, Sat 10:00-6:00, Thu 10:00-7:00

A very nice selection of equestrian books, new and used.

SPORTS WORDS LTD.

1475 Third Avenue, New York, NY 10028 • Tel: (212) 772-8729/(800)
778-7937 • Fax: (212) 772-8809 • Mon-Fri 11:00-8:00, Sat 10:30-
7:00, Sun 11:00-5:45 • Marty Laufer

New hardcover and paperback books: sports; equestrian, fishing,
golf, skiing. 1,000 volumes.

Travel and Voyages of Discovery

BRITISH TRAVEL BOOKSHOP

551 Fifth Avenue, 7th floor, New York, NY 10176 • Tel: (212) 490-6688/
(212) 448-3039 • Fax: (212) 490-0219 • Mon-Fri 9:00-5:00 • Gerlinde
Woititz

New travel publications on the UK and Ireland. Hotel and sight-
seeing guides. Maps and atlases. 500 titles. Annual catalog.

THE CIVILIZED TRAVELER

2003 Broadway, New York, NY 10023 • Tel: (212) 875-0306 • Mon-Sat
10:00-9:00, Sun 12:00-7:00
864 Lexington Avenue, New York, NY 10021 • Tel: (212) 288-9190 •
Mon-Sat 10:00-9:00, Sun 12:00-7:00
2 World Financial Center, New York, NY 10281 • Tel: (212) 786-3301 •
Mon-Fri 10:00-7:00, Sat 11:00-6:00, Sun 12:00-5:00

New books on travel, maps and atlases. Videos, tapes, travel accessories and globes.

COMPLETE TRAVELLER BOOKSTORE

199 Madison Avenue, New York, NY 10016 • Tel: (212) 685-9007 •
Fax: (212) 481-3253 • Mon-Fri 9:00-7:00, Sat 10:00-6:00, Sun 11:00-
5:00 • Arnold and Harriet Greenberg

New and old hardcover and paperback travel books, imported
books, used foreign language books. Maps and atlases. 10,000
volumes. Mail order.

HAGSTROM MAP AND TRAVEL CENTER

57 West 43rd Street, New York, NY 10036 • Tel: (212) 398-1222 •
Mon-Fri 9:30-5:30

Books on travel. A great selection of maps, atlases, globes and guides. Nautical and maritime, boating, geography, New York City, hiking, fishing, bicycling. 60,000 volumes.

RAND MCNALLY, THE MAP AND TRAVEL STORE

150 East 52nd Street, New York, NY 10022 • Tel: (212) 758-7488 •
Mon-Wed, Fri 9:00-6:00, Thu 9:00-7:00, Sat 11:00-5:00

One of New York's best traveller's book shops. Travel, maps, atlases, globes, dictionaries, encyclopedia, foreign language instruction, cartography. Children's travel books. Travel guides. U.S.G.S. topographic maps, videotapes, language tapes, framed maps, gifts, travel accessories, geographic games and toys. Biannual gift catalog. 5,000 volumes.

TRAVELLER'S BOOKSTORE

22 West 52nd Street, New York, NY 10019 • Tel: (212) 397-3984 •
Mon-Fri 9:00-6:00, Sat-Sun 11:00-5:00 • Diane Wells

Travel: maps, atlases, foreign language instruction, natural history, mountaineering, outdoor sports activities, travel memoirs. Maps, guides, language tapes, historical and archaeological works. Mail orders. 30,000 volumes. Catalogs.

Superstores and Large Chains

BARNES & NOBLE BOOKSTORE (MAIN STORES)

105 Fifth Avenue, New York, NY 10003 • Tel: (212)-807-0099 • Mon-Fri
9:30-7:45, Sat 9:30-6:15, Sun 11:00-5:45
600 Fifth Avenue, New York, NY 10020 • Tel: (212) 765-0590
1 Penn Plaza, New York, NY 10019 • Tel: (212) 695-1677
750 Third Avenue, New York, NY 10017 • Tel: (212) 697-2251
2105 Broadway, New York, NY 10023 • Tel: (212) 873-0819
38 Park Row, New York, NY 10038 • Tel: (212) 964-2865
109 East 42nd Street, New York, NY 10017 • Tel: (212) 818-0973
170 Broadway, New York, NY 10038 • Tel: (212) 571-3340
879 Avenue of the Americas, New York, NY 10001 • Tel: (212) 268-
2505/2506
120 East 86th Street., New York, NY 10028 • Tel: (212) 427-0686
2289 Broadway, New York, NY 10024 • Tel: (212) 362-8835
1280 Lexington Avenue, New York, NY 10028 • Tel: (212) 423-9900
Annex / 128 Fifth Avenue, New York, NY 10011 • Tel: (212) 633-3500
105 Fifth Avenue, New York, NY 10003 • Tel: (212) 807-0099

New hardcover and paperback bookseller, fiction, nonfiction, reference in-print books. Most stores have cafes and reading facilities.
Astonishing collection of books outside of a major library. 3,000,000
volumes.

BORDERS BOOKS AND MUSIC

5 World Trade Center, New York, NY 10048 • Tel: (212) 839-8049 •
Fax: (212) 839-0806 • Mon-Fri 7:00-8:30, Sat 10:00-8:30, Sun 11:00-
8:30 • Many languages spoken

This is an interesting experience. A great bookstore with a delightful cafe. Please note the early opening hours to accommodate the
eager beavers on Wall Street. An enormous selection of fiction and
nonfiction. The works.

B. DALTON BOOKSELLER

A Division of Barnes and Noble
396 Avenue of the Americas, New York, NY 10011 • Tel: (212) 674-
8780 • Mon-Sat 9:30-11:00, Sun 12:00-8:00

New books in print, general, fiction and all subjects.

WALDENBOOKS

270 Park Avenue, New York, NY 10017 • Tel: (212) 370-3758 • Mon-Fri
8:30-6:00
57 Broadway, New York, NY 10036 • Tel: (212) 269-1139
614 Columbus Avenue, New York, NY 10024 • Tel: (212) 874-5090

New in-print hardcover and paperback books, fiction, nonfiction,
all categories.

THE BUILDINGS

The phenomenon of The Design Building is unique to America. These buildings that cater to the "Trade Only" are concentrations of the highest quality and most treasured materials of the professional decorators. Access to the buildings is normally limited to the professional who carries a designer's card and has a resale number.

This has been terribly frustrating to the out-of-towner and the foreign visitor who rarely carry such credentials. Recognizing this problem, most of the design buildings across the country have set up in-house services to accommodate the buyer. It is a good idea to telephone the showroom first.

⚎Architects & Designers Building

150 East 58th Street, New York, NY 10155 • Tel: (212) 644-6555 • Fax: (212) 750-1934 • Mon-Fri 9:00-5:00 • Open to the public

The ultimate design resource for architects and designers, including contract furnishings and accessories, floor coverings, wallcoverings, residential furnishings and accessories, kitchen and bath.

Audio Visual Equipment

INNOVATIVE AUDIO

Ground floor • Tel: (212) 619-6400/(718) 596-0888 • Fax: (718) 625-5687

Audio equipment.

Carpets

BRINTONS CARPETS USA LTD.
7th floor • Tel: (212) 832-0121 • Fax: (212) 980-1505

Carpets.

DURKAN PATTERNED
3rd floor • Tel: (212) 752-2520/(800) 241-4580 • Fax: (212) 752-2692

Printed patterned carpet for hotels, restaurants, retail stores, country clubs. More than 3,000 patterns available.

MAYA CARPETS
3rd floor • Tel: (212) 759-0022

Carpets.

EINSTEIN MOOMJY, INC.
Ground floor • Tel: (212) 758-0900 • Fax: (212) 980-8611

One-of-a-kind Oriental rugs from all over the world in wool and silk. Wall-to-wall carpet in wools, sisals and synthetic fibers.

DAVID SHAW NICHOLLS STUDIO OF DESIGN
11th floor • Tel: (212) 223-2999 • Fax: (212) 750-4656

Original designs of rugs and carpets.

THAI DYNASTY CARPET, INC.
7th floor • Tel: (212) 371-4560 • Fax: (212) 826-6562

Floor covering and supplies: braided and rag, custom woven, imported Oriental, Chinese and Moroccan, wool, custom tufted, carpets and rugs.

Custom Cabinetry

AMERICAN CLASSIC KITCHENS/WOODMODE
9th floor • Tel: (212) 838-9308 • Fax: (212) 838-9318

Woodmode custom cabinetry, kitchens and bath; Brookhaven cabinetry. Appliances. Counter surfacing materials: Corian, avonite, granite and marble. Flooring materials: limestone, travertine, ceramic tile, wood flooring, granite. Residential furniture: entertainment units, hutches, bookcases.

BETA CUSTOM FURNITURE

4th floor • Tel: (212) 750-9222 • Fax: (212) 750-5844

High-end, quality custom cabinetry: residential and commercial; unlimited designs and a variety of finishes. Furniture for every room.

RUTT CUSTOM CABINETRY

9th floor • Tel: (212) 752-7888 • Fax: (212) 644-2086

Kitchen and bathroom cabinets, library cabinetry, closets, wall units, bars, built-in cabinetry, counter surface materials. Construction services.

Fabrics

ARC-COM FABRICS, INC.

10th floor • Tel: (212) 751-1590 • Fax: (212) 751-2434

Contract fabrics: for upholstery, draperies, hospital privacy curtains, panels, wallcoverings.

JM LYNNE CO., INC.

3rd floor • Tel: (212) 751-3258 • Fax: (212) 751-0280

Contract fabrics: commercial vinyl and textiles.

PALLAS TEXTILES

2nd floor • Tel: (212) 371-9596 • Fax: (212) 371-9617

Contract textiles: fabrics, upholstery, wallcoverings.

Floor Covering & Supplies

AMERICA LS INDUSTRIES

11th floor • Tel: (212) 355-0008 • Fax: (212) 355-0009

Marble fabrications.

AMSTERDAM CORPORATION

9th floor • Tel: (212) 644-1350 • Fax: (212) 935-6291

Ceramic tiles, quarry tiles, mosaic tiles, residential, commercial and institutional floor tiles, swimming pool tiles, tumbled marble. Kitchen and bath: hand-painted Dutch tiles, English Victorian tiles, arts and crafts tiles, wall tiles.

ELON INC.

8th floor • Tel: (212) 759-6996 • Fax: (212) 207-8023

Handmade ceramic tiles and terra cottas imported from Mexico and Europe. Limestone and antiqued marbles.

PARIS CERAMICS, INC.

7th floor • Tel: (212) 644-2782 • Fax: (212) 644-2785

Decorative ceramics, limestone, exquisite reclaimed antique limestone, terra-cotta floors and terrazzo.

Furniture

B & B ITALIA

Ground floor • Tel: (212) 758-4046/(800) 872-1697 • Fax: (212) 758-2530

Contract and residential furniture and accessories: casegoods, chairs, decorative accessories, office furniture, shelves, shelf/wall systems, sofas.

BROWN JORDAN CO.

4th floor • Tel: (212) 593-1390 • Fax: (212) 935-2173

Indoor and outdoor residential and contract furniture.

CREATIVE DIMENSIONS

3rd floor • Tel: (212) 223-4102/(800) 669-2431

Contract furniture: seating collection in a variety of fabrics, leather and finishes.

GIRSBERGER OFFICE SEATING

10th floor • Tel: (212) 750-7760 • Fax: (212) 223-0340

Contract furniture and accessories. Ergonomic office seating: executive, stacking, conference and guest seating.

HARTER/PRECISION

11th floor • Tel: (212) 688-0044 • Fax: (212) 688-9877

Contract furniture including casegoods and seating.

KI/MEMMO FRESCHI & COX

2nd floor • Tel: (212) 371-9595 • Fax: (212) 371-9617

Contract furniture, accessories and textiles. Ergonomic seating, stack chairs, files and filing systems, computer support furniture, hotel, motel and dormitory, restaurant and school furniture. Panel systems and dividers.

KIMBALL INTERNATIONAL
6th floor • Tel: (212) 753-6161 • Fax: (212) 593-0837

Contract furniture and accessories: casegoods, chairs, wardrobes, computer support furniture and work stations.

NAPIER+JOSEPH+MCNAMARA
2nd floor • Tel: (212) 753-8906 • Fax: (212) 888-6128

Contract furniture and accessories: contemporary, transitional and traditional casegoods, conference tables, executive seating and lounge seating.

OR ASSOCIATES
5th floor • Tel: (212) 758-1861 • Fax: (212) 935-1746

Contract furniture and accessories: files: lateral, vertical, and pedestal. Desks, tables, seating, visual boards, lecterns, video consoles, accessories.

PANEL CONCEPTS
10th floor • Tel: (212) 644-0700/(800) 624-6118 • Fax: (212) 644-0732

Contract furniture: open-plan panel systems and seating; wood and laminate casegoods and conference room tables.

PAOLI INC.
10th floor • Tel: (212) 644-6842 • Fax: (201) 838-4794

Contract furniture: wood casegoods, seating, traditional, transitional and contemporary.

U. SCHAERER SONS, INC./HALLER SYSTEMS
12th floor • Tel: (212) 371-1230 • Fax: (212) 371-1251

Contract furniture: desks and storage systems.

SHELBY WILLIAMS INDUSTRIES, INC.
3rd floor • Tel: (212) 888-9050 • Fax: (212) 421-4328

Contract furniture and accessories: booths, chairs, fabrics.

TRENDWAY CORPORATION
7th floor • Tel: (212) 223-3350 • Fax: (212) 223-3779

Contract furniture and accessories: computer support furniture, files and file systems, office furniture, panel systems and dividers.

UNITED CHAIR/FURNITURE SOURCE INTERNATIONAL
7th floor • Tel: (212) 935-7040 • Fax: (212) 935-7220

Contract seating: Chairs, ergonomic seating. Designer stools, shop stools, lounge room seating, side chairs.

WILKHAHN, INC.

11th/12th floor • Tel: (212) 486-4333 • Fax: (212) 486-4334

Contract furniture: environmentally conscious seating and tables for offices, conference rooms, reception areas, lobbies, airports, healthcare facilities and educational institutions.

General

INTERIORS BY ROYALE

Ground floor • Tel: (212) 753-4600 • Fax: (212) 753-3343

Custom workroom: window treatments, custom upholstery and re-upholstery. Imported and domestic decorative fabrics and trimmings. Drapery hardware and accessories.

POLIFORM USA INC.

9th floor • Tel: (212) 421-1220 • Fax: (212) 421-1225

Poliform products: closet systems, wall units, bed and dining room furniture, Indian mats.

SMALLBONE

9th floor • Tel: (212) 838-4884 • Fax: (212) 838-4936

Handmade English kitchens, bedrooms and bathrooms including furniture and cabinetry.

STVDIVM V

7th floor • Tel: (212) 486-1811 • Fax: (212) 486-0898

Architectural and stone elements, furniture, upholstery, lighting, linens, beds and bedding, desks, flooring, just about everything. Both contract and residential.

WHOLESALE MARBLE AND GRANITE IMPORTERS, INC.

4th floor • Tel: (212) 223-4068 • Fax: (212) 688-8079

Marble, granite, tile and fabrications: custom tabletops and base separates. Floor coverings: limestone, granite, tile, marble for kitchen and bath. Flooring for bathroom and kitchen. Residential furniture and accessories: fireplaces, marble, and travertine.

Kitchen and Bath

BOFFI USA INC.

9th floor • Tel: (212) 421-1800 • Fax: (212) 421-1225

Italy's finest manufacturers of high-end, contemporary kitchens and baths. Award winning.

CHRISTIANS

8th floor • Tel: (212) 308-3554 • Fax: (212) 308-7316

Kitchen and bath cabinetry, bathrooms, bedrooms, libraries, media units, bars: in various wood species from England. Collection includes classic, traditional line of custom furniture.

DAVIS & WARSHOW, INC.

Ground and 4th floors • Tel: (212) 688-5990 • Fax: (212) 593-0446

Kohler, American Standard, Dorbracht, Kallista and Cherry Creek plumbing parts.

EUROPEAN KITCHEN STUDIO

8th floor • Tel: (212) 308-9674 • Fax: (212) 308-9681

Design custom cabinets and furniture for kitchen and every room of the home: libraries, bathrooms, closets, entertainment centers.

SIEMATIC CORPORATION

8th floor • Tel: (212) 593-4915 • Fax: (212) 593-7209

Design cabinets and counters: kitchen appliances, media rooms and installation. Kitchen products, counter surfacing materials, kitchen accessories, bar and kitchen faucets and sinks.

ST. CHARLES OF NEW YORK, INC.

8th floor • Tel: (212) 838-2812 • Fax: (212) 308-4951

Design and installation of custom kitchen and millwork.

⚏ Decoration & Design Building

979 Third Avenue, New York, NY 10022 • Tel: (212) 759-2964 • Fax: (212) 751-8130 • Mon-Fri 9:00-5:00 • Strictly trade only

This centrally located building is the professional designer's shopping mall. These showrooms do not deal directly with the public at large but reserve access to professional decorators and architects. The D&D building has emerged as a prestigious center for new innovations in the design world and the place where the best and the newest can be found.

Serious buyers will always find a way to penetrate the sacred precincts of the D&D. They'll hire a decorator to provide advice and do their buying for them. Many professional decorators work on fees in addition to cost-plus on purchases, some on a flat fee basis. However, the business is going through some changes and more and more people develop their own methods for seeking, selecting and buying. There are also open days to the public, so call the office for information about these days.

There are more than 100 very attractive and comfortable showrooms. The sales people are almost always helpful and gracious, ready to give advice on your needs.

There is a designers' lounge on the 14th floor. You can check your coat and use the fully equipped lounge with its telephones, fax and copy machines, as well as relax and talk over your decoration problems with your client. The restaurant, ASTRA, is open from 8:30 to 4:30.

There are, on each floor of the building, anywhere from two to six or more showrooms; thus, we have organized our information by specialty.

Accessories

AQUARIUM DESIGN

17th floor • Tel: (212) 308-5224 • Fax: (914) 352-1506 • Richard Goldberg

Custom designs of aquariums and ecological life support systems. Installations and maintenance.

CROSS HARRIS FINE CRAFTS

3rd floor • Telfax: (212) 888-7878 • Rise Cross, Freda Harris

Hand-crafted accessories by American artists. Custom orders. Wicker, baskets, decorative boxes.

Antiques

JULIA GRAY LTD.

7th floor • Tel: (212) 223-4454 • Fax: (212) 223-4503 • French, Spanish and Russian spoken • Prices high to very high • Visa and MC

18th- and 19th-century antique furniture, lighting and accessories. Reproductions of antique furniture. Specialist in painted furniture and decorations.

KM ANTIQUES OF LONDON

17th floor • Tel: (212) 888-7950 • Fax: (212) 888-3837

Antique furniture.

NICHOLAS ANTIQUES

10th floor • Tel: (212) 688-3312 • Fax: (212) 688-0425 • Tom Sandleitner • French spoken • Prices medium to high

Antique and reproduction furniture. Small furniture and lighting.

Architectural Elements

ARCHITECTURAL PANELING

9th floor • Tel: (212) 371-9632 • Fax: (212) 759-0276 • Victor Guirguis • Italian and Spanish spoken • Prices high

Finely detailed reproductions of hand-carved wall paneling and furniture.

KETCHAM ENCLOSURES/SPECIAL IMAGES

8th floor • Tel: (212) 421-3190 • Fax: (212) 421-3193

Custom enclosures for showers, tubs. Carved or clear divider panels. Built-ins. Elegant glass for tabletops. Wall units, windows, especially doors. Hand-carved glass and Lalique used.

SONIA'S PLACE

10th floor • Tel: (212) 355-5211 • Fax: (212) 355-0288 • Steve Hyman • Spanish spoken • Prices low to medium

Cork for walls and architectural mouldings; wallcoverings, wallpaper and fabric.

Art Galleries

ARLEEN G. BECKER GALLERY
8th floor • Tel: (212) 832-5144 • Fax: (212) 832-5354
Collection of traditional paintings from all over the world.

GALLERIA LA SERRA
15th floor • Telfax: (212) 758-1335
Antique prints, reproductions, custom Italian frames.

BETTY GINSBERG GALLERY
5th floor • Tel: (212) 980-3370 • Fax: (212) 223-2643
Fine art prints from Asia and Europe and decorative wall hangings.

DAN GREENBLAT ART & FRAMING & MIRRORS
7th floor • Tel: (212) 421-5970 • Fax: (212) 750-5328
Works on paper, frames, framing and mirrors.

JAIN MARUNOUCHI GALLERY
15th floor • Tel: (212) 355-8606 • Fax: (212) 355-8308 • Ashok Jain
Contemporary art for corporate and residential needs.

S.E. ART & DESIGN, INC.
3rd floor • Tel: (212) 980-1914 • Fax: (212) 980-1559
Works on paper, limited-edition graphics, lithographs and hand-colored engravings. Framing and custom mirrors.

TROUBETZKOY PAINTINGS LTD.
17th floor • Tel: (212) 688-6544 • Fax: (212) 688-6225 • Christopher Moore • French spoken
Custom paintings from originals. Custom frames and gold leaf gilding studio. Restoration of frames. Paintings for movie rental. Catalog available with choice of 15,000 subjects.

Audio Visual

LOWELL/EDWARDS
5th floor • Tel: (212) 980-2862 • Fax: (212) 980-2864 • Lowell Kaps • Spanish spoken • Prices medium to high
Home theatre audio and video equipment installed, hand-crafted custom cabinetry, entertainment centers, many units in stock, traditional to contemporary styles.

Carpets

CASA DOS TAPETES DE ARRAIOLOS, INC.

15th floor • Tel: (212) 688-9330 • Fax: (212) 688-9802 • Jenny Prata • Portuguese spoken

Handmade Portuguese needlepoint rugs. Stock and custom.

A. MORJIKIAN CO., INC.

4th floor • Tel: (212) 753-8695 • Fax: (212) 753-9877 • Allan Morjikian • Prices high

Decorative floor covering, antique and new carpets from all major weaving centers. Broadloom carpeting in stock.

PATTERSON, FLYNN, MARTIN & MANGES

6th floor • Tel: (212) 688-7700 • Fax: (212) 826-6740 • David B. Martin

Specialists in floor covering. Unusual and exciting designs for contemporary and traditional requirements. Carpets, rugs, custom floors.

ROSECORE CARPET CO., INC.

10th floor • Tel: (212) 421-7272 • Fax: (212) 421-7847

Wilton carpets and rugs, handmade Aubusson weave, needlepoint, Oriental rugs, hand-tufted rugs, braided and cotton rugs, sisal; tapestry borders, wool broadloom; stock and custom. Synthetic broadloom; wood flooring; marble and tile. Hard surface and broadloom installations.

SAXONY CARPET COMPANY, INC.

9th floor • Tel: (212) 755-7100 • Fax: (212) 223-8130

Floor-covering products custom made for the design trade.

STARK CARPET CORPORATION/OLD WORLD WEAVERS

11th floor • Tel: (212) 752-9000 • Fax: (212) 888-4257

Carpets: Axminster and Wilton woven carpet, needlepoints. Rugs: antique Oriental rugs, custom carpet and rugs. Wood flooring and tiles. Fabric and furniture.

VINCE CARPET COMPANY

3rd floor • Tel: (212) 826-6580 • Fax: (212) 826 6584

Floor coverings.

Chairs

ARTISTIC FRAME COMPANY
17th floor • Tel: (212) 289-2100 • Fax: (212) 289-2101
All kinds of chairs.

J. ROBERT SCOTT: CHAIRS, CHAIRS, CHAIRS
2nd floor • Tel: (212) 755-4910 • Fax: (212) 888-9537
Chairs, lots of chairs.

Fabrics and Wallcoverings

BERGAMO FABRICS
17th floor • Tel: (212) 888-3333 • Fax: (212) 888-3837
Sahco-Hesslein, Rubelli and Bises-Novita collections.

BLUMENTHAL, INC.
2nd floor • Tel: (212) 752-2535
Wallcoverings and fabrics.

BOUSSAC OF FRANCE
16th floor • Tel: (212) 421-0534 • Fax: (212) 826-9236
French cotton textiles. Specialist in large prints, wovens, jacquards, wallcoverings, borders. Represent Chotard formal fabrics. These are extraordinary.

BRUNSCHWIG & FILS, INC.
11th and 12th floors • Tel: (212) 838-7878 • Fax: (212) 371-3026
Beautiful selection of all types of fabrics and trimmings.

MANUEL CANOVAS, INC.
17th floor • Tel: (212) 752-9588 • Fax: (212) 754-0937
Decorative textiles, wallpapers, trims, borders and chairs. One of the best-known names in the world.

CARLETON V. LTD.
10th floor • Tel: (212) 355-4525 • Fax: (212) 838-0553
Fabrics, wallcoverings, trimmings, drapery hardware.

CHINA SEAS, INC.

5th floor • Tel: (212) 752-5555 • Fax: (212) 371-6530

Fabrics: prints and woven designs; wallpaper: hand screened and rotary printed.

CLARENCE HOUSE

211 East 58th Street and 2nd floor • Tel: (212) 752-2890 • Fax: (212) 755-3314

Marvellous textiles, trimmings and wallpapers.

CORAGGIO TEXTILES

5th floor • Tel: (212) 758-9885 • Fax: (212) 371-1973

Textiles for upholstery, drapery, sheers, casements. Exclusive representatives for Missoni and Valentino. Also wallcoverings, some hand painted.

COWTAN & TOUT

10th floor • Tel: (212) 753-4488 • Fax: (212) 593-1839

Excellent selection of fabrics and wallpapers.

CRAIG FABRICS QUILTESSENCE

15th floor • Tel: (212) 371-0827 • Craig Goldman

Fabrics.

IAN CRAWFORD, LTD.

10th floor • Tel: (212) 355-2228 • Fax: (212) 355-2229

Wallcoverings, hand-screened vinyls, stries, chenilles, silks, velvets, chintz, tapestries, jacquards and trimmings.

DURALEE MULTIFABRICS

8th floor • Tel: (212) 752-4040 • Fax: (212) 644-3530

Fabrics for drapery, upholstery, bedspreads, extensive line. Bedspread program.

FIRST EDITIONS

15th floor • Tel: (212) 355-1150 • Fax: (212) 838-0749

Hand-printed fabrics and wallcoverings. Fabrics for upholstery, draperies and bedspreads.

FONTHILL LTD.

17th floor • Tel: (212) 755-6700 • Fax: (212) 371-2358 • Tod Vasse

Superb line of fabrics including the lines of Pierre Frey, Dufour Ltd. and The Twigs.

FORTUNY, INC.
16th floor • Tel: (212) 753-7153 • Fax: (212) 935-7487
Fantastic Italian fabrics.

GREY WATKINS LTD.
17th floor • Tel: (212) 371-2333 • Fax: (212) 371-2358
Decorative fabrics and wallpapers.

S. HARRIS/FABRICUT
2nd floor • Tel: (212) 838-5238 • Fax: (212) 838-5278
Fabrics and trims.

HINES
10th floor • Tel: (212) 754-5880 • Fax: (212) 758-4881
Fabrics.

LEE JOFA
2nd floor • Tel: (212) 688-0444 • Fax: (212) 759-3658
High-quality fabrics.

KRAVET FABRICS, INC.
3rd floor • Tel: (212) 421-6363 • Fax: (212) 751-7196
Decorative fabrics, wallcoverings, trimmings, furniture.

NUNO
2nd floor • Tel: (212) 421-9114 • Fax: (212) 421-9115
High-end Japanese textiles. Fabrics designed by the Nuno Design
Team.

OSBORNE & LITTLE
5th floor • Tel: (212) 751-3333 • Fax: (212) 752-6027
Printed, woven and silk fabrics; trimmings and wallpapers.

PAYNE FABRICS
15th floor • Tel: (212) 752-1960 • Fax: (212) 308-5866
Drapery and upholstery fabrics. Wallcoverings.

POLLACK & ASSOCIATES
17th floor • Tel: (212) 427-8396
Textiles for upholstery and windows.

ROGERS & GOFFIGON LTD.

17th floor • Tel: (212) 888-3242 • Fax: (212) 888-3315

Custom-designed and milled fabrics by Rogers & Goffigon. Trimmings. Almost all from natural fibers.

SANDERSON

4th floor • Tel: (212) 319-7220 • Fax: (212) 593-6184

Fabrics and wallcoverings, mostly from England. Furniture, antiques and accessories.

SONIA'S PLACE

19th floor • Tel: (212) 355-5211 • Fax: (212) 355-0288

Wallcoverings, wallpaper, fabrics, cork for walls and architectural mouldings.

JIM THOMPSON

10th floor • Tel: (212) 758-5357 • Fax: (212) 753-4372

Fabrics for home furnishings. Household name in silks.

TRAVERS

15th floor • Tel: (212) 888-7900 • Fax: (212) 888-6488

Decorative fabrics and wallcoverings.

WESTGATE FABRICS, INC.

4th floor • Tel: (212) 421-3142 • Fax: (212) 421-4245

Fabrics.

WHITTAKER & WOODS

14th floor • Tel: (212) 593-9787 • Fax: (212) 593-9771

Decorative fabrics and wallpaper from England.

WOLF-GORDON

15th Floor • Tel: (212) 319-6800 • Fax: (212) 319-7262

Wallcoverings and upholstery fabrics.

ZIMMER + ROHDE

16th floor • Tel: (212) 758-5357 • Fax: (212) 753-4372

Multi-line fabric showroom and a line of reproduction antique furniture.

Flooring

HOBOKEN FLOORS, INC.
2nd floor • Tel: (212) 759-5917 • Fax: (212) 593-0268
Custom hardwood flooring, installation and refinishing.

LOCKWOOD, HERRING, ROYCE
15th floor • Tel: (212) 644-0440 • Dan D'Allara
Floor covering: carpet, wood and tile.

SHELLY TILE LTD.
8th floor • Tel: (212) 832-2255 • Fax: (212) 832-0434 • Shelly Cohen
Ceramic, tile, marble, granite, limestone and other stone materials
for floors and walls. Custom fabrication of tabletops and
countertops.

Furniture

AMBIENCE/ISABEL MITCHELL
9th floor • Tel: (212) 688-0170 • Fax: (212) 421-5879
Custom furniture for residential and contract.

AVERY BOARDMAN/HEAD-BED
4th floor • Tel: (212) 688-6611 • Fax: (212) 838-9046
Sofas, sofa beds, chairs and all forms of custom bedding.

BIELECKY BROTHERS, INC.
8th floor • Tel: (212) 753-2355 • Fax: (212) 751-9369
Fine quality wicker, cane and rattan furniture handmade in New York.

BRUETON INDUSTRIES, INC.
8th floor • Tel: (212) 838-1630 • Fax: (212) 838-1652
Large selection of fine furniture for residential and commercial installations utilizing stainless steel, stone, glass. Tables, seating and
lighting.

ILANA GOOR
2nd floor • Tel: (212) 421-9114 • Fax (212) 421-9115
Fountains and garden furniture.

CAROL GRATALE INC.

9th floor • Tel: (212) 838-8670 • Fax: (212) 593-9047

Bronze and iron furniture, tables, lamps, lighting.

JULIA GRAY LTD.

7th floor • Tel: (212) 223-4454 • Fax: (212) 223-4503 • Julia Gray • French, Spanish and Russian spoken

18th- and 19th-century antique furniture, lighting and accessories. Reproductions of antique furniture. Specialist in painted furniture and decorations.

DAKOTA JACKSON, INC.

5th floor • Tel: (212) 838-9444 • Fax: (212) 758-6413

Dining chairs, lounge seating, library chairs, desks and occasional tables.

MASON-ART INC.

4th floor • Tel: (212) 371-6868 • Fax: (212) 371-6597

Designers and manufacturers of custom-upholstered furniture.

LEWIS MITTMAN INC.

9th floor • Tel: (212) 888-5580 • Fax: (212) 371-5061 • Steven Mittman • Spanish spoken

Reproduction furniture, antiques and upholstery.

NICHOLAS ANTIQUES

10th floor • Tel: (212) 688-3312 • Fax: (212) 688-0425

Antique and reproduction furniture. Small furniture, lighting.

PALISANDER, LTD.

8th floor • Tel: (212) 755-0120 • Fax: (212) 755-1893

Furniture and accessories from the Far East, including antiques and some reproductions.

SILAS SEANDEL STUDIO

15th floor • Tel: (212) 371-6726 • Fax: (212) 750-0914

Sculptured furniture, sculpture and fountains.

TUITE DIGIORGIO TABLES & CHAIRS

3rd floor • Telfax: (212) 751-7470 • Denise Tuite, Terri DiGiorgio

Reproductions of custom tables, chairs of the 18th and 19th centuries, French, Italian, English and Biedermeier. Desks, iron beds.

WALTERS WICKER

15th floor • Tel: (212) 758-0472 • Fax: (212) 826-6775

Excellent collection of wicker, bamboo and rattan furniture. Also fabrics and other furniture lines.

General

ALFINO/FINE ARTS

9th floor • Tel: (212) 832-2880 • Fax: (212) 754-2186 • Robert O. Longo • Spanish spoken

Complete custom-upholstery service and casegoods. Fine furniture reproductions, fabric and leather. Specialist in hand-stitched construction and the use of white goose down and feathers.

ROGER ARLINGTON, INC.

14th floor • Tel: (212) 752-5288 • Fax: (212) 935-5195

Fabric, furniture, wallcoverings, lamps, lighting, metal furniture and accessories.

BEACON HILL

3rd floor • Tel: (212) 421-1200 • Fax: (212) 826-5053

Furniture, fabrics, accessories and some antiques.

NANCY CORZINE

8th floor • Tel: (212) 758-4240 • Fax: (212) 758-5644

Furniture, fabrics, accessories, all Corzine designs.

CROSBY-MCNEILL LIMITED

4th floor • Tel: (212) 355-5587 • Fax: (212) 308-1067

Fabrics, wallcoverings, murals, contract and residential furnishings.

DECORATORS WALK

18th floor • Tel: (212) 319-7100 • Fax: (212) 752-5781   .

Fabrics, furniture, wallpaper, accessories.

DESIGN 18

4th floor • Tel: (212) 753-8666 • Fax: (212) 753-1088

Reproductions, antique furniture, paintings, prints.

DONGHIA FURNITURE/TEXTILES

12th floor • Tel: (212) 935-3713 • Fax: (212) 935-9707

Furniture and fabrics.

ESPACE TRIANON

16th floor • Tel: (212) 317-8909 • Fax: (212) 317-8911

French decorative products: country and traditional furniture, fabrics, trimmings, lighting and objets d'art.

EDWARD FERRELL LTD.

5th floor • Tel: (212) 758-5000 • Fax: (212) 758-5021

Custom upholstery and casegoods, sleep chairs and sofas.

THE FRIENDLY LYON

14th floor • Tel: (212) 319-3005 • Fax: (212) 750-5767

Furniture, fine art, fabrics and wallpaper.

HINSON & COMPANY

7th floor • Tel: (212) 688-5538 • Fax: (212) 753-8092

Wallpapers, fabrics, decorative accessories and lighting. Representative for Ralph Lauren fabrics and wallpaper.

HOLLY HUNT NEW YORK

6th floor • Tel: (212) 755-6555 • Fax: (212) 755-6578

Furniture, accessories and fabrics.

CHRISTOPHER HYLAND INCORPORATED

17th floor • Tel: (212) 688-6121 • Fax: (212) 688-6176

Fabrics, wallpaper, trimmings, furniture.

INNOVATIONS IN WALLCOVERINGS INC.

17th floor • Tel: (212) 308-1179 • Fax: (212) 832-3876

Wallcoverings, lighting, furniture and textiles.

KIRK-BRUMMEL

5th floor • Tel: (212) 477-8590 • Fax: (212) 752-7914

Fabrics, wallcoverings, furniture, lamps and lighting, decorative accessories.

LORIN MARSH LTD.

7th floor • Tel: (212) 759-8700 • Fax: (212) 644-5849

Custom tables to specifications.

THE MASLOW GROUP

5th floor • Tel: (212) 753-7920 • Fax: (212) 421-7079

Furniture, accessories and lighting.

J.R. MILLER ASSOCIATES
15th floor • Tel: (212) 980-2037 • Fax: (212) 223-0251
Fabrics, wallpaper, furniture, accessories.

MIRAK
5th floor • Tel: (212) 759-7656 • Fax: (212) 759-7665
Contemporary and traditional furniture, lighting and textiles.

CHRISTOPHER NORMAN
16th floor • Tel: (212) 644-4100 • Fax: (212) 644-4124
This showroom represents some of the best lines from France. Fabrics, furniture, lighting, carpets. Custom upholstery.

JOHN ROSSELLI & ASSOCIATES
7th floor • Tel: (212) 593-2060 • Fax: (212) 832-3687
Top showroom: furniture, lighting, upholstery, decorative accessories. Represents Keller Williams, Niermann Weeks, Ironware International and John Stefanides. Nice people.

SANDERSON
4th floor • Tel: (212) 319-7220 • Fax: (212) 593-6184
Fabrics, wallcoverings, furniture, antiques, decorative accessories.

J. ROBERT SCOTT & ASSOCIATES
2nd floor • Tel: (212) 755-4910 • Fax: (212) 755-4957
Furniture, textiles and accessories. A great pleasure.

SIRMOS
16th floor • Tel: (212) 371-0910 • Fax: (212) 752-0121
Lighting: chandeliers, pendants, table lamps; furniture, mirrors, tables, accessories, consoles. Custom fabrication.

STARK CARPET CORPORATION/OLD WORLD WEAVERS
11th floor • Tel: (212) 752-9000 • Fax: (212) 888-4257
Carpets, fabrics, furniture, antiques, cocktail tables, wood flooring, custom carpets, Axminster and Wilton woven carpet, needlepoints, Oriental and antique rugs.

SUMMERHILL LTD.
5th floor • Tel: (212) 935-6376 • Fax: (212) 935-7957
Fabric, wallcoverings, bed linen, lamps, contemporary furniture.

VAUGHAN/CHELSEA TEXTILES
9th floor • Tel: (212) 319-7070 • Fax: (212) 319-7766
Reproduction antique furniture, rugs, all types of lighting, custom lampshades, needlepoint pillows in vintage designs, accessories.

Leather

EDELMAN LEATHER, LTD.
2nd floor • Tel: (212) 751-3339 • Fax: (212) 319-7108 • Cheryl Mendenhall

Specialists in leather. High-quality leathers for upholstery, walls and floors. Decorative leathers; antiqued leathers.

Lighting

AMERICAN GLASS LIGHT COMPANY
5th floor • Tel: (212) 371-4800 • Fax: (212) 371-4874

Residential lighting. Wallpaper and trimmings.

LAMPWORKS INC.
4th floor • Tel: (212) 750-1500 • Fax: (212) 750-1671 • Bebe Regnier

Hand-crafted classic and antique lighting; custom silk shades; American and primitive antiques.

SANDER LAMPS
2nd floor • Tel: (212) 752-9150 • John Sander

Lamps.

Marble

FORO MARBLE CO., INC.
4th floor • Tel: (212) 752-2677 • Fax: (212) 371-6954

Importers, fabricators and installers of marble and fine stone.

MARBLE & STONE CREATIONS, INC.

Telfax: (212) 750-6872

Marble/stone sculptural fountains, sinks, fireplaces, furniture. Gregory Muller's carving is superb.

Pillows

PILLOW FINERY
8th floor • Telfax: (212) 752-9603 • Anika Reiner • Prices high

Stock and custom-made throw pillows, antique and vintage.

Sculpture

SILAS SEANDEL STUDIO, INC.
15th floor • Tel: (212) 371-6726 • Fax: (212) 750-0919
Furniture in metal, brass, copper, bronze, pewter. Decorative accessories in metal. Metal sculptures.

Tapestries

PLACE DES ARTES
6th floor • Tel: (212) 750-8092 • Fax: (212) 832-2118
French tapestries of the 17th, 18th and 20th centuries.

Trimmings

HOULES-USA
1st floor • Tel: (212) 935-3900 • Fax: (212) 935-3923
French handmade trimmings, tassels, braids, home accessories, stools and screens. Very high quality.

PASSEMENTERIE, INC.
2nd floor • Tel: (212) 355-7600 • Fax: (212) 355-1350
American made trimmings, tassels, braids, ropes.

Wallcoverings

GENERAL WALLCOVERINGS
14th floor • Tel: (212) 826-0030 • Fax: (212) 755-9812
Featuring wallcoverings by Sanitas, Fashion, Essex, Genan, Bolta.

QUADRILLE WALLPAPERS & FABRICS, INC.
14th floor • Tel: (212) 753-2995 • Fax: (212) 826-3316
Quadrille designs of wallpapers and fabrics and the lighting, tables and accesssories of M.E. Dupont from France.

WHITTAKER & WOODS
14th floor • Tel: (212) 593-9787 • Fax: (212) 593-9771
Decorative fabrics and wallpaper from England. Four manufacturers: Cole & Son, Harlequin, Warner of London and Zoffany.

ZUBER & CIE

1st floor • Tel: (212) 486-9226 • Fax: (212) 754-6166 • Gina Farahnick
• French spoken

Superb quality wallpaper, scenes, wall murals, architectural elements, trompe l'oeil, ceiling papers, fabrics, trimmings, borders.

Windows

HANMARS POTPOURI/WINDOWS PLUS, INC.

14th floor • Tel: (212) 355-5115

Custom window treatments: shutters, Romans, draperies. Genuine and stenciled fur, rugs, bedspreads and skins for upholstery.

WINDOW MODES LTD.

16th floor • Tel: (212) 752-1140 • Fax: (212) 355-7764

Custom window treatments, manually operated and motorized shutters, wood blinds, draperies, valances, solar shading systems, handwoven blinds and Shoji screens.

WINDOW TECH, INC.

1st floor • Tel: (212) 688-1181 • Fax: (212) 688-1182

Custom window treatments.

✠ Decorative Arts Center

305 East 63rd Street, New York, NY 10021 • Tel: (212) 838-7736 •
Mon-Fri 9:00-5:00 • Hours vary: call first • Trade only

Art Galleries

HARTMAN • RARE ART, INC.

16th floor • Tel: (212) 207-3800 • Fax: (212) 207-4452

Chinese and Japanese works of art; European and American silver.

REHS GALLERIES

9th floor • Tel: (212) 355-5710 • Fax: (212) 355-5742

Fine British, European and American paintings from the 19th and 20th centuries.

Furniture

CUMBERLAND INTERNATIONAL, INC.

11th floor • Tel: (212) 207-4700 • Fax: (212) 207-8399

Contemporary furniture for residential and contract. Seating, conference tables, dining tables, low tables, desks, credenzas and cabinet wall systems.

DUX

1st floor • Tel: (212) 752-3897

Contemporary furniture. European manufacturer of upholstery, bedding and wall systems. Contract and residential.

ICF • UNIKA VAEV • NIENKAMPER

7th floor • Tel: (212) 750-0900 • Fax: (212) 593-1152

Modern furniture by international designers for residential and contract; upholstery fabrics.

CY MANN INTERNATIONAL

6th floor • Tel: (212) 758-6830 • Fax: (212) 758-6735

A collection of contract and residential contemporary furniture, lighting and accessories.

M2L, INC.

11th floor • Tel: (212) 832-8222 • Fax: (212) 832-8276

Internationally recognized distributor of fine furnishings for residential and commercial applications. Custom facilities available.

SMITH & WATSON

10th floor • Tel: (212) 355-5615 • Fax: (212) 371-5624

Fine English 18th- and early 19th-century antiques and reproductions: residential and contract. Restoration of antiques and reproductions. Superb cabinetmakers. Their round dining tables are remarkable.

General

DAVID BARRETT, INC.

12th floor • Tel: (212) 688-0950 • Fax: (212) 752-4102

Antiques, reproductions, custom furnishings, accessories and lighting. Great imaginative choice and fine custom work.

YALE R. BURGE

1st floor • Tel: (212) 838-4005 • Fax: (212) 838-4390

French, English and Oriental antique and reproduction furniture. Lamps, mirrors and decorative accessories.

NANCY CORZINE

4th floor • Tel: (212) 758-4240 • Fax: (212) 758-5644 • Denise Kirsch • Prices high

Furniture, fabrics, antiques, lamps, mirrors and accessories.

ANTHONY LAWRENCE

9th floor • Tel: (212) 888-1771 • Fax: (212) 888-1975

Upholstered furniture, custom upholstery, window treatments, wall upholstery and slip covers.

P D DESIGN STUDIO LTD./PHILIP DANIEL

9th floor • Tel: (212) 832-0333 • Fax: (212) 832-0336

Custom upholstery, furniture, accessories, fabrics and rugs: residential and contract.

JOHN F. SALADINO FURNITURE, INC.

14th floor • Tel: (212) 752-2440 • Fax: (212) 838-4933

Distinguished furnishings, antiques: residential and contract.

TROUVAILLES, INC./MEYER GUNTHER MARTINI, INC.

12th floor • Tel: (212) 759-7330

Manufacturer of reproductions of traditional and country French and English furniture. Antiques and accessories. All periods of French upholstered and occasional furniture.

WOOD & HOGAN

5th floor • Tel: (212) 355-1335 • Fax: (212) 752-1526

Top-quality English reproductions, made in England, and upholstered furniture.

♜ Decorators Center Building

315 East 62nd Street • 3rd floor • New York, NY 10021 • Mon-Fri • Mostly trade only

MARVIN ALEXANDER, INC.

Tel: (212) 838-2320 • Fax: (212) 754-0173 • Mon-Fri 9:00-5:00 • David Reitner • Prices high

Extensive and very fine collection of 18th century through Art Deco lighting and accessories in crystal, wood, iron, tole and bronze, plus a very large selection of reproduction sconces.

CHRYSTIAN AUBUSSON, INC.

Tel: (212) 755-2432 • Mon-Fri 9:30-5:00 • French and German spoken • Prices high

French furniture, mirrors, decorative accessories and bibelots of the 18th and 19th centuries.

OBJETS PLUS INC.

Telfax: (212) 832-3386 • Mon-Fri 10:00-5:00 • Victor Alonzo and Roger Gross • French, Italian, Spanish, Portuguese and German spoken • Prices high

Fine French and Continental furniture of the 18th and 19th centuries. Mirrors, bronzes, lamps, porcelains and chandeliers.

OLD VERSAILLES ANTIQUES

Tel: (212) 421-3663 • Mon-Fri 12:00-5:00 • Charles Kriz • Prices high

French and Continental furniture, paintings and objets d'art.

PARIS ANTIQUES, INC.

Telfax: (212) 421-3340 • Mon-Fri 11:00-5:00 • Ben Passalacqua • French and Italian spoken • Prices medium

French and Continental furniture and accessories of the 18th and 19th centuries.

♛ The Fine Arts Building

232 East 59th Street, New York, NY 10022 • Tel: (212) 759-6935 • Fax: (212) 758-7598 • Mon-Fri 9:00-5:00 • Trade only

Antiques

FRANK KAY LTD.

6th floor • Tel: (212) 758-0917 • Fay Kay • Prices medium

18th- and 19th-century Oriental and European decorative accessories: porcelain, bronze, lacquer, brass, vases, boxes, planters, lamp bases, figures, bowls, chargers.

Carpets and Tapestries

EDWARD FIELDS, INC.

2nd floor • Tel: (212) 310-0400

Manufacturer of custom wool and silk carpets, rugs and tapestries for residential and commercial interiors. Large selection of plain carpet custom made to size and color.

Fabrics

CHELSEA EDITIONS

6th floor • Tel: (212) 758-0005 • Fax: (212) 758-0006 • Mon-Fri 9:00-5:30 • Russell Bowden • Prices medium to very high

Hand-embroidered textiles, bed covers and cushions; glazed linens and sheers.

TASSELS & TRIMS

6th floor • Tel: (212) 754-6000 • Fax: (212) 754-6002

French and Italian fabrics, wallpapers and trimmings. Furnishings and decorative accessories.

Furniture

RON SEFF

4th floor • Tel: (212) 935-0970

Contemporary custom furnishings in metal, glass, stone, exotic woods, shagreen, parchment, fantasy, faux.

Lampshades

ABAT-JOUR CUSTOM LAMPSHADES CORP.

6th floor • Tel: (212) 753-5455 • Fax: (212) 753-5456 • Patricia Sullivan • Spanish, German, Portuguese and Korean spoken • Prices high

Custom lampshades to the decorating trade.

General

RUTH CAPLAN LTD.

4th floor • Tel: (212) 826-3756 • Fax: (212) 826-3792 • Mon-Fri 9:00-5:00 • Ruth Caplan • Prices medium to high

Exclusive unique fabrics, custom trimmings, wallcoverings and furnishings for high-end residential interiors.

ROSE CUMMING

5th floor • Tel: (212) 758-0844 • Fax: (212) 888-2837

Fabrics: chintz, silk, and woven; wallpaper; custom-made sofas, chairs and other furniture; antiques and decorative accessories.

JACK LENOR LARSEN

Street entrance and mezzanine • Tel: (212) 462-1300

A fabric legend: textiles, leather, carpets and furniture. Conrad sunshades, silk dynasty fabrics and wallcoverings, and the European textiles of Zimmer + Rhode.

RANDOLPH & HEIN, INC.

Lobby, lower lobby and 3rd floor • Tel: (212) 826-9898 • Fax: (212) 826-1033

High quality furnishings, wide fabric line, leather, lighting, mirrors, wallcoverings and accessories. Manufacture a collection of fine upholstery and casegoods. Their oversized sofas and armchairs are marvellous.

♛ 56th Street Art and Antiques Center

160 East 56th Street, New York, NY 10022 • Tel: (212) 755-4252 • Fax: (212) 207-4107 • Mon-Sat 10:00-6:00 • Open to the public

ANTIQUE INTERIORS

Gallery C1 • Tel: (212) 486-1673

Collection of superb antique European rugs and tapestries. Restoration services.

BEST OF FRANCE ANTIQUES

Gallery C4 • Tel: (609) 397-9891

Fine 19th-century furniture, bronze and marble sculpture.

MARIE E. BETTELEY

Gallery 6 • Tel: (212) 888-7796

Specializing in Faberge, Imperial Russian works of art, antique and estate jewelry.

MERCIA BROSS ANTIQUES

Gallery 4 • Tel: (212) 355-4422

Antique furniture, ceramics, paintings and art objects.

THE CONSIGNMENT SHOP

Gallery M1 • Tel: (212) 317-1180

Fine decorative furniture and accessories.

GALLE GALLERY

Gallery 7 • Tel: (212) 752-5203 • Fax: (212) 207-4107 • Rosa Soleimani and Roya Farassat • Persian and some French spoken

Hand-painted lamps, lampshades; antique Aubusson and tapestry pillows; custom work and repair.

J.M.S. & EVA, LTD.

Gallery 8 • Tel: (212) 593-1113

Antique jewelry and objets de vertu.

LENORE MONLEON

Gallery 8 • Tel: (212) 750-0470

18th- and 19th-century art and decorative objects.

RARITY COLLECTORS

Gallery C3 • Tel: (212) 755-4252

18th- and 19th-century furniture, silver, and accessories.

NEIL J. SCHERER

Gallery 3 • Tel: (212) 759-8394

19th- and 20th-century American and European paintings. Marine paintings.

BENNETT SMITH

Gallery M2 • Tel: (212) 319-2223

Museum quality custom frames and restoration.

SOLEIMANI ANTIQUES

Gallery C6 • Tel: (212) 755-4252 • Fax: (212) 207-4107 • Ben Soleimani • Spanish, French and Italian spoken

Baroque and Rococco antiques with rich veneers and gilt.

TURNER ANTIQUES, LTD.

Gallery 2 • Tel: (212) 935-1099 • William Turner

High-quality late 19th-century English and American furniture and decorative arts: Aesthetic, Neo-Gothic, Anglo-Japanese. Masterpieces by Herter Brothers, Morris, Dresser and others.

WINDSOR ANTIQUES

Gallery C7 • Tel: (212) 319-1077 • Fax: (212) 319-1169 • Mousa Khouli

Antiquities, seals and cylinder seals, terra cotta. Ancient jewelry, Roman glass, European porcelain, Judaic and Islamic artifacts. 19th-century artifacts and relics.

♨ Interior Design Building

306 East 61st Street, New York, NY 10021 • Tel: (212) 838-7042 • Fax: (212) 755-3987 • Mon-Fri 9:00-5:00 • Mainly trade • Street level open to the public

AGN INC.

3rd floor • Tel: (212) 826-1080 • Fax: (212) 593-3863 • Antoinette Nizza

Custom window treatments, full line of draperies, shutters, motorized window treatments, wood blinds, custom woven woods and solar shades.

CHARLES H. BECKLEY

4th floor • Tel: (212) 759-8450 • Fax: (212) 759-8806 • Ted Marschke

Complete line of custom-made bedding.

BUDD LOOMS

6th floor • Tel: (212) 758-4460 • Fax: (212) 888-2845

Fine quality rugs and carpets: contract and residential.

DELIA ASSOCIATES AND NEW HEARTH SHOWROOM

6th floor • Tel: (212) 753-5345 • Fax: (212) 753-5391 • Spanish spoken

Display showroom for high-end kitchen appliances: Asko, Viking, Abbaka Hoods, Dakor, Vent-A-Hood, Venmar Hoods.

THE DINING TRADE, INC.

3rd floor • Tel: (212) 755-2304 • Fax: (212) 755-2305 • Claudia Aronow-Roush • French and Italian spoken

Antique dining tables from England, Scotland and France and complete sets of chairs; new and old accessories.

EPEL & LACROZE, INC.

2nd floor • Tel: (212) 355-0050 • Fax: (212) 355-4895 • French and Spanish spoken

17th- and 18th-century English and Continental antiques.

GORALNICK-BUCHANAN

2nd floor • Tel: (212) 644-0334 • Fax: (212) 644-0904 • French spoken

Architecture and design studio in 4,000-square-foot loft space of decorative furniture and arts.

MEL HAMMOCK & CO.

6th floor • Tel: (212) 755-7317 • Fax: (212) 755-8410 • Mel Hammock

Designers of interior displays and decorations for interior merchandising.

HISTORICAL DESIGN COLLECTION

Street level • Tel: (212) 593-4528 • Fax: (212) 715-9905

Gallery of 20th-century decorative arts, 1880 to 1960.

KRAFT HARDWARE, INC.

Street level • Tel: (212) 838-2214 • Fax: (212) 644-9254 • Jack Randolph • Visa and MC

Kitchen, bath and architectural decorative door and window hardware and bath accessories.

DENNIS MILLER ASSOCIATES, INC.

4th floor • Tel: (212) 355-4550 • Fax: (212) 355-4495 • Dennis Miller • French and Italian spoken

Contemporary and classic modern furniture, American and European designs.

SENTIMENTO, INC.

3rd floor • Tel: (212) 750-3111 • Fax: (212) 750-3839 • Toby Landey

French, English and Continental furniture and decorative accessories, primarily 18th and 19th centuries. Original drawings.

TOWN AND COUNTRY ANTIQUES

6th floor • Tel: (212) 752-1677 • Marlene Benninger

English and Continental antique furniture and accessories.

UNCOMMON DESIGN

3rd floor • Tel: (212) 751-5566 • Fax: (212) 752-8782

Contemporary and custom designs; transitional furniture and accessories.

BUNNY WILLIAMS INCORPORATED

5th floor • Tel: (212) 207-4040 • Fax (212) 207-4353 • Bunny Williams

Interior design and furnishings.

♛ The Manhattan Art & Antiques Center

1050 Second Avenue, New York, NY 10022 • Tel: (212) 355-4400 • Fax: (212) 355-4403 • Mon-Sat 10:30-6:00, Sun 12:00-6:00 • Open to the public

Over 100 major antique shops and galleries under one roof.

ADDITIONS, LTD./RITA SACKS

Gallery #66 • Tel: (212) 421-8132

20th-century furniture, decorations, art glass, paintings, jewelry.

AFRICAN HEMINGWAY GALLERY

Galleries #96-97 • Telfax: (212) 838-3650 • Brian Gaisford • Spanish and French spoken

African art: sculptures in wood and stone, paintings. African photographic safaris arranged.

ALEXANDER'S ANTIQUES

Gallery #43 • Tel: (212) 935-9386

Islamic art and antiques.

ALTER SILVER GALLERY CORP.

Gallery #50 • Tel: (212) 750-1928 • Fax: (718) 991-6706

American and European silver, Imperial Russian art and objets de vertu; orders and military decorations.

ANGELA & J. GALLERY

Gallery #68 • Tel: (212) 838-1688

19th-century Chinese art and furniture, jades and art objects.

THE ANTIQUARIAN

Gallery #14 • Tel: (212) 230-1349

Fine and rare antiques.

ANTIQUE CACHE/TILLIE STEINBERG

Gallery #64 • Tel: (212) 752-0838

English antiques, boxes, bamboo furniture, desks and decorative accessories.

NATALIE BADER

Gallery #40A • Tel: (212) 486-7673

Antique porcelain, silver, jewelry and collectibles.

CLIFFORD BARON

Gallery #18 • Tel: (212) 355-0767 • Fax: (212) 355-4403

Very fine jewelry, collectibles and silver.

SIDNEY BELL FINE ARTS

Gallery #16 • Tel: (212) 486-0715

19th-century American and European paintings.

BELLA ANTIQUES

Galleries #25-26 • Tel: (212) 308-7330

Period antique furniture and accessories.

BIJAN GALLERY

Gallery #50A • Tel: (212) 752-7287

Antique glass, porcelain, miniatures and clocks.

BLUM ANTIQUES, INC.

Gallery #33 • Tel: (212) 759-2055

Antique silver, jewelry, art glass, paintings and collectibles.

GLORIA BOSCARDIN

Gallery #70 • Tel: (212) 980-3268

Picture frames, textiles, fans, beaded bags, desk items, jewelry and collectibles.

PAUL J. BOSCO

Gallery #89 • Tel: (212) 758-2646 • Fax: (212) 355-4403

Artistic and historical bronze, silver and gilt medallions: Renaissance to recent.

A.R. BROOMER LTD.

Gallery #81 • Tel: (212) 421-9530 • Fax: (212) 758-3840

European works of art from the 16th to the 19th century; Chinese blue and white porcelains, 17th and 18th centuries.

FEDERICO CARRERA

Gallery #28 • Tel: (212) 750-2870

18th- and 19th-century French antiques.

ROSALIE CLAUSON

Gallery #12 • Tel: (212) 888-9078

Antique silver, Tiffany silver, vintage Tiffany jewelry and picture frames.

THE DISCERNING I

Gallery #35 • Tel: (212) 753-0885 • Irma Strasser

Porcelain, silver and collectibles.

ESTATE SILVER COMPANY, LTD.

Gallery #65 • Telfax: (212) 758-4858 • Anthony Mammon

Antique sterling silver, old Sheffield and silver plate; American, English, European and Oriental.

THE FELDMAN COLLECTION

Gallery #40 • Tel: (212) 308-5885 • Fax: (212) 355-4403

20th-century decorative arts and jewelry including Handel and Pairpoint lamps, Meissen, Sèvres, glass and perfume bottles.

F & P ASSOCIATES

Gallery #39 • Tel: (212) 644-5885

19th-century French gilded bronzes; Empire and Regency cande-labras and accessories.

JOAN FISCHEL ANTIQUES

Gallery #57 • Tel: (212) 688-5264

European bronzes, porcelains, tapestries, needlepoint and paint-ings.

LAURA FISHER/ANTIQUE QUILTS AND AMERICANA

Gallery #84 • Tel: (212) 838-2596 • Fax: (212) 355-4403

American antique quilts, hooked rugs, textiles, coverlets, paisley shawls, "Beacon" blankets, Marseilles bedspreads, needlework, lin-ens and folk art.

FLYING CRANES ANTIQUES, LTD.

Galleries #55-56 • Tel: (212) 223-4600 • Fax: (212) 223-4601 • Clifford Schaefer

World-wide reputation for rare, museum quality, 18th- and 19th-century Japanese antiques. Available for appraisals.

BERNICE FRIED

Gallery #15 • Tel: (212) 751-1860

Art Nouveau, Art Deco jewelry, silver and collectibles.

GALLERY 6 ANTIQUES/ENTERPRISE GALLERY

Gallery #6 • Tel: (212) 750-3344

French art glass, 19th-century European porcelain and decorative art.

GALLERY 9 ANTIQUES

Gallery #9 • Tel: (212) 753-7212

European, Islamic and Judaic antiques.

GALLERY 47

Gallery #47 • Tel: (212) 888-0165

Perfume bottles 1910-1950: Art Nouveau, Art Deco objects. 1920s lighting. Fashion jewelry.

GALLERY LES LOOMS/SUZANNE C. NAGY

Gallery #59 • Tel: (212) 752-0995 • Fax: (212) 752-0312

16th- to 18th-century tapestries, textiles, carpets, needlepoint. Marble busts and sculpture. Museum quality restoration and hand cleaning.

GAMBLE & CHEVING

Gallery #14 • Tel: (212) 371-4726

Chinese art and antiques: Neolithic to Qing dynasty, mainly Han and Tang. Russian and Greek icons and antique jewelry.

GLUCKSELIG ANTIQUES

Gallery #90 • Tel: (212) 758-1805 • Fax: (212) 355-4403 • Kurt Gluckselig

16th- to 19th-century European works of art, porcelains, enamels, glass, ivories, textiles, bronzes, furniture. Renaissance wood sculpture and tribal arts.

MARCUS GREENBLATT

Gallery #34 • Tel: (212) 838-7199

Gold, silver, diamonds and antiques. Repair service.

HADASSA ANTIQUES GALLERY/KHAYAM ANTIQUES

Galleries #71-75 • Tel: (212) 751-0009

Islamic art, silver, porcelains, paintings, Oriental rugs.

HOFFMAN/GAMPETRO

Galleries #37 & 91 • Tel: (212) 758-1252

Antique silver, porcelain, jewelry, furniture.

NATHAN HOROWICZ

Gallery #82 • Tel: (212) 755-6320

Silver, flatware, Judaica, holloware, Tiffany and Georg Jensen.

INTERTRUS, S & G ANTIQUES

Gallery #60 • Tel: (212) 888-4885

18th- and 19th-century Continental furniture, decorations and accessories.

JEMAKO

Gallery #10A • Tel: (212) 230-1383

Objects of art, enamels and jewelry.

JOSIE, INC.

Gallery #50F • Tel: (212) 838-6841

Diamond and other precious stone jewelry.

R & P KASSAI

Gallery #1 • Tel: (212) 838-7010

Antique American and Continental silverware, Judaica and art objects.

LILLIE KOMENT

Gallery #19 • Tel: (212) 751-0098

Sterling and Continental silver, overlays and collectibles.

BETTY KORN ANTIQUES & JEWELRY

Gallery #32 • Tel: (212) 759-3507

Antiques, jewelry and paintings.

KUN DAO KNIE ART COMPANY

Gallery #83 • Tel: (212) 752-3633

Oriental antiques. Restoration.

LEAH'S GALLERY

Galleries #42 & 81 • Tel: (212) 838-5590

Fine art and decorative accessories.

HABIB LEBTO GALLERY

Gallery #93 • Tel: (212) 308-3516

Bronzes, paintings, silver, porcelains, Judaica and Persian works of art.

MAN-TIQUES, LTD.

Gallery #51 • Tel: (212) 759-1805 • Eleanor Zelin

Antiques and collectors' items for the man: canes, scientifica, medical instruments and sporting commemoratives.

MICHAEL'S ANTIQUES

Galleries #3-4 • Tel: (212) 838-8780

French and Russian art objects.

MORCEAUX CHOISIS ANTIQUES, LTD.

Gallery #41 • Tel: (212) 888-0657

French furniture, European porcelains, paintings and jewelry.

NELSON & NELSON ANTIQUES

Gallery #58 • Tel: (212) 980-5191

Antiques, silver, glass.

OSTIA, INC.

Gallery #15 • Tel: (212) 371-2424

Watches and jewelry.

PISTON'S

Gallery #92 • Tel: (212) 753-8322 • Fay Piston

17th- to 19th-century antique pewter, brass and copper. Tiebacks and andirons.

REGENCY GALLERY, INC.

Gallery #86 • Tel: (212) 688-0042

European and Oriental art objects: bronzes and jade.

RICHFIELD ANTIQUES, INC.

Galleries #94-95 • Tel: (212) 207-4066

Chinese antiques: furniture, ceramics, jades, bronzes, sculpture and painting.

TERRY RODGERS

Galleries #30-31 • Tel: (212) 758-3164 • Fax: (212) 355-4403

19th- and 20th-century antique, vintage and faux jewelry.

ROVER & LORBER N.Y.C.

Gallery #27 • Tel: (212) 838-1302 • Adrienne Lorber

Costume and fine jewelry, bakelite accessories.

SAMUAL SAIDIAN & SONS

Gallery #48 • Tel: (212) 752-2684

Ancient arts and antique jewelry.

N. SAKIEL & SON

Gallery #88 • Tel: (212) 832-8576

Antique furniture, porcelains, silver and bronzes.

SMALL PLEASURES

Gallery #10 • Tel: (212) 688-8510 • Joseph Caravella and Ralph Furst

Estate jewelry.

PAUL STAMATI

Gallery #38 • Tel: (212) 754-4533

Art Nouveau lamps and glass by Gallé, Daum, Tiffany and Lalique. Furniture, etchings and paintings by Louis Icart.

SUCHOW & SEIGEL ANTIQUES

Gallery #81 • Tel: (212) 888-3489 • Fax: (212) 758-3840

18th- and early 19th-century English and Chinese export porcelain, pottery, glass and objets de vertu.

TIBOR'S ANTIQUES
Gallery #76 • Tel: (212) 759-2513
Silver, porcelains, bronzes, collectibles.

TIME GALLERY
Gallery #54 • Tel: (212) 593-2323 • Fax: (212) 593-0111
17th- to 19th-century rare and unusual clocks. Repairs.

TON YING & COMPANY
Gallery #87 • Tel: (212) 751-0134
Chinese and other Oriental works of art.

TRADITIONAL ART GALLERY
Gallery #62 • Tel: (212) 593-0350
Antiques from India, Nepal and Tibet. Manuscripts and calligraphy art.

TREASURES & PLEASURES/BEA LONDON
Gallery #21 • Tel: (212) 750-1929
Cut glass, silver, porcelain, bronzes, jewelry and paintings.

P.M. TUNG ARTS
Galleries #61 & 95 • Tel: (212) 308-7203
Chinese antiques and works of art.

UNIQUE FINDS, INC.
Gallery #36 • Tel: (212) 751-1983 • Fax: (212) 355-4403 • Dom LaRaia
Objects of art and arms and armour. Japanese ivory, bronze, enamels, porcelain. Some Chinese and much European. Jewelry.

JO VENTO
Gallery #8 • Tel: (212) 308-2973
Jewelry, paintings, silver, bronzes and art objects.

JOHN WALKER
Gallery #17 • Tel: (212) 980-2380 • Fax: (212) 355-4403
Antique ivory and 18th- and 19th-century enamels and snuff boxes.

♛ New York Design Center

200 Lexington Avenue, New York, NY 10016 • Tel: (212) 679-9500 •
Fax: (212) 447-1669 • Mon-Fri 9:00-5:00 • Mostly trade

The New York Design Center is one of New York's better sources for residential and contract furnishings. Sixty showrooms on sixteen floors offer an enormous selection of furniture, floor and wall-coverings, fabrics, lighting and accessories.

The New York Design Center has instituted an exciting new innovation. Interior Options offers the out-of-towner, the foreign visitor and the nonprofessional a guidance and buying service. The amenities of the Center include a design research library, a comfortable designers' lounge and frequent exhibitions.

Art Deco

PIERRE COUNOT BLANDIN
Suite 433 • Tel: (212) 679-3106 • Fax: (212) 679-3217

French Art Deco and traditional collectibles: chairs, armchairs, sofas, consoles, tables, desks and casegoods. French Art Deco fabrics.

Art Galleries

PAULINA RIELOFF GALLERY
"Center for Global Cultural Expression"
Suite 1115 • Telfax: (212) 683-1228

Contemporary art, paintings, drawings and sculpture.

Carpets

DAVITIAN RUG COMPANY, INC.
Suite 434 • Tel: (212) 447-6636 • Fax: (212) 686-4278
Distinctive Oriental rugs and fine needlepoints.

RENAISSANCE CARPET & TAPESTRIES, INC.
Suite 431 • Tel: (212) 696-0080 • Fax: (212) 696-4248

Reproductions of Aubusson and Savonnerie carpets, hand woven in the antique manner. Over 150 Aubusson and 30 Savonnerie designs of museum quality available. Custom orders accepted.

Fabrics

INTERNATIONAL LINEN
Suite 225 • Tel: (212) 685-0424 • Fax: (212) 725-0483

Western European linen fabrics. Wallcoverings and custom linen for the bed, bath, table. Contract and residential.

Flooring

AMTICO
Suite 809 • Tel: (212) 545-1127 • Fax: (212) 545-8382

Flooring systems for both commercial and residential. Synthetic process reproducing wood, granite, marble.

CLASSIC TILE INC.
Suite 1409 • Tel: (212) 686-9741 • Fax: (212) 686-9820

A resilient floor covering distributor. Custom floors and custom designs both traditional and unique.

Furniture

AUFFRAY & CO.
Suite 804 • Tel: (212) 889-4646 • Fax: (212) 889-4739

Fine French furniture reproductions of the 17th and 18th centuries.

CALIFORNIA PACIFIC
Suite 1106 • Tel: (212) 696-0361 • Fax: (212) 696-9352

Transitional custom furniture, upholstery and casegoods.

CASA NOVA
Suite 1111 • Tel: (212) 213-2727 • Fax: (212) 213-2914

Contemporary and reproduction furniture hand crafted in Italy, residential and contract. Custom work and standard collections.

THE CLEARANCE CENTER
Suite 1600 • Tel: (212) 889-3422 • Fax: (212) 889-8196

Floor samples and customer cancellations from showrooms in the Design Center: furniture, sofas, chairs, wall systems. All items discounted 20% to 50%.

CRAFTIQUE

Suite 400 • Tel: (212) 481-9513 • Fax: (212) 684-2663

Collection of 18th-century English and American reproductions. Various finish options, color options and color accenting.

FABRIZI CUSTOM FURNITURE

Suite 1012 • Tel: (212) 685-7861 • Fax: (212) 213-1592

Commercial and residential installations: paneling, upholstery, casegoods. Solid wood furniture; dining and occasional tables, consoles, wall units, buffets and bedroom sets. Original antiques and reproductions.

FREDERIC WILLIAMS INTERIORS INC.

Suite 611 • Tel: (212) 686-6395 • Fax: (212) 679-3359

Italian contemporary design furniture.

GF OFFICE FURNITURE LTD.

Suite 1410 • Tel: (212) 447-0111 • Fax: (212) 545-8171

Complete lines of office furniture systems, furniture, modular furniture, seating, files, storage, CAD design assistance.

GIORGIO COLLECTION

Suite 1112 • Tel: (212) 684-7191 • Fax: (212) 725-2683

Contemporary Italian furniture: bedroom, dining, living room and occasional pieces in exotic woods, leathers and fabrics.

GIRARD-EMILIA

Suite 502 • Tel: (212) 679-4665 • Fax: (212) 447-5780

French reproduction furniture.

GORDON INTERNATIONAL

Suite 610 • Tel: (212) 532-0075 • Fax: (212) 779-0147

Classic 20th-century furniture, specializing in Bauhaus seating and office furniture.

GRANGE FURNITURE

Suite 201 • Tel: (212) 685-9057 • Fax: (212) 213-5132

Fine French furnishings: bedroom, dining, living. Upholstery and occasional pieces.

HARDEN FURNITURE

Suite 904 • Tel: (212) 532-4392 • Fax: (212) 532-4397

Traditional and transitional cherry wood and upholstered furniture.

KPS FURNITURE, INC.

Suite 1210 • Tel: (212) 686-7784 • Fax: (212) 689-2982

High-end residential, traditional reproduction furniture imported from Italy and Spain.

M & M SHOWROOMS

Suite 511 • Tel: (212) 683-4704 • Fax: (212) 683-4750

Custom traditional furniture, dining, and occasional tables, buffets, breakfronts, armoires, dressers and night tables. Sofas, headboards, dining and occasional chairs. Traditional mirrors and desks.

MANOIRS DE FRANCE

Suite 901 • Tel: (212) 447-6464 • Fax: (212) 281-0423

Reproductions of French furniture.

MANOR HOUSE LTD.

Suite 905 • Tel: (212) 532-1127 • Fax: (212) 689-7731

Fine English reproduction furniture, custom furniture, lamps, mirrors, pictures.

MCGUIRE

3rd floor • Tel: (212) 779-8810 • Fax: (212) 689-2827

Hand-crafted and hand-designed furniture in rattan, bamboo, teak, Oriental hardwoods.

J. NORMAN ASSOCIATES INC.

14th floor • Tel: (212) 683-1973 • Fax: (212) 683-0194

Manufacturers representative for contract, healthcare, hospitality and institutional furnishings.

ONE ANGELL DESIGN, INC.

Suite 1411 • Tel: (212) 889-3838 • Fax: (212) 889-7944

Finely crafted custom furniture.

PLEXABILITY, LTD.

Suite 506 • Tel: (212) 679-7826 • Fax: (212) 779-9015

Custom manufacture of furniture in acrylic and solid surfaces; countertops and architectural elements.

PRIMASON SYMCHIK

Suite 1301 • Tel: (212) 679-0300 • Fax: (212) 679-5996

Fine quality office furniture, casegoods, seating, trading desks, library furniture. Representatives of Northwood, Dakota Jackson, CBA, Keilhauer and Prismatique.

T & K FRENCH ANTIQUES INC.

Suite 702 • Tel: (212) 213-2470 • Fax: (212) 213-2464

18th- and 19th-century French antiques, French country reproductions, French Drucker cafe chairs. Lighting fixtures.

WOOD-MODE CABINETRY

Suite 815 • Tel: (212) 679-3535 • Fax: (212) 725-3847

Custom cabinets in fine hand-rubbed woods and laminates.

Pianos

MAXIMILIAAN'S HOUSE OF GRAND PIANOS

Main floor • Tel: (212) 689-2177 • Fax: (212) 689-2178

Art case grand pianos in various styles, designs and finishes of famous makers such as Steinway, Bechstein, Erard, Pleyel.

Sleep

DESIGN FOR SLEEP

Suite 513 • Tel: (212) 685-6556 • Fax: (212) 779-3148

Motion products: Barcalounger motion furniture, recliners, sofa beds, sofas, headboards, bedding. Custom upholstery and installation.

General

APROPOS, INC.

Suite 102 • Tel: (212) 684-6987 • Fax: (212) 689-3684

An eclectic mix of home furnishings specializing in custom lighting, upholstery and wood pieces. Some antiques and objets d'art.

BAKER KNAPP & TUBBS

3rd floor • Tel: (212) 779-8810 • Fax: (212) 689-2827

Custom furniture, limited edition antique reproductions, fabrics, decorative accessories and mirrors.

BLAIR HOUSE

Suite 914 • Tel: (212) 889-5500 • Fax: (212) 725-2729

Country painted furniture; English, French, Italian reproductions; upholstery and casegoods; mosaics in one-of-a-kind pieces.

COLOMBO USA

Suite 1009 • Tel: (212) 683-3771 • Fax: (212) 684-0559

European reproductions manufactured in Italy. Specializing in Biedermeier, Empire, French, English and traditional styles in a variety of wood finishes. Lamps, chandeliers, mirrors and accessories.

CONNOISSEUR GALLERY

Suite 810 • Telfax: (212) 683-0380

Oil paintings, hand-colored engravings, custom mirrors. Empire style seating, dining and occasional furniture. French and English country furniture.

DAVID L.

Main and 2nd Floors • Tel: (212) 684-3760 • Fax: (212) 779-7356

Full-service resource for residential furniture. Custom upholstery, leather upholstery, wood and glass dining tables, dining chairs and armoires. Domestic and imported accessories. Custom bedrooms, dining rooms and accessories.

DIRECTIONAL, INC.

Suite 710 • Tel: (212) 696-1088 • Fax: (212) 685-9156

Fine classic, contemporary and Paris Retro upholstery. Occasional and dining tables, throw pillows and throws.

FLOURISHES INC.

Suite 414 • Tel: (212) 779-4540 • Fax: (212) 779-4542

Fabrics and wallcoverings, some furniture and accessories.

GARGOYLES LTD.

Suite 423 • Tel: (212) 448-0335 • Fax: (212) 448-0336

Theme and package decor, visual merchandising for stores and restaurants. Eclectic one-of-a-kind decoratives.

KRAVET INC.

Suite 401 • Tel: (212) 725-0340 • Fax: (212) 684-7350

Fabrics, trimmings, furniture and wallcoverings.

LIGNE ROSET USA

Suites 601/605 • Tel: (212) 685-2238 • Fax: (212) 779-7812

Headquarters for Ligne Roset. Modern French furniture; contract and residential: sofas, sofa beds, beds, tables, rugs, wall units and accessories.

NICOLETTI/ITALIA

Suite 711 • Tel: (212) 889-7474 • Fax: (212) 689-6463

Leather furniture, Italian furniture, wall systems, lighting, occasional tables: all contemporary.

ODEGARD, INC.

Suite 1206 • Tel: (212) 545-0069 • Fax: (212) 545-0298

Knotted Tibetan carpets, hand-woven flatweaves. Hand-painted silk lampshades (Fortuny reproductions) from Italy, handmade silk lamps from Israel.

PANDE CAMERON

Suite 1313 • Tel: (212) 686-8330 • Fax: (212) 686-9496

Oriental carpets, dhurries and kilims from India. Handmade in all sizes to custom order.

PROFILES

Suite 1211 • Tel: (212) 689-6903 • Fax: (212) 685-1807

Custom upholstery and cabinetry, bedroom and occasional furniture. European as well as American.

LOUIS J. SOLOMON, INC.

Suite 1105 • Tel: (212) 545-9200 • Fax: (212) 545-9438

Antique reproduction furniture: 18th-century French, Regency, Biedermeier, Chippendale. Antique reproduction fireplaces and mantles in wood. 100 different carved wood mirrors, sconces and brackets.

TRICONFORT, INC.

Suite 701 • Tel: (212) 685-7035 • Fax: (212) 447-1835

Complete resource for casual furnishings: wood, resin, aluminium, wicker and stone.

CLIFF YOUNG LTD.

Suite 505 • Tel: (212) 683-8808 • Fax: (212) 683-9286

Contemporary and transitional, residential furniture and accessories. Specializing in building custom cabinetry.

Lighting

CALGER LIGHTING INC.
Suite 801 • Tel: (212) 689-9511 • Fax: (212) 779-0721

Table lamps, floor lamps and wall lamps, chandeliers, pendants and wall sconces.

Services

INTERIOR OPTIONS
Suite 420 • Tel: (212) 726-9708 • Fax: (212) 689-4064 • Ms. Michael Love, ASID • Mon-Fri 10:00-4:00

Purchasing and design referral service. Assistance to the consumer in accessing the products generally available only through designers from the closed-to-the-public showrooms. Interior design and decorating consultants.

CARPETS AND TAPESTRIES

ABC CARPET & HOME

888 Broadway, New York, NY 10003 • Tel: (212) 473-3000 • Fax: (212) 777-3713 • Mon-Fri 10:00-8:00, Sat 10:00-7:00, Sun 11:00-6:30 • Prices low to high • Trade discount • Major credit cards

A very large home-furnishing store specializing in antique Oriental carpets, decorative rugs from every rug-weaving country, broadloom and textiles.

AFKARI RUGS ON STONE INC.

211 East 59th Street, New York, NY 10022 • Tel: (212) 481-0200 • Fax: (212) 481-7012 • Mon-Sat 9:00-6:00 • Richard Afkari • German and Persian spoken • Prices high • Trade discount • Major credit cards

Antique and semi-antique European and Persian carpets from the 17th century to the middle of the 20th century.

⚏ BEAUVAIS CARPETS

201 East 57th Street, New York, NY 10022 • Tel: (212) 688-2265 • Fax: (212) 688-2384 • Mon-Fri 9:00-5:30 • David Amini • French spoken • Prices high • Professional discount

Superb antique Oriental carpets from the 17th to the 19th centuries. Tapestries from the 15th century to the early 19th century. Modern and contemporary handmade area rugs, expert wall-to-wall carpet installations. Restoration of antique carpets and tapestries.

BESHAR'S FINE RUGS & ANTIQUES

1513 First Avenue, New York, NY 10021 • Tel: (212) 288-1998 • Fax: (212) 288-3615 • Mon-Fri 10:00-6:00, Sat 10:00-4:00 • Jackie Mackay • French and Persian spoken • Prices medium to high • Trade discount • Major credit cards

Sales and purchase of antique Oriental rugs and antiques. Cleaning and restoration of rugs.

⚏ DORIS LESLIE BLAU GALLERY

724 Fifth Avenue, 6th floor, New York, NY 10019 • Tel: (212) 586-5511 • Fax: (212) 586-6632 • Appointment suggested • Prices high

Magnificent collection of antique European tapestries and European and Oriental carpets.

SIMONA BLAU TAPESTRIES

524 Broadway, Suite 605, New York, NY 10012 • Tel: (212) 226-5145 • Fax: (212) 274-9520 • By appointment • Simona Blau • Spanish and Italian spoken • Prices medium • Professional discount

Modern and contemporary tapestries. Reproductions and custom designs.

VOJTECH BLAU INC.

41 East 57th Street, New York, NY 10022 • Fax: (212) 249-4525 • Mon-Fri 9:00-4:00 • Czech and German spoken • Prices high • Trade discount

Extensive well known collection of European tapestries from the 16th to the 18th centuries and antique Oriental carpets. Restoration of antique tapestries.

Y & B BOLOUR

595 Madison Avenue, New York, NY 10022 • Tel: (212) 752-0222 • Fax: (212) 752-4200 • Mon-Fri 9:00-5:30 • Nader Bolour • Prices medium to high • Trade discount

Decorative carpets and tapestries specializing in 19th- and early 20th-century oversize carpets. Restoration and carpet cleaning.

BROOKE PICKERING MOROCCAN RUGS & TEXTILES

16 East 23rd Street, New York, NY 10010 • Tel: (212) 780-9125 • Fax: (212) 475-7370 • By appointment • Brooke Pickering • Spanish and French spoken • Prices medium • 15% professional discount

Moroccan tribal rugs and weavings, including pile and flatwoven rugs, kilims, pillows and wall hangings: antique and recent.

CENTRAL CARPET

81 Eighth Avenue, New York, NY 10011 • Tel: (212) 741-3700 • Fax: (212) 633-0849 • 426 Columbus Avenue, New York, NY 10024 • Tel: (212) 787-8813 • 7 days 10:00-7:00 • Ike Timianko • Spanish, Hebrew and French spoken • Prices medium • 15% professional discount • Major credit cards

Antique rugs, new and contemporary rugs, Oriental designs and broadloom.

BEN N. CHAFIEIAN

33 East 33rd Street, #1201, New York, NY 10016 • Tel: (212) 686-0208 • Fax: (212) 686-0925 • Mon-Fri 9:00-5:00 • Prices medium to high • Trade discount

Very large collection of antique Oriental carpets from the 1850s to the 1920s.

FIL CARAVAN INC.

301 East 57th Street, New York, NY 10022 • Tel: (212) 421-5972 • Fax: (212) 421-5976 • Mon-Sat 11:00-6:00 • Nabi Israfil • Polish, Turkish, Spanish and Russian spoken • Prices high • Trade discount • Major credit cards, not Amex

Antique Persian, Turkish and Caucasian carpets, kilims and textiles. Wide range of chandeliers: old and new, including Baccarat, old and new and pink. Antique furniture, lighting, samovars and silver.

FLANDERS INC.

164 East 56th Street, New York, NY 10022 • Tel: (212) 319-6252 • Fax: (212) 980-7563 • Mon-Sat 9:30-6:30 • Zeron Ayvazian • French, Turkish, Armenian and Japanese spoken • Prices medium to high • 20% trade discount

European tapestries of the 14th to the 19th centuries, antique European carpets; oil paintings. Tapestry and carpet restoration.

GHIORDIAN KNOT LTD.

1185 Park Avenue, New York, NY 10028 • Tel: (212) 371-6390 • Fax: (212) 289-2622 • By appointment • Barbara Z. Sedlin • Some French, Swedish and Spanish spoken • Prices medium to very high • Professional discount • Major credit cards

European tapestries from the 16th century to contemporary; Oriental carpets from the 17th to the early 20th centuries.

⚐ F.J. HAKIMIAN

136 East 57th Street, New York, NY 10022 • Tel: (212) 371-6900 • Fax: (212) 753-0277 • Mon-Fri 9:30-5:30 • F. Joseph Hakimian • Prices high • 20% professional discount

Antique European and Oriental carpets from the 18th century to Art Deco; antique tapestries. Restoration of carpets and tapestries.

RENATE HALPERN GALLERIES

325 East 79th Street, New York, NY 10021 • Tel: (212) 988-9316 • Fax: (212) 988-2954 • By appointment • Renate Halpern • German spoken • Prices medium to high • Trade only

Antique textiles, tapestries and rugs from Coptic Egypt to the Arts and Crafts period, 1920s, from many countries: Europe, England, Turkey, the Greek islands, Russia, Japan and China.

⚐ MARVIN KAGAN GALLERY

625 Madison Avenue, New York, NY 10022 • Tel: (212) 535-9000 • Fax: (212) 935-7822 • Mon-Fri 9:30-5:30, Sat 10:00-4:30 • Persian and Spanish spoken • Prices high to very high • Amex

Antique Oriental and European carpets and tapestries from the 17th century to the early 19th century. Roman, Byzantine and Persian glass from the 3rd century B.C. to the 11th century. Restoration and cleaning of carpets and tapestries.

KAMALI ORIENTAL RUGS

151 West 30th Street, New York, NY 10001 • Tel: (212) 564-7000 •
Fax: (212) 947-9290 • Mon-Fri 9:00-6:00 • Barry Kamali • Spanish,
German, Italian and Hebrew spoken • Prices medium • 25% trade dis-
count

Antique and semi-antique Oriental rugs. Antique decorative and collector pieces.

KERMANSHAH

57 Fifth Avenue, New York, NY 10003 • Tel: (212) 627-7077 • Fax:
(212) 627-2939 • Mon-Sat 10:00-6:00 • Hamid Kermanshah • Persian, Arabic and Turkish spoken • Prices medium to very high • Major
credit cards

Antique Persian carpets and kilims; 17th- to 19th-century French
tapestries and needlepoint, Aubussons and Savonneries; 18th-cen-
tury Agra. Cleaning, repair and restoration.

KHALILI ORIENTAL RUGS

150 West 30th Street, New York, NY 10001 • Tel: (212) 239-0033 •
Fax: (212) 239-0268 • Mon-Fri 9:00-5:00 • Arsalan Khalili • Prices medium • MC and Visa

Oriental rugs from the 17th century to the present. The antique rugs
are from Persia, India and Turkey. The new rugs from India and
China.

JERRY LIVIAN ANTIQUE RUGS

148 Madison Avenue, 3rd floor, New York, NY 10016 • Tel: (212) 683-
2666 • Fax: (212) 683-2668 • Mon-Fri 9:00-5:00 • Prices medium •
Trade only

Antique and semi-antique Oriental carpets, mostly 19th and early
20th centuries.

MASTOUR GALLERIES INC.

15 East 30th Street, New York, NY 10016 • Tel: (212) 685-0060 • Mon-
Fri 10:00-5:00 • Joseph Mastour • Prices medium to high • Trade discount • Major credit cards

Antique European and Oriental rugs from the 19th century to contemporary. Cleaning and restoration.

MEGERIAN BROTHERS ORIENTAL RUGS INC.

262 Fifth Avenue, New York, NY 10001 • Tel: (212) 684-7188 • Fax:
(212) 684-8018 • Mon-Fri 9:00-5:00 • Yeran Megerian • French Spanish, Turkish, Arabic and Armenian spoken • Prices high • Trade only •
MC and Visa

All sorts of antique Oriental and decorative rugs, Aubussons, tapestries, Savonneries, needlepoints. Cleaning and restoration.

METROPOLITAN CARPET GALLERY

900 Broadway, Suite 202, New York, NY 10003 • Tel: (212) 529-2200 • Fax: (212) 529-2559 • Sun-Fri 10:00-5:00 • Jacob Galar • Hebrew and Farsi spoken • Prices medium • 20% trade discount • Major credit cards

Antique Oriental rugs and European tapestries; decorative rugs and collectibles. Cleaning, restoration and appraisals.

ABRAHAM MOHEBAN & SON ANTIQUE CARPETS

139 East 59th Street, 3rd floor, New York, NY 10022 • Tel: (212) 758-3900 • Fax: (212) 758-3973 • Mon-Fri 9:30-5:30 • Rom Moheban • Persian and Spanish spoken • Prices high • 25% trade discount

Antique Oriental and European carpets and tapestries. Expert restorations and hand cleaning of carpets.

⚐ FRED MOHEBAN GALLERY

750 Fifth Avenue, New York, NY 10019 • Tel: (212) 397-9060 • Fax: (212) 581-0511 • Mon-Fri 9:30-5:30 • Fred and Janet Moheban • Prices high • 20% trade discount

Rare and unusual decorative Oriental and European carpets; antique tapestries.

⚐ PARVIZ NEMATI ORIENTAL & EUROPEAN RUGS & TAPESTRIES

510 Madison Avenue, New York, NY 10022 • Tel: (212) 486-6900 • Fax: (212) 755-8428 • Mon-Fri 9:00-6:00, Sat 10:00-4:00 • Darius Nemati • Spanish, German and French spoken • Prices high • 20% trade discount

Rare antique tapestries from the 15th to the 19th centuries; European and Oriental carpets from the 16th to the 20th centuries. Restoration and appraisals.

PAK GALLERIES ANTIQUES AND RUGS INC.

30 East 30th Street, New York, NY 10016 • Tel: (212) 532-5658 • Fax: (212) 696-4882 • Mon-Sat 10:00-6:00 • Urdu spoken • Prices medium to very high • Trade discount • Major credit cards

Oriental rugs from the 18th century to the present, kilims and decorative pillows. Cleaning and restoration.

THE PERSIAN CARPET GALLERY

33 East 33rd Street, Suite 706, New York, NY 10016 • Telfax: (212) 686-1100 • Mon-Fri 9:30-5:00 • Jamshid Moadab • Persian spoken • Prices medium • Volume discount

Antique Oriental and Persian rugs.

RAFAEL FINE ART, LTD.

1020 Madison Avenue, New York, NY 10021 • Tel: (212) 744-8988 •
Fax: (212) 879-2527 • Mon-Fri 9:00-6:30 • Benjamin Aryeh • Farsi,
Spanish, Portuguese, French and German spoken • Prices very high •
Trade discount

Antique Oriental rugs and carpets from the Caucases, Iran, Turkey,
Russia, China and India. European tapestries from the 16th to the
19th centuries and European and American paintings with a concentration on the 19th century.

RAHMANAN ORIENTAL RUGS

102 Madison Avenue, 9th floor, New York, NY 10016 • Tel: (212) 683-
0167 • Fax: (212) 683-1437 • Mon-Fri 9:00-6:00, Sun by appointment
• Kevin Rahmanan, Ramin S. Hakimi • French, Russian and many other
languages spoken • Prices low to high • 20% trade discount • Major
credit cards

Antique and decorative rugs from Persia, Afghanistan, Turkey, Pakistan, India, China, Caucases and Europe: 1860s to 1930s. Antique European tapestries. Good selection of hook rugs.

THE RUG WAREHOUSE INC.

220 West 80th Street, New York, NY 10024 • Tel: (212) 787-6665 •
Fax: (212) 787-6628 • Mon-Fri, Sat 10:00-6:00, Thu 10:00-8:00, Sun
11:00-5:00 • Larry Feldman • Spanish and French spoken • Prices
medium to very high • 20% trade discount • Major credit cards

Antique and semi-antique, 18th century to the present, rugs, carpets and textiles from Persia, Turkey, Afghanistan, India and China.

SAFAVIEH CARPETS

238 East 59th Street, New York, NY 10022 • Tel: (212) 888-0626 • Fax:
(212) 753-1261
153 Madison Avenue • Tel: (212) 683-8399
902 Broadway • Tel: (212) 477-1234 • 6 days 9:00-6:00 • Arash Yaraghi
• Persian and most other languages spoken • Prices medium to high •
30% trade discount • Major credit cards

Antique Oriental and European carpets and tapestries. Cleaning
and restoration.

MARK SHILEN GALLERY

109 Greene Street, New York, NY 10012 • Tel: (212) 925-3394 • Fax:
(212) 219-1390 • Mon-Sat 12:30-7:00, Sun 1:00-6:00 • Mark Shilen •
French spoken • Prices high • Major credit cards

Rugs: old and antique especially kilims, tribal rugs and dhurries.
Textiles for wall hangings.

Contemporary Carpets and Rugs

BROADWAY CARPET

1285 Second Avenue, New York, NY 10021 • Tel: (212) 472-6900 •
Fax: (212) 472-0392 • Mon-Fri 9:30-6:30, Sat 9:30-6:00, Sun 11:00-
5:00 • Pamela Crawford Thomson

Wall-to-wall carpeting, sisel, handmade and machine-made area
rugs.

PATRICIA BURLING/WILLOWWEAVE

37 Wells Road, Monroe, CT 06468 • Tel: (203) 268-4794 • By appointment • Prices medium to high • Some trade discounts • MC and Visa

Handwoven rugs, pillows, throws. Available inventory and custom
orders.

ELIZABETH EAKINS, INC.

21 East 65th Street, 5th floor, New York, NY 10021 • Tel: (212) 628-
1950 • Fax: (212) 628-7696 • Mon-Fri 10:00-5:30 • Prices high • Trade
discount • MC and Visa for cotton rugs only

Custom-designed wool rugs, handwoven and hand-hooked; cotton woven rugs.

EINSTEIN MOOMJY

150 East 58th Street, New York, NY 10022 • Tel: (212) 758-0900 •
Mon-Fri 9:30-6:30, Sat 9:30-6:00 • Prices medium to high • Trade discount • Major credit cards

The carpet department store: Oriental rugs, wall-to-wall carpeting
in wools, sisels and synthetic fibers.

FRENCH ACCENTS RUGS & TAPESTRIES, INC.

102 Madison Avenue, 9th floor, New York, NY 10016 • Tel: (212) 686-
6097 • Fax: (212) 683-1437 • Mon-Fri 9:00-6:00 • Danny S. Shafiian •
Prices medium to high • Trade only

Custom handmade reproductions of Aubusson carpets and tapestries. Reproductions of 18th- and 19th-century carpets and 17th-
to 19th-century tapestries. Made in China.

GANGCHEN CARPET GALLERY

236 Fifth Avenue, New York, NY 10001 • Tel: (212) 532-2600 • Fax:
(212) 532-5230 • Mon-Fri 9:00-5:00 • Beverly Thornton • French, Italian and Spanish spoken • Prices high • Trade only

Hand-knotted Tibetan rugs for the designer market.

VICTOR HENSCHEL FLOORS

215 East 59th Street, New York, NY 10022 • Tel: (212) 688-1732 •
Mon-Fri 9:00-6:00, Sat 10:00-4:00 • Suzan Cohen • Spanish spoken •
Prices medium to high

Custom area rugs and wall-to-wall carpeting. Large selection of
stocked items. Custom hand-painted sisal, jute, floor cloths, stocked
sisels and jutes. Quality synthetic carpets. Woven wool designer
carpets. In-house designer to assist in coloration and design. The
best references.

MR. MOTO'S CUSTOM DESIGNED CARPET

104 Franklin Street, New York, NY 10013 • Tel: (212) 343-2930 • Fax:
(212) 941-9131 • Tue-Thu 10:00-6:00 • Tatsuo Tsujimoto • Japanese •
Prices very high • Trade discount • Major credit cards

Rugs in contemporary designs and custom-designed carpets and
rugs. International clients.

ROUBINI INC.

443 Park Avenue South, 2nd floor, New York, NY 10016 • Tel: (212)
576-1145 • Fax: (212) 576-1545 • Mon-Fri 10:00-5:00 • Mark
Karimzadeh • Prices high • 20% trade discount • Major credit cards

Missoni rug collection; Gianni Versace rug collection.

TIBET CARPET CENTER

127 Madison Avenue, New York, NY 10016 • Tel: (212) 686-7661 •
Fax: (212) 686-7811 • Mon-Sat 10:00-6:00 • Tsering • Tibetan, Nepalese
and Spanish spoken • Prices medium to high • Trade discount • Major
credit cards

Carded, spun, dyed and knotted by hand, room-sized Tibetan carpets. Custom fabrication of carpets. Tibetan antique furniture from
the 16th to 19th centuries, antique chests, altar pieces and boxes.
Tibetan ethnic jewelry.

RONALD WEISS CREATIVE FLOORS

274 Madison Avenue, New York, NY 10016 • Tel: (212) 679-1550 •
Fax: (212) 769-1552 • Mon-Fri 9:00-5:00 • Ronald Weiss • Prices
medium to high • Trade only

Custom carpet: American historic designs of the 19th century.

DECORATIVE ARTS OF THE 20TH CENTURY

A & J 20TH CENTURY DESIGNS

255 Lafayette Street, New York, NY 10012 • Tel: (212) 226-6290 • Tue-Thu 11:00-6:00, Fri-Sat 1:00-5:00 • Ana Azevedo, Jerry Hilden • Portuguese spoken • Prices medium to high • Trade discount • Major credit cards

Designer furniture of the 1940s to 1970s; lighting and home accessories.

CITY BARN ANTIQUES

269 Lafayette Street, New York, NY 10012 • Tel: (212) 941-5757 • 362 Atlantic Avenue, Brooklyn, NY 11217 • Tel: (718) 855-8566 • Fax: (718) 624-2199 • Sat-Sun 12:00-6:00, Mon-Fri by appointment • Steve and Harris Gertz, Brenda Benek • Prices low to medium • Trade discount

Blond Heywood Wakefield originals from the 1930s to 1950s, streamlined machine age pieces; 1930s spun-aluminum hanging lights and accessories. Prop rentals for all types of photo shoots.

CROSBY STUDIO

117 Crosby Street, New York, NY 10012 • Telfax: (212) 941-6863 • Mon-Fri 12:00-6:00 by appointment or by chance • Richard Weissenberger • Prices medium • 10 to 20% professional discount

19th- and 20th-century decorative arts specializing in Venetian, Gothic, Art Nouveau and Moorish taste. Lighting, glass, furniture, objects of art and the unusual. Specialty Venetian glass 1900-1970.

DEPRESSION MODERN

150 Sullivan Street, New York, NY 10012 • Tel: (212) 982-5699 • Wed-Sun 12:00-7:00

1930s American furniture, lighting and accessories.

⚘ DONZELLA

90 East 10th Street, New York, NY 10003 • Tel: (212) 598-9675 • Tue-Sat 12:00-6:30 • Paul Donzella • Spanish, German, Italian and French spoken • Prices medium to high • Amex

1930s, 1940s, 1950s furniture by leading designers.

ELAN

345 Lafayette Street, New York, NY 10012 • Tel: (212) 529-2724 •
Mon-Wed 12:00-7:00, Thu-Sat 1:00-7:00 • Jeff Greenberg • Prices
medium • Major credit cards

Art glass, art pottery, furniture, lighting—all in 20th-century design
from Mission to the 1960s. American and European.

FORTY ONE/LIZ O'BRIEN, INC.

41 Wooster Street, New York, NY 10013 • Tel: (212) 343-0935 • Fax:
(212) 343-0837 • Mon-Fri 10:00-6:00, Sat 12:00-6:00 • Liz O'Brien
and Doria Kalt • Prices medium to high • 15% professional discount

Vintage furniture of the 1940s and 1950s, mostly American, some
French. Specialty: pieces created especially for movie stars.

⬢ BARRY FRIEDMAN LTD.

32 East 67th Street, New York, NY 10021 • Tel: (212) 794-8950 • Fax:
(212) 794-8889 • Tue-Sat 10:00-6:00, Mon by appointment • Scott
Cook, Director • French, German, Italian and Spanish spoken • Prices
high

Early 20th-century avant-garde art and design. 20th-century decorative arts; French furniture and accessories of the late 19th century through 1950.

FULL HOUSE

133 Wooster Street, New York, NY 10012 • Tel: (212) 529-2298 • Fax:
(212) 529-9546 • Mon-Sat 12:00-6:00 • Michel Hurst • French and
Spanish spoken • Prices medium • Major credit cards

Designer furniture of the 1920s to the 1980s. Emphasis on the 1940s
and 1950s.

GALERIE DE BEYRIE

393 West Broadway, 3rd floor, New York, NY 10012 • Tel: (212) 219-
9565 • Fax: (212) 965-1348 • By appointment • Catherine and Stephane
de Beyrie • French spoken • Prices medium • 10% professional discount

French furniture and objects of the creators of the 1940s and 1950s.

GANSEVOORT GALLERY/MARK MCDONALD

72 Gansevoort Street, New York, NY 10014 • Tel: (212) 633-0555 •
Fax: (212) 633-1808 • Tue-Sat 11:00-6:00 • Mark McDonald • Prices
high • Major credit cards

The best of classic 20th-century decorative arts: ceramics, glass,
furniture, lighting, metal.

TIM GLEASON GALLERY

77 Sullivan Street, New York, NY 10012 • Telfax: (212) 966-5777 • By appointment • Tim Gleason

American and English turn-of-the-century decorative arts specializing in furniture of Gustav Stickley and his contemporaries.

⛺ GUERIDON

359 Lafayette Street, New York, NY 10012 • Tel: (212) 677-7740 • Fax: (212) 677-0034 • Mon-Fri 12:30-7:00, Sat 12:00-6:00 • Alfonso Munoz • French and Spanish spoken • Prices medium to high • 20% professional discount • Major credit cards

20th-century furniture and accessories from Deco to the present. Pieces by Perriand, Prouvé, Parisi, Pantin and others. Some interesting prototypes by rising stars among the young New York designers. Exclusive representation of the Brazilian designer Antonio Da Motta.

LEO KAPLAN MODERN

965 Madison Avenue, New York, NY 10021 • Tel: (212) 535-2407 • Fax: (212) 535-2495 • Mon-Sat 10:00-5:30 • Scott Jacobson • All major credit cards

Contemporary glass sculpture and studio/functional furniture.

LIN-WEINBERG GALLERY

84 Wooster Street, New York, NY 10012 • Tel: (212) 219-3022 • Fax: (212) 219-1034 • Tue-Sun 12:00-7:00 • Andy Lin and Larry Weinberg • Prices medium to high • Trade discount • Major credit cards

American and European leading designers of the 1940s and 1950s: furniture, glass lighting, ceramics and decorative accessories.

LOST CITY ARTS

275 Lafayette Street, New York, NY 10012 • Tel: (212) 941-8025 • Fax: (212) 219-2570 • Mon-Fri 10:00-6:00, Sat-Sun 12:00-6:00 • Lloyd Goldsmith • Prices medium • 10% professional discount • Major credit cards

Classics of American design, furniture, lighting, advertising art of the 1920s to the 1960s.

MOBILIER

180 Franklin Street, New York, NY 10013 • Telfax: (212) 334-6197 • Tue-Sat 12:00-7:00 • Patrick Marchand • French spoken • Prices medium to high • 15% trade discount

1940s and 1950s furniture, lighting and objects by French architects and artists.

1950

440 Lafayette Street, New York, NY 10003 • Tel: (212) 995-1950 • Fax: (212) 614-0610 • Mon-Fri 11:00-6:30, Sat 12:00-6:00 • Cristina Grajales • Spanish and French spoken • Prices very high • Some trade discounts

French furniture and lighting by designers from the 1940s and 1950s. Furniture by George Nakashima.

PALUMBO

972 Lexington Avenue, New York, NY 10021 • Telfax: (212) 734-7630 • Mon-Fri 11:00-6:00 • Don Silvey • Prices medium • 10% trade discount

20th-century design: furniture, lighting, mirrors, glass and sculpture.

STUART PARR/PARR STUDIOS

67 Vestry Street, #9A, New York, NY 10013 • Tel: (212) 431-0732 • Fax: (212) 431-0733 • By appointment • Stuart Parr • Prices high

Modern furniture of the 1930s. Specialist in Warren McArthur. Art photography. Prop rentals.

PETER-ROBERTS ANTIQUES INC.

134 Spring Street, New York, NY 10012 • Tel: (212) 226-4777 • Fax: (212) 431-6417 • Mon-Sat 11:00-7:00, Sun 12:00-6:00 • Robert Melita • Italian and French spoken • Prices medium • 10% trade discount

Furniture and accessories of the American Arts and Crafts period 1900 to 1920.

FRANK ROGIN INC.

21 Mercer Street, New York, NY 10013 • Tel: (212) 431-6545 • Fax: (212) 431-6632 • Tue-Sat 12:00-6:00 • Prices high • 15% trade discount

European furniture from the 1930s, 1940s and 1950s.

R.S. ANTIQUES

13 Christopher Street, New York, NY 10014 • Tel: (212) 924-5777 • Mon-Sat 12:00-6:00 • Prices medium • Professional discount

20th-century American pottery, art glass, decorative accessories and jewelry, beginning with Art Nouveau.

MIGUEL SACO GALLERY

37 East 18th Street, 6th floor, New York, NY 10003 • Tel: (212) 254-2855 • Fax: (212) 254-2852 • By appointment • Rafael Rovira • Spanish, French and some Portuguese spoken • Prices medium • Trade discount

Furniture and decorative art objects from the 20th century. Pieces by: Jules Leleu, Majorelle, Gallé, Olbrich, Dufrene, Dominique, Dunand, Ruhlmann, Giacometti, Jean Prouvé, Charles Eames and others.

SECONDHAND ROSE

270 Lafayette Street, New York, NY 10012 • Tel: (212) 431-7673 • Mon-Fri 10:00-6:00, Sun 12:00-6:00 • Suzanne Lipschutz, Martin Dinowitz • Prices high • 15% trade discount • Amex

Early 20th- and some 19th-century exotic furnishings and decorative arts: English Colonial furniture, Moroccan, Turkish, Japanese and Chinese lamps, accessories and furnishings.

FRED SILBERMAN CO.

83 Wooster Street, New York, NY 10012 • Tel: (212) 925-9470 • Fax: (212) 925-3856 • Mon-Sat 11:00-6:30 • Thomas Stewart • Prices medium • Trade discount • All major credit cards

Italian furniture, lighting and decorative accessories from 1925 to 1955.

280 MODERN

280 Lafayette Street, New York, NY 10012 • Tel: (212) 941-5825 • Fax: (212) 274-1612 • Mon-Sat 11:00-7:00 • Rick Gallagher • Trade discounts • All major credit cards

20th century decorative arts, 1920 to 1970. Furniture and tribal art.

UPSTAIRS DOWNTOWN ANTIQUES

12 West 19th Street, New York, NY 10011 • Tel: (212) 989-8715 • Mon-Sat 11:00-6:00, Sun 12:00-6:00 • William Straus • Prices medium to high • Professional discount • Major credit cards

20th-century American design: Art Deco through the 1950s to 1970s. 18th- and 19th-century furniture and lighting. Prop rentals. Upholstery.

WYETH

151 Franklin Street, New York, NY 10013 • Tel: (212) 925-5278 • Fax: (212) 925-5314 • Mon-Sat 11:00-6:00 • John Wyeth • Some French, German and Japanese spoken • Prices high • Trade discount • Major credit cards

Mainly original American and European furnishings and decorative arts of the 20th century. Some 19th century. A selection of custom designs. Showroom items are available for rentals.

ZERO TO SIXTIES

75 Thompson Street, New York, NY 10012 • Tel: (212) 925-0932 • Mon-Sat 12:00-7:00 • Robin Lowe • Trade discount • Major credit cards

Furniture, lighting, Italian glass, chrome objects, clocks, folk art, jewelry and unusual objects from 1800 to 1960.

FABRICS

General

BECKENSTEIN

130 Orchard Street, New York, NY 10002 • Tel: (212) 475-4887 • Fax: (212) 673-8809 • Sun-Fri 9:00-5:30 • Spanish and French spoken • Modest prices • Major credit cards

Good buys in decorator fabrics for upholstery, furniture and walls. Also a wide selection of drapery fabrics.

⚑ BENNISON FABRICS, INC.

76 Greene Street, New York, NY 10012 • Tel: (212) 941-1212 • Fax: (212) 941-5587 • Mon-Fri 10:00-6:00 • Sarah E. O'Neil, Gillian Newberry and Geoff Newberry, Directors • French, Italian and Spanish spoken • Prices very high • Trade discount • MC and Visa

Archive printers of 18th- and 19th-century documents. Highest quality reproduction of English and French fabrics. Beautifully drawn large-scale "Indiennes" and "Arboresques" with subtle muted palette of colors. Large stock available from on site warehouse. Custom coloring for a 25-yard minimum. Upholstered furniture and some accessories.

INTERIORS BY ROYALE

964 Third Avenue, New York, NY 10022 • Tel: (212) 753-4600 • Fax: (212) 753-3343 • Mon-Fri 9:30-6:00 • Italian and Polish spoken • Prices medium • 30% trade discount • Major credit cards

Quality lines of imported fabrics for wall and furniture upholstery. Drapery fabrics. Complete window treatment service. Slipcovers, bedding, trimmings and decorative drapery hardware.

JOE'S FABRIC WAREHOUSE

102 Orchard Street, New York, NY 10002 • Tel: (212) 674-7089 • Fax: (212) 674-6961 • Sun-Fri 9:00-6:00 • Spanish spoken • Prices in a wide range • Trade discounts • Visa and MC

A very good selection of upholstery and drapery fabrics at all prices.

LAURA ASHLEY

398 Columbus Avenue, New York, NY 10024 • Tel: (212) 496-5110 • Mon-Wed 11:00-7:00, Thu-Fri 11:00-8:00, Sat 11:00-7:00, Sun 12:00-6:00 • Prices medium to high • Major credit cards

Full line of fabrics and trimmings.

LAURA ASHLEY HOME

714 Madison Avenue, New York, NY 10021 • Tel: (212) 593-2100 •
Fax: (212) 593-0818 • Mon-Sat 10:00-6:00, Thu 10:00-7:00, Sun
12:00-5:00 • Major credit cards

The full line of their famous prints as well as their latest collection.

LE DECOR FRANCAIS

1006 Lexington Avenue, New York, NY 10021 • Tel: (212) 734-0032 •
Fax: (212) 988-0816 • Mon-Fri 9:30-6:00, Sat 11:00-5:00 • Jacqueline
Coumans • French, Portuguese and Spanish spoken • Prices medium
to high • 20% trade discount • Amex

Excellent choice of high-quality fabrics for: upholstery, draperies,
slipcovers, lampshades. Beautiful trimmings.

PIERRE DEUX FABRICS

870 Madison Avenue, New York, NY 10021 • Tel: (212) 570-9343 •
Fax: (212) 472-2931 • Mon-Sat 10:00-6:00, Thu until 7:00 • Prices
medium to high • Major credit cards

Enchanting lines of fabrics: Les Olivades Collection and the Pierre
Deux line of some of the best Toiles de Jouy available anywhere.
Upholstery-weight woven fabrics, fine lace weaves, border fabrics.
Full line of trimmings, tassels and tiebacks. Coordinating
lampshades from stock or custom made.

▦ SCALAMANDRE

942 Third Avenue, New York, NY 10022 • Tel: (212) 980-3888 • Fax:
(212) 688-7531 • Mon-Fri 9:00-5:00 • Prices high • Trade only • Major
credit cards

Marvellous selection of fabrics, wallcoverings and trimmings for the
high end designer and contract industries.

▦ F. SCHUMACHER & CO.

939 Third Avenue, New York, NY 10022 • Tel: (212) 415-3900 • Fax:
(212) 415-3907 • Mon-Fri 9:00-5:00 • Brigitte Ple • Prices very high •
Trade only

Wide variety of classical fabric for upholstery and wallcovering; trimmings, tassels and tiebacks; furniture, carpets, lighting, mirrors and
accessories for design professionals.

SHEILA'S INTERIORS

274 Grand Street, New York, NY 10002 • Tel: (212) 966-1663 • Fax:
(212) 226-0412 • Sun-Fri 9:00-5:00 • Spanish and Yiddish spoken •
Prices modest • Major credit cards

One of the better shopping experiences for the homemaker in New
York. A very extensive line of discounted fabrics for furniture and
wall upholstering. They have wallpapers, custom bedding and a
new line of custom furniture. They also provide a decorating service and complete window treatments.

SILK SURPLUS

255 East 58th Street, New York, NY 10022 • Tel: (212) 753-6511 • Fax: (212) 980-2057 • Mon-Fri 10:00-5:00, Sat 10:00-5:30 • Prices low to quite high • Trade discounts • Major credit cards

An exciting line of decorator fabrics, trimmings, cording, fringes, tassels, wallcoverings, pillows and accessories. The exclusive outlet for Scalamandré.

STROHEIM & ROMANN

31-11 Thomson Avenue, Long Island City, NY 11101 • Tel: (718) 706-7000 • Fax: (718) 361-0159 • Mon-Fri 9:00-5:00 • Prices high • Trade only

Designer and manufacturer of fabrics, wallcoverings, trimmings and rugs for the design profession and the contract market.

HARRY ZARIN

318 Grand Street, New York, NY 10002 • Tel: (212) 825-6112 • Fax: (212) 925-6584 • Every day 9:00-5:30 • Ask for Mike • French, Spanish and Italian spoken • Prices low • All major credit cards

Fabric warehouse. A huge selection and excellent buys in drapery and upholstery fabrics. They also have blinds and trimmings.

See also: DEPARTMENT STORES under HOME FURNISHINGS
　　　　　DESIGN CENTERS
　　　　　UPHOSTERY AND DRAPERY SERVICES

ʬ Antique Textiles

VIRGINIA DI SCIASCO ANTIQUE TEXTILES

Gallery: 799 Madison Avenue, 2nd floor, New York, NY 10021 • Tel: (212) 452-1500 • Mon-Sat 10:00-6:00 • Elaine Springer
Studio: 236 East 78th Street, New York, NY 10021 • Tel: (212) 794-8807 • Mon-Sat 12:00-6:00 • French, German, Spanish and Italian spoken • Prices very high • 20% trade discounts • Major credit cards

Luxury textiles of the 17th century through the early 20th century. Antique silks, damasks, velvets, brocades and tapestry fragments; metallic trims and tassels; period pillows. Custom pillows, throws and table covers. Restoration.

LINDA FRESCO

420 East 86th Street, New York, NY 10028 • Telfax: (212) 772-0244 • By appointment • Italian and French spoken • Prices medium • Trade discounts

Beautiful collection of antique textiles.

CORA GINSBURG INC.

19 East 74th Street, 3rd floor, New York, NY 10021 • Tel: (212) 744-1352 • Fax: (212) 879-1601 • Mon-Fri 9:00-5:00 by appointment only • Tin Halle • French and Portuguese spoken • Prices medium to high • Some trade discounts • Amex

Remarkable collection of antique textiles, embroidery and decoration. Historic costume.

RENATE HALPERN GALLERIES

325 East 79th Street, New York, NY 10021 • Tel: (212) 988-9316 • Fax: (212) 988-2954 • By appointment only • German spoken • Prices medium to high • Trade only

Antique textiles, tapestries and rugs ranging from Coptic Egypt to the Arts and Crafts period of the early part of the 20th century. Wide range of periods and countries of origin: Europe, Turkey, Greek Islands, Russia, Japan, China, England.

GAIL MARTIN GALLERY

310 Riverside Drive, New York, NY 10025 • Tel: (212) 864-3550 • Fax: (212) 663-0940 • By appointment • Polish and Bulgarian spoken, Japanese with advance notice • Prices medium to very high • Trade discounts

Outstanding examples of ancient, antique and ethnographic textiles and objects. Conservation, mounting and collection management.

FRANCOISE NUNNALLE

105 West 55th Street, #6A, New York, NY 10019 • Tel: (212) 246-4281 • By appointment

Magnificent antique textiles. Custom one-of-a-kind pillows made from 17th- to early 20th-century textiles, such as brocade, cut velvet, silk damask, tapestry, needlepoint and embroidery. Many of her treasures have historical significance.

Antique Textile Conservation

STUDIO GINA BIANCO

526 West 26th Street, Studio #823, New York, NY 10001 • Tel: (212) 924-1685 • Mon-Fri 8:30-4:40 by appointment • Gina Bianco speaks Italian, French and Mandarin Chinese • Prices medium to high

Textile and costume conservation of the finest quality. Clients include museums, historic houses and societies, antique dealers, major auction houses and corporate and private collectors.

Custom Fabrics

HANDWOVEN STUDIO/HWS DESIGN GROUP LTD

838 Broadway, New York, NY 10012 • Tel: (212) 253-8735 • Fax: (516) 423-9015 • Mon-Fri 9:00-6:00 • Barbara Anne Grib • Prices very high • Trade only

Very exclusive to the trade custom fabrics: hand-woven sheers, chenille and upholstery weaves. No minimum and no maximum; for residential and commercial use. Custom window treatments. All made in Italy.

Embroidered Fabrics

PENN & FLETCHER INC.

242 West 30th Street, 2nd floor, New York, NY 10001 • Tel: (212) 239-6868 • Fax: (212) 239-6914 • Mon-Fri 9:00-5:00 • Ernest A. Smith • Prices medium to high • Trade only • Major credit cards

Fine embroidery on all fabrics, in single pieces or quantity, by hand and by machine. Drapery borders, valances, bed covers, chair seats and backs, pillows, table covers, throws, monograms and linens. Custom work is to the trade only. Stock patterns available to all. The finest work.

♔ Hand-Painted Fabrics

ATELIER CHRISTINE LAMBERT

912 Fifth Avenue, New York, NY 10021 • Tel: (212) 249-6939 • Fax: (212) 472-6908 • By appointment • French spoken • Prices medium to high • Professional discount

Hand-silk-screened fabrics and wallcoverings for indoor and out-door use. Custom colors and designs also available. Extraordinary.

D.D. TILLETT

New York, NY 10021 • Tel: (212) 737-7313 • Fax: (212) 737-7314 • By appointment

Hand printing and hand painting on all fabrics, especially cottons. The accent is on one-of-a-kind. These are unique paintings on fabric and on pillows. From 1 yard to large quantities. Residential, nautical and commerical installations. Hand-painted flowers in water-colors, framed and unframed. This is all superb work.

Antique Pillows

VIRGINIA DI SCIASCIO — *19 E, 71 794-8807*

799 Madison Avenue, 2nd Floor, New York, NY 10021 • Tel: (212) 452-1500 • Mon-Sat 10:00-6:00 • French, German, Spanish and Italian spoken • Prices very high • Trade discount • Major credit cards

Beautiful pillows, throws and tablecloths made from luxury textiles of the 17th century through the early 20th century. Metallic trims and tassels. Will custom design.

MORTON & COMPANY

146 East 84th Street, New York, NY 10028 • Tel: (212) 472-1446 • Fax: (212) 472-4798 • By appointment • Jill Braufman • Some French and Spanish spoken • Prices high • 25% trade discount

Marvellous antique textile pillows, beautifully trimmed. 500 in stock.

FRANCOISE NUNNALLE

105 West 55th Street, New York, NY 10019 • Tel: (212) 246-4281 • By appointment • Prices high to very high

Magnificent custom one-of-a-kind pillows made from 17th- to early 20th-century textiles: tapestry fragments, brocade, cut velvet, silk damask, needlepoint. The detailing is lavish and the trims and tassels are mostly metallic, many from the late 19th century. The pillow stuffing is half down and half goose feathers to maintain body.

THE PILLOWRY

132 East 61st Street, New York, NY 10021 • Tel: (212) 308-1630 • Mon-Fri 11:30-5:30 • Marjorie Lawrence • French and Italian spoken • Prices medium to very high • Trade discounts • Visa and MC

Antique decorative pillows and textiles. Gorgeous pillows made from antique tapestry fragments, Aubusson, silk damasks, brocades and vintage needlepoint, as well as more contemporary pillows from vintage kilims and knotted rugs. The tapestries are from France and the textiles from Europe, North Africa, Persia and Asia. They range from the 17th century to the 1940s.

Leather

ABRAHAM LEATHER CO.

264 West 40th Street, New York, NY 10018 • Tel: (212) 840-7275 • Call for hours

Good selection of all kinds of leather. Complete skins for replacing leather on desks or large pillows. Good choice of colors.

COSTELLO STUDIO, INC.

315 East 91st Street, New York, NY 10128 • Tel: (212) 410-2083 • Fax: (212) 410-4455 • By appointment

Fine craftsmanship in leather: furniture and decorative objects. Marvellous work.

TEDDY & ARTHUR EDELMAN, LTD.

28 Hawleyville Road, Hawleyville, CT 06440-0110 • Tel: (203) 426-3611 • Fax: (203) 426-3840 • Mon-Fri 9:00-5:00 • Teddy Edelman • Italian, French, Spanish and Portuguese spoken • Prices high • Trade only

High-quality leathers for upholstery, walls and floors. Decorative leathers, antiqued leathers.

HERMES LEATHER CORP.

45 West 34th Street, Room 1108, New York, NY 10001 • Tel: (212) 947-1153 • Fax: (212) 967-2701 • Mon-Fri 9:00-5:00 • Robert Katz and Ralph Elias • Spanish spoken • Prices medium to high • Major credit cards

Wholesalers of finished leathers. Specialists in a variety of smooth and sueded leathers: cowhide, pig, lamb, goat, cabretta. Excellent source.

Trimmings

BRUNSCHWIG & FILS INC.

979 Third Avenue (D&D), New York, NY 10022 • Tel: (212) 838-7878 • Fax: (212) 371-3026 • Mon-Fri 9:00-5:00 • Trade only

Beautiful selection of trimmings.

CLARENCE HOUSE

211 East 58th Street (D&D), New York, NY 10022 • Tel: (212) 752-2890 • Fax: (212) 755-3314 • Mon-Fri 9:00-5:00 • French spoken • Trade only

Extensive line of high-quality trimmings.

COLLECTANIA

1194 Lexington Avenue, New York, NY 10028 • Tel: (212) 327-2176 • Fax: (212) 727-9160 • Sharon Rossano • French spoken • Prices medium • 10% professional discount • Amex and MC

Good collection of large vintage tassels and some sets of antique tiebacks. Pretty pillows.

FONTHILL LTD.

979 Third Avenue (D&D), New York, NY 10022 • Tel: (212) 755-6700 •
Fax: (212) 371-2358 • Mon-Fri 9:00-5:00 • Tod Vasse • Trade only

Full line of top quality trimmings from France, England and India:
cords, tassels, tiebacks, tapes, bullions. Everything.

HYMAN HENDLER & SONS

67 West 38th Street, New York, NY 10018 • Tel: (212) 840-8393 • Fax:
(212) 704-4237 • Mon-Fri 9:00-5:30 • Spanish spoken

A fine stock of European tassels and tiebacks in silk, cotton, solid
colors and exotic mixtures. Ribbons of all kinds; some cords for
pillows.

⚓ HOULES USA

979 Third Avenue (D&D), New York, NY 10022 • Tel: (212) 935-3900 •
Fax: (212) 935-3923 • Mon-Fri 9:30-5:00 • Trade only

Some of the best French handmade trimmings available. Superb
choice of colors in braids, tassels, cords, tiebacks.

CHRISTOPHER HYLAND INCORPORATED

979 Third Avenue (D&D), New York, NY 10022 • Tel: (212) 688-6121 •
Fax: (212) 688-6176 • Mon-Fri 9:00-5:00 • Trade only

Great tassels and tiebacks.

LE DECOR FRANCAIS

1006 Lexington Avenue, New York, NY 10021 • Tel: (212) 734-0032 •
Fax: (212) 988-0816 • Mon-Fri 9:30-6:00, Sat 11:00-5:00 • Jacqueline
Coumans • French, Portuguese and Spanish spoken • Prices medium
to high • 20% trade discount • Amex

Excellent selection of trimmings to coordinate with their fabrics.

M & J TRIMMING CO., INC.

1008 Sixth Avenue, New York, NY 10018 • Tel: (212) 391-6200 • Fax:
(212) 764-5854 • Mon-Fri 9:00-6:00, Sat 10:00-5:00 • Bob Gross •
French, Spanish, German, Yiddish and Arabic spoken • Prices medium
• Trade discount • Major credit cards

Trimmings of every description: cords, laces, fringes, tassels and
tiebacks.

PASSEMENTERIE, INC.

979 Third Avenue (D&D), New York, NY 10022 • Tel: (212) 355-7600 •
Fax: (212) 355-1350 • Mon-Fri 9:00-5:00 • Trade only

American made trimmings, tassels, braids, ropes and cords.

JEANNE E. PEARSON

5 Oaklawn Avenue, Glen Head, NY 11545 • Telfax: (516) 674-4619 • Tue-Sat 10:00-6:00 • Italian and Spanish spoken • Prices high • Trade discount

Hand-crafted passementerie trimmings: tassels, fringes, cords, tie-backs, decorative knots. All variations. Custom.

PENN & FLETCHER INC.

242 West 30th Street, 2nd floor, New York, NY 10001 • Tel: (212) 239-6868 • Fax: (212) 239-6914 • Mon-Fri 9:00-5:00 • Ernest A. Smith • Trade only

Trimmings, laces, Cluny laces, cording, sequins, military fringes, chenilles, metallic braids.

ROGERS & GOFFIGAN LTD.

979 Third Avenue (D&D), New York, NY 10022 • Tel: (212) 888-3242 • Fax: (212) 888-3315 • Mon-Fri 9:00-5:00 • Trade only

Trimmings from all natural fibers, silk, cotton and linen: unusual braids and gimps, bullions, fringes and silk brush fringe.

SCALAMANDRE

942 Third Avenue, New York, NY 10022 • Tel: (212) 980-3888 • Fax: (212) 688-7531 • Mon-Fri 9:00-5:00 • Prices high • Trade only • Major credit cards

Designers and manufacturers of trimmings and fabrics for the high-end interior designer and contract industries. Excellent choice.

F. SCHUMACHER & CO.

939 Third Avenue, New York, NY 10022 • Tel: (212) 415-3900 • Fax: (212) 415-3907 • Mon-Fri 9:00-5:00 • Brigitte Ple • Prices very high • Trade only

Classic selection of trimmings, decorative tiebacks, key tassels.

TASSELS & TRIMS

232 East 59th Street, New York, NY 10022 • Tel: (212) 754-6000 • Fax: (212) 754-6002 • Mon-Fri 9:00-5:00 • Trade only

Trimmings, largely French: tassels, fringes and a large selection of braids and gimps.

TINSEL TRADING COMPANY

47 West 38th Street, New York, NY 10018 • Tel: (212) 730-1030 • Fax: (212) 768-8823 • Mon-Fri 10:00-5:00 • Trade discount • Visa and MC

A treasure house of vintage trimmings largely from the 1930s.

WILLIAM N. GINSBURG COMPANY

242 West 38th Street, New York, NY 10018 • Tel: (212) 244-4539 • Fax: (212) 921-2014 • Mon-Fri 9:00-5:00 • Trade only

Unusual tassels, fringes, gimps, braids, and ropes. Mainly for fashion but will take custom orders from decorators for any kind of trimmings.

FIREPLACES AND ACCESSORIES

ALCAMO MARBLE WORKS

541-543 West 22nd Street, New York, NY 10011 • Tel: (212) 255-5224 • Fax: (212) 255-4060 • Mon-Fri 8:00-4:30 • Onofrio or Nino D'Angelo • Italian and Spanish spoken • Prices medium

Antique fireplaces and mantels and custom fireplaces in marble and granite.

A&R ASTA LTD.

1152 Second Avenue, New York, NY 10021 • Tel: (212) 750-3364 • Fax: (212) 751-5418 • Mon-Fri 9:30-5:00, Sat 11:30-4:00 • French and Italian spoken

Antique and reproduction French and English mantels, fireplaces and fireplace accessories.

₩ DANNY ALESSANDRO LTD.

146 East 57th Street, New York, NY 10022 • Tel: (212) 759-8210 • Fax: (212) 759-3819 • Mon-Fri 10:00-6:00, Sat 12:00-4:00 • Italian spoken • Prices medium to high • Major credit cards

18th- and 19th-century French, English and American fireplaces, mantels and accessories. Tools, screens, fenders and chenets.

BARONE BROS. MARBLE AND CERAMIC TILE, INC.

2905 Review Avenue, Long Island City, NY 11101 • Tel: (718) 786-9880 • Fax: (718) 492-9463 • Mon-Fri 8:00-5:00 • Joseph Barone • Italian spoken • Prices low to high

Custom fireplaces and mantels in marble and granite.

D.M.S. STUDIOS

5-50 51st Avenue, Long Island City, NY 11101 • Tel: (718) 937-5648 • Fax: (718) 937-2609 • Mon-Fri 9:00-6:00 • Daniel Sinclair • Italian spoken • Prices medium

Custom fireplaces in limestone and marble.

ELIZABETH STREET GARDENS & GALLERY

1176 & 1190 Second Avenue, New York, NY 10021 • Tel: (212) 644-6969 • Fax: (212) 644-8090 • Mon-Thu 10:00-6:00, Fri 10:00-5:00 • Michael Garden • Prices high • Major credit cards

18th-, 19th- and 20th-century fireplaces in marble and stone. Great selection of garden ornaments.

IRREPLACEABLE ARTIFACTS

14 Second Avenue, New York, NY 10003 • Tel: (212) 777-2900 • Fax: (212) 780-0642 • Mon-Fri 10:00-6:00, Sat-Sun 11:00-5:00 • Prices medium • Trade discount

Lots of antique fireplaces from demolished buildings.

◀ WILLIAM H. JACKSON

210 East 58th Street, New York, NY 10022 • Tel: (212) 753-9400 • Fax: (212) 753-7872 • Mon-Fri 9:30-5:00 • Marie McDonald • Prices high • Trade discount • Major credit cards

Antique wood, marble and limestone mantels. Reproduction wood mantels. Installation. Full line of fireplace accessories.

FRANK PELLITTERI

201 East 56th Street, New York, NY 10022 • Tel: (212) 486-0545 • Fax: (212) 486-0546 • By appointment • Italian spoken • Prices low to high

Finely carved custom wood fireplaces and mantels.

PIMLICO WAY

1028 Lexington Avenue, New York, NY 10021 • Tel: (212) 439-7855 • Mon-Sat 10:00-6:00 • Judith and Sidney Amdur

Nice selection of fireplace equipment and accessories.

PS CRAFTSMANSHIP CORPORATION

10-40 Jackson Avenue, Long Island City, NY 11101 • Tel: (718) 729-3686 • Fax: (718) 729-3781 • Mon-Fri 9:00-7:00 • Stephan Pousse • French spoken • Prices medium

French limestone fireplace mantels.

PUCCIO MARBLE & ONYX

661 Driggs Avenue, Brooklyn, NY 11211 • Tel: (718) 387-9778 • Fax: (718) 387-5464 • Mon-Fri 8:30-5:00, Sat by appointment • Joseph Puccio • Italian spoken • Prices high • Trade discount

Puccio's own custom designs of fireplaces and mantels.

LOUIS J. SOLOMON

380 Second Avenue, New York, NY 10010 • Tel: (212) 254-4900 • Fax: (212) 477-4351 • Mon-Fri 9:00-5:00 • Italian and Spanish spoken • Prices high • Trade only

Fireplaces and mantels.

FRAMES AND FRAMING

There are hundreds of places in New York City where you can have a picture framed. From all of these the authors have selected some of the best who do the highest quality work and who offer a stock of antique frames or fine period reproductions.

Almost any art supply store can offer framing services and, in addition, scattered throughout the city, are many "do-it-yourself" framing shops.

ALVAREZ FINE ART SERVICES

29 West 36th Street, New York, NY 10018 • Tel: (212) 244-5255 • Mon-Sat 9:30-6:00 • Prices medium to high

Matting and framing of works on paper, conservation and restoration.

APF HOLDINGS INC.

172 East 75th Street, New York, NY 10021 • Tel: (212) 988-1090 • Fax: (212) 794-3254 • Mon-Fri 9:30-5:30 • Nathan Raisen • Prices very high • Professional discount

Custom framing and conservation. Mirrors.

ATLANTIC GALLERY LTD.

1185 Lexington Avenue, New York, NY 10028 • Tel: (212) 772-0634 • Mon-Fri 11:00-6:00 • Rubens Penna • Prices medium • Professional discount • Major credit cards

Hand-painted frames and French matting. 17th- to 20th-century prints in hand-painted frames. 18th- and 19th-century furniture, lamps and chandeliers.

CENTER ART STUDIO

250 West 54th Street, #901, New York, NY 10019 • Tel: (212) 247-3550 • Fax: (212) 586-4045 • Mon-Fri 9:00-6:00 • Lansing Moore • Italian and Spanish spoken • Prices medium to high • Major credit cards

Custom-designed pedestals, display bases and display cases for art objects. Restoration.

FINE ART CONSERVATION SERVICES

419 Third Avenue, New York, NY 10016 • Tel: (212) 889-8173 • Fax: (212) 683-1550 • Mon-Sat 10:00-6:00 • Robert Hammerquist • Spanish and Chinese spoken • Prices medium • Professional discount • Major credit cards

Custom hardwood frames, inlaid and gilded. Restoration and gilding of frames and objects. Museum and gallery clients.

FLEISCHER FRAMES

119 West 40th Street, New York, NY 10018 • Tel: (212) 840-2248 • Mon-Fri 10:00-6:30 • Prices medium • Major credit cards

Custom framing; art frames of the 1920s and 1930s; a large collection of antique prints from the turn of the century.

GILL & LAGODICH

137 Duane Street, No. 5B, New York, NY 10013 • Tel: (212) 619-0631 • Fax: (212) 285-1353 • By appointment

18th- to 20th-century American and European frames and mirrors. Restoration services.

GODEL & CO.

39A East 72nd Street, New York, NY 10021 • Tel: (212) 288-7272 • Fax: (212) 772-0303 • Mon-Fri 10:00-6:00, Sat 10:00-5:00 • Prices high

19th- and 20th-century gilded frames.

GOLDFEDER/KAHAN FRAMING GROUP LTD.

37 West 20th Street, Ground floor, New York, NY 10011 • Tel: (212) 242-5310 • Fax: (212) 242-5326 • Mon-Fri 9:00-6:00, Sat 10:00-5:00 • Elizabeth Goldfeder • Prices very high • Major credit cards

Museum quality archival framing: conservation and restoration in paper, painting, textile, photography. Antique frames. Excellent references.

E. GREENE GALLERY

361 Bleeker Street, New York, NY 10014 • Tel: (212) 366-0643 • Fax: (201) 222-3349 • Tue-Wed 11:00-5:00, Thu 12:00-8:00, Fri-Sat 10:00-6:00 • Ed Greene • Prices medium to high • Trade discount • Major credit cards

Hand-gilded and hand-painted picture frames.

GUTTMAN PICTURE FRAME ASSOCIATES

180 East 73rd Street, New York, NY 10021 • Tel: (212) 744-8600 • Fax: (212) 744-7888 • Mon-Thu 9:00-5:00 • German spoken • Prices very high

One of the largest antique frame collections in the world. Carved reproduction frames. All frames custom made to size. Repair of wood carved frames. Gilding and restoration of frames and furniture.

HOUSE OF HEYDENRYK

417 East 76th Street, New York, NY 10021 • Tel: (212) 249-4903 • Fax: (212) 472-9010 • Mon-Fri 9:30-5:00, Sat 9:30-3:00 • Charles Schreiber • Prices high • Trade discount

Hand-made custom picture frames and mirrors. Framing and restoration of frames and paintings.

JINPRA N.Y.

1208 Lexington Avenue, New York, NY 10028 • Telfax: (212) 988-3903 • Tue-Sat 11:00-6:00 • Prices medium • 10% trade discount • Major credit cards

Picture frames and mouldings, museum conservation framing, period reproduction mirrors. Restoration and gilding.

KEW GALLERY INC.

301 East 56th Street, New York, NY 10022 • Telfax: (212) 688-5035 • Mon-Fri 9:30-6:30, Sat 10:00-5:00 • Alberto Braunstein • French, Italian and Spanish spoken • Prices medium • Visa and MC

Fine custom framing.

LEE'S ART SHOP

220 West 57th Street, New York, NY 11019 • Tel: (212) 247-0110 • Fax: (212) 247-0507 • Mon-Fri 9:00-7:00, Sat 9:30-6:30, Sun 12:00-5:00 • Mike Stone • French, Spanish, German and Italian spoken • Prices medium to high • Trade discount • Major credit cards

Fast same-day framing, glass and mats cut while you wait. Art and needlepoint supplies, conservation framing. Restoration of paintings and photographs.

₩ LOWY

223 East 80th Street, New York, NY 10021 • Tel: (212) 861-8585 • Fax: (212) 988-0443 • Mon-Fri 9:00-5:30 • Larry Shar • Spanish, Italian, French and Chinese spoken • Prices medium to very high • Major credit cards

One of New York's finest dealers in antique and reproduction frames. They gild and restore frames and furniture. Restoration of paintings. See the cover of this book for one of their frames.

PARK SLOPE FRAMING & GALLERY

559 Tenth Street, Brooklyn, NY 11215 • Tel: (718) 768-4883 • Fax: (718) 965-4199 • By appointment (includes evenings) • Phyllis Wrynn • French spoken • Prices medium • 15 to 20% trade discount • Amex

Custom archival framing. A huge selection from which to choose; delivery, installation, fine papers, conservation, painting.

MARGUERITE PHILLIPS GALLERY

1418 Lexington Avenue, New York, NY 10128 • Tel: (212) 831-1416 •
Mon-Fri 10:30-6:30, Sat 10:30-5:00

Custom framing. Good selection of antique prints available.

J. POCKER & SONS, INC.

135 East 63rd Street, New York, NY 10021 • Tel: (212) 838-5488 •
Fax: (212) 750-2053 • Mon-Sat 10:00-5:30 • French spoken • Prices
high • 20% trade discount • Major credit cards

Quality framing and a collection of prints and posters. Nice people.

RIVERDALE GALLERY

450 West 238th Street, New York, NY 10463 • Tel: (718) 549-3800 •
Wed-Sat 10:00-6:00, other times by appointment

Custom framing and restoration of paintings and other works on
paper.

DIEGO SALAZAR PICTURE FRAME CO., INC.

21-25 44th Avenue, Long Island City, NY 11101 • Tel: (718) 937-9077
• Fax: (718) 937-9136 • Mon-Fri 8:00-4:30 • Spanish spoken • Prices
medium • Professional discount

Custom and period picture frames. Clients include top museums
and galleries.

FREDDIE SCHNEIDER CUSTOM PICTURE FRAMING

1272 Third Avenue, New York, NY 10021 • Tel: (212) 535-0160 • Mon-
Fri 9:00-6:00, Sat 10:00-5:30 • Prices medium • 10% trade discount •
Major credit cards

Custom picture framing. Framed mirrors and needlepoint. Restoration of paintings. Excellent references.

70 ART GALLERY

130 East 70th Street, New York, NY 10021 • Tel: (212) 472-2234 • Fax:
(212) 472-2368 • Mon-Fri 10:00-6:00, Sat 12:00-5:00 • Juan Rodriguez
• Spanish spoken • Prices medium to high • Visa and MC

Framing and restoration of frames and paintings.

SHEPHERD GALLERY SERVICES

21 East 84th Street, New York, NY 10028 • Tel: (212) 744-3392 • Fax:
(212) 772-1314 • Mon-Fri 10:00-6:00, Sat 1:00-6:00 • Joseph Gib-
bon, Director • Prices medium to very high

High-quality frames and framing; in particular 19th-century German,
French and American frames. Custom framing of museum quality
and art conservation and restoration.

SOHO PICTURE FRAMING

568 Broadway, New York, NY 10012 • Tel: (212) 431-5600 • Fax: (212) 334-9214 • Mon-Fri 10:00-7:00, Sat 12:00-6:00 • Myung Bae Kim • Italian and Korean spoken and a smattering of lots of other languages • Prices medium • Trade discount • Major credit cards

Largest selection of frames in NYC. Everything from inexpensive metal to 24ct gold leaf. They claim to sell to more than half of the galleries in Soho.

SPIEGEL FRAMING CO.

308 Bowery, New York, NY 10012 • Tel: (212) 475-5630 • Fax: (212) 475-7430 • Mon-Thu 8:00-5:00, Fri 8:00-2:00 • Hebrew, German and Spanish spoken • Prices medium

18th- and 19th-century picture frames. Restoration of period pieces and custom moulding design. Top references. Gold leafing.

♨ ELI WILNER & CO.

1525 York Avenue, New York, NY 10028 • Tel: (212) 744-6521 • Fax: (212) 628-0264 • Mon-Fri 9:30-5:30 • French and Japanese spoken • Prices high • Major credit cards

Superb quality 19th- to early 20th-century American and European frames and mirrors. Frame conservation and restoration.

WINDWOOD GALLERY

1079 Third Avenue, New York, NY 10021 • Tel: (212) 355-2508 • Fax: (212) 355-0176 • Mon-Fri 11:00-7:00, Sat 11:00-6:00 • Eduard Doga • German, French, Hungarian, Rumanian and Italian spoken • Prices medium • Major credit cards

Picture framing as well as contemporary art, lithographs and posters.

Silver Frames

DIONYSIS

1189 Lexington Avenue, New York, NY 10028 • Tel: (212) 861-5616 • Fax: (212) 861-9472 • Mon-Fri 10:00-6:00, Sat 10:00-4:00 • Mike Giordas • Greek spoken • Prices medium to high • Trade discount • Major credit cards

English and Greek antique silver frames of the 19th century to Art Deco.

FRAMED ON MADISON

740 Madison Avenue, New York, NY 10021 • Tel: (212) 734-4680 •
Fax: (212) 988-0128 • Mon-Sat 10:00-6:00, Thu 10:00-7:00, Sun
12:00-5:00 • Prices medium to high • Major credit cards

Very good selection of antique silver frames from the turn of the
century to the 1930s, from England, France, Austria and Central
Europe. Other frames in lacquer, wood, gold and silver leaf and
pewter.

HARRIET'S GIFT & FRAME BOUTIQUE

997 Lexington Avenue, New York, NY 10021 • Tel: (212) 288-2798 •
Mon-Fri 10:00-6:00, Sat 10:00-5:00 • Harriet Kanter, Jane Weisglass •
Prices medium • Major credit cards

Sterling silver and silver plate frames in all shapes and sizes. Frames
in lacquer, wood and fabric.

See also: ANTIQUE DEALERS

FURNITURE

Antique Reproductions

♛ AGOSTINO ANTIQUES, LTD.

808 Broadway, New York, NY 10003 • Tel: (212) 533-3355 • Fax: (212) 477-4128 • Mon-Fri 9:00-5:00 • Salvatore Tropiano • Italian spoken • Prices medium to high

Fine 18th- and 19th-century English and French antique reproductions. An excellent dealer in the real thing.

BARTON SHARPE, LTD.

66 Crosby Street, New York, NY 10012 • Tel: (212) 925-9562 • Fax: (212) 925-9687 • Mon-Sat 11:00-6:00, Sun 12:00-5:00 • Sarah Carlson • Spanish and French spoken • Prices high • 10 to 15% trade discount • Major credit cards

Hand-crafted structurally correct 18th-century American furniture reproductions.

DEVON SHOPS

111 East 27th Street, New York NY 10016 • Tel: (212) 686-1760 • Fax: (212) 686-2970 • Mon-Fri 10:00-6:00, Sat-Sun 10:00-7:00 • Prices medium to high • Trade discount

Fine selection of reproductions of European furniture: tables, chairs, desks and armoires.

FRANCE FURNITURE, INC.

40-09 21st Street, Long Island City, NY 11101 • Tel: (718) 361-0718 • Fax: (718) 937-1377 • Mon-Fri 7:30-4:00 • Cono Monaco • Italian and Spanish spoken • Prices high • Trade discount

Custom antique reproduction furniture, traditional and contemporary.

GLOBAL FINE REPRODUCTIONS, INC.

801 Broadway, New York, NY 10003 • Tel: (212) 533-5810 • Fax: (212) 995-2832 • Syrus Sedge, President • Prices modest

Direct importers of fine antique reproduction furniture.

RESTORATION GILDING & REPRODUCTIONS

129 West 29th Street, 2nd floor, New York, NY 10001 • Tel: (212) 629-5630 • Fax: (212) 268-4577 • Mon-Fri 9:00-5:00 • Joseph Biunno • Spanish, Russian, Hungarian and Italian spoken • Prices high to very high • Major credit cards

Re-creation of any piece of furniture in wood or gilded wood.

JOHN ROSSELLI INTERNATIONAL

523 East 73rd Street, New York, NY 10021 • Tel: (212) 772-2137 • Fax: (212) 535-2989 • Mon-Fri 9:30-5:30 • Prices high • Trade only • Amex

Custom reproduction of antique furniture. If you bring him one chair, he will make three duplicates. Restorations.

RUVOLO & DIMARIA, INC.

121 West 19th Street, New York NY 10011 • Tel: (212) 924-4937 • Fax: (212) 924-5467 • Mon-Fri 8:00-4:30

Reproductions of European furniture.

SLATKIN & CO.

131 East 70th Street, New York, NY 10021 • Tel: (212) 794-1661 • Fax: (212) 794-4249 • Mon-Sat 10:00-6:00 • Mark Flesher • French spoken • Prices high • Boutique at Bergdorf Goodman • Major credit cards

A beautiful showroom featuring reproductions of French 18th- and 19th-century furniture; some French antiques and boudoir and desk accessories. Their workrooms specialize in duplicating 18th- and 19th-century hand-painted furniture. They also feature silk pillows and porcelain botanicals. Check out their Christmas gift baskets.

SMITH & WATSON

305 East 63rd Street, New York, NY 10021 • Tel: (212) 355-5615 • Fax: (212) 371-5624 • Mon-Fri 9:00-5:00 • Robert T. Ryan • Spanish and French spoken • Prices high to very high • Trade only • Amex

Manufacturers and importers of fine traditional reproduction furniture for residential and contract use. Very special round dining tables, which expand.

LOUIS J. SOLOMON INC.

380 Second Avenue, New York, NY 10010 • Tel: (212) 254-4900 • Fax: (212) 477-4341 • Mon-Fri 9:00-5:00

European furniture reproductions.

TIMELESS TREASURES

150 West 25th Street, New York, NY 10001 • Tel: (212) 255-0340 • Fax: (212) 255-6430 • Tue-Sun 10:00-6:00 • Frank Rossetti • Spanish spoken • Prices medium to high • Trade discount • Major credit cards

A huge selection of antique reproductions.

TREILLAGE LTD.

418 East 75th Street, New York, NY 10021 • Tel: (212) 535-2288 • Fax: (212) 517-6589 • Mon-Fri 10:00-6:00, Sat 10:00-5:00 • Tony D'Agostino • Prices high • 20% trade discount • All major credit cards

Reproductions of interior and exterior antique furniture and garden ornaments.

⚘ FREDERICK P. VICTORIA & SON, INC.

154 East 55th Street, New York, NY 10022 • Tel: (212) 755-2549 • Fax: (212) 888-7199 • Mon-Fri 9:00-5:00 • Anthony G. Victoria • French and Spanish spoken • Prices high • 20% trade discount

Superb reproductions of antique furniture. Mainly a marvellous collection of the real thing.

Children's

ART & TAPISSERIE CORP.

1242 Madison Avenue, New York, NY 10128 • Telfax: (212) 722-3222 • Mon-Fri 10:30-6:30, Sat 10:00-6:00, Sun 12:00-5:00 • Flo B. Abbo • French and Spanish spoken • Prices medium • Major credit cards

A children's store with a wide selection of furnishings and room accessories including tables and chairs, rocking chairs, lamps, clocks, stools, mirrors, chests, picture frames. All items can be personalized.

BELLINI

1305 Second Avenue, New York, NY 10021 • Tel: (212) 517-9233 • Fax: (212) 628-2754 • Mon-Fri 10:00-6:00, Thu 10:00-8:00, Sat 10:00-5:30, Sun 12:00-5:00 • Jean Bonaventure • French, Italian and Spanish spoken • Trade discounts • Major credit cards

Juvenile designer furniture: cribs from Italy, custom linens for children. Everything from birth to teens.

THE CHILDREN'S ROOM

140 Varick Street, New York, NY 10013 • Tel: (212) 627-2006 • Mon-Fri 10:00-5:30, Sat 10:00-5:00 • Visa and MC

The largest collection of solid wood furniture for children. All types: beds, bunk beds, loft beds, trundle beds, captain's beds, chests, desks, night tables. From three years up.

FOREMOST FURNITURE

8 West 30th Street, 5th floor, New York, NY 10001 • Tel: (212) 889-6347 • Mon-Fri 10:00-6:00, Thu until 7:00, Sat 10:00-5:00, Sun 11:00-5:00 • Prices low to medium • Major credit cards

This is a discount outlet for various manufacturers' lines of children's furniture.

INTERIEURS

114 Wooster Street, New York, NY 10012 • Tel: (212) 343-0800 • Mon-Sat 10:00-6:00 • Mrs. Kriegel • French spoken

Custom designed and fabricated pine play cabins for kids. Complete with furnishings and on casters to make them mobile.

PORTICO KIDS

1167 Madison Avenue, New York, NY 10128 • Tel (212) 717-1963 • Fax: (212) 717-1983 • Mon-Sat 10:00-6:00, Sun 12:00-5:00 • Marina Benzemann • French, Spanish, Persian and Russian spoken • Prices high • Trade discounts • Major credit cards

Large choice of upscale children's furniture, bedding and accessories.

WICKER GARDEN

1318 Madison Avenue, New York, NY 10128 • Tel: (212) 410-7001 • Fax: (212) 410-6609 • Mon-Sat 10:00-6:00 • Pamela Scurry • Spanish spoken • Prices high • Trade discounts • Major credit cards

Good choice of children's wood furniture. Baby nursery furniture and accessories.

WYNKEN, BLYNKEN & NOD'S

306 East 55th Street, New York, NY 10022 • Tel: (212) 308-9299 • Fax: (212) 355-4403 • Mon-Fri 11:00-6:00, Sat 10:00-5:00 • Deborah Kleman • French and Spanish spoken • Trade discount • Major credit cards

19th- and early 20th-century children's furniture. Early 20th- century paintings and collectibles for children. Contemporary hand-painted children's cabinets. Vintage carousel horses, puppet theatres, wooden toys, rocking horses, puzzles. 19th-century dolls.

Contemporary

BILHUBER INC.

330 East 59th Street, 6th floor, New York, NY 10022 • Tel: (212) 308-4888 • Fax: (212) 223-4590 • Mon-Fri 9:00-7:00 • Courtney Pyle • French and Spanish spoken • Prices in all ranges • 10% trade discount • All major credit cards

Complete interior design, decoration and architectural services and related products. Line of furniture by Jeffrey Bilhuber and accessories.

B.P. ASSOCIATES

155 East 56th Street, New York, NY 10022 • Tel: (212) 759-1300 • Fax: (212) 759-2127 • Mon-Fri 9:00-5:00 • Paul Berglund • Prices medium • Trade only

Desks, office chairs, healthcare furniture, ergonomic seating, computer tables, dining/conference tables.

BRITISH KHAKI FURNITURE

62 Greene Street, New York, NY 10012 • Tel: (212) 343-2299 • Fax: (212) 343-0485 • Mon-Fri 10:00-6:00, Sat 12:00-5:00 • Rod Helm • Spanish spoken • Prices high • Trade discount

Handmade English Colonial furniture in teak and rosewood, in more than sixty styles.

CAMPANIELLO ENTERPRISES, INC.

225 East 57th Street, New York, NY 10022 • Tel: (212) 371-1700 • Fax: (212) 688-6527 • Mon-Fri 9:00-5:00, Sat 10:00-6:00 • Sandra Campaniello • Italian and Spanish spoken • Prices high to very high • Trade only

High-end contemporary Italian residential and executive office furniture, including leather and leather top desks. Four lines of furniture available as well as contemporary fabrics.

CASSINA, INC.

155 East 56th Street, New York, NY 10022 • Tel: (212) 245-2121 • Fax: (212) 245-1340 • Mon-Fri 9:00-5:30 • Hilary Huff • Prices high • Trade discount • Major credit cards

Classic modern furniture, including The Masters Collection of reproductions of original designs by Le Corbusier, Pierre Jeanneret, Charlotte Perriand, Charles Rennie Mackintosh, Gerrit Thomas Rietveld, Erik Gunnar Asplund and Frank Lloyd Wright. In addition there is the collection of pieces designed by contemporary architects such as Mario Bellini, Toshiyuki Kita, Ettore Sottsess and others.

ROGER CROWLEY FURNITURE

207 East 84th Street, Room 205, New York, NY 10028 • Tel: (212) 439-6002 • Fax: (212) 744-7464 • Mon-Fri 9:00-6:00 by appointment • Roger Crowley • Italian spoken • Prices medium to high • 25% trade discount

Contemporary furniture; custom design available.

CURTIS CO. INC.

40 East 19th Street, New York, NY 10003 • Tel: (212) 673-5353 • Fax: (212) 979-9713 • Mon-Sat 10:00-6:00, Sun 12:00-6:00 • Herbert Roberts, CEO • Prices low to medium • Major credit cards

Solid wood furniture center. Home theatre, home office, libraries. Custom and ready made furniture; woodworking and custom cabinetry.

DANISH DESIGNS

319 East 53rd Street, New York, NY 10022 • Tel: (212) 223-7210 • Fax: (212) 223-8177 • Mon-Fri 10:00-6:00, Sat 10:00-5:00, Sun 12:00-5:00 • Joe Donegan • Spanish spoken • Prices medium to high • All major credit cards

Scandinavian imported furniture: contemporary Danish designs in leather, wood, fabric and some metal.

DESIGN STORE AT THE DOOR STORE

1 Park Avenue, New York, NY 10016 • Tel: (212) 679-9700 • Fax: (212) 545-1799
1201 Third Avenue, New York, NY 10021 • Tel: (212) 772-1110 • Fax: (212) 772-3138
123 West 17th Street, New York, NY 10011 • Tel: (212) 627-1515 • Fax: (212) 627-1518
599 Lexington Avenue, New York, NY 10022 • Tel: (212) 832-7500 • Fax: (212) 755-4995
National Ordering 1-800-433-4071
Some locations speak Spanish and French • Prices medium • Trade discount over $5000 • All major credit cards

Furniture for the home and office. A great mix of styles of furniture from around the world.

DIALOGICA

484 Broome Street, New York, NY 10013 • Tel: (212) 966-1934 • Fax: (212) 966-2870 • Tue-Sun 12:00-6:00 • Sara Williams • Prices medium to high • 40% professional discount • All major credit cards
1070 Madison Avenue, New York, NY 10028 • Tel: (212) 737-7811 • Fax: (212) 737-8564 • Tue-Sat 12:00-6:00 • Prices medium to high • Trade discount • All major credit cards

Contemporary furniture, romantic and modern, and accessories.

EINZIG ART & COMPANY

88 Wooster Street, New York, NY 10012 • Tel: (212) 334-4663 • Fax: (212) 334-4665 • Mon-Fri 11:00-7:00, Sat-Sun 12:00-7:00

Specialists in imported European contemporary furniture for the home and commercial purposes. All types of custom work available.

JENSEN-LEWIS

89 Seventh Avenue, New York, NY 10011 • Tel: (212) 929-4880 • Mon-Sat 10:00-7:00, Thu 10:00-8:00, Sun 12:00-5:30 • Spanish spoken • Prices medium • All major credit cards
Outlet Store at 96 Morton Street, West Village, New York, NY 10012 • Tel: (212) 929-1880 • Fri-Sat 11:00-5:00, Sun 12:00-5:00

Wide selection of all sorts of contemporary furniture.

SCOTT JORDAN FURNITURE

137 Varick Street, New York, NY 10013 • Tel: (212) 620-4682 • Fax: (212) 645-0152 • Mon-Sat 11:00-6:00, Thu until 8:00, Sun 12:00-5:00 • Scott Jordan • Italian spoken • Prices medium to high • MC and Visa

Contemporary solid wood furniture in Mission and Shaker traditions in largely cherry and oak.

JOHN KELLY FURNITURE

144 Chambers Street, New York, NY 10007 • Tel: (212) 385-1885 •
Fax: (212) 227-2901 • Mon-Sat 10:00-6:00 • French spoken • Prices
high • MC and Visa

Hand-crafted contemporary indoor and outdoor furniture.

KNOLL   GTH AVE : 212 - 343 - 4000

105 Wooster Street, New York, NY 10026 • Tel: (212) 343-4000 • Fax:
(212) 343-4180 • Mon-Fri 10:00-5:00, Sat-Sun 12:00-5:00 • Prices
high • Professional discount

Product lines include office systems, seating, desks and casegoods;
files and storage, tables, executive furnishings, computer accessories, contract textiles and leathers.

MIYA SHOJI AND INTERIORS

109 West 17th Street, New York 10011 • Tel: (212) 243-6774 • Fax:
(212) 243-6780 • Mon-Fri 9:00-6:00 • Hisao Hanafusa • Japanese
spoken • Prices high • Trade discount • Major credit cards

Hand-crafted classic Japanese furniture in light woods, such as
pale ash, red cedar and cherry. There are shoji screens, different
types of tables, beds, cabinets, light fixtures. There are also some
Japanese antique pieces. Complete Japanese interiors can be custom created.

MODERN AGE

102 Wooster Street, New York, NY 10012 • Tel: (212) 966-0669 • Fax:
(212) 966-4167 • Tue-Fri 11:00-6:00, Sat-Sun 12:00-6:00 • David Hurd
• Prices medium • Major credit cards

Contemporary European furniture: current original designs by
Philippe Starck, Jasper Morrison, James Irvine and Ettore Sottsass.

MODERNICA

57 Greene Street, New York, NY 10012 • Tel: (212) 219-1303 • Fax:
(219) 219-1699 • Fax: (212) 219-1699 • Mon-Sun 11:00-6:00 • Frank
and Jay Novak • All major credit cards

Handmade high quality reproductions of mid-century modern furniture classics and Herman Miller designs.

NEOTU GALLERY

409 West 44th Street, New York, NY 10036 • Tel: (212) 262-9250 •
Fax: (212) 262-9251 • Mon-Sat by appointment • Gerard Dalmon •
French spoken • Prices high • Professional discount • Amex

Contemporary furniture in limited edition. Very high quality.

NORTH CAROLINA FURNITURE SHOWROOMS

12 West 21st Street, 5th floor, New York, NY 10011 • Tel: (212) 645-2524 • Fax: (212) 627-8670 • Mon-Sun 10:00-6:00, Thu 10:00-8:00 • Neil Baser • Prices low to medium • 40% trade discount • All major credit cards

Four hundred different manufacturers of contemporary and traditional furniture designs.

NUOVO MELODROM

60 Greene Street, New York, NY 10012 • Tel: (212) 219-0013 • Fax: (212) 431-3931 • Mon-Fri 9:00-6:30, Sat-Sun 12:00-6:00 • Carolin Funk, VP • German, Italian, French and some Spanish spoken • Prices low to medium • All major credit cards

Contemporary Italian and classic furniture design from the Bauhaus period. Also various accessories.

◀ THE PACE COLLECTION

986 Madison Avenue, New York, NY 10021 • Tel: (212) 535-9616 • Fax: (212) 535-7157 • Mon-Sat 10:00-6:00, Thu 10:00-7:00, Sun 12:00-5:00 • Ron Barth • French, Italian, and Spanish spoken • Prices high to very high • 40% trade discount • All major credit cards

Full line of contemporary designer furniture in unlimited array of fabrics and finishes. Sofas, chairs, tables, bedrooms, desks, office furniture, vitrines, lighting. Designers and manufacturers of custom furniture, inlaid woods, custom upholstery and cabinetry. This 32-year-old nationally recognized company can meet any requirement in contemporary or Art Deco design.

PALAZZETTI INC.

515 Madison Avenue, New York, NY 10022 • Tel: (212) 832-1199 • Fax: (212) 832-1385 • Mon-Fri 10:00-6:00, Sat 11:00-5:00, Sun 12:00-5:00 • Annamaria Fattori • Italian, French and German spoken • Prices medium to high • 10% trade discount • All major credit cards

High-end imported reproduction of modern classics as well as contemporary furniture.

PEIPERS + KOJEN

1023 Lexington Avenue, New York, NY 10021 • Tel: (212) 744-1047 • Mon-Sat 10:00-6:00 • Luda Gerszonowicz • French, Polish, Russian and Spanish spoken • Prices medium to high

Contemporary furniture and collectibles. One-of-a-kind and limited edition Continental furnishings.

REGENERATION—MODERN FURNITURE

223 East 10th Street, New York, NY 10003 • Telfax: (212) 614-9577 •
Tue-Sat 1:00-8:00, Sun 1:00-6:00 • Valerie Guariglia and Christine Miele
• Spanish spoken • Prices low • Visa and MC

20th-century designed furniture from Knoll, Herman Miller, Danish
Modern and industrial stainless steel cabinets.

SAM FLAX ART & DESIGN

12 West 20th Street, New York, NY 10021 • Tel: (212) 620-3000
425 Park Avenue, New York, NY 10022 • Tel: (212) 620-3060
• Mon-Sat 8:30-6:30, Sun 12:00-6:00 (downtown only) • Prices medium to high • Major credit cards

Small office and home-office furniture, art and graphic supplies,
frames and framing and a large selection of filing solutions.

SCHRAGER FURNITURE

1624 First Avenue, New York, NY 10028 • Tel: (212) 879-0400 • Mon,
Wed, Fri 10:00-8:00, Tue, Thu, Sat 10:00-6:00 • Prices medium

New York City's armoire resource: more than 50 styles and 20 finishes. American, Mexican and European styles.

SEE, LTD.

920 Broadway, New York, NY 10010 • Tel: (212) 228-3600 • Fax: (212)
228-0558 • Mon-Sat 10:00-7:00, Sun 12:00-6:00 • Italian and Spanish spoken • Prices high • All major credit cards

High-end contemporary European furniture: sofas, chairs, tables,
lighting, beds.

TENT INC. COLLECTION CARTON

110 Thompson Street, New York, NY 10012 • Telfax: (212) 334-4883 •
Mon-Sat 11:00-7:00, Sun 12:00-7:00 • John Bateman • French spoken • Prices low • All major credit cards

Cardboard furniture in all sizes. Designer Olivier Le Blois.

MAURICE VILLENCY INC.

200 Madison Avenue, New York, NY 10016 • Tel: (212) 725-4640 •
Fax: (212) 779-2461 • Mon, Thu 10:00-9:00, Tue, Wed, Fri, Sat 10:00-
6:00, Sun 12:00-5:00 • French, Italian, Spanish, Russian and Farsi spoken • Prices medium to very high • All major credit cards

Upscale contemporary furniture at all locations.

WORKBENCH

470 Park Avenue South, New York, NY 10016 • Tel: (212) 481-5454 •
Mon-Fri 9:00-8:00, Sat 10:00-6:00, Sun 12:00-6:00
336 East 86th Street, New York, NY 10028 • Mon, Thu 9:00-8:00, Tue,
Wed, Fri 9:00-6:00, Sat 10:00-6:00, Sun 12:00-5:00
2091 Broadway, New York, NY 10023 • Mon-Thu 10:00-8:00, Tue, Wed,
Thu 10:00-6:30, Sat 10:00-6:00, Sun 12:00-5:00
176 Sixth Avenue, New York, NY 10013 • Mon-Sat 10:00-7:00, Sun
12:00-6:00 • All major credit cards

For the young in heart. Mostly simple contemporary furniture in
graceful, functional designs.

Custom

⚜ ATELIER VIOLLET

505 Driggs Avenue, Brooklyn, NY 11211 • Tel: (718) 782-1727 • Fax:
(718) 782-1602 • Mon-Fri 7:30-6:00 • Jean-Paul Viollet • French spoken • Prices high

A very special designer and fabricator of fine custom furniture in
wood, parchment, shagreen, metal.

EVANSON STUDIOS

1 Bond Street, New York, NY 10012 • Tel: (212) 777-6943 • Fax: (212)
473-2604 • Mon-Fri 9:00-5:00 • James Evanson • Prices medium •
Trade discount

Fabricator of contemporary and transitional furniture: chairs, tables,
lights. They work with exotic woods and veneers, gold and silver
leafing. Also refinishing of antiques and French polishing.

HAF LIMITED

68 Thompson Street, New York, NY 10012 • Telfax: (212) 925-3100 •
Tue-Fri 10:00-6:00, Sat 11:00-6:00 • Meredith Clapp • Arabic and French
spoken • Prices high • 10 to 20% trade discount • Amex and Visa

Contemporary, architect designed, one-of-a-kind custom furniture.
Japanese influence. Will soon be making some models in large editions.

⚜ TODD HASE FURNITURE, INC.

51 Wooster Street, New York, NY 10013 • Tel: (212) 334-3568 • Fax:
(212) 274-1479 • Mon-Fri 10:00-6:00, Sat 12:00-6:00 • Amy and Todd
Hase • Prices high • Trade discount • Major credit cards

Entire collection of superb upholstered furniture and tables designed
by Todd Hase. Some antiques.

TERRY HIRST

313 Church Street, New York, NY 10013 • Tel: (212) 966-2609 • Fax: (212) 941-1702 • Mon-Fri 7:30-6:00 • Terry Hirst • Spanish and French spoken • Prices high • Some trade discounts

Fine furniture and cabinetry for clients looking for design as well as construction.

IKERU LTD. THE DESIGN WORKSHOP

466 Washington Street, New York, NY 10013 • Tel: (212) 219-3757 • Fax: (212) 274-0115 • Mon-Fri 9:00-5:00 • Many languages spoken • Prices medium to high • 20% trade discounts • Major credit cards

One-of-a-kind custom furniture; dinnerware; tableware; ceramics.

HOWARD KAPLAN ANTIQUES

827-831 Broadway, New York, NY 10003 • Tel: (212) 674-1000 • Fax: (212) 220-7204 • Mon-Fri 9:00-6:00 • David B. Kyner • Prices high • MC and Visa

Very special custom tables made from old woods. Custom iron work.

METALWORK ARCHITECTURE DESIGN

28 Richardson Street, Brooklyn, NY 11211 • Telfax: (718) 384-2985 • By appointment • James Coleman • Prices high

Custom furniture and fixtures and display designs for retail stores and restaurants. In metal and wood.

METROPOLITAN DESIGN CENTER INTERNATIONAL

450 Broome Street, New York, NY 10013 • Tel: (212) 941-8600 • Fax: (212) 941-8723 • Tue-Sat 11:00-7:00, Sun-Mon 12:00-6:00 • Yiannis Georgopoulos • Greek, Spanish and Italian spoken • Prices medium • Major credit cards

Design and custom fabrication of contemporary and classical furniture. No stock.

♔ FRANK POLLARO

356 Glenwood Avenue, East Orange, NJ 07017 • Tel: (201) 748-5353 • Fax: (212) 675-7778 • Mon-Fri 8:00-6:00 and by appointment • Prices very high

Custom-made museum quality furniture, specializing in French Art Deco, particularly the work of Ruhlmann. Restoration and replications.

POMPANOOSUC MILLS

470 Broome Street, New York, NY 10013 • Tel: (212) 226-5960 • Fax: (212) 226-6086 • Mon-Fri 10:00-7:00, Sat-Sun 11:00-6:00 • Robert Chapin • Prices medium to high • Some trade discounts • Major credit cards

Hardwood furniture custom built to order in a choice of five North American hardwoods. Lamps, some rugs and other accessories.

ROBERT RUSSELL FURNITURE DESIGN

12 Waverly Place, New York, NY 10003 • Telfax: (718) 388-3055 • By appointment • Robert Russell • Prices high

Fine hand-crafted furniture made to order.

GINGER SCHMIDT

130 Ryerson Avenue, #118, Wayne, NJ 07470 • Tel: (201) 696-2620 • By appointment • Prices medium to high • Trade discounts • Major credit cards

Custom designed unique hand-painted furniture in whimsical animal and floral designs.

DAVID SMOLEN/DRS INTERIORS

P.O. Box 156, Deposit, New York 13754 • Telfax: (607) 467-2572 • By appointment • Prices medium to high

One of the best artisans in the New York area. He designs and makes custom furniture, does wood sculpture for artists and does custom millwork for the top architects and designers in New York.

WALTER STEVENS WOODWORKING & DESIGN

497 Route 55, Eldred, NY 12732 • Tel: (914) 557-6437 • By appointment • Walter Stevens • Prices medium to high

Marquetry furniture in contemporary styles made from the woods native to the Catskills region. A unique style of polished rustic marquetry. Extraordinary work. Will take custom orders. Photos of his work are available.

T & T WOODWORKING, INC.

37 West 20th Street, New York, NY 10011 • Tel: (212) 255-6005 • Fax: (212) 255-6006 • Mon-Sat 8:30-4:30 • Josef Tomahatsch • Hungarian, French and Spanish spoken • Prices high

Custom antique reproduction furniture.

THE WOODSHOP OF ENRIQUE MARTINEZ

322 Dean Street, Brooklyn, NY 11217 • Tel: (718) 643-4003 • Mon-Fri 9:00-5:00 • Enrique Martinez • Spanish spoken • Prices high • Trade discounts

Hand-crafted custom furniture using old-world techniques in solid woods. Country designs, home entertainment centers, armoires, book units, tables, custom cabinetry.

Painted

ELLEN BERENSON ANTIQUES AND FINE ARTS, INC.

988 Lexington Avenue, New York, NY 10021 • Telfax: (212) 288-5302 • Mon-Fri 10:30-6:00, Sat 11:00-5:30 • French spoken • Prices medium to high • Trade discount • Major credit cards

Fine period and antique European painted furniture.

ERCOLE

116 Franklin Street, New York, NY 10013 • Tel: (212) 941-6098 • Fax: (212) 941-6720 • Mon-Fri 10:00-6:00 • French, Italian, Spanish and Portuguese spoken • Prices very high

Mosaic and hand-painted furniture. These are one of a kind, especially tables, chests and bureaus. A special technique of "picassiette" is used on vintage pieces of furniture where broken china is applied in a mosaic style. Very unusual and great fun.

GREY GARDENS

461 Broome Street, New York, NY 10013 • Tel: (212) 966-7116 • Fax: (212) 965-9787 • Mon-Fri 12:00-7:00, Sat-Sun 12:00-6:00 • Terry Ross and Jennifer Jager • Prices high • Trade discount • Major credit cards

European and American painted furniture, 18th century to the 1940s. Marvellous mirrors, chandeliers and English transferware.

OSMUNDO ECHEVARRIA & ASSOC. INC.

130 West 29th Street, 10th floor, New York, 10001 • Tel: (212) 868-3029 • Fax: (212) 868-3037 • Mon-Fri 9:00-6:00 • Spanish spoken • Prices medium to high • Trade only

This is a decorative painting studio that specializes in hand-painted and decorative finishes on furniture and screens. Works especially with decorators and designers to create and re-create their project designs.

Plexi

LEPAGE NEW YORK GALLERY

72 Thompson Street, New York, NY 10012 • Tel: (212) 966-2646 • Tue-Sat 12:00-7:00, Sun 12:00-6:00 • Susanne Hassenstein • French and German spoken • Prices medium to high • Trade discount • Major credit cards

Manhattan made, acrylic signature collection of home accessories designed by Cec LePage: candleholders, vases, bookends, bath accessories, napkin rings, trays. Custom furniture ranges from foot stools to 36-inch consoles, side tables and pool benches. Custom coloring and will match any color swatch. One-of-a-kind and limited editions available.

PLEXI-CRAFT QUALITY PRODUCTS CORP.

514 West 24th Street, New York, NY 10011 • Tel: (212) 924-3244 • Fax: (212) 924-3508 • Mon-Fri 9:30-5:00 • Prices low to medium • MC and Visa

Stock and custom plexi furniture: all kinds of tables, dining, cocktail, parson's tables, TV tables, snack, side. Bases for rolling carts, all kinds of chairs, computer stands, pedestals, vanities. Absolutely everything.

Rattan and Wicker

BIELECKY BROTHERS

979 Third Avenue (D&D), New York, NY 10022 • Tel: (212) 753-2355 • Fax: (212) 751-9369 • Mon-Fri 9:30-4:30 • Anthony Melkun • Prices very high • Trade only

Cane, wicker and rattan furniture; all handmade in the U.S. Living room, dining room, bedrooms; chairs, sofas, tables, cabinets. Has served New York's top interior designers.

WALTERS WICKER INC.

979 Third Avenue (D&D) New York, NY 10022 • Tel: (212) 758-0472 • Fax: (212) 826-6775 • Mon-Fri 9:00-5:00 • David S. Laurence • Prices high • Trade only

Excellent collection of good quality bamboo and rattan furniture. They also carry fabrics and other furniture items.

WICKER GARDEN

1318 Madison Avenue, New York, NY 10128 • Tel: (212) 410-7001 • Fax: (212) 410-6609 • Mon-Sat 10:00-6:00 • Pamela Scurry • Spanish spoken • Prices high • Trade discount • Major credit cards

Pamela Scurry's line of reproduction antique wicker furniture and some antique wicker. Home furnishings and children's furniture.

Upholstered and Convertibles

CARLYLE CUSTOM CONVERTIBLES, LTD.

1056 Third Avenue, New York, NY 10021 • Tel: (212) 838-1525
1375 Third Avenue, New York, NY 10021 • Tel: (212) 570-2236
122 West 18th Street, New York, NY 10011 • Tel: (212) 675-3212
• Mon-Fri 10:00-7:00, Thu 10:00-8:00, Sat 10:00-6:00, Sun 12:00-5:00 • Many languages spoken • Prices medium to high • All major credit cards

Manufacturers and retailers of good quality custom-made sleep sofas, sofas, chair beds, chairs, ottoman beds and ottomans.

CLASSIC SOFA LTD.

5 West 22nd Street, New York, NY 10010 • Tel: (212) 620-0485 • Fax: (212) 924-0953 • Mon, Wed, Fri-Sat 10:00-6:00, Tue, Thu 10:00-8:00, Sun 12:00-5:00 • Prices high • Major credit cards

Custom-upholstered furniture. Down filled sofas made in two weeks.

COCONUT COMPANY

131 Greene Street, New York, NY 10012 • Tel: (212) 539-1940 • Fax: (212) 539-1935 • Mon-Sat 10:30-6:30, Sun 12:00-6:00 • Philippe M. Trang • French, German, Spanish and Japanese spoken • 20% trade discount • Major credit cards

An extensive collection of generously proportioned English style sofas. A wide selection of upholstery fabrics. Great imports from the Far East, antique and new, Dutch Colonial furniture, 19th-century French antiques and fabrics from England.

HOPE & WILDER

90 Grand Street, New York, NY 10013 • Tel: (212) 966-9010 • Tue-Sat 11:00-7:00, Sun 12:00-7:00 • Eileen Applebaum • Prices medium to high • Trade discount • Major credit cards

Upholstered furniture, fabric, slipcovers, custom sewing work, draperies, skirts, duvets. 19th- and 20th-century cupboards, dressers, beds, tables, chairs and smalls galore.

JENNIFER CONVERTIBLES

893 Broadway, New York, NY 10003 • Tel: (212) 614-0837 • Fax: (212) 614-0851 • Mon-Fri 10:00-9:00, Sat 10:00-6:00, Sun 12:00-5:00 • Prices medium • Major credit cards

This is a vast chain with 200 retail outlets. Call or fax the above number for the location nearest you. They manufacture and distribute sofa beds, furniture and leather upholstery.

LEATHER CENTER

44 East 32nd Street, New York, NY 10017 • Tel: (212) 696-4100 • Fax: (212) 696-5120 • Mon-Thu 10:00-8:00, Fri-Sat 10:00-6:00, Sun 12:00-6:00 • Prices medium to high • Major credit cards

Major manufacturer and retailer of leather seating, sofas, chairs.

PEMBROOKE & IVES

149 Wooster Street, New York, NY 10012 • Tel: (212) 995-0555 • Fax: (212) 995-2678 • Mon-Fri 9:00-6:00 and by appointment • Andrew Sheinman • Prices high to very high

Upholstered furniture custom made to order, created to fill a particular space. Follow-up maintenance provided for pillows, wood and fabric. Full drapery services.

POLTRONA FRAU

145 Wooster Street, New York, NY 10012 • Tel: (212) 777-7592 • Fax: (212) 777-8481 • Mon-Fri 10:00-6:00, Sat 12:00-5:00 • French, Spanish and Italian spoken • Prices high to very high

Fine leather upholstered furniture from Italy.

SHABBY CHIC

93 Greene Street, New York, NY 10012 • Tel: (212) 274-9842 • Fax: (212) 274-9845 • Mon-Sat 10:00-7:00, Sun 11:00-7:00 • Wendi Brighton • Italian spoken • Prices high • Major credit cards

Oversized, overstuffed, feather and down filled, faded slipcovered furniture. Also antique accessories.

SOFA SO GOOD

106 Wooster Street, New York, NY 10012 • Tel: (212) 219-8860 • Fax: (212) 219-8674 • Mon-Fri 10:00-7:00, Sat-Sun 11:00-6:00 • Prices high • 30% trade discount • MC and Visa

Designer leather furniture. Molinari trade showroom open to the public.

THE UPHOLSTERED ROOM

412-416 Atlantic Avenue, Brooklyn, NY 11217 • Tel: (718) 875-7084 • Wed-Sun 12:00-6:00 by appointment • David Marshall • Spanish spoken • Trade discounts • Major credit cards

Fine upholstery of 18th- and 19th-century furniture and draperies. He also sells high-style Victorian furniture and lace from the Victorian period.

GARDENS

Garden Accessories and Furniture

ACE PUMP CORP.

57 West 21st Street, New York, NY 10010 • Tel: (212) 242-1787 •
Mon-Thu 7:30-4:30, Fri 7:30-2:00 • Prices medium

Pumps for fountains and accessories. Sales and service.

CENTRUM

225 Fifth Avenue, New York, NY 10010 • Tel: (212) 779-8827 • Fax:
(212) 689-9662 • Mon-Fri 9:00-5:00 • Joan Cosgrove • Prices medium
• Trade only

Garden accessories, stools, cache-pots, watering cans, umbrellas,
lacquer trays, marble cheeseboards, needlepoint pillows.

ELIZABETH STREET GARDENS & GALLERY

1176 & 1196 Second Avenue, New York, NY 10021 • Tel: (212) 644-
6969 • Fax: (212) 644-8090 • Mon-Fri 10:00-5:00 • Michael Garden •
Prices high • Trade discount • Major credit cards

Antique and re-creations of 18th- , 19th- and 20th-century garden
ornaments, fountains, statuary and decorative objects.

EMBEE SUNSHADE COMPANY

722 Metropolitan Avenue, Brooklyn, NY 11211 • Tel: (718) 387-8566 •
Mon-Thu 8:30-5:00, Fri 8:30-3:00 • Spanish spoken • Prices medium
• Trade discount

Garden, lawn, pool, patio and beach umbrellas.

FLORENTINE CRAFTSMEN

46-24 28th Street, Long Island City, NY 11101 • Tel: (718) 937-7632 •
Fax: (718) 937-9858 • Mon-Fri 8:00-4:30 • Graham "Skip" Brown II •
Trade discounts • Major credit cards

High quality hand-crafted garden fountains, statuary, planters, urns
and accessories.

⚏ FOLLY

13 White Street, New York, NY 10013 • Tel: (212) 925-5012 • Fax:
(212) 925-0240 • Mon-Fri 11:00-5:00 and by appointment • Paul Flores
• Spanish spoken • Prices high • 20% trade discount

17th- , 18th- and 19th-century antique garden ornaments; the David
Anthony Easton furniture line.

THE GARDEN ANTIQUARY

724 Fifth Avenue, New York, NY 10019 • Tel: (212) 757-3008 • Fax: (212) 757-3904 • Mon-Fri 10:00-6:00 • Moshe Bronstein • Trade discount

16th- to 19th-century garden sculpture, ornaments and garden furniture.

THE GARDEN ROOM

1179 Lexington Avenue, New York, NY 10028 • Telfax: (212) 879-1179 • Mon-Fri 9:00-6:00 • Mark J. McCarty • Prices medium • Trade discount • Major credit cards

Garden furniture in metal and iron, very good selection of garden statuary, urns, benches and accessories. Antique and custom wrought iron railings, gates and table bases.

THE GARDENER'S TOUCH

1545 Second Avenue, New York, NY 10028 • Tel: (212) 288-1418 • Mon-Sat 11:00-7:00, Sun 12:00-5:00 • Jim Manning • German spoken • Trade discount • Prices medium to high • Major credit cards

Decorative accessories for the garden, upscale hand tools, chimes, small statuary, watering cans, hand-painted decoupage pots, large selection of books on landscaping and gardening.

GENERAL FOUNTAIN COMPANY

264 West 40th Street, New York, NY 10018 • Tel: (212) 391-3920 • Fax: (212) 391-3923 • Mon-Fri 9:00-4:00 • Jeanne Hodge • Prices medium to high • Trade discount

Fountains and garden ornaments.

IRREPLACEABLE ARTIFACTS

14 Second Avenue, New York, NY 10003 • Tel: (212) 777-2900 • Fax: (212) 780-0642 • Mon-Fri 10:00-6:00, Sat-Sun 11:00-5:00 • David Callegeros • 10 to 20% trade discount

An enormous collection of architectural ornaments from demolished buildings, including garden ornaments, carved stone figures and wrought iron elements.

LEXINGTON GARDENS

1011 Lexington Avenue, New York, NY 10021 • Tel: (212) 861-4310 • Fax: (212) 988-0943 • Mon-Fri 10:00-6:00, Sat 11:00-5:00 • Debbie Dunn and Rosa Szule • French, German, Spanish, Turkish and Italian spoken • 20% trade discount • Major credit cards

An astonishing display of antique garden furniture; some oversized urns, planters, indoor and outdoor lanterns, gargoyles, tole and decoupage mirrors, plinthes, brackets, sconces, pedestals, Haddonstone benches and some botanical prints.

MUNDER-SKILES

799 Madison Avenue, New York, NY 10021 • Tel: (212) 717-0150 • Fax: (212) 717-0149 • Mon-Fri 9:00-5:00 • John G. Danzer • Prices high • 20% trade discount

Garden furniture and outdoor decorative objects in wood, masonry and cold-rolled steel. Their standard line of furniture is in mahogany and they will custom make in teak and oak. They ship world-wide.

ROOMS & GARDENS

290 Lafayette Street, New York, NY 10012 • Tel: (212) 431-1297 • Fax: (212) 431-0945 • Mon-Fri 10:00-6:00, Sat 11:00-6:00, Sun 12:00-5:00 • Jim Gardner • French and Japanese spoken • Prices high • 20% trade discount • Major credit cards

French antique furniture, accessories; folk art with an emphasis on garden; exterior pieces.

SMITH & HAWKEN

394 West Broadway, New York, NY 10012 • Tel: (212) 925-1190 • Fax: (212) 925-4894 • Mon-Sat 10:00-7:00, Sun 12:00-6:00 • Paul Barthel • Prices medium to high • 20% discount on furniture • Major credit cards

High-quality and large choice of teak garden furniture, benches, plant stands, caste stone statuary, fountains, garden ornaments. Full line of trellises, terra-cotta containers; English garden tools, boots and apparel. Full line of orchids and orchid products, wide selection of indoor plants and planting materials. Topiaries and herbs.

BRIAN WINDSOR ART, ANTIQUES & GARDENING FURNISH-INGS

272 Lafayette Street, New York, NY 10012 • Tel: (212) 274-0411 • Mon-Fri 11:00-6:00, Sat-Sun 12:00-5:00 • Some French spoken • Prices medium • Trade discount • Major credit cards

Antique and vintage wrought iron garden furniture; folk art and Americana.

Garden and Terrace Design and Planting

ALPINE FLORIST

999 Lexington Avenue, New York, NY 10021 • Tel: (212) 879-6932 • Fax: (212) 628-7581 • Mon-Sat 9:00-6:00 • Paul MacDonnell • French and Spanish spoken • Prices medium • Trade discounts • Major credit cards

Terrace landscaping services; flower arrangements and contract flower service.

ANTHONY GARDEN BOUTIQUE LTD.

134 East 70th Street, New York, NY 10021 • Tel: (212) 737-3303 • Fax: (212) 717-5170 • Mon-Sat 9:00-6:00 • Prices high • 10% trade discount • Major credit cards

Terrace landscaping, flowers and decorative antiques.

CHELSEA GARDEN CENTER

205 Ninth Avenue, New York, NY 10011 • Tel: (212) 929-2477 • Fax: (212) 645-9400 • Daily 9:00-6:00 • David Protell • French, Hebrew, Spanish and Portuguese spoken • Prices medium to high • 15% trade discount • Major credit cards

Complete garden center: fully stocked nursery with plants, ivy, flowering plants. Garden design and installations. Garden furniture and furnishings.

FARM & GARDEN NURSERY

2 Sixth Avenue, New York, NY 10013 • Tel: (212) 431-3577 • Fax: (212) 431-4162 • Daily 9:00-6:00 • Prices medium to high

Terrace landscaping and planting. Spring clean-ups and winterizing services.

JAMIE GIBBS & ASSOCIATES

340 East 93rd Street, New York, NY 10128 • Tel: (212) 722-7508 • Fax: (212) 369-6332 • Mon-Fri 10:00-6:00 • Claudio Yanes • Spanish, some French, Italian and Russian spoken • Prices high • 15% trade discount

Landscape architects for fine homes.

THE GRASS ROOTS GARDEN

131 Spring Street, New York, NY 10012 • Tel: (212) 226-2662 • Fax: (212) 274-1887 • Tue-Sat 9:00-6:00, Sun 12:00-6:00 • Larry Nathanson • Major credit cards

Specimen and rare tropical foliage and flowering plants. Pottery, garden goods, baskets, accessories and books on gardening. Indoor and outdoor landscaping services: residential and commercial.

DAVID MADISON HORTICULTURAL DESIGN INC.

219 East 60th Street, New York, NY 10022 • Tel: (212) 421-8110 • Fax: (212) 688-6652 • Mon-Sat 9:00-5:00 • David Madison • Prices very high • 20% trade discount • Major credit cards

Antique garden furniture and accessories. Plants, flowers, garden and party design.

RONALDO MAIA LTD.

27 East 67th Street, New York, NY 10021 • Tel: (212) 288-1049 • Mon-Fri 9:00-6:00, Sat 11:00-5:00 • French, Spanish, Italian and Portuguese spoken • Prices high • Major credit cards

The author of two fabulous books on decorating with flowers, Ronaldo Maia is the acknowledged master of the classic as well as the innovative flower arrangement. His shop offers unusual containers, holiday decorations and his own potpourris and fragrances for the house. He also has a small collection of antiques and crafts from all over the world.

PLANT SPECIALISTS INC.

42-25 Vernon Boulevard, Long Island City, NY 11101 • Tel: (718) 392-9404 • Fax: (718) 706-1169 • Mon-Fri 9:00-5:00 • Spanish spoken • Prices high • Major credit cards

Garden design, construction and maintenance. Garden planting and lighting.

POTTED GARDENS LTD.

27 Bedford Street, New York, NY 10014 • Tel: (212) 255-4797 • Fax: (212) 255-4680 • Tue-Sun 12:00-7:00 • Amy Wanggaard • Spanish spoken • Prices medium to high • 10% trade discount • Major credit cards

Full-scale florist and antique store: antique garden furniture in wood and metal and accessories. Terrace services, weekly floral contracts; weddings and events.

STUDIO 19

21 Commerce Street, New York, NY 10014 • Tel: (212) 337-0085 • Fax: (212) 337-0774 • By appointment • David Walker, Herman Fugate • Prices medium to high • MC and Visa

A garden shop that offers landscaping services. They have planted flowers, special containers in custom colors, glazed terra-cotta pots and decorative objects.

Decorative Hardware: Door, Window, Cabinet and Bath

AF SUPPLY CORP.

22 West 21st Street, New York, NY 10010 • Tel: (212) 243-5400 • Fax: (212) 423-2403 • Mon-Fri 8:00-5:00 • Bennett Friedman • French spoken • Prices medium to very high • Major credit cards

Distributors of fine bath fixtures and quality door and window hardware. Excellent choice.

THE BRASS CENTER

248 East 58th Street, New York, NY 10021 • Tel: (212) 421-0090 • Fax: (212) 371-7088 • Mon-Fri 8:30-5:00 • Spanish spoken • Prices medium to high • 25% trade discount • Major credit cards

Complete line of good quality bath, door and cabinet hardware. All standard finishes.

DAVIS & WARSHOW

150 East 58th Street, New York, NY 10155 • Tel: (212) 593-0438 • Fax: (212) 593-0446 • Mon-Fri 8:00-5:30 • Prices medium to high • Trade discount

High-quality bathroom fittings and fixtures in standard finishes, brass, chrome, nickel. The showroom represents Kohler, Broadway and Kallista.

THE DECORATIVE HARDWARE STUDIO

P.O. Box 627, Chappaqua, New York 10514 • Tel: (914) 238-5251 • Fax: (914) 238-4880 • Mon-Fri 10:00-5:00 • Ron and Marie Prezner • Spanish spoken • Prices high • Trade only

Custom manufacturers of decorative door, window, cabinet and drapery hardware. Will restore, re-finish and duplicate hardware. Catalog available upon request.

DECO WARE, INC.

944 McDonald Avenue, Brooklyn, NY 11218 • Tel: (718) 871-1212 • Fax: (718) 972-3277 • Mon, Tue, Wed 9:00-6:00, Thu 9:00-7:00, Fri 9:00-2:00, Sun 10:00-5:00 • Aaron Taub • Prices medium • 25 to 30% trade discount • Major credit cards

Decorative hardware for doors, cabinets and windows; locks; plumbing fixtures; accessories, tubs, sinks, pedestals, toilets, shower doors.

DESIGN SOURCE BY DAVE SANDERS

115 The Bowery, New York, NY 10002 • Tel: (212) 274-0022 • Fax: (212) 274-0627 • Mon-Fri 8:00-5:00 • Sheik Anif • Spanish spoken • Prices medium to high • Trade discounts • Major credit cards

Large selection of imported door, cabinet and window hardware in all standard finishes. Plumbing fixtures and accessories.

MICHAEL DOTZEL & SON

402 East 63rd Street, New York, NY 10021 • Tel: (212) 838-2890 • Fax: (212) 371-4839 • Mon-Fri 8:00-5:00 • Michael Dotzel • Prices medium to high

Reproduction casting of decorative hardware and gilding and refinishing of bronze and brass.

GRACIOUS HOME

1220 Third Avenue, New York, NY 10021 • Tel: (212) 517-6300 • Fax: (212) 249-1534 • Mon-Fri 8:00-7:00, Sat 9:00-7:00, Sun 10:00-6:00 • Prices medium to high • Major credit cards

A very extensive selection of decorative hardware: door, window, bath, cabinet and drapery, both American and European. Everything in standard or more exotic finishes.

⚎ P.E. GUERIN, INC.

21-23 Jane Street, New York, NY 10014 • Tel: (212) 243-5270 • Fax: (212) 727-2290 • Mon-Fri 9:00-5:00 by appointment • Prices medium to very high • Trade discount

High-quality decorative hardware for doors, windows and cabinets in classic and contemporary designs. One of New York's best sources.

⚎ ILE DE FRANCE IMPORTS

Upper East Side, New York, NY 10021 • Tel: (212) 439-0194 • Fax: (212) 249-9501 • By appointment only • French spoken • Prices high to extremely high

French chateau and palace quality hardware for doors and windows. Consultation and specifications for major contracts only. Very likely the most beautiful hardware in the world.

KRAFT

306 East 61st Street, New York, NY 10021 • Tel: (212) 838-2214 • Fax: (212) 644-9254 • Mon-Fri 9:00-5:00 • Jack Randolph • 25% trade discount • MC and Visa

Door, window and cabinet hardware. Wide range of contemporary and antique reproduction hardware. Extensive lines of locks as well as bathroom and kitchen fixtures. Variety of finishes.

LOCKS AND KEYS UNLIMITED

129 West 29th Street, 12th floor, New York, NY 10001 • Tel: (212) 629-5630 • Fax: (212) 268-4577 • Mon-Fri 9:00-5:00 • Joseph Biunno • Spanish, Russian, Hungarian and Italian spoken • Prices medium to very high • Major credit cards

Replacements and repairs of antique locks and keys.

NANZ CUSTOM HARDWARE, INC.

20 Vandam Street, New York, NY 10013 • Tel: (212) 367-7000 • Fax: (212) 367-7375 • Mon-Fri by appointment • Carl Sorenson • Prices very high • Catalog available for $20

Manufacturer and distributor of decorative door and window hardware, locks, hinges, knobs, levers. Consultation, specification and scheduling.

RAJACK DESIGNS, LTD.

43-45 Rome Street, Farmingdale, NY 11735 • Tel: (516) 293-8273 • Fax: (516) 293-8717 • Mon-Fri 7:00-3:30 • Prices medium • Trade only

Manufacturer of high-quality bronze and brass door and cabinet hardware in custom finishes. Architectural and builders' hardware.

SHERLE WAGNER INTERNATIONAL, INC.

60 East 57th Street, New York, NY 10022 • Tel: (212) 758-3300 • Fax: (212) 207-8010 • Mon-Fri 9:30-5:00 • Vincent Geoffroy • Spanish spoken • Prices high to very high

Decorative door and window hardware, much of it reproduced from classic European period hardware. Bathroom fixtures and accessories. Unique designs.

SIMON'S HARDWARE & BATH

421 Third Avenue, New York, NY 10016 • Tel: (212) 532-9220 • Fax: (212) 481-0564 • Mon-Fri 8:00-5:30, Thu 8:00-7:00, Sat 10:00-6:00 • Spanish, French and Italian spoken • Prices medium to high • 20 to 25% trade discount • Major credit cards

A very large selection of decorative door and window hardware; contemporary styles and reproductions of European period hardware; architectural hardware; bath fixtures and accessories. Marble stone and tile.

SMITH WOODWORKS AND DESIGN

101 Farmersville Road, Califon, NJ 07830 • Tel: (908) 832-2723 • Fax: (908) 832-6994 • Mon-Fri 8:00-5:00 • Barbara and Todd Smith • French spoken • Prices medium to high • Visa and MC

Custom turned wooden knobs in maple, walnut, cherry, oak and pine. They also carry a line of French furniture hardware, door hardware and door knockers.

Drapery Hardware

THE DECORATIVE HARDWARE STUDIO

P.O. Box 627, Chappaqua, NY 10514 • Tel: (914) 238-5251 • Fax: (914) 238-4880 • Mon-Fri 10:00-5:00 • Ron and Marie Prezner • Spanish spoken • Prices high • Trade only

Custom manufacturers of drapery hardware, stair rods and door, window and cabinet hardware. All finishes and refinishing.

FINIALS UNLIMITED

129 West 29th Street, 2nd floor, New York, NY 10001 • Tel: (212) 629-5630 • Fax: (212) 268-4577 • Mon-Fri 9:00-5:00 • Joseph Biunno • Spanish, Russian, Hungarian and Italian spoken • Prices medium to very high • Trade discount • Major credit cards

Custom drapery hardware.

GRACIOUS HOME

1220 Third Avenue, New York, NY 10021 • Tel: (212) 517-6300 • Fax: (212) 249-1534 • Mon-Fri 8:00-7:00, Sat 9:00-7:00, Sun 10:00-6:00 • French and Spanish spoken • Prices medium to high • Trade discount • Major credit cards

A wide selection of drapery hardware as well as the proper tools for installation.

HOULES USA

979 Third Avenue (D&D), 1st floor, New York, NY 10022 • Tel: (212) 935-3900 • Fax: (212) 935-3923 • Mon-Fri 9:00-5:00 • Denise Nassar • French spoken • Prices high • Trade only

Good selection of French drapery hardware as well as their marvellous collection of trimmings.

CHRISTOPHER HYLAND, INC.

979 Third Avenue (D&D), 17th floor, New York, NY 10022 • Tel: (212) 688-6121 • Fax: (212) 688-6176 • Mon-Fri 9:00-5:00 • Prices high • Trade only

High-quality imported drapery hardware and trimmings from France, England and Germany.

KRAFT

306 East 61st Street, New York, NY 10021 • Tel: (212) 838-2214 • Fax: (212) 644-9254 • Mon-Fri 9:00-5:00 • Jack Randolph • Prices medium to high • Trade discounts • MC and Visa

Good commercial quality drapery hardware.

FRANCOISE NUNNALLE

105 West 55th Street, New York, NY 10019 • Tel: (212) 246-4281 • By appointment • Prices high

Beautiful antique tiebacks from the 19th century, some with interesting historic provenance.

SIMON'S HARDWARE & BATH

421 Third Avenue, New York, NY 10016 • Tel: (212) 532-9220 • Fax: (212) 481-0564 • Mon-Fri 8:00-5:30, Thu 8:00-7:00, Sat 10:00-6:00 • Spanish, French and Italian spoken • Prices medium to high • Trade discounts • Major credit cards

A substantial line of good drapery hardware.

WAINLANDS INC.

453 West 17th Street, New York, NY 10011 • Tel: (212) 243-7717 • Fax: (212) 243-7722 • Mon-Fri 7:00-4:00 • Robert E. Lee • Spanish, Italian, Polish, Hungarian and Rumanian spoken • Prices high • Trade discount

A 25-man shop producing custom curtain hardware: poles, brackets and finials. Metal polishing and finishing. Faux painting and patinas. Custom grilles and registers, stair railings, lanterns and lighting, étagères, tables, desks and consoles. Restoration and repair.

WINDOW MODES LTD.

979 Third Avenue (D&D), 16th floor, New York, NY 10022 • Tel: (212) 752-1140 • Fax: (212) 355-7764 • Trade only

Full line of drapery hardware.

HOME FURNISHINGS, DECORATIVE ACCESSORIES, HOUSEWARES

ABC CARPET & HOME

888 Broadway at East 19th Street, New York, NY 10003 • Tel: (212) 473-3000 • Fax: (212) 777-3713 • Mon-Fri 10:00-8:00, Sat 10:00-7:00, Sun 11:00-6:30 • French and Spanish spoken • Prices medium to very high • 10% trade discount • Major credit cards

A ten-floor home furnishings specialty store with broadloom, rugs, antiques, Orientals, furniture, fabrics, linens, gifts, accessories, lighting, tabletop, etc.

AD HOC SOFTWARES

410 West Broadway, New York, NY 10012 • Tel: (212) 925-2652 • Fax: (212) 941-6910 • Mon-Sat 11:00-7:00, Sun 11:30-7:00 • Michelle Hebert • Prices medium • Major credit cards

Household linens, bed and bath products, china, glass, clothing accessories, robes and gift items.

ADRIEN LINFORD

927 Madison Avenue, New York, NY 10021 • Tel: (212) 628-4500 • Fax: (212) 628-1322
1320 Madison Avenue, New York, NY 10128 • Tel: (212) 289-4427 • Perry Layton • French, Spanish and German spoken • Prices medium • Major credit cards

Hand-crafted decorative accessories, small furniture and gifts for the home, as well as great selection in table arts and books on the decorative arts. You will also find jewelry and personal items designed primarily by American artists. Visually exciting.

AERO LTD.

132 Spring Street, New York, NY 10012 • Tel: (212) 966-1500 • Fax: (212) 966-4701 • Mon-Sat 11:00-6:00 • Spanish spoken • Prices high • 10% trade discount • Major credit cards

Custom-designed lamps and furniture, vintage pieces from a range of periods. Jonathon Adler ceramics, small silver tea sets, lots of Depression colored glass, hand blown glass and more.

AFTER THE RAIN

149 Mercer Street, New York, NY 10012 • Tel: (212) 431-1044 • Fax: (212) 431-1570 • Mon-Sat 11:00-7:00, Sun 12:00-6:00 • Agnieszka Potoczek • Prices medium • Major credit cards

Fine craft gallery, unique objects from around the world: glass, boxes, jewelry, tapestries and gargoyles. Their specialty is fine kaleidoscopes and optical toys by over 100 artisans. Visit their second location with handmade toys, books and folk art: THE ENCHANTED FOREST, 85 Mercer Street, Soho • Tel: (212) 925-6677.

APARTMENT 48

48 West 17th Street, New York, NY 10011 • Tel: (212) 807-1391 • Fax: (212) 807-1989 • Tue-Fri 11:00-8:00, Sat 11:00-7:00, Sun 1:00-6:00 • Rayman Boozer • Prices medium • 10% professional discount • Major credit cards

Home accessories for every room: rustic furniture, garden and bath gifts.

ARKITEKTURA

96 Greene Street, New York, NY 10012 • Tel: (212) 334-5570 • Fax: (212) 334-8028 • Mon-Fri 10:30-5:30, Sat 12:00-5:00 • Lynn Adams • Trade discount • Major credit cards

In-house designs of furniture, lighting and accessories.

BEDFORD & COMPANY

995 Lexington Avenue, New York, NY 10021 • Tel: (212) 772-7000 • Fax: (212) 772-3513 • Mon-Fri 10:00-6:00, Sat 11:00-5:00 • Martha Bedford • Prices medium to high • Major credit cards

Decorative furnishings for the home: everything from upholstered furniture to mirrors, lamps and unique accessories.

BETTER YOUR HOME INC.

1295 Second Avenue, New York, NY 10021 • Tel: (212) 734-5800 • Fax: (212) 734-5355 • Mon-Sat 10:00-7:00, Sun 11:00-6:00 • Vanida Chawla • Prices medium • Major credit cards
103 West 96th Street, New York, NY 10025 • Tel: (212) 866-8700 • Fax: (212) 866-9277 • Prices medium • Major credit cards

Kitchen furniture, carts, housewares, bathware, frames.

BLOOMINGDALE'S

1000 Third Avenue/Lexington Avenue at 59th Street, New York, NY 10022 • Tel: (212) 705-2000 • Mon-Fri 10:00-8:30, Sat 10:00-7:00, Sun 11:00-7:00 • All price levels • Major credit cards

Everything in home furnishings, from furniture to appliances, linens and tableware. In-house decorating service.

BOCA GRANDE

89 Spring Street, New York, NY 10012 • Tel: (212) 966-7716 • Fax: (212) 941-6061 • 7 days 11:00-7:45 • Marcello Duek • Spanish, Portuguese and Italian spoken • Prices high • 15-25% trade discount • Major credit cards

Crafts and furniture from around the globe.

THE BOMBAY COMPANY

900 Broadway, New York, NY 10003 • Tel: (212) 420-1315 • Tue-Fri 10:00-7:00, Mon-Thu until 8:00, Sat 10:00-6:00, Sun 12:00-6:00
2001 Broadway, New York, NY 10023 • Tel: (212) 721-7701 • Mon-Fri 10:00-8:00, Sat 10:00-7:00, Sun 12:00-5:00
1062A Third Avenue, New York, NY 10021 • Tel: (212) 759-7217 • Mon-Fri 10:00-8:00, Sat 10:00-6:00, Sun 12:00-6:00 • Prices medium to high • Major credit cards

Reproductions of 18th- and 19th-century English and French furniture. Some antique pine furniture and lots of decorative accessories.

JOHN BOONE INC.

1059 Third Avenue, New York, NY 10021 • Tel: (212) 758-0012 • Fax: (212) 758-0260 • Mon-Fri 8:30-5:30 • John Boone and Christopher Lockwood • Prices high • Trade only

Custom designed furniture, lighting and decorative accessories: Lockwood/Boone Collection as well as Paul M. Jones Collection and Jerome Sutter Lighting Collection. Ever changing mix of antiques and accessories.

SHEILA BRITZ HOME

1196 Lexington Avenue, New York, NY 10028 • Tel: (212) 517-5153 • Fax: (212) 517-5103 • Mon-Sun 10:00-6:00 • Caroline Fuchs and Sheila Britz • Prices medium • Trade discount • Visa and MC

Antiques and decorative accessories. Here you will find fabrics that are not normally available to the public.

THE BRODEAN STORE, NEW YORK

338 Columbus Avenue, New York, NY 10023 • Tel: (212) 877-4000 • Fax: (212) 877-0274 • Daily 10:00-8:00 • Bernadette Hitt • Prices medium to high • Trade discount • Major credit cards

Antique furniture, china, crystal, linens, flatware and housewares.

CALDONIA ANTIQUES

1685 Third Avenue, New York, NY 10128 • Tel: (212) 534-3307 • Mon-Fri 12:00-7:00 • Trevor Caldonia • Prices low • Trade discount • Major credit cards

Brocante: from the late 19th century through the 1940s: furniture, mirrors, chandeliers, crystal, cut glass and collectibles.

CAP SUD

50 Bond Street, New York, NY 10012 • Tel: (212) 260-9114 • Fax: (212) 260-9014 • Mon-Sun 11:00-7:00 • Catherine Glazer and Annick de Lorme • French spoken • Prices high • 20% trade discount • Major credit cards

A line of French furniture by Garouste and Bonetti, Gatti bistro chairs, antiques. Custom order and French Haute Epoque reproductions: Louis XIII and Louis XIV style furniture adapted to contemporary styles. Mirrors, screens and general accessories, old tables and doors.

C.I.T.E. DESIGN CORP.

100 Wooster Street, New York, NY 10012 • Tel: (212) 431-7272 • Fax: (212) 226-6507 • Mon-Sat 11:00-7:00, Sun 12:00-6:00 • P.J. Casey • French spoken • Prices medium • Trade discount • Major credit cards

Home furnishings: antique metal and stainless steel industrial furniture, lighting in stone and stainless steel. Contemporary toys and accessories.

A COUNTRY

30-55 Vernon Blvd., Long Island City, NY 11102 • Tel: (718) 777-7400 • Fax: (718) 777-7365 • Daily 10:00-5:00 • Prices medium • Trade discount • Major credit cards

Warehouse store carrying constantly changing line of imported antique and reproduction furniture and home furnishings. Custom woodworking and visual displays for stores.

CRAFT CARAVAN INC.

63 Greene Street, New York, NY 10012 • Tel: (212) 431-6669 • Mon-Fri 10:00-6:00, Sat-Sun 11:00-6:00 • Ignacio Villarreal • French and Spanish spoken • Prices medium • Major credit cards

Traditional imports from Africa, Afghanistan and the Philippines: textiles, furniture and jewelry.

CRATE & BARREL

650 Madison Avenue, New York, NY 10022 • Tel: (212) 308-0011 • Fax: (212) 843-0949 • Mon-Fri 10:00-8:00, Sat 10:00-7:00, Sun 12:00-6:00 • Lisa Smith, Tammy Dorward • Multilingual staff • Prices medium • Major credit cards

Housewares and furniture. Gift registry.

CULLMAN & KRAVIS

790 Madison Avenue, Suite 700, New York, NY 10021 • Tel: (212) 249-3871 • Fax: (212) 249-3881 • Mon-Fri 9:00-5:00 • French, Italian, Spanish and some German spoken • Prices very high

Original designs of hand-painted picture frames, waste baskets, lamps, hampers, candlesticks. Will custom make to match fabrics or color schemes.

MICHAEL DAWKINS

33 East 65th Street, New York, NY 10021 • Telfax: (212) 639-9827 •
Mon-Sat 10:00-6:00 • Mark S. Morin • Prices high • Visa and MC

Sculpture, found objects and home furnishings. 14 ct. and sterling
silver jewelry designed by Michael Dawkins.

JOHN DERIAN COMPANY INC.

6 East Second Street, New York, NY 10003 • Tel: (212) 677-3917 •
Fax: (212) 677-7197 • Tue-Sun 10:00-7:00 • John Derian • Prices high
• Trade discount • Major credit cards

Antiques, decorative accessories, découpage plates, lamps, platters, place mats and frames.

DESIGN & COMFORT

464 Park Avenue South, New York, NY 10016 • Tel: (212) 679-9088 •
Fax: (212) 779-0084 • Mon-Fri 10:00-7:00, Thu 10:00-8:00, Sat 10:00-
6:00, Sun 12:00-5:00 • Major credit cards

DESIGN & COMFORT SOHO

380 West Broadway, New York, NY 10012 • Tel: (212) 334-1000 • Fax:
(212) 334-0184 • Mon-Wed 11:00-6:00, Thu-Sat 11:00-8:00, Sun
11:00-6:00 • Farley Kemler • Spanish spoken • Prices medium to high
• Professional discount • Major credit cards

A full range of sofas, tables, wall units, dining tables, contemporary
designs, domestic and imported products.

DISTANT ORIGIN

153 Mercer Street, New York, NY 10012 • Tel: (212) 941-0024 • Fax:
(212) 941-8502 • Mon-Sat 11:30-6:30, Thu 11:30-7:00, Sun 12:00-
6:00 • Alex Hernandez • Spanish spoken • Prices medium • Trade discount • Major credit cards

Blend of humor with style, a mix of old and new 20th-century accessories and home furnishings from around the world: Turkey,
Egypt, South and Central America. Fortuny silk lampshades, ceramics from Italy and antique furniture from Mexico.

DOMAIN HOME FASHIONS

938 Broadway, New York, NY 10002 • Tel: (212) 228-7450 • Fax: (212)
228-8591 • Mon-Fri 10:00-8:00, Sat 10:00-7:00, Sun 12:00-6:00 •
Susan Plaskow
Trump Palace, 1179 Third Avenue, New York, NY 10021 • Tel: (212)
639-1101 • Fax: (212) 639-1106 • Yasmine Chourbagoi • Prices medium • Trade discount • Major credit cards

Specialty retailer of exclusive designer home furnishings including
upholstery, dining, bedroom and decorative accessories.

DOMUS DESIGN CENTER

215 East 58th Street, New York, NY 10022 • Tel: (212) 421-2800 • Fax: (212) 308-8795 • Mon-Fri 9:30-6:00, Sat 11:00-5:00 • B. Hakakian • Spanish and Hebrew spoken • Prices high • Trade discount • Major credit cards

Large showroom of high-end Italian, Swiss and German contemporary furniture and accessories.

DREXEL HERITAGE MANHATTAN

32 West 18th Street, New York, NY 10011 • Tel: (212) 463-0088 • Fax: (212) 463-0099 • Mon & Thu 10:00-8:00, Tue, Wed, Fri 10:00-6:00, Sat 10:00-5:00, Sun 12:00-5:00 • Maryann DiGregorio • Chinese, Spanish and Italian spoken • Prices high • Trade discount • Major credit cards

High-end retail store with furniture, accessories, area rugs, carpeting, bedding and window treatments.

ECLECTIC HOME

224 Eighth Avenue, New York, NY 10011 • Tel: (212) 255-2373 • Fax: (212) 255-3603 • Mon-Sat 12:00-9:00, Sun 12:00-7:00 • Dan Duttinger • Spanish and Portuguese spoken • Prices medium • 10% trade discount • Major credit cards

Funky, whimsical home furnishings, accessories and gifts.

EQUATOR

98 Greene Street, New York, NY 10012 • Fax: (212) 219-3708 • Fax: (212) 219-9313 • Sun-Mon 12:00-6:00, Tue-Sat 11:00-7:00 • Gregory Carson • French spoken • Prices medium • Major credit cards

An eclectic selection of world furnishings and accessories.

ERCOLE

116 Franklin Street, New York, NY 10013 • Tel: (212) 941-6098 • Fax: (212) 941-6720 • By appointment • Raphael Kastoriano • French, Italian and Spanish spoken • Prices high • Trade only

Mosaic tabletops and home accessories.

ETHAN ALLEN

192 Lexington Avenue, New York, NY 10016 • Tel: (212) 213-0600 • Fax: (212) 889-8900 • Louise Tanis • Mon & Thu 10:00-8:00, Tue, Wed, Fri 10:00-6:30, Sat 10:00-6:00, Sun 12:00-5:00
1107 Third Avenue, New York, NY 10021 • Tel: (212) 308-7703 • Mon-Sat 10:00-6:00, Thu 10:00-8:00, Sun 1:00-5:00 • French, Italian and Spanish spoken • Prices medium to high • Trade discount • Major credit cards

Large retail home furnishings store with furniture, accessories, and lighting.

ETRO MILANO

720 Madison Avenue, New York, NY 10021 • Tel: (212) 317-9096 • Fax: (212) 317-1550 • Mon-Sat 10:00-6:00 • Jorgelina Leone • French, Italian, Russian and Japanese spoken • Major credit cards

Home furnishings, metal tables, lamps, metal trays, cache-pots, magazine racks, decorative ceramics, cushions in silk or cotton, bed and table linens.

EVANSON STUDIOS

One Bond Street, New York, NY 10012 • Tel: (212) 777-6943 • Fax: (212) 473-2604 • Mon-Fri 9:00-5:00 • James Evanson • Prices medium • Trade discount

Contemporary and transitional furniture: chairs, tables, lights, rugs, suitable for residential and contract. Custom projects. Work with exotic woods and veneers, gold and silver leaf; custom built-in cabinets. Antique refinishing.

FELISSIMO

10 West 56th Street, New York, NY 10019 • Tel: (212) 247-5656 • Fax: (212) 956-0081 • Mon-Sat 10:00-6:00, Thu 10:00-8:00 • Arthur Doermer • Multilingual staff • Prices high • Major credit cards

Felissimo's turn-of-the-century townhouse offers four floors of objects for the home: antiques, furniture, gardening essentials, bed linens and table items, gifts, books, stationery and apothecary items.

THE FINISHED ROOM

1027 Lexington Avenue, New York, NY 10021 • Tel: (212) 717-7626 • 1200 Madison Avenue, New York, NY 10128 • Tel: (212) 996-9610 • Mon-Sat 10:00-6:00, Sun 12:00-6:00 • Fran Mandalari and Susan Weiss • Prices medium • Trade discount • All major cards

Home furnishings and delightful accessories with some linens.

FOREMOST FURNITURE

8 West 30th Street, New York, NY 10001 • Tel: (212) 889-6347 • Fax: (212) 213-8260 • Mon-Fri 10:00-6:00, Thu 10:00-7:00, Sat 10:00-5:00, Sun 11:00-5:00 • Richard Broderson • Prices medium to high • Trade discount • Major credit cards

Five floors of furniture: contemporary, transitional and country furniture for every room; carpeting, drapery, lighting, wall systems. One floor of leather furniture. Complete decorating service.

GORDON FOSTER

1322 Third Avenue, New York, NY 10021 • Tel: (212) 744-4922 • Fax: (212) 737-1703 • Mon-Fri 10:00-5:45, Sat by appointment • Miguel Pons • Spanish and French spoken • Trade discount

Exceptional accessories including antique and contemporary baskets, antique Chinese and Japanese ceramics, African and Primitive art. Contemporary American porcelain can be custom made in many colorful glazes, platinum and gold for tableware, and lamps.

THE GAZEBO OF NEW YORK

114 East 57th Street, New York, NY 10022 • Tel: (212) 832-7077 • Fax: (212) 754-0571 • Mon-Sat 10:00-7:00, Sun 12:00-6:00 • Major credit cards

Country home furnishings: quilts, rugs, pillows, wall hangings, American 1920s to 1930s furniture, wicker furniture, needlepoint, frames, ceramics and their famous fabric ornaments by Gladys Boalt depicting various fairy tales and historical figures.

GOLDMAN'S TREASURES

655 Avenue of the Americas, New York, NY 10010 • Tel: (212) 924-4900 • Fax: (212) 924-4611 • Mon-Thu 10:00-9:00, Fri 10:00-3:00, Sun 11:00-6:00 • Hansi Brody • Spanish, German, Hebrew, Russian and Polish spoken • Prices low to medium • 15% trade discount • Major credit cards

Decorative accessories, furniture, lighting, full line of tabletop, mirrors and gifts.

GRACIOUS HOME

1220 Third Avenue and 1217 Third Avenue, New York, NY 10021 • Tel: (212) 517-6300 • Fax: (212) 249-1534 • Mon-Fri 8:00-7:00, Sat 9:00-7:00, Sun 10:00-6:00 • Robert Battista, Robert Gambassi • Spanish, French, Arabic, Russian and Italian spoken • Prices low to very high • 10 to 25% professional discount • Major credit cards

More than 125,000 products for all home categories including decorative hardware, lighting, accessories, home supplies, kitchenware, electrical, plumbing, painting, appliances, tools, rugs, fabrics, household linens, wallpapers and a selection of housewares. Everything. World-wide delivery.

GREGORY'S CHATEAU HIP

110 Greene Street, New York, NY 10012 • Tel: (212) 941-8080 • Fax: (212) 941-0651 • Mon-Sun 11:00-7:00 • Gregory G. Smith • French and Spanish spoken • Prices low to high • Major credit cards

Complete furnishings for the home, slipcovered sofas, chairs, custom wood pieces.

HAMMACHER SCHLEMMER

147 East 57th Street, New York, NY 10022 • Tel: (212) 421-9000 • Fax: (212) 644-3875 • Mon-Sat 10:00-6:00 • Robert Kieffer • Spanish spoken • Prices high to very high • Major credit cards

Unique, unusual functional items not found at the standard retail store. Travel items, electronic gadgets, classic traditional games, high-end leather shiatsu chair, fire-resistant hearth rugs. An adventure.

HOLD EVERYTHING

1311 Second Avenue, New York, NY 10021 • Tel: (212) 535-9446 •
Mon-Fri 10:00-8:00, Sat 10:00-7:00, Sun 12:00-6:00
104 Seventh Avenue, New York, NY 10011 • Tel: (212) 633-1674 •
Mon-Fri 10:00-9:00, Sat 10:00-8:00, Sun 11:00-6:00
2109 Broadway, New York, NY 10023 • Tel: (212) 595-5573 • Mon-Fri
10:00-8:00, Sat 10:00-7:00, Sun 11:00-6:00 • Prices medium • Major
credit cards

Hold Everything means what it says! Boxes, bags, cartons, recep-
tacles to store everything from a toothbrush to a steamer trunk.
Provides the right things to hold everything.

KELTER-MALCE ANTIQUES

74 Jane Street, New York, NY 10014 • Tel: (212) 675-7380 • Jolie
Kelter and Michael Malce • By appointment • Prices medium to high •
Professional discount

American antiques, furnishings and folk art: textiles, Native American pottery, Christmas ornaments, furniture, rugs, lighting fixtures,
Navajo weavings, quilts. Sporting antiques specifically photographs
and game boards.

KESSIE & CO.

163 East 87th Street, New York, NY 10128 • Tel: (212) 987-1732 •
Mon-Fri 11:00-7:00, Sat 11:00-6:00, Sun 12:00-5:00 • Linda Kessler
• French, Italian and Spanish spoken

Fun bric-a-brac, old and new collectibles, second-hand furniture
and lamps, glass and crystal, vintage clothes and costume jewelry.

KITSCHEN

380 Bleecker Street, New York, NY 10014 • Tel: (212) 727-0430 • Fax:
(212) 680-9219 • Daily 1:00-8:00, closed Tue • Celio Ledo • Portuguese, French and Spanish spoken • Prices low • Trade discount •
Major credit cards

Vintage decorative accessories, collectibles; housewares including
dishware, glassware, linens. Appliances and small furniture.

KREISS COLLECTION

141 East 56th Street, New York, NY 10022 • Tel: (212) 593-2005 • Fax:
(212) 593-1901 • Mon-Fri 10:00-6:00, Sat 10:00-5:00 • Madalyn Dean
• Prices high • Trade discount • Major credit cards

Custom home furnishings, imported accessories and fine cotton
bedding.

LANCELOTTI HOUSEWARES

66 Avenue A, New York, NY 10009 • Tel: (212) 475-6851 • Fax: (212)
475-6883 • Mon-Sat 12:00-8:00, Sun 12:00-7:00 • Ben Schneider •
Prices medium • Major credit cards

Housewares for the 90s.

LAZARO

112 Mercer Street, New York, NY 10012 • Tel: (212) 219-8494 • Fax: (212) 219-0790 • Mon-Fri 10:00-6:00, Sat-Sun 12:00-7:00 • Spanish and Italian spoken • Prices medium to high • Major credit cards

Collection of accessories custom made on the premises. All items made of solid pewter or pewter dipped in 24ct gold: candlesticks, vases, as well as contemporary jewelry with antique stones.

LEO DESIGN

413 Bleecker Street, New York, NY 10014 • Tel: (212) 929-8466 • Tue-Sat 12:00-8:00, Sun 12:00-6:00 • Kimo Jung • Prices medium to high • Trade discount • Major credit cards

Gifts and home furnishings including arts and crafts decor, pottery, lighting, dinnerware.

THE LIVELY SET

33 Bedford Street, New York, NY 10014 • Tel: (212) 807-8417 • Mon-Sun 11:00-7:00 • Steve Lohr and Marcelo Soriano • Prices medium • Trade discount • Major credit cards

Country and modern mix in furnishings and accessories dating from 1900-1950. American antiques, enamelware, furniture and lighting from the 40s and 50s. Pottery from the 30s and 40s.

THE LYNN HOLLYN STORE

520 Madison Avenue, New York, NY 10022 • Tel: (212) 319-0520 • Fax: (212) 223-3791 • Mon-Wed, Fri, Sat 10:30-6:00, Thu 10:30-8:00 • Diane Hadel • Prices medium to high • Trade discount • Major credit cards

Home furnishings including reproductions, upholstered sofas and chairs, accessories for the home, bedroom, decorative pillows, lamps, candlesticks.

MACKENZIE-CHILDS OF NEW YORK

824 Madison Avenue, New York, NY 10021 • Tel: (212) 570-6050 • Fax: (212) 570-2485 • Mon-Sat 10:00-6:00 • Margaret Imrie • Limited German, Spanish and French spoken • Prices high • Major credit cards

The designs of Victoria and Richard Mackenzie-Childs in ceramicware, glassware, furniture and accessories for the home.

MACY'S

151 West 34th Street, New York, NY 10001 • Tel: (212) 695-4400 • Mon-Sat 10:00-8:30, Sun 11:00-7:00 • Major credit cards

Macy's is one of the most famous stores in the world and offers literally everything for the home. All prices, all styles, all tastes.

MODERN AGE

102 Wooster Street, New York, NY 10012 • Tel: (212) 966-0669 • Fax: (212) 966-4167 • Tue-Fri 11:00-6:00, Sat-Sun 12:00-6:00 • Erwin de Leon • Prices high • Major credit cards

Contemporary furnishings for the home.

MODERN STONE AGE

111 Greene Street, New York, NY 10012 • Telfax: (212) 966-2570 • Fax: (212) 966-2578 • Mon-Fri 10:00-7:00, Sat 11:00-7:00, Sun 12:00-6:00 • Carole Boy Ferron • French and Lithuanian spoken • Prices medium • Trade discount • Major credit cards.

Stone, metal, glass and some wood furniture; lighting and home accessories.

MOSS

146 Greene Street, New York, NY 10012 • Tel: (212) 226-2190 • Fax: (212) 226-8473 • Tue-Sat 11:00-7:00, Sun 12:00-6:00 • Murray Moss • Prices high • Major credit cards

An industrial design store, carrying a broad selection of objects currently in production, including aluminum ironing boards, flatware, glassware, lighting, furniture and home accessories. Numerous manufacturers represented here.

MXYPLYZYK

125 Greenwich Avenue, New York, NY 10014 • Tel: (212) 989-4300 • Fax: (212) 989-0336 • Mon-Sat 11:00-7:00, Sun 12:00-5:00 • Kevin Terpstra and Kevin Brynan • Prices medium • Major credit cards

Modern contemporary design for the home: tabletop, bath, stationery, general giftware, furniture, lighting, toys, and dog accessories.

123 Greenwich Avenue, New York, NY 10014 • Tel: (212) 647-0777 • Mon-Sat 11:00-7:00, Sun 12:00-5:00 • Major credit cards

Expanding the concept, this location offers more bedding and a colorful selection of housewares.

NIEDERMAIER

120 Wooster Street, New York, NY 10012 • Tel: (212) 966-8631 • Fax: (212) 966-8608 • Sun-Mon 12:00-6:00, Tue-Sat 11:00-7:00 • Prices high • Trade discounts • Major credit cards

Contemporary furniture with a Deco feel; accessories replicating traditional styles in gold and silver leafing; fabrics; custom upholstery and custom wood finishes. Their trademark Venetian masks.

OAK SMITH & JONES

1510 Second Avenue, New York, NY 10021 • Tel: (212) 327-3462 •
Mon-Sat 10:00-9:00, Sun 12:00-5:00 • Prices medium • Trade discount • Major credit cards

Three-level upper East Side home emporium with a broad mix of home furnishings from around the world. The collection includes antiques and collectibles. Will custom modify their own armoires for entertainment centers and home offices.

PAN AMERICAN PHOENIX

857 Lexington Avenue, New York, NY 10021 • Tel: (212) 570-0300 •
Fax: (212) 535-3383 • Mon-Fri 10:30-6:30, Sat 10:00-6:00 • Martha and Mary Bartos • Spanish spoken

Mexican home furnishings and decorative items. Tableware, mirrors, accessories from Peru and fabrics from Guatemala.

PIER I IMPORTS

1550 Third Avenue, New York, NY 10128 • Tel: (212) 987-1746 • Mon-Fri 9:30-9:00, Sun 11:00-7:00
71 Fifth Avenue, New York, NY 10003 • Tel: (212) 206-1911 • Mon-Fri 9:00-9:00, Sat 10:00-7:00, Sun 11:00-7:00
461 Fifth Avenue, New York, NY 10017 • Tel: (212) 447-1610 • Mon-Fri 9:00-8:00, Sat 10:00-7:00, Sun 12:00-7:00 • Prices medium • Major credit cards

Furnishings for the home, tabletop, glassware, china, ceramics, decorative accessories.

PIERRE DEUX

870 Madison Avenue, New York, NY 10021 • Tel: (212) 570-9343 •
Fax: (212) 472-2931 • Mon-Sat 10:00-6:00, Thu 10:00-7:00 • French spoken • Prices medium to high • Major credit cards

Home furnishings with a wide selection of Provencal fabrics and Toiles de Jouy, French country home furnishings, antique furniture, superb antique armoires from Normandy and Brittany and decorative accessories.

PLATYPUS

126 Spring Street, New York, NY 10012 • Tel: (212) 219-3919 • Daily 11:00-6:00 • Thomas Wodock • Spanish and French spoken • Prices medium to high • Major credit cards

Home furnishings and tabletop with food themes.

PLAZA FURNITURE & MIRROR COMPANY

226 East 59th Street, New York, NY 10022 • Tel: (212) 759-9877 •
Mon-Sat 12:00-7:00 • Sydney Silberman • Some Hungarian and some Yiddish spoken • Prices low to medium • Trade discount • Visa and MC

Traditional and some antique furniture, chandeliers, mirrors, lamps and bric-a-brac.

PORTICO HOME

379 West Broadway, New York, NY 10012 • Tel: (212) 941-7800 • Fax: (212) 925-4279 • Mon-Sat 11:00-7:00, Sun 12:00-6:30 • Stephen Wether • French and Spanish spoken • Prices medium to high • Trade discount • Major credit cards

American made wood and upholstered furniture, lamps, candles and a large choice of accessories.

POTTERY BARN

600 Broadway, New York, NY 10012 • Tel: (212) 219-2420 • Fax: (212) 219-1416 • Mon-Sat 10:00-9:00, Sun 11:00-8:00
1965 Broadway, New York, NY 10025 • Tel: (212) 579-8477 • Mon-Sat 10:00-9:00, Sun 11:00-7:00
51 Greenwich Avenue, New York, NY 10014 • Tel: (212) 807-6321 • Mon-Sat 11:00-8:00, Sun 12:00-6:00
1451 Second Avenue, New York, NY 10021 • Tel: (212) 988-4228 • Mon-Fri 10:00-8:00, Sat 10:00-7:00, Sun 11:00-6:00
117 East 59th Street, New York, NY 10022 • Tel: (212) 753-5424 • Mon-Sat 10:00-8:00, Sun 12:00-6:00
100 Seventh Avenue, New York, NY 10011 • Tel: (212) 633-8405 • Mon-Sat 10:00-8:00, Sun 12:00-6:00
250 West 57th Street, New York, NY 10019 • Tel: (212) 315-1855 • Mon-Fri 10:00-8:00, Sat 10:00-7:00, Sun 12:00-6:00

Glassware, pottery, ceramics, kitchenware, utensils, candles, ornaments: a huge ever-changing selection. The best of the basics.

A REPEAT PERFORMANCE

156 First Avenue, New York, NY 10009 • Tel: (212) 529-0832 • Mon-Sat 12:00-8:00, Sun 2:00-8:00 • Beverly Bronson • Prices medium • Professional discount • Major credit cards

Whimsical, unusual furnishings including Continental and European furniture from the 1900s to the 1960s: specializing in European lampshades and lighting with a wide selection of bric-a-brac and English accessories.

ROCHE BOBOIS

200 Madison Avenue, New York, NY 10016 • Tel: (212) 725-5513 • Fax: (212) 779-2461 • Mon and Thu 10:00-9:00, Tue, Wed, Fri, Sat 10:00-6:00, Sun 12:00-5:00 • Prices high • Major credit cards

A major outlet for French furniture and home furnishings, including carpeting, window treatments, fabrics, lighting, wall panels. Custom work and installations.

DENNIS ROLAND INC.

405 East 54th Street, New York, NY 10022 • Tel: (212) 644-0537 • Fax: (212) 486-9189 • Mon-Fri 10:00-6:00 by appointment only • Dennis Roland • Italian, French, Russian and Chinese spoken • Prices high • Trade discount • Major credit cards

Unique home accessories, lamps, antique and new, occasional furniture.

SALON MODERNE

281 Lafayette Street, New York, NY 10007 • Tel: (212) 219-3439 • Fax: (212) 219-9852 • Mon-Fri 11:00-7:00, Sat-Sun 12:00-6:00 • Sabrina Schilcher • Italian, French and German spoken • Prices medium to high • Trade discount • Major credit cards

Home furnishings including rugs, accessories, glass, ceramics, lighting, upholstery, chairs and sofas. Epoque Moderne and custom reproductions. Special woodwork and finishes. Custom design.

SAM'S SOUK, INC.

979 Lexington Avenue, New York, NY 10021 • Tel: (212) 535-7210 • Fax: (212) 517-8871 • Mon-Sat 10:00-7:00 • Sam Ben Safi 321-1/2 Bleecker Street, New York, NY 10014 • Tel: (212) 691-0726 • Mon-Sun 12:00-8:00, Thu-Fri 12:00- 9:00 • Prices medium • Major credit cards

Decorative Mediterranean furniture, art, handicrafts, exotic and fun accessories. Trade warehouse open by appointment at 626 West 28th Street, NY 10001.

SARAJO

98 Prince Street, New York, NY 10012 • Tel: (212) 966-6165 • Fax: (212) 274-0462 • Mon-Sat 11:00-7:00, Sun 12:00-7:00 • Stephen S. Gomez • Spanish, Urdu and Israeli spoken • Prices medium to high • Trade discount • Major credit cards

Textiles, furniture, decorative arts and jewelry from all over the world.

⚌ SCULLY & SCULLY

504 Park Avenue, New York, NY 10022 • Tel: (212) 755-2590 • Fax: (212) 486-1430 • Mon-Sat 9:00-6:00 • Spanish spoken • Professional discount • Major credit cards

Very fine selection of traditional home furnishings and decorative accessories including classic, high-end reproductions, top of the line in China, crystal, flatware, prints and lighting. A selection of children's accessories: sterling silver rattles and picture frames. Bridal registry.

SEMINOLE FURNITURE SHOPS, INC.

44 East 32nd Street, New York, NY 10016 • Tel: (212) 683-6464 • Fax: (212) 683-6484 • Mon-Fri 9:00-5:00 • Henry Bensen • Trade only • Prices medium to high • Major credit cards

Full range of traditional home furnishings: bedding, lamps, leather furniture and accessories from all over the world. Crystal chandeliers, ceramic plates and vases. Oriental accessories: screens, lamps, chests. Furniture: largely antique reproductions of English styles of the 17th and 18th centuries as well as a line of rustic country furniture.

SHI

233 Elizabeth Street, New York, NY 10012 • Telfax: (212) 334-4330 • Tue-Sat 12:00-7:00, Sun 12:00-6:00 • Laurie McLendon • Prices medium to high • Some trade discounts • Major credit cards

New and vintage home furnishings and furniture from France, Asia and the U.S. Lighting, ceramics, hand-blown glass, French bistroware, furniture designs, original artwork, handmade stationery and more.

SIN KEN KEN FURNITURE

401 Washington Street, Suite 6C, New York, NY 10013 • Tel: (212) 226-1641 • Fax: (212) 965-1044 • Mon-Fri 10:00-6:00, Sat by appointment • Vanessa Murphy • Some French spoken • Prices medium • Visa, MC

Teak furniture from Bali, accessories and handmade tabletop items, paper and textural products.

THE SOHO FUTON SHOP

491 Broadway, New York, NY 10012 • Tel: (212) 219-0055 • Fax: (212) 431-1590 • Mon-Sat 11:00-7:00, Sun 12:00-6:00 • Russian and Hebrew spoken • Prices medium • Trade discount • Major credit cards

Large selection of futons and futon frames, decorative accessories and Oriental kilims.

STRAIGHT FROM THE CRATE

261 Madison Avenue, New York, NY 10016 • Tel: (212) 867-4050 • Fax: (212) 867-4060 • Mon-Fri 10:00-8:00, Sat 10:00-7:00, Sun 12:00-6:00 • Marc Saban
344 West 57th Street, New York, NY 10019 • Tel: (212) 541-4350
1251 Lexington Avenue, New York, NY 10028 • Tel: (212) 717-4227 • Prices medium • Major credit cards

Furniture and furnishings, ceramics, pottery, utensils and kitchenware. Constantly changing selections.

DAVID STYPMANN

192 Sixth Avenue, New York, NY 10013 • Tel: (212) 226-5717 • Daily 12:00-7:00 • Prices medium • Trade discount • Amex

19th- and mid-20th-century decorative objects, American and European art pottery, small tables, lamps, mirrors.

TAKASHIMAYA

693 Fifth Avenue, New York, NY 10022 • Tel: (212) 350-0100 • Fax: (212) 350-0192 • Mon-Sat 10:00-6:00, Thu 10:00-8:00 • Multilingual • Prices very high • Major credit cards

Unique, limited edition and antique home furnishings. Some remarkable art objects from Japan, linens, accessories and floral arrangements.

TROY

138 Greene Street, New York, NY 10012 • Tel: (212) 941-4777 • Tue-Sat 11:00-7:00, Sun 12:00-6:00 • Troy Halterman • Spanish spoken • Prices high • Trade discount • Major credit cards

Home furnishings and decorative accessories by 20th-century Scandinavian designers.

JAMSON WHYTE

47 Wooster Street, New York, NY 10013 • Tel: (212) 965-9405 • Fax: (212) 965-9407 • Daily 11:00-7:00 • David Traub • Prices medium • Professional discount • Major credit cards

Unique home furnishings from Asia: specializing in carved teak furniture from Indonesia and India. Four poster beds, benches, dining tables, chairs, lazy chairs, primitive cabinets, TV cabinets, bronze and lacquer pieces and more.

WICKER GARDEN

1318 Madison Avenue, New York, NY 10128 • Tel: (212) 410-7001 • Fax: (212) 410-6609 • Mon-Sat 10:00-6:00 • Pamela Scurry • Spanish spoken • Prices high • 10% trade discount • Major credit cards

Furniture and accessories; specialists in children's furniture in wood. Pamela Scurry's line of reproduction wicker furniture with some antique wicker.

WILLIAM-WAYNE & CO.

850 Lexington Avenue, New York, NY 10021 • Tel: (212) 737-8934 • Fax: (212) 288-8915 • Mon-Sat 10:30-6:30 • Wayne Adler • French spoken • Prices medium • 10% trade discount • Amex, Visa, MC
40 University Place, New York, NY 10003 • Tel: (212) 533-4711 • Mon-Sat 11:00-7:00, Sun 12:00-6:00 • Major credit cards

Home furnishings and decorative accessories. Extensive selection of imported and domestic table linens; dishware, pottery, ceramics, white restaurant china and china in colors, pottery; mostly French flatware and some Asian in silver plate and stainless steel.

WOLFMAN-GOLD & GOOD COMPANY

117 Mercer Street, New York, NY 10012 • Tel: (212) 431-1888 • Fax: (212) 966-8268 • Mon-Sat 11:00-6:00, Sun 12:00-5:00 • Peri Wolfman • Prices medium to high • Major credit cards

Great selection of furniture, slipcovered sofas, chairs, tables and general home furnishings. White, gold, earth-tone and colored dishware and pottery. Imported and domestic table linens, French and Asian flatware in silver plate and stainless steel. Intricate bird houses.

ZONA

97 Greene Street, New York, NY 10012 • Tel: (212) 925-6750 • Fax: (212) 941-1792 • Mon-Sat 11:00-7:00, Sun 12:00-6:00 • French, Spanish, Italian and Russian spoken • Prices medium to high • 10% trade discount • Major credit cards

Remarkable store: home furnishings, specialty gifts and found objects in earth friendly materials. Furniture from the American Southwest and the Italian countryside, and garden furniture.

The Designer Home Collections

CALVIN KLEIN

654 Madison Avenue, New York, NY 10021 • Tel: (212) 292-9000 • Fax: (212) 292-9002 • Mon, Tue, Wed, Fri 10:00-8:00, Thu and Sat 10:00-6:00 • Spanish, French, Portuguese, German and Chinese spoken • Prices medium to very high • Trade discount • Major credit cards

A full range of bedding, bath, tabletop, home fragrances and giftware.

RALPH LAUREN

867 Madison Avenue, New York, NY 10021 • Tel: (212) 606-2100 • Fax: (212) 606-2171 • Mon-Sat 10:00-6:00, Thu until 8:00 • Trade discounts • Major credit cards

Furniture, fabrics, wallcoverings, tabletop including china, crystal and flatware.

VERSACE FIFTH AVENUE

647 Fifth Avenue, 5th floor, New York, NY 10022 • Tel: (212) 317-0224 • Fax: (212) 317-0227 • French, Italian, Spanish and Hebrew spoken • Major credit cards

Tabletop including crystal, china, flatware, china accessories and placements. A large selection of fabric for upholstery and a small line of furniture: sofas and chairs and accessories.

KITCHENS

BOFFI USA, INC.

150 East 58th Street, (A&D), 9th floor, New York, NY 10155 • Tel: (212) 421-1800 • Fax: (212) 421-1225 • Mon-Fri 9:00-5:00 • David A. Yarom • Italian spoken • Prices very high • Trade discount • Major credit cards

Italy's finest manufacturer of high-end contemporary kitchens and baths.

CARDINAL KITCHENS INC.

301 East 58th Street, New York, NY 10022 • Tel: (212) 888-8400 • Fax: (212) 486-6379 • Mon-Sat 10:00-5:00 • Prices medium to high • Trade discount

Kitchen specialists: complete installations of cabinetry and appliances.

♔ CHRISTIANS

150 East 58th Street (A&D), 8th floor, New York, NY 10155 • Tel: (212) 308-3554 • Fax: (212) 308-7316 • Mon-Fri 9:00-6:00 • Peter Harris • German and French spoken • Prices high • 15% trade discount

Complete furniture interior design, including kitchens, bathrooms, bedrooms, library and study. Bespoke custom English furniture. Will install cabinetry as well as kitchen equipment and appliances. All technical and architectural skills available. Excellent references.

CUSTOM DESIGN PLUS INC.

1388 Lexington Avenue, New York, NY 10128 • Telfax: (212) 410-0634 • Mon-Fri 8:30-5:00 • Joseph Jimenez • Spanish spoken • Prices medium • 5% trade discount

Custom kitchens and bathrooms. Cabinets, appliances, countertops, granite, corian, painting, appliances. Kitchen and bath renovation.

ELGOT

937 Lexington Avenue, New York, NY 10021 • Tel: (212) 879-1200 • Fax: (212) 794-9228 • Mon-Fri 9:30-5:30, Sat 10:00-4:00 • Spanish spoken • Prices medium to high • MC and Visa

Custom kitchens and bathrooms installed, air conditioning and major kitchen appliances such as Dynasty, Garland, Viking, Sub-Zero.

EUROPEAN KITCHEN STUDIO

150 East 58th Street (A&D), 8th floor, New York, NY 10022 • Tel: (212) 308-9674 • Fax: (212) 308-9681 • Mon-Fri 9:00-5:00 • Prices medium to very high • 30% trade discount

Designs custom cabinets and furniture for kitchens and every room of the home including libraries, bathrooms, closets and entertainment centers.

R. GASPARRE CUSTOM FURNITURE

32-45 62nd Street, Woodside, NY 11377 • Tel: (718) 726-7348 • (718) 274-4994 • Mon-Fri 9:00-5:00 • Bruce Gasparre • Prices high

Designs and builds custom kitchens and supplies kitchen cabinetry of the major manufacturers, such as Wood-Mode.

GENESIS CUSTOM CABINETRY

568 Second Avenue, 2nd floor, New York, NY 10028 • Tel: (212) 517-7020 • Fax: (212) 517-7029 • Mon-Fri 9:00-6:00 and by appointment • Lee J. Stahl • Prices medium to high • 20% trade discount • Visa and MC

Complete installation of kitchens and bathrooms, from design to installation with all appliances. Fully licensed and insured for all co-ops and condos.

GRINGER & SONS INC.

29 First Avenue, New York, NY 10003 • Tel: (212) 475-0600 • Fax: (212) 982-1935 • Mon-Fri 8:00-5:30, Sat 8:00-4:30 • Lewis Shenker • Spanish spoken • Prices low • Wholesale • MC and Visa

Sale of all major kitchen appliances, domestic and foreign. Delivery and installation.

KAMWAY DISTRIBUTING CORP.

175 Lexington Avenue, New York, NY 10016 • Tel: (212) 779-1000 • Fax: (212) 779-1002 • Mon-Fri 9:00-5:00 • Kambiz Hakim • Persian and Spanish spoken • Prices medium • 10% trade discount • Major credit cards

Kitchen cabinets, specialty floors and marble restoration. References upon request.

KITCHEN REJUVENATION

167-15 Union Turnpike, Flushing, NY 11366 • Tel: (718) 380-8481 • Fax: (718) 380-5760 • Mon-Thu 11:00-7:00, Fri 11:00-3:00 • Jonathan Wiener • Spanish, Hebrew and Yiddish spoken • Prices low • 10% trade discount • Major credit cards

All major appliances for kitchens and bathrooms, cabinets. Next day delivery.

KITCHEN SOLUTIONS INC.

1086 East Gunhill Road, Bronx, NY 10469 • Tel: (718) 547-6100 • Fax: (718) 547-7732 • Mon-Fri 9:00-5:00, Sat 9:00-4:00 • Glenn Muller • Prices very high • Professional discount

Thirty-nine years in business representing manufacturers of custom kitchen cabinets from around the world including Rutt and SieMatic. Specialty is very complex custom kitchens. Large showroom with full displays of cabinets, granite, European appliances. Professional appliances and the AGA Cooker from England.

KRUPS KITCHENS & BATH LTD.

11 West 18th Street, New York, NY 10011 • Tel: (212) 243-5787 • Fax: (212) 243-3205 • Mon-Fri 9:00-6:00, Sat 9:00-5:00 • Prices medium • Trade discount • Major credit cards

Collection of all kitchen and bath appliances, fixtures, custom cabinetry and countertops. Installation available.

POGGENPOHL U.S. INC.

230 Park Avenue South, New York, NY 10003 • Tel: (212) 228-3334 • Fax: (212) 358-9893 • Mon-Fri 9:30-5:30, Sat 10:00-5:00 • Michael K. Storms, Design Director • Spanish and German spoken • Prices high to very high • Trade discount • Major credit cards

The kitchen design studio for cabinetry and accessories for the kitchen and bath including countertops, and all major kitchen appliances. Complete installation. Also custom cabinetry for entertainment centers, dining and living rooms. Clients world-wide.

REGENCY KITCHENS & CUSTOM INTERIORS

4204 14th Avenue, Brooklyn, NY 11219 • Tel: (718) 435-4266 • Fax: (718) 435-5411 • Sun-Thu 10:00-5:00 • Russian, Hungarian, Spanish, Hebrew, German and Yiddish • Prices medium to very high • Trade discount

Certified kitchen designers on staff offering full services from inception of project to final installation. Design, build and install kitchens. Complete bathroom installation. Custom cabinetry for any room.

SIGNATURE KITCHENS

1602 Richmond Road, Staten Island, NY 10304 • Tel: (718) 351-5576 • (718) 351-5548 • Mon-Sat 9:00-6:00, Tue-Thu 9:00-8:00 • Richard W. Clift • Spanish spoken • Prices medium to high

Kitchen design showroom with cabinet lines by Neff, Omega, Dynasty, Bertch, Kabinart, all solid surface. Can supply appliance package. References upon request.

SMALLBONE

150 East 58th Street (A&D), 9th floor, New York, NY 10155 • Tel: (212) 838-4884 • Fax: (212) 838-4936 • Mon-Fri 9:00-6:00 • Robert Hughes • French and Spanish spoken • Prices very high • Trade discount • Amex

Handmade English kitchens, bedrooms and bathrooms with full design and installation service. Handmade English cabinetry. Excellent references.

SNAIDERO BY REGBA DIRAN

1100 Second Avenue, New York, NY 10022 • Tel: (212) 980-6023 • Fax: (212) 980-6064 • Mon-Fri 10:00-5:00 • Uri Lev • Prices medium to high • Trade discount

Kitchen and bath design and installation.

ST. CHARLES OF NEW YORK INC.

150 East 58th Street (A&D), 8th floor, New York, NY 10155 • Tel: (212) 838-2812 • Fax: (212) 308-4951 • Mon-Fri 9:00-5:00 • Robert Schwartz • Spanish and Italian spoken • Prices very high

Design, planning, manufacture and implementation of custom kitchens and architectural millwork.

Kitchenware

BRIDGE KITCHENWARE

214 East 52nd Street, New York, NY 10022 • Tel: (212) 688-4220 • Fax: (212) 758-5387 • Mon-Fri 9:00-5:30, Sat 10:00-4:30 • French spoken • Prices medium to high • Professional discount • Major credit cards

A collection of professional level imported cookware: copper pots, porcelain and bakeware, French casseroles, coffeepots, teapots. A treasure house of the best.

BROADWAY PANHANDLER

477 Broome Street, New York, NY 10013 • Tel: (212) 966-3434 • Fax: (212) 966-9017 • Mon-Fri 10:30-7:00, Sat 11:00-7:00, Sun 11:00-6:00 • Prices low • Major credit cards

Select collection of the best in kitchenware, baking equipment, coffee equipment and chocolate-making equipment.

CRATE & BARREL

650 Madison Avenue, New York, NY 10022 • Tel: (212) 308-0011 • Fax: (212) 843-0949 • Mon-Fri 10:00-8:00, Sat 10:00-7:00, Sun 12:00-6:00 • Lisa Smith and Tammy Dorward • Many languages spoken • Prices medium • Major credit cards and Crate & Barrel Card

Large selection of kitchen and tableware.

CUTLERY WORLD

World Trade Center, Building #5, 324 World Trade Center Concourse, New York, NY 10048 • Tel: (212) 938-1936 • Mon-Fri 8:00-6:00 • Bill Warden • Prices medium to high • Major credit cards

Kitchen cutlery, scissors, sporting and pocket knives, personal care items.

DEAN & DELUCA

560 Broadway, New York, NY 10012 • Tel: (212) 431-1691 • Mon-Sat 10:00-8:00, Sun 10:00-7:00 • Prices medium to high • Major credit cards

Commercial cookware with an extensive line of bakeware, stainless steel, cutlery, utensils, gadgets and table linens. French porcelain, pottery and ceramics imported from Europe. One of the largest selections of teapots and copper cookware imported from Italy and France.

FORZANO

128 Mulberry Street, New York, NY 10013 • Tel: (212) 925-2525 • Fax: (212) 334-6719 • Mon-Thu 10:00-10:00, Fri-Sun 10:00-midnight • Dino Forzano • Italian spoken • Prices medium • Major credit cards

Specialty store for fine imported kitchenware, traditional to contemporary. Cappuccino machines, pasta bowls, pasta makers, demitasse cups and more.

GRACIOUS HOME

1220 Third Avenue and 1217 Third Avenue, New York, NY 10021 • Tel: (212) 517-6300 • Fax: (212) 249-1534 • Mon-Fri 8:00-7:00, Sat 9:00-7:00, Sun 10:00-6:00 • French, Spanish, Arabic, Russian and Italian spoken • Prices low to very high in each product line • 10%-25% trade discount • Major credit cards

Kitchenware of every type, shape and size; all appliances, from toasters to refrigerators, pots, pans, gadgets and utensils.

HAMMACHER SCHLEMMER

147 East 57th Street, New York, NY 10022 • Tel: (212) 421-9000 • Fax: (212) 644-3875 • Mon-Sat 10:00-6:00 • Robert Kieffer • Spanish spoken • Prices high to very high • Major credit cards

Unique and unusual but functional items not found at standard retail stores, including cookware. Merchandise is constantly changing and ranges from travel items, electronic gadgets, to classical traditional games, high-end leather Shiatsu chairs, fire resistant hearth rugs, and more.

HOUSE OF WARES

1071 Madison Avenue, New York, NY 10028 • Tel: (212) 249-4300 •
Fax: (212) 744-2686 • Mon-Fri 9:00-6:30, Sat 9:00-5:00, Sun 12:00-
5:00 • Jack Sebastian • Russian spoken • Prices high • All major credit
cards

Top-of-the-line cookware, cutlery, appliances, gadgets, knife sharp-
ening; free delivery in the city.

KAUFMAN APPLIANCES

365 Grand Street, New York, NY 10002 • Tel: (212) 475-8313 • Fax:
(212) 260-6625 • Sun-Thu 10:00-5:00 • Prices low • MC and Visa

Major kitchen appliances and housewares.

LAMALLE KITCHENWARE

36 West 25th Street, 6th floor, New York, NY 10010 • Tel: (212) 242-
0750 • Fax: (212) 645-2996 • Mon-Fri 9:00-6:00, Sat 1:00-6:00 • Trade
discount • Major credit cards

Importers from France, Italy and Germany of high-end kitchen cookware and tools. Selection of copper and steel cookware. Ovenware
and stovetop. Will re-tin copper.

LECHTERS, INC.

250 West 57th Street, New York, NY 10107 • Tel: (212) 956-7290 •
Mon-Fri 8:00-8:30, Sat 11:00-7:00
536 Broadway, New York, NY 10012 • Tel: (212) 274-0890 • Mon-Sat
9:30-8:30, Sun 11:00-7:00
291 First Avenue, New York, NY 10009 • Tel: (212) 677-6481 • Mon-Fri
9:00-8:00, Sat 10:00-7:00, Sun 11:00-6:00 • Prices low to medium •
Major credit cards

The country's only specialty housewares retailer with national cov-
erage operating over 600 stores in 42 states, with continuing ex-
pansion. Since inception in 1975, they have become the problem
solver and specialist in basic products for the kitchen. You will find
everything for the kitchen.

NEW CATHAY HARDWARE CORP.

49 Mott Street, New York, NY 10013 • Telfax: (212) 962-6648 • Mon-
Sun 10:00-7:00 • Wing Lam • Chinese spoken • 10% professional
discount • Major credit cards

Extensive collection of Chinese kitchen utensils and cookware as
well as traditional kitchen supplies for the home or restaurant.

WILLIAMS-SONOMA, INC.

20 East 60th Street, New York, NY 10022 • Tel: (212) 980-5155 • Fax: (212) 753-8170 • Mon-Fri 10:00-7:00, Sat 10:00-6:00, Sun 12:00-5:00

110 Seventh Avenue, New York, NY 10011 • Tel: (212) 633-2203 • Fax: (212) 206-0862 • Mon-Fri 10:00-8:00, Sat 10:00-7:00, Sun 12:00-6:00

1309 Second Avenue, New York, NY 10021 • Tel: (212) 288-8408 • Fax: (212) 327-3749 • Mon-Fri 10:00-8:00, Sat 10:00-7:00, Sun 12:00-6:00

1175 Madison Avenue, New York, NY 10028 • Tel: (212) 289-6832 • Fax: (212) 831-1330 • Mon-Fri 10:00-7:00, Sat 10:00-6:00, Sun 12:00-6:00

580 Broadway, New York, NY 10012 • Tel: (212) 343-7330 • Fax: (212) 343-7327 • Mon-Sat 10:00-8:00, Sun 12:00-7:00

A huge selection of cookware, kitchenware, glassware and appliances. Marvellous selection of copper pots and pans. They also carry basic essentials, such as spices, chocolates, oils and vinegars.

WILLIAMS-SONOMA, INC.'S OUTLET STORE

231 Tenth Avenue at 23rd Street, New York, NY 10011 • Mon-Fri 11:00-6:00, Sat-Sun 10:00-5:00 • Spanish and Creole spoken • Prices low • 30-70% discounts • Major credit cards

Discontinued and sales merchandise of kitchen accessories and tableware. Lots of surprises! Three floors of merchandise with constant change.

ZABARS

2245 Broadway, New York, NY 10024 • Tel: (212) 787-2000 • Fax: (212) 580-4477 • Mon-Fri 8:00-7:30, Sat 8:00-8:00, Sun 9:00-6:00 • Spanish, Russian and Chinese spoken • Prices medium • Major credit cards

A New York institution for gourmet food. They also carry an excellent selection of housewares, cookware, utensils and appliances.

Antique Kitchenware

BOB PRYOR ANTIQUES—DECORATIONS

1023 Lexington Avenue, New York, NY 10021 • Tel: (212) 688-1516 • Mon-Sat 10:30-5:30 • Prices medium to high

Antique kitchenware, largely English and French 18th and 19th centuries: moulds, strainers, ladels, large copper and brass pots and pans. Copper funnels used in the kitchen and in wine making; brass graters. Cobalt blue glass plates, finger bowls and cruet sets. Antique decanters, some in colored glass, from the 18th and 19th centuries. "Gourmet" magazine visits regularly for their shoots.

COBBLESTONES

314 East 9th Street, New York, NY 10003 • Tel: (212) 673-5372 • Tue-Sat 1:00-7:00, Sun 1:00-5:00 • Delanee Koppersmith • Prices medium • Trade discount • Major credit cards

Some amusing vintage kitchenware and housewares; Fire King and Fiestaware, much from the 1930s. Old printed linens and tablecloths. Canister sets, cookie jars and cutters, glass butter dishes, spice sets, vintage cookbooks from various countries and some glassware sets and lots of other surprise collectibles.

LIGHTING

▣ MARVIN ALEXANDER, INC.

315 East 62nd Street, New York, NY 10021 • Tel: (212) 838-2320 •
Fax: (212) 754-0173 • Mon-Fri 9:00-5:00 • David Reitner • Prices high
• Trade only

Extensive and very fine collections of antique lighting and accessories in crystal, wood, iron, tole and bronze. A large collection of reproduction sconces.

ANTIQUE ACCENTS, LTD.

1175 Second Avenue, New York, NY 10021 • Tel: (212) 755-6540 •
Fax: (212) 755-9604 • Mon-Fri 10:00-5:00, Sat 10:00-4:00 • David
Weinbaum • Prices medium to high • Trade discount

19th- to 20th-century lighting fixtures and sconces in bronze. 19th-century paneling, bronze statuary and Louis XV and Louis XVI style occasional furniture.

ARTEMIDE SOHO

46 Greene Street, New York, NY 10013 • Tel: (212) 925-1588 • Fax:
(212) 925-2429 • Mon-Fri 10:00-5:00, Sat 11:00-6:00 • Trade only

New showroom with large selection of all types of contemporary lighting for indoors and outdoors; track and linear systems; incandescent, fluorescent, halogen and energy saving.

BACCARAT, INC.

625 Madison Avenue, New York, NY 10021 • Tel: (212) 826-4100 •
Fax: (212) 826-5043 • Mon-Sat 10:00-6:00 • Francois Mainetti • French,
German, Spanish, Italian and Japanese spoken • Prices high • Corporate discounts • Major credit cards

Superb crystal chandeliers and wall sconces.

BARRY OF CHELSEA ANTIQUES

154 Ninth Avenue, New York, NY 10011 • Tel: (212) 242-2666 • Tue-Fri
12:00-7:00, Sat 12:00-6:00 • Prices medium • Major credit cards

Antique lighting from the 1890s to 1930s. Restored antique lamps, Art Deco; milk glass hanging lamps; schoolhouse globes; desk, table and bedroom lamps from the forties; electrified gaslight chandeliers; art glass shades.

BENNY'S DE LIGHT

141 Bowery, New York, NY 10002 • Tel: (212) 226-8069 • Fax: (212) 226-9591 • Mon-Fri 9:00-5:00 • Spanish spoken • Prices medium to high • Trade discounts • All major credit cards

A huge selection of traditional and contemporary lighting fixtures, reproductions of antique lighting, chandeliers, lamps, wall sconces. Halogen and track.

DANIEL BERGLUND

141 Grassy Hill Road, Lyme, CT 06371 • Telfax: (860) 434-5162 • NYC Tel: (212) 243-1718 • By appointment • Prices very high

One-of-a-kind and limited edition light fixtures from sconces to chandeliers.

BOWERY LIGHTING

148 Bowery, New York, NY 10002 • Tel: (212) 941-8244 • Fax: (212) 226-7046 • Mon-Fri 9:00-5:30 • Spanish spoken • Prices medium to high • 30% trade discounts • All major credit cards

Almost a full city block of everything to do with lighting: traditional, contemporary, antique reproductions, standing lamps, wall sconces, track lighting, halogens, large institutional lighting.

H.M. BRANDSTON & PARTNERS, INC.

141 West 24th Street, New York, NY 10011 • Tel: (212) 924-4050 • Fax: (212) 691-5418 • Mon-Fri 9:00-5:00 • Chinese and Korean spoken

Antique lighting, lighting design, contemporary and custom. Landscape lighting.

EAGLES ANTIQUES

1097 Madison Avenue, New York, NY 10128 • Tel: (212) 772-3266 • Mon-Fri 9:30-5:30, Sat 10:00-5:30 • Mrs. Carol Feinberg, Christopher Dziadosz • Prices medium to high • 20% professional discount

Antique Oriental and cloisonné vases converted into lamps.

FIL CARAVAN

301 East 57th Street, New York, NY 10022 • Tel: (212) 421-5972 • Fax: (212) 421-5976 • Mon-Sat 11:00-6:00 • Nabi Israfil • Polish, Turkish, Spanish and Russian spoken • Prices high • Visa and MC

A wide range of chandeliers, antique and new. Some Baccarat chandeliers, antique, contemporary and pink.

HUBERT DES FORGES

1193 Lexington Avenue, New York, NY 10028 • Tel: (212) 744-1857 • Mon-Fri 10:00-6:00 • Hubert Des Forges and Oscar Moore • French spoken • Prices medium • 20% trade discount • Major credit cards

Lots of lamps, antique and contemporary; decorative accessories, Italian gilded tassel furniture of the 1930s and 1940s.

GALLERIA HUGO

304 East 76th Street, New York, NY 10021 • Tel: (212) 288-8444 • Fax: (212) 570-9041 • By appointment • Hugo Ramirez • Spanish spoken • Prices very high • 20% trade discount • Major credit cards

A huge selection of restored lighting and decorative bronze items. Most of their restoration work takes place at this location.

GASLIGHT TIME

5 Plaza Street West, Brooklyn, NY 11217 • Tel: (718) 789-7185 • Fax: (718) 789-6185 • Sat 12:00-5:00, other times by appointment • Prices high

Sale and restoration of antique lighting fixtures 1830-1930.

GRAY GARDENS

461 Broome Street, New York, NY 10013 • Tel: (212) 966-7116 • Fax: (212) 965-9787 • Mon-Fri 12:00-7:00, Sat-Sun 12:00-6:00 • Terry Ross, Jennifer Tager • Prices high • 10% trade discount • All major credit cards

17th century to 1940s: Venetian chandeliers, gilded mirrors and other antiques.

GREENE'S LIGHTING FIXTURES, INC.

1059 Third Avenue, New York, NY 10021 • Tel: (212) 753-2507 • Fax: (212) 688-6389 • Mon-Fri 9:00-5:30 • Trade only

A large and fine selection of some antique lighting fixtures and high-quality reproductions. Specialists in chandeliers.

GREGORY

158 Bowery, New York, NY 10002 • Tel: (212) 226-1276 • Fax: (212) 226-2705 • Mon-Fri 9:00-5:30 • Clifford Starr, Lighting Consultant • Russian, Spanish, Hebrew, German, French and Polish spoken • Prices low to very high • All major credit cards

A complete range of residential and commercial lighting. Contemporary, traditional, antique reproductions. Lights for the garden, for parking lots, lights for just about anything.

HUGO LTD.

233 East 59th Street, New York, NY 10022 • Tel: (212) 750-6877 • Fax: (212) 750-7346 • Tue-Wed 10:00-5:00 or by appointment • Hugo Ramirez • Spanish spoken • Prices very high • 20% trade discount • Major credit cards

Original and antique reproductions in brass, glass, cranberry glass. Electrified gas lamps, chandeliers and desk and table lamps. Styles from the 19th through the 20th centuries.

IRREPLACEABLE ARTIFACTS

14 Second Avenue, New York, NY 10003 • Tel: (212) 777-2900 • Fax: (212) 780-0642 • Mon-Fri 10:00-6:00, Sat-Sun 11:00-5:00 • David Callegeros • Prices medium • 10-20% trade discount

Antique lighting, Victorian to Art Deco. Sconces, chandeliers, oversized lighting fixtures from commercial spaces. Enormous choice.

HOWARD KAPLAN ANTIQUES

827-831 Broadway, New York, NY 10012 • Tel: (212) 674-1000 • Fax: (212) 228-7204 • Mon-Fri 9:00-6:00 • David B. Kyner • Prices high • MC and Visa

Custom lighting and custom lampshades.

MRS. KAY LAMPSHADES

237 East 59th Street, New York, NY 10022 • Tel: (212) 388-1111 • Fax: (212) 317-0909 • Mon-Sat 10:00-7:00 • Claire Portes • Spanish and Portuguese spoken • Prices medium • Major credit cards

Small selection of stock lamps and chandeliers. Mounting of lamps and repairs. Lampshades.

LAKS LAMP MOUNTING CO, INC.

1059 Second Avenue, New York, NY 10022 • Tel: (212) 688-4161 • Mon-Fri 10:00-6:00, Sat 12:00-4:00 • Milton Laks • Russian, German, Yiddish, Polish spoken • Prices medium • 15% trade discount

They buy and sell antique chandeliers, lamps, wall sconces. They also do mounting of lamps, chandeliers and sconces.

LALIQUE BOUTIQUE

680 Madison Avenue, New York, NY 10021 • Tel: (212) 355-6550 • Fax: (212) 752-0203 • Mon-Fri 10:00-6:00, Sat 10:00-5:00 • Rosalyn Rand • French spoken • Prices high • Corporate discounts • Major credit cards

Beautiful art glass crystal chandeliers, sconces and lamps.

⚏ EILEEN LANE ANTIQUES

150 Thompson Street, New York, NY 10012 • Tel: (212) 475-2988 • Fax: (212) 673-8669 • Mon-Sun 11:00-7:00 • Bo Linstrad • French, German and Spanish spoken • Prices medium to high • Trade discount • Amex, Visa and MC

Extraordinary collection of alabaster light fixtures of the 1900s; custom wired.

LEE'S STUDIO

1755 Broadway, New York, NY 10019 • Tel: (212) 581-4400 • Mon-Sat 10:00-7:00, Sun 12:00-5:00
1069 Third Avenue, New York, NY 10021 • Tel: (212) 371-1122 • Fax: (212) 826-1493 • Mon-Sat 10:00-6:30 • Mike Stone • Prices medium to high • Trade discount • Major credit cards

French, Italian, German, Spanish and domestic lighting: all contemporary styles and models; some traditional styles; some Art Deco reproductions. Picture lighting and some outdoor lighting.

LIGHTFORMS, INC.

168 Eighth Avenue, New York, NY 10011 • Tel: (212) 255-4664 • Fax: (212) 627-7678 • Mon-Fri 11:00-7:00, Sat 10:00-6:00, Sun 12:00-5:00 • Spanish spoken • Prices medium to high • Trade discounts • All major credit cards

A full range of residential and commercial lighting: track, halogens, contemporary, traditional, antique reproductions, standing and table lamps, wall sconces and chandeliers.

WILLIAM LIPTON LTD.

27 East 61st Street, New York, NY 10021 • Tel: (212) 751-8131 • Fax: (212) 751-8133 • Mon-Fri 10:00-6:00, Sat 12:00-5:00 • Yvonne Wong • Chinese spoken • Prices very high • 20% trade discounts • Major credit cards

Wide range of bronze lights commissioned in Paris, including the popular Architects' Lamp. Early Chinese furniture. High quality.

MIDTOWN LIGHTING

155 West 18th Street, New York, NY 10003 • Tel: (212) 255-7701 • Fax: (212) 255-6889 • Mon-Fri 8:00-5:00, Sat 8:00-2:00 • Trade discount • Major credit cards

Brand new state-of-the-art lighting showroom. The largest Lightolier stock in Manhattan.

LILLIAN NASSAU

220 East 57th Street, New York, NY 10022 • Tel: (212) 759-6062 • Fax: (212) 842-9493 • Mon-Sat 10:00-6:00 • Paul Nassau, Henry Wallace, Arlie Sulka • Prices high

Original works by Tiffany; including lamps, glass, paintings, pottery, decorative objects and furniture of the Art Nouveau and Art Deco periods. American sculpture.

NESLE

151 East 57th Street, New York, NY 10022 • Tel: (212) 755-0515 • Fax: (212) 644-2583 • Mon-Fri 9:00-5:00 • Italian, French and German spoken • Prices low to medium

Extraordinary 18th- and 19th-century chandeliers and lighting, most from France and Russia. Candelabra, girandoles, hurricane globes, sconces and lanterns.

NEWEL ART GALLERIES

425 East 53rd Street, New York, NY 10022 • Tel: (212) 758-1970 • Fax: (212) 371-0166 • Mon-Fri 9:00-5:00 • Bruce Newman • Spanish spoken • Prices medium to very high • Major credit cards

Superb examples of antique chandeliers and sconces from all sources, all periods.

ORIENTAL DECORATIONS

253 East 72nd Street, New York, NY 10021 • Tel: (212) 439-1573 • Mon-Fri 11:00-6:30, Sat 11:00-5:30 • Some French and Russian spoken • Prices medium to high • Major credit cards

19th-century Chinese antique lamps. Custom lamps made from hand- painted Oriental porcelain. All styles of custom lampshades.

PELL ARTIFEX

653 11th Avenue, 10th floor, New York, NY 10036 • Tel: (212) 582-7099 • Fax: (212) 265-6497 • Mon-Thu 8:00-4:00, Fri 8:00-3:00 • Mario Esguerra • Trade only

Anything to do with antique lighting, reproductions, rewiring.

PIMLICO WAY

1028 Lexington Avenue, New York, NY 10021 • Tel: (212) 439-7855 • Mon-Fri 11:00-5:30, Sat 12:00-4:00

Nice selection of antique lamps and lighting.

A.W. PISTOL, INC.

375 Fairfield Avenue, Stamford, CT 06902 • Tel: (203) 348-6597 • Fax: (203) 325-0798 • Mon-Fri 8:00-6:00 • Morton Weintraub • Some French spoken • Prices high

Custom fabrication of lighting fixtures, lamps and decorative metalwork to architects' and designers' specifications. Renovate existing fixtures to use newer lighting sources. All materials used.

J. DIXON PRENTICE ANTIQUES

1036 Lexington Avenue, New York, NY 10021 • Tel: (212) 249-0458 • Mon-Fri 11:00-5:00 • Prices medium to high • Trade discounts • Amex

Antique chandeliers of the 18th and 19th centuries, sconces, decorative objects and mirrors.

⚘ PRICE GLOVER, INC.

59 East 79th Street, New York, NY 10021 • Tel: (212) 772-1740 • Fax: (212) 772-1962 • Mon-Fri 10:00-5:00 • Isobel Glover • Prices high • 20% trade discount

18th- and 19th-century English lighting and decorative arts. Antique sconces in bronze, hurricane lamps, brass chandeliers and some reproductions. They also sell their own line of reproduction 18th- and 19th-century English lighting fixtures.

THOMAS P. RICHMOND, INC.

79 Longview Avenue, White Plains, NY 10605 • Tel: (914) 428-2511 •
Fax: (914) 428-1343 • By appointment • Prices high

Lighting design and installation. Specialists in the Wendel optical
framing projector system for the illumination of fine art. Clients include museums and collectors.

JOSEPH RICHTER, INC.

249 East 57th Street, New York, NY 10022 • Tel: (212) 755-6094 • Fax:
(212) 755-6229 • Mon-Fri 9:30-5:30 • Todd Atkinson • French and
Spanish spoken • Prices medium to high • Trade only • Trade discounts

Chandeliers, sconces, table, standing and desk lamps: antiques
and reproductions. Custom mounting. Very high quality.

SHEBA ANTIQUES, INC.

233 East 59th Street, New York, NY 10022 • Tel: (212) 421-4848 • Fax:
(212) 421-4862 • Mon-Fri 9:30-5:00 • Sajid Ali Mirza Khan • Prices
medium • 20% trade discount • Major credit cards

A very fine array of French, English, Italian and American chandeliers and sconces. They also have some antique furniture.

UPLIFT LIGHTING

506 Hudson Street, New York, NY 10014 • Tel: (212) 939-3632 • Fax:
(212) 255-1439 • 7 days 12:00-8:00 • Randy Wicker • Some Spanish
spoken • Prices medium • Major credit cards

Very large collection of American Art Deco chandeliers and wall
sconces. Full line of restored original and quality reproduction table
lamps.

URBAN ARCHAEOLOGY

285 Lafayette Street, New York, NY 10012 • Tel: (212) 431-6969 • Fax:
(212) 941-1918 • Mon-Fri 8:00-6:00, Sat 10:00-4:00 • Amex, Visa and
MC

Art Deco and Victorian lighting fixtures, chandeliers, sconces. Antique and reproduction. Restoration.

VERSAILLES LIGHTING

224 West 30th Street, New York, NY 10001 • Tel: (212) 564-0240 •
Fax: (212) 268-7473 • Mon-Fri 8:30-5:00 • Maurine Locke • French,
Spanish, Arabic and Vietnamese spoken • Prices medium • Trade dis-
counts • Visa and MC

Manufacturer of decorative lighting fixtures. Custom design to specification. Restoration of antiques. New York landmark status. Residential and commercial work. Restoration.

WATERFORD-WEDGEWOOD STORE

713 Madison Avenue, New York, NY 10021 • Tel: (212) 759-0500 • Fax: (212) 486-6570 • Mon-Sat 10:00-6:00 • Japanese spoken • Prices high • Trade discounts • Major credit cards

Crystal chandeliers and beautiful wall sconces. Lots of crystal lamps.

⌘ CHARLES J. WINSTON & CO., INC.

515 Madison Avenue, New York, NY 10022 • Tel: (212) 753-3612 • Mon-Fri 9:30-4:30 • John J. Winston • French and Spanish spoken • Prices high • Trade only

A marvellous selection of antique chandeliers and sconces. Also porcelains, furniture and accessories. Crystal, rock crystal and French, English and Chinese bronzes.

WYETH

151 Franklin Street, New York, NY 10013 • Tel: (212) 925-5278 • Fax: (212) 925-5314 • Mon-Sat 11:00-6:00 • French and Japanese spoken • Prices medium to high • Trade discount • Major credit cards

Contemporary lighting and special purpose lighting, as well as contemporary wood, metal and upholstered furniture.

Lighting Restoration

MICHAEL DOTZEL & SON INC.

402 East 63rd Street, New York, NY 10021 • Tel: (212) 838-2890 • Fax: (212) 371-4839 • Mon-Fri 8:00-5:00

Refinishing bronze and brass parts of antique chandeliers and all types of lighting. Rewiring and remounting.

GRAND BRASS LAMP PARTS, INC.

221 Grand Street, New York, NY 10013 • Tel: (212) 226-2567 • Fax: (212) 226-2573 • Tue-Sat 8:00-5:00, Thu 8:00-8:00

A huge selection of all kinds of lamp parts.

LAMP DOCTOR

1944 Coney Island Avenue, Brooklyn, NY 11223 • Telfax: (718) 627-0448 • Mon-Sat 10:00-5:00, Sun 11:00-5:00

Specialists in the restoration of lighting fixtures, including rewiring, polishing, plating and remounting. Shades.

RESTORATION & DESIGN STUDIO

249 East 77th Street, New York, NY 10021 • Tel: (212) 517-9742 •
Mon-Fri 10:00-5:00, Wed 1:00-5:00 • Paul Karner

Restoration of lamps and chandeliers. Rewiring. All patinas on metal.

SWAROVSKI LIGHTING PARTS LTD.

230 Fifth Avenue, New York, NY 10001 • Tel: (212) 683-6991 • Mon-Fri
9:00-5:00

An enormous assortment of chandelier parts.

Lampshades

ABAT-JOUR CUSTOM LAMPSHADE CORP.

232 East 59th Street, 6th floor, New York, NY 10022 • Tel: (212) 753-5455
• Fax: (212) 753-5456 • Mon-Fri 9:00-5:00 • Patricia Sullivan • Spanish,
German, Portuguese and Korean spoken • Prices high • Trade only

Custom lampshades to the decorating trade.

OSMUNDO ECHEVARRIA & ASSOC. INC.

130 West 29th Street, 10th floor, New York, NY 10001 • Tel: (212) 868-
3029 • Fax: (212) 868-3037 • Mon-Fri 9:00-6:00 • Osmundo Echevarria
• Spanish spoken • Prices very high • Trade only

A decorative painting studio creating custom order hand-painted
lampshades.

GRACIOUS HOME

1220 Third Avenue, New York, NY 10021 • Tel: (212) 517-6300 • Fax:
(212) 249-1534 • Mon-Fri 8:00-7:00, Sat 9:00-7:00, Sun 10:00-6:00 •
Robert Battista and Robert Gambassi • Spanish, French, Arabic, Russian and Italian spoken • Prices medium to very high • 10% to 25%
trade discount • Major credit cards

500 stocked lampshades in various sizes, materials and colors.

JUST SHADES INC.

21 Spring Street, New York, NY 10012 • Tel: (212) 966-2757 • Fax:
(212) 334-6129 • Thu-Tue 9:30-4:00 • Prices medium • MC and Visa

Lampshades: stock and custom. Silk, parchment, linen, hide (sheep
skin). 4,000 in stock. Plain and pleated.

MRS. KAY LAMPSHADES

237 East 59th Street, New York, NY 10022 • Telfax: (212) 317-0909 •
Mon-Sat 10:00-7:00 • Claire Portes • Spanish and Portuguese spoken
• Prices medium • Trade discount • Major credit cards

Custom lampshades: choice of 150 different sizes and styles. Repair and rewiring of lamps.

LE DECOR FRANCAIS

1006 Lexington Avenue, New York, 10021 • Tel: (212) 734-0032 • Fax: (212) 988-0816 • Mon-Fri 9:30-6:00, Sat 11:00-5:00 • Jacqueline Coumans • French, Portuguese and Spanish spoken • Prices medium to high • 20% trade discount • Amex

Custom-made lampshades from a wide selection of fine fabrics.

ORIENTAL LAMP SHADE CO.

223 West 79th Street, New York, NY 10024 • Tel: (212) 873-0812 • Mon-Sat 10:00-6:00 • Spanish, Chinese and some French spoken 816 Lexington Avenue, New York, NY 10021 • Tel: (212) 832-8190 • Fax: (212) 758-5367 • Mon-Sat 10:00-6:00 • Trade discount • MC and Visa

Custom and stock lampshades in a selection of styles and colors. 100% silk, parchment and string shades. Lamp repair, restoration and custom mountings.

PIERRE DEUX FABRICS

870 Madison Avenue, New York, NY 10021 • Tel: (212) 570-9343 • Fax: (212) 472-2931 • Mon-Sat 10:00-6:00, Thu until 7:00 • Prices medium to high • Major credit cards

Coordinating lampshades to Pierre Deux lines of fabrics, from stock or custom.

M & H REISMAN LAMPSHADES

735 Lorimer Street, Brooklyn, NY 11211 • Tel: (718) 768-7508 • Fax: (718) 768-4133 • Mon-Thu 8:00-5:30, Fri 8:00-1:30 • Chayim Kramer • Spanish, Yiddish, French, Hebrew and Italian spoken • Prices high to very high • Trade only

Manufacturer of custom lampshades, any shape, any style.

UNIQUE CUSTOM LAMPSHADES

247 East 77th Street, New York, NY 10021 • Telfax: (212) 472-1140 • Mon-Fri 9:00-5:00 • Ron Megown • French spoken • Prices high

Hand-sewn, made-to-order, custom lampshades in silk, string and parchment.

RUTH VITOW INC.

351 East 61st Street, 2nd floor, New York, NY 10021 • Tel: (212) 355-6881 • Fax: (212) 753-5021 • Mon-Fri 8:30-4:30 • Prices high • Trade only

Custom-made lampshades; fixtures; chandeliers and lamp mountings.

LINEN

Household and Table

BED, BATH & BEYOND

620 Avenue of the Americas, New York, NY 10011 • Tel: (212) 255-3550 • Fax: (212) 229-1040 • Mon-Sat 9:30-9:00, Sun 10:00-8:00 • Many languages spoken • Prices medium • Major credit cards

Enormous choice of bedding; linens for bed, bath and table. Lifestyles closet department and housewares.

BERGDORF GOODMAN

754 Fifth Avenue, 7th floor, New York, NY 10019 • Tel: (212) 753-7300 • Direct: (212) 753-7352 • Fax: (212) 872-8971 • Mon-Sat 10:00-6:00, Thu until 8:00 • Professional discount • Major credit cards

Linens for bed, bath and table: full selection of domestic and imported lines.

♨ E. BRAUN & CO.

717 Madison Avenue, New York, NY 10021 • Tel: (212) 838-0650 • Fax: (212) 832-5640 • Mon-Sat 10:00-6:00 • Stephanie Barbatelli • Spanish spoken • Prices very high • Professional discount • Major credit cards

Luxury bedding. Custom sizes and colors as well as stock. Imported, hand-embroidered table linens and everything for the bath.

JEANNE-AELIA DESPARMET-HART PAINTED LINENS

19 Roosevelt Avenue, Larchmont, NY 10538 • Telfax: (914) 834-7442 • By appointment • French spoken • Prices high • Professional discount

Hand-painted 100% cotton and 100% linen table and bedroom linens and accessories. All custom orders.

DOWN FACTORY OUTLET

32 West 40th Street, New York, NY 10018 • Tel: (212) 840-2550 • Fax: (212) 840-2241 • Mon-Fri 10:00-6:00 • Some French and Spanish spoken • Prices medium to very high • Trade discount • Major credit cards

World-class luxury down comforters, pillows, pillow forms, sofa cushions, travel pillows and feather beds. Duvet covers and fillers. Services offered for cleaning, refurbishing and restoring.

DOWN & QUILT SHOP

1225 Madison Avenue, New York, NY 10128 • Tel: (212) 423-9358 •
Fax: (212) 423-9359 • Mon-Fri 10:00-6:00, Sat 11:00-6:00, Sun 12:30-
5:00 • Gregory Holland • Prices medium to high • Major credit cards
518 Columbus Avenue, New York, NY 10024 • Telfax: (212) 496-8980
• Mon-Fri 10:00-7:00, Sat-Sun 12:00-6:00 • Major credit cards

**Patchwork quilts, decorative pillows, cushions, fine linens for the
bed and antique iron beds.**

ELDRIDGE TEXTILE CO. INC.

277 Grand Street, New York, NY 10002 • Tel: (212) 925-1523 • Fax:
(212) 219-9542 • Sun-Fri 9:00-5:30 • Spanish spoken • Prices medium to high • Trade discount • Major credit cards

**Discounted prices on sheets, towels, blankets, rugs, table linens
and bathroom accessories. Custom and ready-made bedspreads,
comforters and draperies. Mail order catalog available.**

FINE LINENS

1193 Lexington Avenue, New York, NY 10028 • Tel: (212) 737-0520 •
Fax: (212) 737-0054 • Mon-Fri 9:30-5:30, Sat 10:00-4:00 • Steven
Hirsch • Some German spoken • Prices medium to high • Trade dis-
count • Major credit cards

**Bed, bath and table linens: custom designs, sizes and colors to
your specifications.**

DAVID FORSTER & CO.

750 Madison Avenue, New York, NY 10021 • Tel: (212) 861-8989 •
Fax: (212) 861-8352 • Mon-Fri 9:00-5:00 • David Forster • Prices medium to very high • Trade discount

**Fine linens (bed, bath, table) for hotels, private clubs, executive
dining rooms. Also boardroom accessories such as leather mats,
lacquered trays.**

FRETTE, INC.

799 Madison Avenue, New York, NY 10021 • Tel: (212) 988-5221 •
Fax: (212) 988-5257 • Mon-Sat 10:00-6:00 • Lupe Biasiolo • Japanese, Italian, French and Spanish spoken • Prices very high • Professional discount • Major credit cards

Fine Italian bed, table and bath linens since 1860.

LAYTNER'S LINEN & HOME

2270 Broadway, New York, NY 10024 • Tel: (212) 724-0180
237 East 86th Street, New York, NY 10028 • Tel: (212) 996-4439
512 Broadway, New York, NY 10012 • Tel: (212) 965-9382 • Mon-Fri
10:00-7:30, Sat 10:00-6:30, Sun 12:00-6:00 • Spanish, French, Chinese and Hebrew spoken • Prices medium • Major credit cards

Bed and bath linens and accessories.

♛ LERON

750 Madison Avenue, New York, NY 10021 • Tel: (212) 753-6700 •
Fax: (212) 249-3610 • Mon-Fri 10:00-6:00, Sat 10:30-5:30 • Caroline
Donadio • French and Spanish spoken • Prices medium to very high •
Trade discount • Major credit cards

Luxury linen for bed, bath and table. Luxury lingerie, in stock or
custom order. Léron was founded at the turn of the century, and
their artisans in France, Madeira, Italy and the U.S.A. produce this
beautiful collection.

HARRIS LEVY INC.

278 Grand Street, New York, NY 10002 • Tel: (212) 226-3102 • Fax:
(212) 334-9360 • Mon-Thu 9:00-5:00, Fri 9:00-4:00, Sun 9:00-5:00 •
Spanish, Russian, French, Portuguese and Chinese spoken • Prices
medium to high • Major credit cards

Family owned and operated since 1894, fine imported and domestic linens for table, bed and bath. Selections include Crown Crafts,
Fieldcrest, Palais Royal and Wamsutta.

PONDICHERRI

454 Columbus Avenue, New York, NY 10024 • Tel: (212) 875-1609 •
Fax: (212) 875-1679 • Sun-Wed 11:00-7:00, Thu-Sat 11:00-8:00 •
Amba Singh • Spanish and Hindu spoken • Prices medium • Trade
discount • Major credit cards

A large selection of printed, woven and embroidered table, bed and
linen.

D. PORTHAULT INC./JANE BORTHWICK

18 East 69th Street, New York, NY 10021 • Tel: (212) 688-1660 • Fax:
(212) 772-8450 • Mon-Fri 10:00-5:30, Sat 10:00-5:00 • Jane Borthwick
• French, German and Italian spoken • Prices very high • Trade discount
• Major credit cards

Luxury linens and decorative accessories.

PORTICO BED & BATH

139 Spring Street, New York, NY 10012 • Tel: (212) 941-7722 • Mon-
Sat 11:00-7:00, Sun 12:00-6:00 • Prices medium to high
903 Broadway, New York, NY 10010 • Tel: (212) 328-4343
450 Columbus Avenue, New York, NY 10024 • Tel: (212) 579-9500 •
Trade discount • Major credit cards

Linens, blankets, comforters, home accessories, bath products, bath
accessories.

♛ PRATESI LINENS

829 Madison Avenue, New York, NY 10021 • Tel: (212) 288-2315 •
Fax: (212) 628-4038 • Mon-Sat 10:00-6:00 • Priscilla Fabiano • French
and Italian spoken • Prices very high • Major credit cards

Luxury bed, bath and table linens, robes and fragrances.

ROSETREE

295 Fifth Avenue, #1518, New York, NY 10016 • Telfax: (212) 481-6426 • Mon-Fri 9:00-5:00 • Robert Lovely • Prices medium to high • Trade only

Luxury bedding (excluding sheets) and table linens.

Z. SCHWEITZER LINENS

1132 Madison Avenue, New York, NY 10028 • Tel: (212) 249-8361 • Mon-Sat 10:00-6:00
457 Columbus Avenue, New York, NY 10024 • Tel: (212) 799-9629 • Mon-Sat 10:00-6:00, Sun 12:00-5:00
1053 Lexington Avenue, New York, NY 10021 • Tel: (212) 570-0236 • Mon-Sat 10:00-6:00 • Prices medium to high • Major credit cards

Luxury linen collection created by skilled artisans from around the world: bed, bath and table.

SLEEPING PARTNERS

63 Greene Street, Suite 502, New York, NY 10012 • Tel: (212) 274-1211 • Fax: (212) 274-1226 • Mon-Fri 9:00-7:00 by appointment • Salvo Stoch • Spanish and French spoken • Prices high • Trade discount • MC and Visa

Bed linens, baby bedding with an urban fashion accent. Collection includes textiles for the home, pajamas, shower curtains, throws, pillows, baby gifts and custom orders.

Antique Linen

VIRGINIA DI SCIASCIO, ANTIQUE TEXTILES

799 Madison Avenue, 2nd floor, New York, NY 10021 • Tel: (212) 452-1500 • Mon-Sat 10:00-6:00 • Elaine Springer • French, German and Italian spoken • Prices very high • Major credit cards

Antique linens and lace, largely European from the 19th century. Luxury textiles of the 17th century through early 20th century.

JEAN HOFFMAN ANTIQUES

207 East 66th Street, New York, NY 10021 • Tel: (212) 535-6930/(212) 535-6925 • Mon-Sat 12:00-6:00 and by appointment • Jean Hoffman • German, French and Spanish spoken • Prices medium to high • Trade discount • Major credit cards

Extensive collection of antique linens, including handmade lace items, for the bed and the table. Large selection of sterling silver turn-of-the-century dressing table accessories; antique parasols, canes and paisley shawls.

♕ FRANCOISE NUNNALLE

105 West 55th Street, New York, NY 10019 • Tel: (212) 246-4281 • By appointment • Francoise Nunnallé

Exquisite collection of antique linens from Italy, Belgium, France, Germany, Switzerland and Ireland of museum quality. The crafting includes openwork, drawnwork, punchwork, raised embroidery and lace.

JANA STARR ANTIQUES LTD.

236 East 80th Street, New York, NY 10021 • Tel: (212) 861-8256 • Mon-Sat 12:00-6:00 • Jana Starr • Prices medium • Trade discount • Major credit cards

Antique linens for the table and bed, hand-embroidered, laces, lace curtains, paisley shawls, needlepoint and antique textiles.

TROUVAILLE FRANCAISE

Upper East Side • Tel: (212) 737-6015 • By appointment • Muriel Clarke • Prices low to medium

Vintage and antique bed linens and table linens, both town and country in style. Some textiles as well as antique Victorian white clothes: nightgowns, shirts, bloomers, dresses.

See also: THE DESIGNER COLLECTIONS in HOME FURNISHINGS

MIRROR AND GLASS

AAA GLASS

152 West 26th Street, New York, NY 10001 • Tel: (212) 463-8000 •
Fax: (212) 675-5777 • Mon-Fri 9:00-5:00 • Spanish spoken • MC and
Visa

40 different types of imported patterned glass and colored mirrors.
Many colors, textures, thicknesses and shapes available. Good references.

ABALON

1571 York Avenue, New York, NY 10028 • Tel: (212) 744-0556 • Mon-
Fri 8:00-5:00, Sat 9:00-2:00 • Prices medium • Trade discount

Installation of mirrors, shades and blinds. Custom-made picture
frames and Venetian blinds.

ABBEY SHADE & GLASS

1336 Second Avenue, New York, NY 10021 • Tel: (212) 879-8500 •
Fax: (212) 879-8909 • Mon-Fri 10:00-5:30, Sat 10:00-3:30 • Prices
medium to high • Trade discount • Major credit cards

Custom mirror and glass. Window shades: woven woods, Roman
and bamboo. Venetian blinds in metal and wood, all types.

AGGRESSIVE GLASS CO.

546 East 92nd Street, New York, NY 10128 • Tel: (212) 860-3333 •
Fax: (212) 534-4662 • Mon-Fri 8:30-5:00, closed 12:00-1:00 • Major
credit cards

Mirrors, glass, blinds and shades installed. Homes and offices.

BIBICOFF MIRROR & GLASS

724 Coney Island Avenue, Brooklyn, NY 11218 • Tel: (718) 941-9100 •
Fax: (718) 941-1815 • By appointment • Prices medium

Custom mirror installations, painted glass, mirrored furniture, bath
and shower enclosures.

BROADWAY GLASS & MIRROR

2350 Broadway, New York, NY 10024 • Tel: (212) 721-7878 • Mon-Fri
7:00-4:00, Sat 9:30-4:00 • Spanish spoken

Wall-to-wall mirrors, mirrored doors, glass shelves, picture glass
and installations.

COUNTRY CITY

28 East 10th Street, New York, NY 10003 • Tel: (212) 473-8861 • Daily 10:00-2:00 • Don True • Prices medium • Trade discount • Amex

Interesting mirrors. Vases, lamps and some furniture.

CROSSTOWN CUSTOM SHADE & GLASS INC.

200 West 86th Street, New York, NY 10024 • Tel: (212) 787-8040 • Fax: (212) 787-8467
115 West 10th Street, New York, NY 10011 • Tel: (212) 647-1519 • Fax: (212) 647-1570 • Tue and Thu 9:30-7:00, Wed and Fri 9:30-5:00, Sat 9:30-4:00 • Prices low to high • Trade discount • Major credit cards

Glass and mirror installation; shower and tub enclosures; radiator enclosures in wood or metal; window treatments.

EXQUISITE GLASS

123 Allen Street, New York, NY 10002 • Tel: (212) 674-7069 • Fax: (212) 473-4808 • Mon-Fri 10:00-6:00 • Buz Vaultz • Spanish spoken

Etched glass and mirror; carved stone. Custom engraving on crystal goblets or anything in glass or mirror.

THE FRENCH REFLECTION INC./KRAFT

306 East 61st Street, New York, NY 10021 • Tel: (212) 838-2214 • Fax: (212) 644-9254 • Mon-Fri 9:00-5:00 • Spanish spoken • Prices medium to high • Major credit cards

Magnifying mirrors.

BARRY LONDON GLASS COMPANY

53 West 106th Street, New York, NY 10025 • Tel: (212) 662-1900 • Mon-Fri 7:30-4:00 • Prices medium • Trade discount • Major credit cards

Wall and ceiling mirrors, mirrored doors, antique mirrors and mirror installation.

MANHATTAN SHADE & GLASS CO.

1299 Third Avenue, New York, NY 10021 • Tel: (212) 288-5616 • Fax: (212) 288-7241 • Mon-Fri 8:30-5:30, Sat 10:00-4:00 • Prices medium to high • Major credit cards

Custom fabrication of mirrors for walls and doors; glass table-tops, sand blasting and beveling. Full line of window treatments.

MIRROR FAIR/S. CAVALLO INC.

1495 Third Avenue, New York, NY 10028 • Tel: (212) 288-5050 • Fax: (212) 772-7936 • Mon-Fri 9:00-5:00 • Prices medium to high • Trade discounts

Manufacturer of antique reproduction mirrors and restoration of antique mirrors.

MIRRORS BY JORDAN

38-27 28th Street, Long Island City, NY 11101 • Telfax: (718) 729-3267
• Mon-Fri 8:00-4:30 • Jordan Goldstein • Prices medium to high • Trade
discount

Custom mirror work; custom-made mercury reproduction antique
mirrors; colored mirrors in bronze, grey, peach, black. Glass tops
for tables. Framed or frameless bath and shower enclosures.

NARCISSUS

406 East 9th Street, New York, NY 10009 • Tel: (212) 677-7105 • Fax:
(212) 673-5248 • Mon-Fri 9:00-5:00 • Michael Carbonelli • Spanish
and Italian spoken • Trade discounts

Furnish, install and renovate glass and mirror for small and large
projects.

SHEFTS

697 East 132nd Street, Bronx, NY 10454 • Tel: (718) 665-6240 • Fax:
(718) 993-5062 • Mon-Fri 8:30-5:00 • Neal Shefts • Trade discounts

Etching, carving and gilding on glass, mirror, marble and stone. From
very large projects to a single goblet.

For ANTIQUE MIRRORS see ANTIQUE DEALERS

SHIPPERS AND PACKERS

AARON'S RELOCATIONS

44-01 Eleventh Street, Long Island City, NY 11101 • Tel: (212) 752-2976 • Fax: (212) 745-9292 • Mon-Fri 9:00-5:00 • Derek N. Durka • Prices medium

Expert packing, crating and transport of fine art, antiques and the things their clients care about. 15 years of experience moving antiques for the British Government.

AEI-RADIX FINE ART

Building 75, Room 212, JFK Airport, Jamaica, NY 11430 • Tel: (718) 244-4880 • Fax: (718) 656-0640 • Mon-Fri 8:00-6:00 • Dirk Friedkin • Spanish, Italian and Portuguese spoken • Prices medium • Visa and MC

Complete fine art and antique transport services, international and domestic. Packing, crating and customs clearances.

RACINE BERKOW ASSOCIATES

156 Williams Street, New York, NY 10038 • Tel: (212) 553-6046 • Fax: (212) 791-0622 • Mon-Fri 9:00-5:00 • Racine Berkow • Spanish and French spoken • Prices medium to high • Trade discount

Expert packing and shipping of fine art and antiques.

JAMES BOURLET

21-41 45th Road, Long Island City, NY 11101 • Tel: (718) 392-9770 • Fax: (718) 392-2470 • Mon-Fri 8:00-5:30 • Robert Linley • Prices medium • Major credit cards

Packing and shipping of fine art and antiques.

D.A.D. TRUCKING

76 Varick Street, New York, NY 10013 • Tel: (212) 226-0054 • Fax: (212) 226-1070 • Mon-Fri 9:00-5:00 • Michael Leonard • Spanish spoken • Trade discount • Amex

Packing, crating and storage of fine art and antiques. Pre-shipping advice and estimates.

DAY & MEYER, MURRAY & YOUNG

1166 Second Avenue, New York, NY 10021 • Tel: (212) 838-5151 • Fax: (212) 759-4901 • Mon-Fri 9:00-12:00, Sat 1:00-4:00 • John Miles • Spanish spoken

Packing, moving, storage and shipping of furniture, fine art and antiques.

FERRARI LORENZI LTD.

400 East 54th Street, Suite 21C, New York, NY 10022 • Tel: (212) 826-8261 • Fax: (212) 826-8355 • Mon-Fri 9:00-5:00 • Gianni Renosi • Italian and French spoken • Prices medium • Trade discount

Fine art, collectibles and antiques shipping. Customs arranged.

GANDER & WHITE

21-44 44th Road, Long Island City, NY 11101 • Tel: (718) 784-8444 • Fax: (718) 784-9337 • Mon-Fri 9:00-5:00 • Michael Jaque • Prices medium to high • Trade discounts • Amex

Packing, crating and shipping of fine art and antiques.

GROSSO ART PACKERS

1400 York Avenue, New York, NY 10021 • Tel: (212) 734-8879 • Fax: (212) 288-9009 • Mon-Fri 9:00-5:00 • Gregory Gallo • Prices medium

Expert packing and shipping of fine art.

HAHN BROTHERS WAREHOUSE

190 Christopher Columbus Drive, Jersey City, NJ 07302 • Tel: (201) 432-8488 • Fax: (201) 432-9547 • Mon-Fri 8:00-5:00 • Prices medium

Crating, shipping and climate-controlled storage of antiques and works of fine art.

CHARLES HAPPEL, INC.

17 Battery Place, Suite 1230, New York, NY 10004 • Tel: (212) 487-2629 • Fax: (212) 487-2637 • Mon-Fri 9:00-5:00 • Aphrodite Gavrilis • Spanish and German spoken • Prices high

Fine art customs brokerage, expert packing and international shipping.

HEDLEY'S INC.

30 Thompson Street, New York, NY 10013 • Tel: (212) 219-2877 • Fax: (212) 219-2826 • Mon-Fri 9:00-6:00 • Michael Thomas • French spoken • Prices high • Trade discount negotiable

Packing, crating and shipping of antiques and fine art: world-wide, sea and air. Well known in the Paris Flea Market.

LEBRON BROS. INC.

31-36 58th Street, Woodside, NY 11377 • Tel: (718) 274-0532 • Mon-Fri 9:00-5:00 • James Lebron • Spanish spoken • Prices medium

Shipping of fine art and antiques.

MAGNA FINE ARTS

47-15 Fifth Street, Long Island City, NY 11101 • Tel: (718) 937-0373 • Fax: (718) 786-2143 • Mon-Fri 9:00-5:00

Skillful packing and crating. Shipping, local and long distance.

OLLENDORF FINE ARTS

780 East 138th Street, Bronx, NY 10454 • Tel: (718) 665-8666 • Fax: (718) 665-8555 • Mon-Sat 6:00-10:00 • Many languages spoken • Prices medium • Major credit cards

International ocean and air shipments of fine art and antiques.

THE PADDED WAGON

120 West 107th Street, New York, NY 10025 • Tel: (212) 222-4880 • Fax: (212) 222-8564 • Mon-Fri 9:00-5:00, Sat 9:00-3:00 • Barry Weinstein and Ed Dowling • Spanish spoken • Prices medium • Trade discounts negotiable • Major credit cards

Packing and crating, moving and storage; specializing in fine art and antiques. Local, long distance and overseas.

RAINBOW MOVERS

19 Leonard Street, New York, NY 10013 • Tel: (212) 431-8550/(800) 660-2929 • Mon-Fri 8:00-5:00, Sat 8:00-12:00 • All major credit cards

Packing and moving for households and offices. Moves for antique dealers.

SCAC TRANSPORT

North Hangar Road, Suite 242, Jamaica, NY 11430 • Tel: (718) 656-8100 • Fax: (718) 917-8425 • Mon-Fri 9:00-5:00 • Peter Bernacki • French and Spanish spoken • Prices medium

Air and sea freight forwarding.

SOUTH PASS TRANSART

466 Washington Street, New York, NY 10013 • Tel: (212) 925-3067 • Fax: (212) 966-8757 • Mon-Fri 8:30-5:30 • Paul Sipos • Spanish and French spoken • Prices medium

Fine arts and antiques crating, shipping, storage.

SPARTACUS MOVERS

46-09 11th Street, Long Island City, NY 11101 • Tel: (718) 706-8888 • Fax: (718) 937-8481 • Daily 7:30-9:00 • Neil Deutsch, Peter Brown • Professional discount • Major credit cards

Moving of unique furniture and antiques.

TABLE ARTS

The arts of the table have been refined over thousands of years; and whether we are outdoors enjoying a picnic or sitting down to a formal meal, we cannot but feel pleasure at the sight of a fine repast set out and served in an attractive manner.

There is a vast difference between eating and dining. Eating is basically the necessity of re-fueling the body when it demands sustenance to continue the daily race.

Dining, however, is another story. Good food and the time to enjoy it requires atmosphere and setting. Elegant linen, beautiful silver, fine porcelain and delicate crystal all serve to make sharing a meal a pleasurable experience.

The origins of these arts of the table go back to the time of the Ancient Egyptians, the Chinese and the Persians. Many of the great crafts came back to Europe with the Crusaders. Catherine de Medici then brought the taste and style of Renaissance Italy to France with her.

Now fine tableware can be found everywhere in the world and the 20th century has brought a new wrinkle: without a dowry system, the new brides get started in life with gifts of tableware from friends and family.

Crystal and Glass

♔ BACCARAT

625 Madison Avenue, New York, NY 10021 • Tel: (212) 826-4100 • Fax: (212) 826-5043 • Mon-Sat 10:00-6:00, Thu 10:00-7:00 • Francois Mainetti • French, German, Spanish, Italian and Japanese spoken • Prices high • Corporate discounts • Major credit cards

Baccarat crystal, crafted in France since 1764, is world renowned for its exceptional quality and innovative design. This collection includes stemware, barware, vases, decanters, pitchers, lighting and re-creations from The Baccarat Museum Collection. They also carry Limoges and Haviland china, Gien faience and stemware and hollowware from Puiforcat and Christofle.

DAUM BOUTIQUE

694 Madison Avenue, New York, NY 10021 • Tel: (212) 355-2060 • Fax: (212) 355-2074 • Mon-Sat 10:00-6:00 • Evelyne Dreyfus • French spoken • Prices medium to high • Major credit cards

Decorative crystal and accessories. Stemware, barware, limited edition objets d'art. Many of the decorative objects are in pate de verre, a glassmaking technique used by Daum's craftsmen since 1870. Features work of Salvador Dali, Hilton McConnico and Philippe Starck.

GALLERI ORREFORS KOSTA BODA

58 East 57th Street, New York, NY 10022 • Tel: (212) 752-1095 • Fax: (212) 752-3705 • Mon-Fri 10:00-6:00, Sat 10:00-5:00 • Irene Shyberger • Swedish, German, Spanish and Italian spoken • Prices medium to high • Major credit cards

This company has been making crystal for 250 years. They carry crystal, glass, glass sculpture and glass art. One-of-a-kind and limited edition ornamental pieces by the 16 artists of Orrefors Kosta Boda, such as Bertil Vallien, Ulrica Hydman Vallien, Kjell Engman and Ann Wahlstrom.

HOYA CRYSTAL GALLERY

689 Madison Avenue, New York, NY 10021 • Tel: (212) 223-6335 • Fax: (212) 371-9129 • Mon-Sat 10:00-6:00 • Major credit cards

Fifteen in-house artists, along with Sugasawa, Hoya's design leader, have created crystal art sculptures as well as functional stemware, barware, saki glasses, vases, bowls.

D. KING IRWIN

225 Fifth Avenue, Suite 721, New York, NY 10010 • Tel: (212) 683-0619 • Fax: (212) 683-0634 • Mon-Fri 9:30-4:30 • Tony Falutico • Spanish spoken • Prices medium to high • Trade only • MC and Visa

Excellent choice of crystal and glass stemware, barware, vases, bowls and decorative color cut crystal.

LALIQUE

680 Madison Avenue, New York, NY 10021 • Tel: (212) 355-6550 • Fax: (212) 752-0203 • Mon-Fri 10:00-6:00, Sat 10:00-5:30 • Rosalyn Hand • French spoken • Prices high • Corporate discounts • Major credit cards

Superb examples of the fine art of blown and cut crystal continuing the tradition begun by René Lalique in 1921. Stemware, barware and china. Crystal sculptures, lighting and extraordinary tables and consoles.

SIMON PEARCE

500 Park Avenue, New York, NY 10022 • Tel: (212) 421-8801 • Fax: (212) 421-8802 • Mon-Sat 10:00-6:00 • Kim Bratton Share
120 Wooster Street, New York, NY 10012 • Tel: (212) 334-2393 • Mon-Sat 11:00-7:00, Sun 12:00-6:00 • Prices medium • Major credit cards

Simon Pearce is a designer and blower of glass. He established his own workshop in Kilkenny, Ireland, in 1970. In 1981 he moved his operations to The Mill in Quechee, Vermont, where he harnessed the hydro-power of the Ottauquechee River to fuel his glass furnace. These two shops sell this line of fine crystal as well as their pottery and glass.

ROGASKA

685 Madison Avenue, New York, NY 10021 • Tel: (212) 980-6200 • Fax: (212) 980-5588 • Mon-Fri 10:00-6:00, Sat 11:00-5:00 • French, Italian and Croation spoken • Prices medium • Major credit cards

Stemware and glassware produced in Slovenia by Rogaska for more than 50 years. A large choice for the table including paperweights and other decorative items. Custom orders possible. Bridal registry.

STEUBEN

715 Fifth Avenue, New York, NY 10022 • Tel: (212) 752-1441 • Fax: (212) 753-1354 • Mon-Sat 10:00-6:00, Thu 10:00-7:00 • Joan Baret • Prices medium to high • Major credit cards

Steuben crystal and glass has been made in New York since 1918. The company is especially known for design and craftsmanship of its glass sculptures. They carry tableware such as bowls, vases and decorative pieces.

⚏ WATERFORD-WEDGEWOOD STORE

713 Madison Avenue, New York, NY 10021 • Tel: (212) 759-0500 • Fax: (212) 486-6570 • Mon-Sat 10:00-6:00 • Japanese spoken • Prices high • Major credit cards

For over 200 years Waterford crystal and Wedgewood china have graced some of the most elegant tables of Europe and America and have become the classic favorites. Splendid crystal sculpture, crystal tableware, barware, decanters, crystal chandeliers and lamps; excellent choice of Wedgewood fine china.

Engraving of Crystal and Glass

YOUR NAME HERE, INC./CALLARI CRYSTAL GLASS ENGRAVING

39 West 14th Street, Suite 201, New York, NY 10011 • Tel: (212) 255-7229 • Fax: (212) 229-1021 • Mon-Fri 11:00-6:00 • Joseph A. Callari • Wholesale discount • Major credit cards

Personalized engraving of crystal and glass. Etching of crystal and glass awards and corporate giftware. Top references.

See also: ART GLASS

General

⚜ ASPREY

725 Fifth Avenue, New York, NY 10022 • Tel: (212)688-1811 • Fax: (212) 826-3746 • Mon-Sat 10:00-5:30 • Philip Warner • Japanese, French and Spanish spoken • Prices medium to high • Major credit cards

Superb silver, antique and contemporary; porcelain, crystal, glassware, everything for the table; jewelry; leather goods. Custom made gifts. Bridal registry; corporate gifts.

AVVENTURA

463 Amsterdam Avenue, New York, NY 10024 • Tel: (212) 769-2510 • Fax: (212) 769-2511 • Mon-Thu 10:30-7:00, Fri 10:30-4:00, Sun 11:00-6:00, closed Sat • Major credit cards

Carlo Moretti barware, stemware and decanters, Venini bottles, Morano crystal, Alessi cruet sets, Ricci and Georg Jensen flatware. Formal dinnerware, vases, bowls, candlesticks, serving pieces, coffee pots.

NIELS BAMBERGER INC.

1070 Madison Avenue, New York, NY 10028 • Tel: (212) 737-7118 • Mon-Fri 9:00-5:30 • Prices medium to high • Professional discount • Major credit cards

Agents for Royal Copenhagen, Bing & Grondahl, and Dahl-Jensen porcelains; Georg Jensen silver. Outstanding inventory of new and out-of-production older pieces. Flora Danica sets.

BARDITH LTD.

31 East 72 Street, New York, NY 10021 • Tel: (212) 737-8660 • Fax: (212) 650-9228 • Mon-Fri 11:00-5:30 • Prices high

Complete sets of formal china services by all the legendary companies, platters, majolica. The 901 Madison Avenue store specializes in mid-18th- to mid-19th-century English porcelain and pottery. No complete sets.

CHRISTINE BELFOR DESIGN LTD.

304 Hudson Street, Studio 600, New York, NY 10013 • Tel: (212) 633-6680 • Fax: (212) 645-2759 • Mon-Fri 10:00-5:00 • Prices high • Trade discount • Major credit cards

Custom-designed, hand-painted dinner services and glassware. From one-of-a-kind pieces to complete services.

⚜ BERNARDAUD

499 Park Avenue, New York, NY 10022 • Tel: (212) 371-4300 • Fax: (212) 758-8444 • Mon-Fri 10:00-7:00, Sat 10:00-6:00 • French, Italian and Spanish spoken • Professional discount • Major credit cards

Manufacturer of superb Limoges porcelain displayed in a beautiful setting resembling "home". Full lines of flatware and crystal.

CARDEL LTD.

621 Madison Avenue, New York, NY 10022 • Tel: (212) 753-8880 • Fax: (212) 826-6685 • Mon-Sat 9:30-6:00 • Jo Elliott-Smith • French and German spoken • Prices medium to high • Trade discount • Major credit cards

A superb offering of very fine crystal, china and silver. Meissen, Herend, Minton, and Limoges as well as bone china from the English companies. Stemware: Saint-Louis, Stuart, Baccarat, Moser, Peill, and Val St. Lambert. Sterling silver flatware is hand-forged by the Old Newbury Crafters.

CARTIER

2 East 52nd Street, New York, NY 10022 • Tel: (212) 446-3428 • Fax: (212) 832-2234 • Mon-Sat 10:00-5:30 • Lorraine Littles • French, Spanish and Italian spoken • Prices high • Major credit cards

A small exclusive line of French china, crystal and flatware. Bridal registry.

CERAMICA

59 Thompson Street, New York, NY 10012 • Tel: (212) 941-1307 • Fax: (212) 941-1308 • Mon-Sat 11:30-7:00, Sun 11:30-6:00 • Prices medium to high • Trade discount • Major credit cards

Contemporary Italian hand-painted ceramic tableware and decorative accessories based on Renaissance designs. Some Moroccan earthenware items such as planters and dishes.

CITY EAST ANTIQUES CENTER

201 East 31st Street, New York, NY 10016 • Tel: (212) 779-0979 •
Mon-Fri 11:00-6:00, Sat 11:00-5:00 • Renee Braverman • Prices medium • Trade discount • MC and Visa

Small antiques center. The china and glassware dates from the 1880s to the 1940s. Complete china sets in florals or Art Deco geometrics. Glassware that ranges from long-stemmed crystal goblets to cranberry cordials to kitschy glasses with flamingoes.

EASTSIDE CHINA LTD.

5002 Twelth Avenue, Brooklyn, NY 11219 • Tel: (718) 633-8672 • Fax: (718) 972-5071 • Mon 10:00-7:00, Tue-Wed 10:00-6:00, Thu 10:00-8:00, Fri 10:00-2:00 • MC and Visa

Everything for the table: Mikasa, Royal Doulton, Royal Worcester, Spode, Lenox and many more; crystal, glass and flatware from the great names. Bridal registry.

EASTSIDE GIFTS AND DINNERWARE INC.

351 Grand Street, New York, NY 10012 • Tel: (212) 982-7200 • National Bridal Registry Tel: (800) GIFTS-11 • Sun-Thu 10:00-6:00, Fri 10:00-2:00 • Trade discount • Major credit cards

Full line of tableware: Mikasa, Fitz and Floyd, Royal Doulton, Wedgewood, Haviland, Hutchenreuther and Lalique at savings. Selection of stemware and flatware.

ENAMELED GLASS

2 Bowers Lane, Closter, NJ 07624 • Tel: (201) 767-1572 • By appointment • Richard Knopf • Prices medium

Custom enameled glass dinnerware and serving pieces. Also glass lamp shades.

FELISSIMO

10 West 56th Street, 3rd floor, New York, NY 10019 • Tel: (212) 247-5656 • Fax: (212) 956-0081 • Mon-Sat 10:00-6:00, Thu 10:00-8:00 • Most languages spoken • Prices high • Major credit cards

Charming selection of tableware in this delightful turn-of-the-century townhouse.

MICHAEL C. FINA

580 Fifth Avenue, New York, NY 10036 • Tel: (212) 869-5050 • Fax: (212) 575-4621 • Mon-Fri 9:30-6:00, Thu until 7:00, Sat 10:30-6:00 • Tracey Wekar • French and Spanish spoken • Major credit cards

Well-known vendor of tableware and giftware. Very large choice of lines of famous names such as Baccarat, Wedgewood, etc. Bridal registry.

FISHS EDDY

889 Broadway, New York, NY 10003 • Tel: (212) 420-9020 • Fax: (212) 353-1454 • Owners: Julie Gaines, David Lenovitz

2176 Broadway, New York, NY 10024 • Tel: (212) 873-8819 • Fax: (212) 873-4169 • P.J. Singh and Lillian Francescini, Managers • Mon-Thu 10:00-8:00, Fri-Sat 10:00-9:00, Sun 11:00-7:00 • Major credit cards

Store, named after a Catskill town, filled with china, new and old, from diners in Mississippi and all across the country, from country clubs and country day schools, colleges, hotels. In addition to the vintage collection, the stores are stocked with earthenware reproduced from 1920s designs and china reproduced from 1940s moulds. Large selection of glassware.

GOLDMANS TREASURES

655 Avenue of the Americas, New York, NY 10010 • Tel: (212) 924-4900 • Bridal Registry: (800) 221-7457 • Fax: (212) 924-4611 • Mon-Thu 10:00-9:00, Fri 10:00-3:00, Sun 11:00-6:00 • Hansi Braudy • Most languages spoken • Trade discount • Major credit cards

China, stemware, flatware, giftware, lighting, furniture and decorative accessories.

GUCCI

685 Fifth Avenue, New York, NY 10022 • Tel: (212) 230-0804 • Fax: (212) 230-0894 • Mon-Sat 9:30-6:00, Thu until 7:00 • Major credit cards

Gucci's Bamboo service and a line of stemware and flatware.

JUDY HENDERSON STUDIO

70 Kellogg Hill, Weston, CT 06883 • Tel: (203) 221-0731 • By appointment

Beautiful and unique handmade limited editions of ceramic tableware.

HERMES

11 East 57th Street, 2nd floor, New York, NY 10022 • Tel: (212) 751-3181 • Fax: (212) 751-8143 • Mon-Sat 10:00-6:00, Thu 10:00-8:00 • French spoken • Prices high • Major credit cards

Seven patterns of porcelain services; three patterns of barware; several patterns of Saint-Louis crystal; two silver plate and two stainless steel flatware patterns. Bridal registry.

LINDA HORN ANTIQUES

1015 Madison Avenue, New York, NY 10021 • Tel: (212) 772-1122 • Fax: (212) 288-0449 • Mon-Sat 10:00-6:00 • Professional discount • Major credit cards

English, French and European antiques: crystal decanters, silver boxes and exceptional majolica.

IKERU LTD.

466 Washington Street, Suite 4W, New York, NY 10013 • Tel: (212) 219-3757 • Fax: (212) 274-0115 • Mon-Fri 9:00-5:00 • Many languages spoken • Trade discount • Major credit cards

One-of-a-kind custom work: dinnerware, glassware, ceramics.

JAMES II GALLERIES

11 East 57th Street, 4th floor, New York, NY 10022 • Tel: (212) 355-7040 • Fax: (212) 593-0341 • Barbara Munves, Owner • Mon-Fri 10:00-5:30, Sat 10:30-4:30 • Prices very high • Major credit cards

19th-century English decorative arts: Wedgewood drabware, Ridgeway and Mason ironstone, Staffordshire, Spode and Worcester. Full dinner services, covered vegetable dishes and compotes, dessert sets and children's tea sets. Crystal claret jugs, hyacinth vases, cut and clear decanters and jugs, cranberry glass bowls and goblets, crystal candlesticks. Sterling silver and Victorian plate: trays, pitchers, candlesticks, bowls, selection of stuffing spoons, soup ladles, berry spoons, and mother-of-pearl handled fish forks and knives. Collectibles: silver-topped perfume bottles and sterling silver frames. Antique jewelry.

LA TERRINE

1024 Lexington Avenue, New York, NY 10021 • Tel: (212) 988-3366 • Mon-Sat 10:30-6:00 • Yvette Goddard and Marcia Goldstein • Prices medium • Major credit cards

Hand-painted ceramics for tabletop from: France, Greece, Hungary, Italy, Mexico and Portugal.

THE L•S• COLLECTION

469 West Broadway, New York, NY 10012 • Tel: (212) 673-4575 • Fax: (212) 673-4108 • Mon-Fri 11:30-7:00, Sat 11:30-8:00, Sun 12:00-6:00 • Portuguese and Spanish spoken • Prices medium to high • Major credit cards

Contemporary china, glassware, flatware and ceramics. International inventory, some of which include: stemware and barware by Murano of Italy, sterling silver flatware from West German silversmiths, Robbe & Berking, china from Italian architect Paoli Portoghesi and others. Lots of art glass.

MOOD INDIGO

181 Prince Street, New York, NY 10012 • Tel: (212) 254-1176 • Tues-Sat 12:00-7:00, Sun 1:00-6:00 • Diane Petipas • Major credit cards

Decorative accessories from the 1930s, 1940s and 1950s. City's largest supply of Fiestaware, Hall china, Russel Wright dinnerware, Depression glass plates and bowls, chrome-topped glass martini shakers and kitchen glasses from the 30s and 40s.

THE MEDITERRANEAN SHOP

780 Madison Avenue, New York, NY 10021 • Tel: (212) 879-3120 •
Mon-Sat 10:00-5:30 • Spanish spoken • Prices medium to high • Trade
discount • Visa and MC

A beautiful choice of Italian and French faience; Italian paper items
and ceramic tiles. Bridal registry.

MUD

East: 1566 Second Avenue, New York, NY 10028 • Tel: (212) 570-
6868
West: 506 Amsterdam Avenue, New York, NY 10024 • Tel: (212) 579-
5575 • Mon-Sat 11:30-8:00, Thu until 9:00, Sun until 6:00 • Lorrie
Hammond • Some French and Spanish spoken • Prices low to medium
• Major credit cards

This is a retail store where pottery is made on site. Emerging artists
are represented who also work in glass, metal and wood. They do a
large amount of custom and personalized work for restaurants,
decorators and individuals. References upon request.

NORTH RIVER POTTERY

107 Hall Street, Brooklyn, NY 11205 • Telfax: (718) 636-8608 • By
appointment • Ragnar Dixon Naess • Major credit cards

Handmade stoneware: tableware and pots. Custom orders.

FRANCOISE NUNNALLE

105 West 55th Street, New York, NY 10019 • Tel: (212) 246-4281 • By
appointment • Prices high

Extraordinary collection of mid-18th-century and mid-19th-century
soup tureens and other antique porcelain.

PAVILLON CHRISTOFLE

680 Madison Avenue, New York, NY 10021 • Tel: (212) 308-9390 •
Mon-Sat 10:00-6:00 • Major credit cards

Christofle has been a leader in "Arts de la Table" since its creation
in Paris in 1830 and its appointment as purveyor of King Louis-
Philippe and Emperor Napoleon. In addition to the beautiful lines of
silver flatware, there are classic designs of Limoges porcelain and
the latest innovation of Microgold, hand-adorned Limoges porcelain with 24ct gold that is microwavable. A collection of fine cotton
table linens inspired by the archives of the Christofle Museum.

THE POTTERY BARN

600 Broadway, New York, NY 10012 • Tel: (212) 219-2420 • Mon-Sat 10:00-9:00, Sun 11:00-8:00
1965 Broadway, New York, NY 10025 • Tel: (212) 579-8477 • Mon-Sat 10:00-9:00, Sun 11:00-7:00
51 Greenwich Avenue, New York, NY 10014 • Tel: (212) 807-6321 • Mon-Sat 11:00-8:00, Sun 12:00-6:00
1451 Second Avenue, New York, NY 10021 • Tel: (212) 988-4228 • Mon-Fri 10:00-8:00, Sat 10:00-7:00, Sun 11:00-6:00
100 Seventh Avenue, New York, NY 10011 • Tel: (212) 633-8405 • Mon-Sat 10:00-8:00, Sun 12:00-6:00
250 West 57th Street, New York, NY 10019 • Tel: (212) 315-1855 • Mon-Fri 10:00-8:00, Sat 10:00-7:00, Sun 12:00-6:00
117 East 59th Street, New York, NY 10022 • Tel: (212) 753-5424 • Mon-Sat 10:00-8:00, Sun 12:00-6:00
• Prices medium • Major credit cards

A large and ever-changing selection of medium priced, good quality, contemporary designed glassware, earthenware, tableware and barware. Lots of useful items for the table and the home.

THE QUEENS ART AND ANTIQUES CENTER

37-27 32nd Street, Long Island City, NY 11415 • Tel: (718) 784-1959 • Fax: (718) 784-2179 • Tue-Sat 10:00-6:00 • Prices low to medium • Major credit cards

Collections of crystal and porcelain in addition to a variety of antiques. Zsolnay irridescent glazed porcelain.

SOLANEE

866 Lexington Avenue, New York, NY 10021 • Tel: (212) 439-6109 • Fax: (212) 288-3065 • Mon-Fri 10:00-6:00, Sat 11:00-5:00 • Georgie McConnell • French spoken • Prices high • Trade discount • Major credit cards

Hand-painted French dinnerware from Moustiers, Quimper and Provence. Glassware from Biot and Brittany. Painted wood furniture, iron and glass tables, linens and more.

STUPELL LTD.

29 East 22nd Street, New York, NY 10010 • Tel: (212) 260-3100 • Mon-Sat 10:00-6:00 • Keith Stupell • All major credit cards

Carole Stupell's son now runs the shop. Fine quality china, glassware, and silver, and his mother's designs: plates in the shape of lobsters and leaves, bowls like acorns.

☷ TIFFANY & CO.

727 Fifth Avenue, New York, NY 10022 • Tel: (212) 755-8000 • Fax: (212) 605-4356 • Mon-Sat 10:00-5:30 • Prices medium to high • All major credit cards

An international legend since their acclaim in 1867 at the Paris Exposition Universelle. Beautiful choice of porcelain by the top names and special patterns made exclusively for Tiffany's. More than 20 superb flatware designs and a large choice of barware and stemware. Bridal registry.

TRIBECA POTTERS

443 Greenwich Street, New York, NY 10013 • Tel: (212) 431-7631 • Fax: (212) 431-8938 • 7 days 10:00-5:30 • Judy Jackson • French spoken • Prices medium • Major credit cards

Custom made ceramics: high-fire stoneware, low-fire slipcast ware and majolica. 10 professional artists who take commissions for everything for the table, oven and serving dishes; masks and sculpture.

VILLEROY & BOCH

974 Madison Avenue, New York, NY 10021 • Tel: (212) 535-2500 • Mon-Sat 10:00-6:00 • French spoken • Major credit cards

Wide selection of fine French china, crystal, art glass and accessories.

WATERFORD-WEDGEWOOD STORE

713 Madison Avenue, New York, NY 10021 • Tel: (212) 759-0500 • Fax: (212) 486-6570 • Mon-Sat 10:00-6:00 • Major credit cards

Magnificent crystal and china from these noted manufacturers who have more than 200 years experience in production. Excellent choice.

Department Stores

BARNEYS NEW YORK

154 West 17th Street, New York, NY 10011 • Chelsea Passage • Tel: (212) 593-7800 • Mon-Thu 10:00-9:00, Fri 10:00-8:00, Sat 10:00-7:00, Sun 12:00-6:00 • Major credit cards
660 Madison Avenue, New York, NY 10021 • Chelsea Passage • Tel: (212) 826-8900 • Mon-Fri 10:00-8:00, Sat-Sun 12:00-6:00 • Major credit cards

Selections of crystal and china from the major names: Baccarat, Haviland, Lalique; Christofle flatware. From formal porcelains to everyday ceramics. Some one of a kind. Bridal registry.

HENRI BENDEL

712 Fifth Avenue, New York, NY 10019 • Tel: (212) 247-1100 • Mon-Sat 10:00-7:00, Thu 10:00-8:00, Sun 12:00-6:00 • Prices medium to high • Major credit cards

The Frank McIntosh Home Collection: unusual and imaginative selection of tableware.

BERGDORF GOODMAN

754 Fifth Avenue, 7th floor, New York, NY 10019 • Tel: (212) 753-7300 • Bridal registry: (212) 872-8868 • Mon-Sat 10:00-6:00, Thu 10:00-8:00 • Major credit cards

Excellent choice of porcelain patterns, crystal and flatware. Vintage blue and white, English, French and early American lines. Full line of table linens. Antique table items in the Kentshire Galleries. Bridal registry.

BLOOMINGDALE'S

1000 Third Avenue/Lexington at 59th, 6th floor, New York, NY 10022 • Tel: (212) 705-2000 • Bridal registry: (212) 705-2800 • Fax: (212) 705-3684 • Mon-Fri 10:00-8:30, Sat 10:00-7:00, Sun 11:00-7:00 • Major credit cards

Kitchen and table, most wanted names in glassware, china, and silver. Bridal registry.

MACY'S

151 West 34th Street, New York, NY 10001 • Tel: (212) 695-4400 • Bridal registry: (212) 494-3800 • Mon-Sat 10:00-8:30, Sun 11:00-7:00 • Prices medium to high • Major credit cards

Large choice of most lines of china, crystal and flatware. Bridal registry. Difficult to get through by telephone. It's best to go there.

TAKASHIMAYA NEW YORK

693 Fifth Avenue, 3rd floor, New York, NY 10022 • Tel: (212) 350-0100 • Fax: (212) 350-0192 • Mon-Sat 10:00-6:00, Thu 10:00-8:00 • Prices medium to high • Major credit cards

Very attractive selection of tableware from international sources. Bridal registry.

The Wholesalers

225 FIFTH AVENUE

225 Fifth Avenue, New York, NY 10010 • Tel: (212) 685-6377 • Mon-Fri 9:00-5:00 • Trade only

This building is set aside exclusively for the trade. It houses the headquarters and wholesale showrooms of many of the international tableware manufacturers. They do have regular shows and you can call the office for these dates.

NEW YORK MERCHANDISE MART

41 Madison Avenue, New York, NY 10010 • Tel: (212) 686-1203 • Mon-Fri 9:00-5:00 • Trade only

This building is open to wholesale buyers, designers and architects only. Many of the tableware manufacturers are located here. You can call for information about shows but admittance is restricted to professionals.

See also: ANTIQUE DEALERS, ANTIQUE PORCELAIN, HOME FUR-NISHINGS

Silver

AARON'S

576 Fifth Avenue, 4th floor, New York, NY 10036 • Tel: (212) 764-7929 • Fax: (212) 764-7931 • Mon-Fri 11:00-6:00 • Prices medium to high • Trade discounts • Major credit cards

Their specialty is active and discontinued patterns in sterling silver flatware from the 1850s to the present. There are tea services and a large selection of serving dishes. They will replace missing pieces.

⚎ BUCCELLATI

46 East 57th Street, New York, NY 10022 • Tel: (212) 308-2900 • Fax: (212) 750-1323 • Mon-Fri 10:00-6:00, Sat 10:00-5:30 • Major credit cards

Silver by Mario Buccellati who modeled his designs after antique Florentine silver. Sterling silver objects and flatware patterns, hollowware, bowls, tureens, trays, candlesticks and coffee services. Seven designs of silver plate flatware available.

MICHAEL FEINBERG

225 Fifth Avenue, Room 514, New York, NY 10010 • Tel: (212) 532-0311 • Fax: (212) 889-7394 • Mon-Fri 9:00-5:00 • Shelly Ludlow • Spanish spoken • Prices high • Trade only • MC and Visa

High-end sterling silver, silver plate and pewter. Everything in silver from flatware to silver trays and serving dishes to picture frames.

FORTUNOFF

681 Fifth Avenue, New York, NY 10019 • Tel: (212) 758-6660 • Mon and Thu 10:00-7:00, Tue-Wed, Fri-Sat 10:00-6:00 • Major credit cards

Wonderful selection of antique and estate silver: Chinese export, American and English tea services, Old Sheffield and Old Victorian plate sweetmeat dishes, wine coasters, biscuit boxes, spoon warmers, candlesticks, candelabra, covered serving dishes. Assortment of 19th-century Chinese and antique Tiffany silver patterns. Hundreds of contemporary flatware patterns in sterling, stainless steel, gold and silver plate. China and crystal selection.

FORTY SEVENTH STREET SILVER

21 West 47th Street, New York, NY 10036 • Tel: (212) 840-6904 •
Mon-Thu 10:00-5:00, Fri 10:00-3:00 • Prices medium to high • Trade
discount

All kinds of silver, old and new. Antique Tiffany, English and Jensen;
Judaica. Will arrange for repairs. Free estimates.

I. FREEMAN & SON

60 East 56th Street, New York, NY 10022 • Tel: (212) 759-6900 • Fax:
(212) 759-6905 • Mon-Fri 9:00-5:00 • Carole Gliedman • French and
Spanish spoken • All price ranges • Trade discounts

Antique silver of all periods and all countries and modern silver.
Everything for the table. Old Sheffield and Victorian plate. Bridal
registry.

GEORG JENSEN

683 Madison Avenue, New York, NY 10021 • Mon-Sat 10:00-6:00 •
Tel: (212) 759-6457 • Mon-Sat 10:00-6:00 • Prices high • Major credit
cards

Georg Jensen sterling silver and stainless flatware patterns. Many
of his early designs.

F. GOREVIC & SON

635 Madison Avenue, New York, NY 10022 • Tel: (212) 832-9000 •
Fax: (212) 832-1509 • Mon-Sat 10:00-5:30 • Prices high • Trade discount • Amex

Antique European and American silver from the 17th to the 19th
centuries; Old Sheffield and Victorian plate. Antique jewelry. 19th-
century bronzes.

GRAND STERLING SILVER CO.

345 Grand Street, New York, NY 10002 • Tel: (212) 674-6450 • Fax:
(212) 979-0578 • Sun-Thu 10:30-5:30 • All major credit cards

Sterling silver in every shape and size: bowls, vases, cake and fruit
plates, wine cups and candlesticks, frames and flatware.

HISTORICAL DESIGN COLLECTION

305 East 61st Street, New York, NY 10021 • Tel: (212) 593-4528 • Fax:
(212) 486-3188 • Mon-Sat 10:00-6:00 • Prices high

Silver and decorative arts, 1880-1960. Special exhibitions of silver
items by world famous designers, such as Archibald Knox. Exhibitions change regularly but there is always a special selection of art
in silver available to see and buy.

ALICE KWARTLER

123 East 57th Street, New York, NY 10022 • Tel: (212) 752-3590 •
Mon-Sat 11:00-6:00 • Major credit cards

Old Tiffany silver is a specialty. Art Nouveau sterling coffee sets,
dresser and desk accessories, candlesticks, picture frames, flasks,
enameled Austrian stemware and English fruit sets with tusk handles.
19th-century crystal.

J. MAVEC & CO.

625 Madison Avenue, New York, NY 10022 • Tel: (212) 888-8100 •
Fax: (212) 888-0418 • Mon-Fri 10:00-5:30, Sat by appointment • Major
credit cards

Antique silver: Georgian and Victorian candlesticks and candelabra, tea-caddy spoons, snuff mulls and boxes, tartanware, frames,
castors, serving pieces, and infant mugs and spoons. Old Sheffield
plate wine coasters and trays. Jewelry from the Georgian period to
the 1940s and glass.

﷼ NELSON & NELSON ANTIQUES, INC.

445 Park Avenue, New York, NY 10022 • Tel: (212) 980-5825 • Fax:
(212) 980-5827 • Mon-Sat 10:30-5:30 • Pat Nelson • Spanish spoken
• Prices low to high • 20% trade discount • Major credit cards

Antique and estate silver, objets d'art and jewelry. Engraving, repair
for silver and jewelry. Bridal registry. Corporate gifts.

﷼ PAVILLON CRISTOFLE

680 Madison Avenue, New York, NY 10021 • Tel: (212) 308-9390 •
Mon-Fri 10:00-6:00, Sat 10:00-5:30 • Major credit cards

Christofle has been a leader in "Arts de la Table" since their creation in 1830 and their appointment as purveyor of King Louis-
Philippe and Emperor Napoleon. They have been the silversmith
for countless families, embassies, luxury hotels, corporate dining
rooms and ocean liners. They created 40,000 pieces of silverware
for the "Normandie" alone. Many of their classic designs are still in
production. Sterling, gold and silver plate flatware, tea services, ice
buckets, bowls, trays, pitchers, silver rattles, forks, mugs and spoons
for babies. They also carry the top French lines of porcelain as well
as crystal from Baccarat and Saint-Louis.

﷼ JAMES ROBINSON

480 Park Avenue, New York, NY 10022 • Tel: (212) 752-6166 • Mon-Fri
10:00-5:00, Sat 10:30-4:30 • Prices high to very high • Major credit
cards

Antique silver, antique porcelain services, antique table glass and
antique jewelry. 17th- to 19th-century English hallmark silver: each
period of silver, Georgian to Victorian, is represented. Porcelain dinner sets from Coalport, Spode, Derby, Minton, Worcester and 19th-
century jewelry.

S. J. SHRUBSOLE

104 East 57th Street, New York, NY 10022 • Tel: (212) 753-8920 • Fax: (212) 754-5192 • Mon-Fri 9:30-5:30, Sat 10:00-5:00 • Prices medium to high • Some trade discounts • Major credit cards

Antique English and American silver; antique and estate jewelry; antique English and Irish glass. This English company has been on 57th Street for more than fifty years, the most distinguished silver purveyor in the country. Items from the 16th through the early 19th centuries. Work of the silversmiths: Paul de Lamerie, Hester Bateman, Paul Storr, Myer Myers and Paul Revere. American, English, and Scottish silver. Old Sheffield plate.

TIFFANY & CO.

727 Fifth Avenue, New York, NY 10022 • Tel: (212) 755-8000 • Fax: (212) 605-4356 • Mon-Sat 10:00-5:30, Thu until 7:00 • Prices high • Major credit cards

Tiffany & Co. was founded by Charles Lewis Tiffany in 1837 when he was 25 years old. The company went on to create the "American style" after achieving international recognition in 1867 at the Paris Exposition Universelle. This award resulted in Tiffany becoming the silversmith and goldsmith to 17 crowned heads of Europe, as well as the premier American silversmith. More than 20 of the 60 flatware designs created are available today. The choice of silver is enormous and the quality impeccable. Bridal registry.

TOUT LE MONDE

1178 Lexington Avenue, New York, NY 10021 • Tel: (212) 439-8487 • Fax: (212) 439-8490 • Mon-Sat 10:00-5:30 • Prices medium to high • Major credit cards

An interesting collection of silver pieces. Large silver trays, carving tables, servers, flatware, bowls, candlesticks, ink stands and lamp bases.

TUDOR ROSE ANTIQUES

28 East 10th Street, New York, NY 10003 • Telfax: (212) 677-5239 • Mon-Sat 10:30-6:00 • Major credit cards

Antique sterling silver decorative items: candlesticks, frames, dressing table items, candy dishes, trays, wine coasters, pill boxes, baby mugs and serving spoons. Much more.

S. WYLER

941 Lexington Avenue, New York, NY 10021 • Tel: (212) 879-9848 • Fax: (212) 472-8018 • Mon-Sat 9:45-5:30 • Prices high • Amex

The country's oldest silver dealer has a superb collection of antique English silver and porcelain, Sheffield plate, Chinese export porcelain and English Georgian crystal.

Silversmiths

ARTISTIC SILVER RESTORATION

37 West 47th Street, New York, NY 10036 • Tel: (212) 719-1330 •
Mon-Thu 9:30-5:00, Fri 9:30-12:00 • Morty • Prices medium

Repair and replating of silver, gold, brass, bronze and copper. Polishing and complete restoration. Monogram removal. Good references.

BRANDT & OPIS INC.

46 West 46th Street, 5th floor, New York, NY 10036 • Tel: (212) 245-9237 • Fax: (212) 302-0892 • Mon-Thu 8:00-5:00, Fri 8:00-2:00 •
Prices reasonable

Expert repair and replating of silver.

JEAN'S SILVERSMITHS

16 West 45th Street, New York, NY 10036 • Tel: (212) 575-0723 •
Mon-Thu 9:00-4:30, Fri 9:00-3:30 • Prices medium to high • MC and
Visa

Specialty is discontinued flatware patterns. Jean's offers more than 900, some of which have not been produced in over fifty years. Other stock includes: candy dishes, pitchers, candlesticks, silver goblets and cordial glasses, lots of trays, early American, Georgian and Victorian hollowware. Repairs, polishing and replating. Great source.

THOME SILVERSMITH INC.

49 West 37th Street, Room 605, New York, NY 10018 • Tel: (212) 764-5426 • Mon-Fri 8:30-5:30, closed 1:00-2:30 • Robert Routh • French and German spoken • Trade discount

Silversmith: expert repair of antique silver objects of art and gold. Silver and gold plating and repair of brass and bronze, copper and pewter. Can custom make to order. Established 1931.

Repair and Replating

BIANCA

638 Lexington Avenue, New York, NY 10022 • Tel: (212) 753-2343 •
Mon-Fri 9:00-7:00, Sat 10:00-6:00, Sun 10:00-5:00

Repair, polishing and replating of silver. Appraisals for insurance. Service for over 25 years. They sell jewelry.

See also: ANTIQUE DEALERS

UPHOLSTERY AND DRAPERY SERVICES

MARTIN ALBERT INTERIORS, INC.

9 East 19th Street, New York, NY 10003 • Tel: (212) 673-8000 • Fax: (212) 673-8006 • 7 Days 9:00-6:00 • Martin Zeliger • Prices medium to high • 20% trade discount • Major credit cards

Custom window treatments, custom re-upholstery, new custom upholstered furniture, slipcovers. Measurements and installations.

ALDO DI ROMA

327 East 94th Street, New York, NY 10128 • Tel: (212) 688-3564 • Fax: (212) 410-6174 • Mon-Fri 8:00-4:00 • Italian and Spanish spoken

Fine custom upholstery of chairs and furniture. All window treatments and shades. Bedspreads and skirts.

BARON UPHOLSTERERS, INC.

6 East 32nd Street, New York, NY 10016 • Tel: (212) 683-0101 • Fax: (212) 683-0147 • Mon-Fri 8:00-4:30 • Stephen Urban • Spanish and Italian spoken • Prices high • Trade discounts

Upholstery, draperies, wall upholstery, pillows and bedspreads. Works for top designers. References on request.

MARIO BASCIANO

1197 Castleton Avenue, Staten Island, NY 10310 • Telfax: (718) 442-5816 • Mon-Fri 8:30-5:30, Sat 8:30-2:00 • Mario Basciano • Italian spoken • Prices low to medium

Custom-upholstered furniture. Re-upholstery, upholstered walls, upholstered headboards and bases. Window treatments, bedspreads. Restoration of upholstery. Excellent references.

BERGEN UPHOLSTERY AND FURNITURE CO., INC.

283 Main Street, Hackensack, NJ 07601 • Tel: (201) 489-0555 • Mon-Wed, Fri-Sat 9:30-5:30, Thu 9:30-8:30 • Stan Sinowitz • Spanish spoken • Prices high • Major credit cards

Upholstered furniture, slipcovers, draperies, re-upholstery. Upholstery shop for both trade and retail. They are an ASID Industry Foundation member.

BERTHOLD'S UPHOLSTERY, INC.

119 West 25th Street, New York, NY 10001 • Tel: (212) 633-0071 •
Fax: (212) 633-2670 • Mon-Fri 8:00-5:00 • Berthold • Spanish and
French spoken • Prices medium

Custom upholstery of contemporary and traditionl furniture. Works
for leading decorators. References upon request.

CASA NOVA

243 East 78th Street, New York, NY 10021 • Tel: (212) 639-9486 • Fax:
(212) 639-9586 • Mon-Sat 10:00-6:00 • Patricia Kahane • Portuguese,
French and Spanish spoken • Prices medium • 20% trade discount •
Visa and MC

Custom made draperies, upholstering services and interior design
services. References on request.

HENRY CHAN UPHOLSTERY, INC.

11 East 26th Street, New York, NY 10010 • Tel: (212) 689-1845 • Fax:
(212) 689-2786 • Mon-Fri 8:30-5:00 • Henry Chan • Mandarin spoken
• Trade only

All upholstered furniture: special styles and sizes in the best quality. Wall upholstery and draperies. 100 pieces in the showroom.
They custom make any piece you choose in the size you want.
Work for the show houses and top designers. References upon request.

CREATIVE WINDOWS

69 Saugatuck Avenue, Westport, CT 06880 • Tel: (203) 226-8114 •
Fax: (203) 226-0546 • Mon-Fri 9:00-5:00 • Elizabeth W. Kiester, Owner
• German and Spanish spoken • Prices very high • 20% trade discount

High-end custom drapery workroom and retail showroom. Designer
fabrics, trimmings and wallpapers. Distinctive and creative fabrications of the finest workmanship.

DE ANGELIS

312 East 95th Street, New York, NY 10128 • Tel: (212) 348-8225 • Fax:
(212) 876-1850 • Mon-Fri 9:00-5:00 and by appointment • Guido De
Angelis • Italian spoken • Prices high • Trade discount

High-quality workmanship in all types of upholstery, including walls.

DOREEN INTERIORS LTD.

221 West 17th Street, New York, NY 10011 • Tel: (212) 255-9008 •
Fax: (212) 255-8946 • Mon-Fri 9:00-5:00 by appointment • French
spoken • Prices high • Major credit cards

Custom upholstery and drapery workroom.

THE FRENCH NEEDLE

152 West 25th Street, New York, NY 10001 • Tel: (212) 647-0848 •
Fax: (212) 647-0847 • By appointment • Serge L'Hermite • Prices high
• Trade discount

All upholstery services.

GENERAL DRAPERY SERVICES

135 East 144th Street, Bronx, NY 10451 • Tel: (718) 665-9200 • Fax:
(718) 665-9672 • Mon-Fri 8:00-5:00 • Jim Belmont • French and Spanish
spoken • Prices medium

All types of window coverings.

HOPE & WILDER

90 Grand Street, New York, NY 10013 • Tel: (212) 966-9010 • Tue-Sat
11:00-7:00, Sun 12:00-7:00 • Eileen Applebaum • Prices medium to
high • 10% trade discount • Major credit cards

Upholstered furniture, fabric, slipcovers. Custom sewing work: draperies, bedspreads, duvets.

INTERIORS BY ROYALE

964 Third Avenue, New York, NY 10022 • Tel: (212) 753-4600 • Fax:
(212) 753-3343 • Mon-Fri 9:30-6:00 • Italian and Polish spoken • Prices
medium • Trade discount • Major credit cards

Custom upholstery, fine decorator fabrics, custom window treatments, slipcovers, custom bedding, trimmings and decorative hardware. Works for top decorators. References on request.

LANGSAM & BREUER CUSTOM UPHOLSTERERS

657 Amsterdam Avenue, New York, NY 10025 • Tel: (212) 362-8600 •
Fax: (212) 362-8635 • Mon-Tue, Thu 11:00-6:00, Wed 11:00-7:30,
Sun 2:30-6:00 • Leon Breuer • Yiddish and Spanish spoken • Prices
high

Re-upholstery, slipcovers, window treatments. References on request.

LAURA DRAPERY CONTRACTING CO., INC.

5-19 48th Avenue, Long Island City, NY 11101 • Telfax: (718) 706-8003
• Mon-Fri 8:00-5:00 and by appointment • Joseph J. Decker • Prices
medium • Trade only

Draperies, curtains, vertical blinds, mini-blinds, solar shades, all
types of window treatments and upholstery. Complete architectural
and designers' workroom.

ANTHONY LAWRENCE

305 East 63rd Street, 9th floor, New York, NY 10021 • Tel: (212) 888-1771 • Fax: (212) 888-1975 • Mon-Fri 9:30-4:30 • Prices medium to high • Trade only

Fine custom upholstery, window treatments, wall upholstery and slipcovers. They also have a workroom in Cos Cob, CT • Tel: (203) 869-9775.

LE DECOR FRANCAIS

1006 Lexington Avenue, New York, NY 10021 • Tel: (212) 734-0032 • Fax: (212) 988-0816 • Mon-Fri 9:30-6:00, Sat 11:00-5:00 • Jacqueline Coumans • French, Portuguese and Spanish spoken • Prices medium to high • 20% trade discount • Amex

All work with fabrics: upholstery, draperies, pillows, lampshades. Fine fabrics and trimmings.

OLEK LEJBZON & CO.

210 11th Avenue, New York, NY 10001 • Tel: (212) 243-3363 • Fax: (212) 243-3432 • Mon-Sat 7:30-6:00 • Peter Triestman • Many languages spoken in the workroom

There are 35 skilled artisans in this extraordinry workroom. Their skills include upholstering.

RAY MURRAY, INC.

121 East 24th Street, New York, NY 10010 • Tel: (212) 838-3752 • Fax: (212) 477-2122 • Mon-Thu 9:00-5:00, Fri 8:00-3:30 • Rita Blake • Spanish spoken • Prices high • Trade only

Fine custom draperies, upholstery, re-upholstery, wall upholstery.

P.D. DESIGN STUDIO LTD.

305 East 63rd Street, New York, NY 10021 • Tel: (212) 832-0333 • Fax: (212) 832-0336 • Mon-Fri 9:00-5:00 • Audrey Leshin • Prices medium • Trade only • Amex

Showroom, upholstery and accessories.

RICHARD'S INTERIOR DESIGN

1390 Lexington Avenue, New York, NY 10128 • Tel: (212) 831-9000 • Fax: (212) 427-0287 • Mon-Fri 10:00-6:00, Thu 10:00-7:00, Sat 10:00-5:00 • Prices medium to high • Trade discount • Major credit cards

High-quality upholstery: furniture, drapery and walls. Good choice of reasonably priced fabrics and decorative window hardware.

20TH CENTURY DRAPERY

70 Wooster Street, New York, NY 10012 • Tel: (212) 925-7707 • Fax: (212) 274-0134 • Mon-Fri 8:00-5:00 • Martin Schnell • Prices medium • Some trade discounts

Custom drapery and window coverings. Upholstery.

VERSAILLES DRAPERY & UPHOLSTERY

37 East 18th Street, New York, NY 10003 • Tel: (212) 533-2059 • Fax: (212) 995-1681 • Mon-Fri 8:00-4:00 • Mr. Bernard • French and Spanish spoken • Prices medium

All types of custom decorative drapery; re-upholstery, upholstered walls with braid finish and custom designed upholstered sofas, armchairs and ottomans. Top references.

WHITE WORKROOM FOR SOFT FURNISHINGS

529 Broadway, Suite 702, New York, NY 10012 • Tel: (212) 941-5910 • Fax: (212) 941-1354 • Mon-Fri 9:00-6:00 • Gary Meisner • French and Spanish spoken • Prices high • Some trade discounts

Very high-end drapery workroom: anything made of fabric and re-upholstering. Top references.

For additional WINDOW TREATMENTS see MIRROR AND GLASS

♚ WALLCOVERINGS AND WALLPAPERS

CHARLES R. GRACIE & SONS, INC.

1010 Lexington Avenue, New York, NY 10021 • Tel: (212) 861-1150 •
Fax: (212) 861-1944 • Mon-Fri 9:30-5:30, Sat 11:00-4:00 • Brian Gracie
• French, Spanish, Chinese and Japanese spoken • Prices high • Trade
discount • Major credit cards

Outstanding selection of hand-painted wallpapers. Distinguished
client list.

ELIZABETH DOW LTD.

580 Broadway, Suite 1206, New York, NY 10012 • Tel: (212) 219-8822
• Fax: (212) 941-1331 • Mon-Fri 9:00-5:00 • Mark Sheppill • Prices
high • Trade discount

Hand-painted wallcoverings and decorative painting. Top references

ANYA LARKIN

39 West 28th Street, 8th floor, New York, NY 10001 • Tel: (212) 532-
3263 • Fax: (212) 532-2854 • Mon-Fri 9:00-5:00 • Hellen Fatherley •
German spoken • Prices very high • Trade only

Handmade wallpaper. Anya has important references.

CAROLLE THIBAUT-POMERANTZ

New York Tel: (212) 759-6048 • Fax: (212) 308-3486 • Paris Fax: (33
1) 42 86 04 87 • By appointment only • French spoken • Prices high •
Trade discount • Amex

French antique wallpaper panels and decorative arts. Clients in
clude museums.

ZUBER & CIE.

979 Third Avenue (D&D), 1st floor, New York, NY 10022 • Tel: (212)
486-9226 • Fax: (212) 754-6166 • Mon-Fri 9:00-5:00 • Gina Farahnic
• French spoken • Prices high • Trade only

The best-known name in scenic wallpapers. Wall murals, architec
tural themes, trompe l'oeil, ceiling papers, fabrics and trimmings.

Note: For a more extensive selection of wallpapers and wallcoverings
please see FABRICS and THE DESIGN BUILDINGS

Experts in Scenic Wallpaper Installation

JOSEPH BAUMEISTER

113 Hillcrest Drive, Marlboro, NY 12542 • Tel: (914) 236-1249 • Fax: (914) 236-1017 • Mon-Fri 9:00-5:00 • Hungarian, Spanish, German and Rumanian spoken • Prices medium to high

Specialized installation of wallpaper and high-quality painting.

JOHN NALEWAJA

170 West 74th Street, New York, NY 10023 • Tel: (212) 496-6135 • Fax: (212) 496-5549 • Mon-Fri 8:00-7:00 • Jim Francis • Greek, Spanish and French spoken • Prices high

Wallpaper installations specializing in Zuber scenic wallpaper, Gracie Chinese scenic wallpaper, De Gournay silk panels and fabric installations. Removal and re-installation of antique wallpaper, appraisal of condition; ceiling wallpaper installation, such as silver and gold tea leaf paper. Top references.

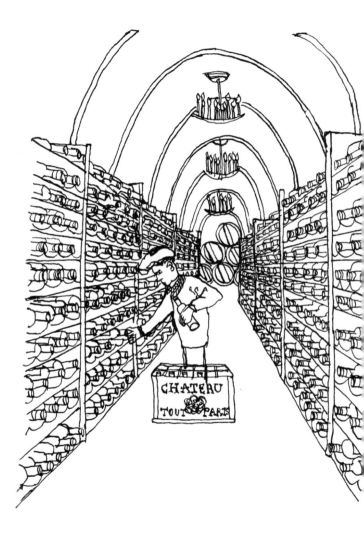

WINE CELLARS AND EQUIPMENT

CRAMER PRODUCTS

381 Park Avenue South, New York, NY 10019 • Tel: (212) 532-0871 • Fax: (212) 725-6914 • Mon-Fri 9:00-5:00 • French spoken • Prices high

Wine storage systems. Systems and cabinets for the protection of valuable collectibles: cigars, musical instruments, documents. Custom made to specifications.

KEDCO WINE STORAGE SYSTEMS

564 Smith Street, Farmingdale, NY 11735 • Tel: (516) 454-7800 • (516) 454-4876 • Mon-Fri 9:00-5:30, Sat 9:00-5:00 • Spanish spoken • Prices medium to high • Major credit cards

Temperature-controlled wine cellars and components; self-contained wine storage cabinets; wine racks in wrought iron and wood; wine and beer-making equipment and supplies. America's largest wine related showroom open to the public.

THE WINE ENTHUSIAST

8 Saw Mill River Road, Hawthorne, NY 10532 • Tel: (914) 345-8463 • Fax: (914) 345-3129 • Mon-Fri 9:00-6:00, Sat 10:00-5:00 • Spanish spoken • Prices medium • Trade discounts • Major credit cards

Temperature-controlled wine cellars, wine racks, accessories.

WINE SERVICES, INC.

1825 River Drive, Riverhead, NY 11901 • Tel: (800) 955-9463 • (516) 722-3800 • Fax: (516) 722-8770 • Mon-Fri 10:00-4:00, closed 1:00-2:00

Temperature-controlled wine storage.

THE FLEA MARKETS OF
NEW YORK

The most important flea markets of New York City are concentrated in the Chelsea area just to the north and south of West 23rd Street. Most are open on weekends and are easy to reach by subway or bus.

During the late spring, summer and early autumn, street markets pop up nearly every weekend. It's great fun to saunter along one of the avenues and take in the good cooking smells while sharing your city time with literally thousands of friendly strangers.

Dealers are not only native New Yorkers but arrivals from all over the Eastern Seaboard who come to sell their wares.

While you are visiting the Chelsea area, take time for a visit to the Chelsea Pier. There you will find the occasional big antique show and you can indulge in all sorts of recreational activities.

The Chelsea Antiques Building

110 West 25th Street, New York, NY 10001 • Tel: (212) 929-0909 • Fax: (212) 924-8535 • Seven days 10:00-6:00 • Leslie Dezer • Spanish spoken • Prices medium • Trade discounts • Major credit cards

More than 100 dealers on 12 floors. Antiques, collectibles of every kind, and a truly convivial neighborhood atmosphere. You'll find casual browsers, serious collectors and the occasional design professional looking for hidden treasures.

OF PARTICULAR INTEREST IN THE BUILDING:

ANTIQUARIAN BOOK ARCADE

9th floor • Tel: (212) 620-5627 • Fax: (212) 620-5688

A marvellous place to find rare and out-of-print books on many subjects. Some in fine bindings and the occasional beautifully bound complete set.

CHERUBS ANTIQUES AND COLLECTIBLES

11th floor • Tel: (212) 627-7097 • Fax: (212) 924-8535 • Daily 10:00-6:00 • Gary Felsher and Alex Auver • French, Spanish and Italian spoken • Prices medium • Major credit cards

French, English and German turn-of-the-century porcelains. American and Continental furniture and decorative arts.

THE CHRIS ELLIS COLLECTION

12th floor • Tel: (212) 647-1700 • Fax: (212) 647-1704 • 7 Days 10:00-6:00 • Nina S. Wittling • Prices medium to high • Visa and MC

The Chris Ellis Collection occupies an entire floor of the building and offers antique furniture, lighting, mirrors, art and accessories. The collection can also be seen at their showroom at 160 East 56th Street in Gallery #5. Tel: (212) 223-3770.

City East Antiques Center

201 East 31st Street, New York, NY 10016 • Tel: (212) 779-0979 • Fax: (212) 545-1761 • Mon-Fri 11:00-6:00, Sat 11:00-5:00 • Renee Braverman • Prices medium • Trade discounts • MC and Visa

This is a center for five or six dealers who specialize in folk art, art pottery, art glass, antique advertising posters and materials, stained glass and what they call salesman's samples.

International Antiques & Collectibles

30 West 26th Street, New York, NY 10010 • Tel: (212) 255-7615 • Fax: (212) 929-0802 • Tue-Fri 9:00-5:30, Sat-Sun 7:30-5:30

An indoor market with dealers offering fine and unusual 19th- and 20th-century furniture, porcelain, paintings, bronzes, silver, carpets, Orientalia and objets d'art.

Manhattan Castles & Props, Inc.

76 East Houston Street, New York, NY 10012 • Tel: (212) 505-8699 • Daily, weather permitting, 10:00-7:00 • Robert Fennick • French, Japanese, German and Italian spoken • Prices low to medium • Major credit cards

General antiques, important trunks and luggage. Architectural elements and furniture. Prop rentals for theatre and films.

The Showplace

40 West 25th Street, New York, NY 10011 • Tel: (212) 633-6033 • Sat-Sun 8:30-5:30

100 dealers in antiques and collectibles.

Soho Antiques Fair and Collectibles

Broadway and Grand Street in Soho • Tel: (212) 682-2000 • Sat-Sun 9:00-5:00

Weather permitting, an outdoor fair offering antiques, collectibles and crafts.

The Annex

6th Avenue from 24th to 27th Street • Tel: (212) 243-5343 • Sat-Sun 9:00-5:00

Outdoor fair and flea market. Just about everything is offered here, from fine antique silver to antique baby carriages.

The Garage

112 West 25th Street, New York, NY 10001 • Tel: (212) 647-0707 • Sat-Sun 9:00-5:00

Indoor market with nearly 100 dealers offering interesting collectibles.

The Green Flea In/Outdoor Market

Saturdays on 67th Street between 1st and York Avenues • Tel: (212) 721-0900 • Sat 6:00-6:00
Sundays on Columbus Avenue at 77th Street • Sun 10:00-6:00

Antiques, collectibles, crafts, a farmers market and plants and flower dealers.

The New Yorkville Antique Market

351 East 74th Street, New York, NY 10021 • Tel: (718) 897-5992 • Sat 6:00-5:00

Indoor market with antiques, collectibles, folk art and crafts.

Alphabetical Index